Globalization and Global History

This new volume argues that globalization is not a new and exotic phenomenon. Instead it emphasizes that globalization is something that has been with us as long as there have been people who are both interdependent and aware of that fact.

Contemporary concerns about globalization are hard to avoid. Growing interdependence benefits some and marginalizes others. History is often described from a local perspective, making events seem particularistic and disconnected, rather than being enmeshed in a much larger network of interdependent events. Studying globalization from the vantage point of long-term global history permits theoretical and empirical investigation allowing the contributors to this volume to assess the extent of ongoing transformations and to compare them to earlier iterations. With this historical advantage, the extent of ongoing changes – which previously appeared unprecedented – can be contrasted to similar episodes in the past.

This interdisciplinary volume includes chapters written by economists, historians, sociologists and political scientists. It will appeal to anyone interested in globalization and its origins.

Barry K. Gills is Reader in International Politics at the University of Newcastle upon Tyne, UK.

William R. Thompson is Rogers Professor of Political Science at the University of Indiana, USA.

Rethinking globalizations

Edited by Barry K. Gills

University of Newcastle upon Tyne, UK

This series is designed to break new ground in the literature on globalization and its academic and popular understanding. Rather than perpetuating or simply reacting to the economistic understanding of globalization, this series seeks to capture the term and broaden its meaning to encompass a wide range of issues and disciplines, and convey a sense of alternative possibilities for the future.

The tone of the series will be problem oriented, practical and accessible, assuming the role of the public intellectual as well as the specialized academic. It will seek to identify a set of global problems and address these in a way that allows readers to receive needed and essential information as well as encounter new ideas about practical solutions and alternatives.

1 **Whither Globalization?**
The vortex of knowledge and ideology
James H. Mittelman

2 **Globalization and Global History**
Edited by Barry K. Gills and William R. Thompson

Globalization and Global History

Edited by Barry K. Gills and
William R. Thompson

Routledge
Taylor & Francis Group
LONDON AND NEW YORK

First published 2006 by Routledge
2 Park Square, Milton Park, Abingdon, Oxon, OX14 4RN

Simultaneously published in the USA and Canada
by Routledge
270 Madison Avenue, New York, NY 10016

Routledge is an imprint of the Taylor & Francis Group

Typeset in Baskerville by Prepress Projects Ltd, Perth
Printed and bound in Great Britain by TJ International Ltd, Padstow, Cornwall

British Library Cataloguing in Publication Data
A catalogue record for this book is available from the British Library

Library of Congress Cataloging in Publication Data
Globalization and global history / edited by Barry K. Gills and William R. Thompson.
p. cm. – (Rehinking globalization ; 2)
Includes bibliographical references and index.
1. Globalization. 2. International trade. 3. Economic history. I. Gills, Barry K., 1956– II. Thompson, William R. III. Series.
JZ1318.G578625 2006
909–dc22
2005015668

ISBN10: 0-415-70137-6 (hbk)
ISBN10: 0-415-70136-8 (pbk)

ISBN13: 9-78-0-415-70137-2 (hbk)
ISBN13: 9-78-0-415-70136-5 (pbk)

For Andre Gunder Frank, who was always ahead of us

Contents

Figures

Tables

Contributors

Alexis Alvarez is a published poet fluent in four languages, a graduate of the University of California, Riverside, and a teacher of sociology at the community college level. His interests include sociolinguistics and macrosociological/world systems paradigms. His empirical interests include the pre-gunpowder periods of the Islamic, Mesoamerican, Chinese and western civilizations. His methodology includes both a quantitative/statistical approach as well as anecdotal content analysis and artefact analysis.

Jerry H. Bentley is Professor of History at the University of Hawai'i and editor of the *Journal of World History*. His research on the religious, moral and political writings of Renaissance humanists led to the publication of *Humanists and Holy Writ: New Testament Scholarship in the Renaissance* (Princeton, 1983) and *Politics and Culture in Renaissance Naples* (Princeton, 1987). More recently, his research has concentrated on global history and particularly on processes of cross-cultural interaction. His book *Old World Encounters: Cross-Cultural Contacts and Exchanges in Pre-Modern Times* (New York, 1993) examines processes of cultural exchange and religious conversion before the modern era, and his pamphlet *Shapes of World History in Twentieth-Century Scholarship* (Washington, DC, 1996) discusses the historiography of world history. His current interests include processes of cross-cultural interaction and cultural exchanges in modern times.

Christopher Chase-Dunn is Distinguished Professor of Sociology and Director of the Institute for Research on World-Systems at the University of California, Riverside. His recent research focuses on the causes of empire expansion and urban growth (and decline) in the Afro-Eurasian world system over the last 3,000 years. His studies of structural globalization in the modern world system since 1800 are supported by the National Science Foundation.

Sing C. Chew is Professor of Sociology at Humboldt State University, Arcata, California. He is presently finishing the sequel to *World Ecological Degradation, 3000 BC–AD 2000*.

Claudio Cioffi-Revilla earned his doctorate in political and social sciences at the Cesare Alfieri School of the University of Florence, Italy, and his PhD in international relations at the State University of New York. His interests are in origins of social complexity and long-term world system analysis. He has taught at the University of North Carolina (Chapel Hill), the University of Illinois (Urbana-Champaign) and the University of Colorado (Boulder). He presently teaches at George Mason University where he is Professor of Computational Social Science and Director of the Center for Social Complexity. He is also founder and director of the Long-Range Analysis of War (LORANOW) Project, as well as author of numerous articles and books. Professor Cioffi is a Visiting Scientist at the National Museum of Natural History, Smithsonian Institution, and a member of the ISA, APSA, IPSA, AAG, SAA, NAACSOS, the Washington Academy of Sciences, Accademia Internazionale Medicea and other learned societies.

Dennis O. Flynn is Alexander R. Heron Professor of Economics at the University of the Pacific. He has written/edited eight books and 40 articles on global trade history since 1978, with an initial focus on monetary history. He has organized several 'Pacific Centuries' Conferences and is co-General Editor of an 18-volume series *The Pacific World: Lands, Peoples, and History of the Pacific, 1500–1900* (Aldershot, 2001–07). Convinced that world history is a multidisciplinary enterprise, work in recent years has focused on the birth of globalization and interconnections among ecological, economic, epidemiological, cultural and demographic variables.

Andre Gunder Frank was an Associate of the Luxembourg Institute of European and International Studies, a Visiting Professor at the University di Calabria Dipto di Sociologia in Italy and a Senior Fellow of the World History Center at Northeastern University. He was the author of *ReOrient* (California, 1998), among other works, and was working on its nineteenth-century sequel at his death in 2005.

Barry K. Gills is currently Reader in International Politics in the School of Geography, Politics and Sociology at the University of Newcastle upon Tyne, UK. He was recently Acting Director of the Globalization Research Center of the University of Hawaii and is the founding Editor of the journal *Globalizations*, published by Routledge, and series editor of the Rethinking Globalizations series, also published by Routledge. He is a fellow of the World Academy of Art and Science, and co-founder of the World Historical Systems Theory group (with David Wilkinson) of the International Studies Association. He was co-author/editor with Andre Gunder Frank of *The World System: Five Hundred Years or Five Thousand?* (Routledge, 1993; Chinese and Turkish editions, 2004); co-editor (with Robert Denemark, Jonathan Friedman and George Modelski) of *World System History: The Social Science of Long-term Change* (Routledge, 2000); and editor of *Globalization and the*

Politics of Resistance (Palgrave, 2000). He is currently writing a monograph on historical dialectics in global history entitled *Capital and Power: a Global History*.

Arturo Giráldez is a Professor in Modern Languages and the School of International Studies at the University of the Pacific (Stockton, California). He received his BA and MA 'Universidad Complutense' at Madrid (Spain) and his PhD in Spanish at the Universiteit van Amsterdam (the Netherlands). In collaboration with D.O. Flynn, he has published articles and edited volumes in modern economic history and the origins of globalization.

Thomas D. Hall is Lester M. Jones Professor of Sociology at DePauw University in Greencastle, Indiana. His recent works include *A World-Systems Reader* (Rowman & Littlefield, 2000) and *Rise and Demise: Comparing World-Systems* (Westview, 1997) with Christopher Chase-Dunn. Recently, he has published a number of articles with James V. Fenelon on indigenous peoples, and they are completing a book on indigenous peoples and globalization.

David Inglis is Senior Lecturer in Sociology at the University of Aberdeen. He writes in the areas of social theory and the sociology of culture, and has particular research interests in the sociology of knowledge as applied to ancient Greece and Rome. He is the author of *Confronting Culture: Sociological Vistas* (Polity, 2003) and *Culture and Everyday Life* (Routledge, 2005).

Andrew Linklater is Woodrow Wilson Professor of International Politics at the University of Wales, Aberystwyth. Main publications include *Men and Citizens in the Theory of International Relations* (Macmillan, 1982/1990), *Beyond Realism and Marxism: Critical Theory and International Relations* (Macmillan, 1990) and *The Transformation of World Politics: Ethical Foundations of the Post-Westphalian Era* (Polity, 1998). His next book, *The English School: A Contemporary Assessment*, co-written with Hidemi Suganami, will be published in 2005.

Patrick Karl O'Brien is Centennial Professor of Economic History and Convenor of the Network in Global Economic History (GEHN) at the Department of Economic History, London School of Economics, and Emeritus Fellow, St Antony's College, Oxford. A Fellow of the British Academy, Academia Europaea, Royal Historical Society and Royal Society of Arts, he is also a past president of the British Economic History Society and former director of the University of London's Institute of Historical Research. Most recently, he has co-edited *The Political Economy of British Historical Experience, 1688–1914* (Oxford, 2002), *Two Hegemonies: Britain, 1846–1914 and the United States, 1941–1989* (Ashgate, 2002) and *The Formation and Efficiency of Fiscal States in Europe and Asia, 1500–1914* (Cambridge,

2006). Two of his books in progress include *European Traditions in Writing the Global History of Material Progress from Herodutus to Pomeranz* and *The Long Run History of World Trade*.

Daniel Pasciuti is a graduate from the University of California, Riverside, and is currently a graduate student at the Johns Hopkins University. He is a research assistant for the Cities and Empires Project of the Institute for Research on World-Systems (at UC, Riverside) and for the Danwei Project at Johns Hopkins University. A former sergeant in the US Army, his interests include macrohistorical analysis/world systems and historical and modern urbanization.

Joachim Karl Rennstich is Assistant Professor at the Political Science Department at Fordham University with degrees from the University of Gottingen and Indiana University. His work focuses on issues surrounding the global economy, as well as the development of the global system as a whole. His main interests lie in the global political economy, past and present, and the long-term development of the global world system, at the moment especially with regard to new digital technologies. In addition, Rennstich looks at rivalry behaviour of major power states and the geopolitical restructuring of the modern global system, as well as the development of a new political and human geography. He is also co-founder and director of the Center for the Study of Long-term Change in World History (LTC) and is currently engaged in a study of generational change.

Roland Robertson is Professor of Sociology and Director of the Centre for the Study of Globalization at the University of Aberdeen. He is the author of many works on global social change including *Globalization: Social Theory and Global Culture* (Sage, 1992), *Globality and Modernities* (Sage, 2004) and, with David Inglis, *Globalization and Social Theory: Redefining Social Science* (Open University Press, forthcoming).

William R. Thompson is the Rogers Professor of Political Science at Indiana University. Recent books include *Growth, Trade and Systemic Leadership* (Michigan, 2004) with Rafael Reuveny and *Puzzles of the Democratic Peace* (Palgrave-Macmillan, 2005) with Karen Rasler. He is President of the International Studies Association (2005–06).

David Wilkinson is a Professor of Political Science at the University of California, Los Angeles. He has been concerned with the political problems of civilizations/world systems since encountering the Somervell abridgement of Toynbee about 1950.

Acknowledgements

Our thanks for permission to reprint Jerry H. Bentley, 'Globalizing history and historicizing globalization', *Globalizations* 1 (1) (September 2004): 69–81; Roland Robertson and David Inglis, 'The global *Animus*: in the tracks of historical consciousness', *Globalizations* 1 (1) (September 2004): 38–49; David Wilkinson, 'Globalizations: the first ten, hundred, five thousand, and million years', *Comparative Civilizations Review* 49 (Fall 2003): 132–45; and an earlier version of the Dennis O. Flynn and Arturo Giráldez chapter first appeared as 'Cycles of silver: globalization as historical process', *World Economics* 3 (2) (April–June 2002): 1–16. We would like to thank Craig Fowlie, Harriet Brinton and Heidi Bagtazo of Routledge for their commitment to this volume and the series *Rethinking Globalizations* and Andrew R. Davidson for his assistance with the proofs and production of this volume. Thanks are also due to the International Studies Association, and its International Political Economy Section in particular, for many years of support for the World Historical Systems Theory group, and to all the members and contributors to the group over the years since its founding in 1989/90. Thanks also to Neil Harris for his help on the index for this book.

1 Globalizations, global histories and historical globalities

Barry K. Gills and William R. Thompson

Contemporary concerns about globalization are rather difficult to avoid. Growing interdependence enriches some people and marginalizes others. Some professional observers counsel that these economic changes are inevitable, while others mobilize in protest and opposition to unregulated and often rapid change. There are clear gains in community sensitivities. Genocide in Rwanda or a destructive tsunami in the Indian Ocean are events that are no longer 'too distant' to heed. There are mixed gains in activities such as outsourcing. Selected poorer areas gain new jobs while other areas lose employment to places with lower wage structures. There are also clear losses in terms of such activities as globalized crime and pollution, as well as the more rapid dissemination of disease.

Our book, however, is not about the gains and losses of globalization. We address instead its alleged novelty. Too many observers regard these dislocating changes as something spawned only recently. We suggest instead that the globalization processes that have caused so much concern have long pedigrees. Their pace and scale may have accelerated, but they are anything but novel. Maximally, they have been ongoing ever since *Homo sapiens* began migrating from the African continent ultimately to populate the rest of the world. Minimally, they have been ongoing since the sixteenth-century's connection of the Americas to Afro-Eurasia.

One reason why our position remains contested has to do with the way we tell stories about the past. For many, history – even 'world history' – constitutes stories about relatively local and largely disconnected events. Ancient history fixates on the Greeks and Romans as if they were the only people on earth in their respective centuries of visible activity. Medieval history often reduces to post-Roman dark ages and chivalrous European knights. Modern history is about the European 'discoveries' of the rest of the world and the subsequent conflicts over how best to divide the new spoils.

There can be no denying that the Graeco-Roman world has its interests but less well known is that both Greeks and Romans went to some trouble attempting to develop closer trade connections with Asia, just as their European successors did almost two millennia later. Those chivalrous European knights may have inherited their heavy armour and combat styles – along with the political–economic implications of supporting heavily armoured cavalry – from Central Asian nomads who first developed heavy cavalry to deal with other nomads specializing in light cavalry. Subsequent conflict with Rome led to the spread of heavy cavalry units (and Central Asians) throughout the Roman Empire. Mid-second millennium CE Europeans did not so much discover the Americas as they increased the connectivity of the 'New' and 'Old' Worlds, while, at the same time, they developed still new routes for increasing the connectivity of eastern and western Eurasia.

History is a matter of perspective. Local perspectives yield local histories. Global perspectives yield global histories. One of the advantages of a global perspective is that phenomena that were once thought to be particularistic and disconnected turn out to be anything but purely local affairs. Rather, they are, at least in part, a product of people and regions being enmeshed in larger networks. 'Things' do occur locally but not necessarily solely as a result of local influences. Similarly, local changes can alter the nature of wider networks. Local–global interactions and influences are reciprocal, at least potentially.[1]

Developing global history(ies) is a relatively new and fairly recent undertaking. It is also one closely linked to developing a better understanding of globalization processes. To the extent that we can develop an improved appreciation for how things have been connected in the past, we should be better able to evaluate intensified connections in the present. But the issues are more complicated than simply developing less particularistic history. How should we go about it? What and where should we emphasize? Are there recurring processes that permit generalization? Or is everything that has happened unlike anything that has happened? Various approaches to developing global history and explaining globalization processes are what this volume is about. We will certainly not be the last word on the subject but, by bringing together different points of view, we can hope to influence and accelerate the analytical probes towards developing more global perspectives on human interactions in the past, present and future.

To some, globalization and global history cannot and should not be conflated, in the sense that some want to argue that all of global history is in fact part of the same processes that we may call 'globalization'. Therefore, the latest stage of globalization is in fact just that – the latest stage – with deep antecedents in all of global history – culminating in the present expressions of the processes of globalization.

Others reject this view entirely and argue that, if this were indeed the case (conflation), we would have no need for a new concept such as globalization at all as it would serve no useful purpose – because all global history *is* globalization and vice versa. Alternatively, then, this position sees a necessary and useful separation of these two concepts. Globalization is therefore to be defined as a qualitatively distinctive set of phenomena. Therefore, it requires new concepts and theories to explain. Globalization is *not* global history.

The third position, naturally, seeks to find some middle ground or reconciliation between these two opposing views on the relationship between globalization and global history. At the very least, it can be argued that there are deeply embedded patterns, structural forces, mentalities and perhaps more that we can analyse in the course of 'global history' that are relevant to and instructive for our emerging comprehension of contemporary 'globalization'. So, therefore, it is not necessary to argue that there is a strict separation between the two analytically and historically; but rather that they inform one another theoretically and empirically. In this sense, the search for patterns or patterned processes in global history is part of the intellectual preparation for a theory or understanding of globalization as a set of processes not necessarily entirely without precedent, although of course 'different' and therefore needing to be clearly distinguished from the whole continuum of 'global history'. That is to say, we have seen instances of 'globalizing' patterns in the past, and the study of these can at least cast further light upon processes in the present to which they can be legitimately compared as being similar in some aspects.

Of course, all three of these positions still beg the question of definition. For some, 'global history' encompasses all human history going back to the year dot. For others, however, the only true 'global' history is very much a product of modern forces of change and cannot be projected all the way back to the very beginning. Some argue that 'global history' is therefore only very recent history – some even maintaining that it is not more than a couple of decades old. The definition of 'globalization' is no more set in stone than global history and, as a concept, is accompanied here by other concepts such as 'network society', 'information society', 'post-industrial age', 'post-modern age' and so on.

Further complicating matters, there are also perennial issues in the social sciences that are entailed in/by this debate. The 'agency–structure', 'idealist–materialist', 'free will–determinist' dichotomizations all have a relevance to this globalization/global history discussion. Different authors take very different methodological and philosophical positions on these issues – as with any other serious discussion in the social sciences in the past or present. We may not be able to resolve these differences here or certainly not portray any sort of consensus on them, but at least we can point to their existence and their continued relevance in the present circumstances.

There is also finally an even larger controversy that remains in all this discussion, and that is for what purposes or with what aims or intentions do we try to link 'globalization' and 'global history' closely together? Who or what is this type of research for? One take on this argument is that we seek neutral objectivity and simply seek to establish positive knowledge about the 'real' processes, structures and outcomes of these processes and identify the 'real' nature of their historical and contemporary relationship. In effect, this is a kind of mapping exercise on which a cumulative body of knowledge can be established. In this sense, 'objective' or 'positive' knowledge about the past is valuable in itself, as it is the foundation for an objective global history and thus of a comprehension of contemporary globalization as well.

An alternative view would be to assert that the debate is not really about the past but actually about the future. It is about the future of the whole planet, that is a 'global future' and the future of all humanity and not any national, ethnic, religious, cultural or political fragment of it. In this sense, we need to make the link between global history and globalization because the real issues are about the present and future direction of the world as a 'single' place and a 'single' human community. The more we understand the past, therefore, the more it may inform the present and the future. In this sense, this kind of knowledge construction may be more self-consciously engaged and concerned with normative and moral questions, and with 'critical' analysis of both past and present forces of history.

Our view on this is ecumenical and tolerant. This diversity is reflected in the contributions to this volume. This is one of the beginnings of what will be a long conversation, not the end of one. The debate about the relationship between globalization and global history, which is actually about our self-understanding of the past, the present and the future of humanity, is pivotal. We believe that it will remain so for quite some time to come. The outcome of these debates and discussions is by no means predetermined or clear from the standpoint of where we are today. We hope that this volume will make a small contribution in the direction of forming new self-understandings and that these will in fact have some bearing not only on how we reinterpret the relevance of the past to the present, but how we understand and shape our common human future.

We do not begin our discussions from an assumption that there is a single globalization, non-controversial and well established. Rather, we begin from a position that accepts the inherently undecided nature of the ongoing globalization debates both historically and in the contemporary context. This in itself signifies something of a paradigmatic shift from the type of thinking about the historical 'singularity' of globalization (as opposed to the multiplicity of 'globalizations' invoked above) that predominated in the first phase of the globalization debate. This move is intrinsically more inclusive intellectually and allows us to address a much wider range of perspectives in many fields of knowledge.

However, it is the obvious intention and purpose of this volume to have a serious examination of those perspectives that attempt to relate the 'globalization(s)' concept directly to that of 'global history'. Global history implies a global framework and a global perspective, which should make such approaches fairly compatible with a globalization research interest. Our sense of global history implies moreover that we are interested in understanding human development in the long term, something that many of the researchers in this volume have been concerned with for quite a long time.[2] The evolution or development of the entire human community is likewise the main subject of our understanding.[3]

The deliberate pairing of global history and globalization that characterizes this volume leads to further ideas about their association in real history such as 'the historicization of globalization' and the 'globalization (or 'globalizing') of history'.[4] Potentially, all of this is indicative of a potential remaking of world history as 'global history', which in turn contributes to the remaking of global education, escaping the parochial confines of nineteenth-century inspired nationalisms and national historical narratives and mythologies. It may also, we hope, contribute something of value to the contemporary evolution of 'global consciousness' or 'world consciousness', which in fact is not unique to our present age, but itself has a long and extremely interesting 'global history'.[5]

We are indeed witnessing, in our own times, a renewed impetus to the formation of a 'world consciousness', as globalization processes bring more and more of humanity into greater physical and communicative proximity to one another. These same processes of global history/globalization(s) are rapidly and perhaps profoundly altering the social relations and social networks of existence that compose the very basis of the human community, whether locally or globally constituted. Globalization(s) and, thus, global history, as a reality and not just a concept, are now something that every person has to deal with in one way or another, in their everyday life as well as in their comprehension of the world and the way that they choose to act in it. Therefore, 'globality' comes with globalization(s) and global history, again both as a concept and as a reality. This implies recognizing human unity at least at some levels, while however simultaneously negotiating and maintaining identity and social relationships at the individual, family, community and national levels, thus ensuring the continuation of human and cultural diversity. This is not a paradox, but rather the nature of real existence under the conditions of globality.

Insofar as the idea of human identity is concerned here, it is based on two fundamental facts. The first is our own genealogy and how genetic science has demonstrated our common membership in a single species and discredited ideas based on fundamental categorization into supposed 'races' or 'nations' of humanity. We are in fact all closely related and members of a single species all sharing a common heritage from our remote (and not so remote) ancestors, despite millennia of migration and the formation of myriad groups, languages and cultures.

The second fact is our mutual inhabitancy of a single, integrated, common natural environment – our planet and its single biosphere, in reality undifferentiated by political, ideological or other artificial human-imposed boundaries. The image of the earth seen from outer space is the image of this reality of our globality and our common global history. Thus, the evolution of human understanding of this global condition is a subject worthy of the closest attention by scholars and public alike, and it is to this understanding that we dedicate this volume.

The evolution of our comprehension of the world is also an aspect of the evolution of a common global identity, symbolized in the image of globality represented by planet earth suspended in space. The evolution of world-consciousness, and awareness of the history of globalization(s) understood as a common global history, brings us finally to the concept of 'global civilization', the ultimate repository of all that has come down the ages and which combines all the streams of history into that single great river we call 'global history', which is no other in fact than real 'human history' itself.

The chapters

The 'order of battle' for our chapters begins with the more abstract arguments about globalization and globality and moves towards more specific applications of arguments on the observed history of globalization. Jerry Bentley's chapter briefly reviews academic propensities towards fixations on national communities and European modernity. The former tends to frame much of our knowledge acquisition. What happens within the territorial boundaries of political communities? Any such focus will give short shrift to influences and processes that operate across multiple boundaries. Then, too, as long as European history and development is viewed as the evaluation standard for appraising activity outside Europe, non-European activity will tend to be regarded as somehow secondary to our understanding of world development and developments.

The antidote is genuinely to globalize history and genuinely to historicize globalization. That means rethinking the inclination to study the world in ways that further the interests of foreign policy, commerce and missionary work. It means more globalizing history which, so far, has been making significant progress. Less successful, again so far, is the need to historicize globalization. Eurocentricity remains well entrenched. To overcome this strong bias, two alternative strategies are being pursued. One is to 'go local' and focus exclusively on microbehaviour. The obvious risk is that non-microbehaviour and processes will be ignored altogether. The other strategy is to 'go global' and focus primarily on macrobehaviour. The risks here are that historical messiness and contingency will be obscured by commitments to macrotheories and that these macrotheories may also prove to be Trojan horses for maintaining Eurocentric conceptualization.

Neither approach, therefore, is without its liabilities. Analysts will need to choose their strategies carefully. But, for Bentley, one central assumption is salient. If communities were never totally unconnected, there is an obvious need to examine how and to what extent their interactions (globalization) have shaped global history. It is unlikely that any single macrotheory will manage to organize the heterogeneity of world history, but that is a poor excuse for not trying to capture global and globalizing processes.

The existence of globalizing processes is one thing. Yet, commensurate with globalization are processes of recognition that one's world is becoming more closely interconnected. Roland Robertson and David Inglis argue that a globalization consciousness is anything but a new phenomenon. They argue that sensitivities to interconnectedness emerged quite clearly in the Graeco-Roman world in response to early globalization developments. The successes of Alexander the Great and Roman imperialism created politico-economic systems that spanned the area from the Mediterranean to India, with increasing connections to areas further away in Afro-Eurasia.

This increasing sense of an interconnected world, even if not fully global or planetary in scope, had several concrete manifestations. Attempts to write universal historiographies or histories of the world began in this era. Some Greek philosophical schools began to emphasize cosmopolitan identities that transcended home city states. Similarly, imperial conquests opened up worlds of trade and administration that took Greeks and Romans far from their home towns. Not only were their new tasks to be undertaken in managing imperial activities, the basic ability to travel to farflung territories became more feasible and safer.

In many respects, Rome itself may have epitomized these early globalizing processes. Roman citizens viewed their city as the capital of the known world. Its population hailed from all corners of the empire and beyond the imperial frontiers. The very density of the Roman urban population, combined with the ethnic heterogeneity, guaranteed a sense of greater interconnectedness. Roman trade networks (and balance of payment problems) extended to India and China. Roman food became more varied. Roman entertainments (for example gladiators and exotic animals) were recruited from all over the known world. As a consequence, a sense of interconnectedness and global consciousness became commonplace, especially in the centre of the Roman empire, at least two millennia before our own time. Thus, globality is nothing new.

A greater awareness of interconnectivity is one facet of globalization. Another related dimension, however, is the emergence of norms that constrain behaviours considered harmful or undesirable to the functioning of society. In the study of globalization, one question is whether these norms spread beyond their initially local environs and become more widely and more deeply entrenched. Andrew Linklater's perspective is that all societies develop 'civilizing/civility' processes that maintain order and constrain violence and suffering. People are socialized into these expectations and internalize them. Along with the development of mutual identifications as members of the same society and empathy, the internal constraints help to make it possible for individuals to adapt to other peoples' legitimate needs and demands.

But this civilizational consciousness can be two-faced. For instance, it tends to emerge along with a sense that the civilized are superior to the non-civilized. The standards of civilization can then be used to justify the subordination of outsiders until they attain the level of development enjoyed by the 'more civilized' group – a process that describes the interactions between the West and the non-West in recent centuries. Alternatively, increased interactions between different groups can also lead to defensive reactions against what are viewed as highly undesirable and alien cultural encroachments. In either case, the weakening of the applicability of civilizational norms on a global scale is conceivable. Norms may apply to one's own group but not the categorical others.

Despite the risks, Linklater is moderately optimistic that norms pertaining to various types of human suffering are becoming global. Norms applying to the undesirability of slavery, colonial domination and forced labour have been developing for some time. Sentiments against the persecution of minorities, civilian suffering in wartime and the employment of excessive military force appear to be emerging on a global scale. Nevertheless, the jury is still out on the full extent to which a global civilizing process will develop that is capable of constraining the inflicting of intentional and unintentional harm perpetrated by states and non-state actors throughout a globalizing planet.

David Wilkinson's emphasis is on the development of increased complexity within nested system levels and the 'scaling up' of initially local processes. Like Linklater, he is interested in civilizations, but norms would constitute only one type of process that can be globalized. Globalization, for Wilkinson, therefore, is about the scaling up of local processes towards limits ultimately imposed by the dimensions of the planet Earth. He acknowledges that the 'norm' in globalization analyses is to stress more recent (post-1945 to post-Cold War) increases in the flow of commodities across national borders. These increases in economic activities have meant corresponding changes in banking, marketing, investing, production, media and corporate mobility. Such ongoing changes are certainly real, but they only scratch the surface of longer term globalization processes. The scaling up of population diasporas, anti-globalization political movements and crime all predate the Second World War. Some warfare encompassed multiple regions of fighting long before 1939. Even longer term processes of globalization characterize the fusion of 'civilizations/world systems' – a process that began around 1500 BCE when Mesopotamia and the Nile Valley lost their political–military autonomy. Parts of the world economy began to integrate before 1500 BCE, as did schemes to conquer the known world. Wilkinson dates the expanding scope of imperialism efforts to the twenty-third century BCE.

Even older globalization processes can be tracked back to the emergence of *Homo sapiens* and the migrations out of Africa to the rest of the world. In fact, Wilkinson suggests that this early process, in important ways, became the central globalization driver, in the sense that it initiated linked processes of demographic expansion and increasing density of human habitation. As humans became more numerous, living within a finite space, pressures to adapt became inescapable. Continued population growth means, moreover, that old adaptations eventually become obsolete. New adaptations must replace older ones. But for how long can globalization processes persist? Once some point of density and complexity is attained, must the system crash in response to widespread famine or disease? Is there no limit to the level of density that can be sustained? Or will the system create counteracting pressures to regulate its own growth that do not depend on increased mortality?

Whatever answers to these questions emerge, it is likely that some problems will persist. Some proportion of the population will continue to be marginalized by upscaling changes. New strategies for coping with the costs of change will be needed. New social configurations will be constructed. Globalization, in other words, has been going on for some time in some spheres of activity and will continue into the future in old and new ways, creating novel opportunities and age-old problems to resolve.

Claudio Cioffi-Revilla's chapter advances a specific model of historical globalization processes that emphasizes multiple origins, differential timing, a common political development sequence and an outcome that represents the largest human-built, complex, adaptive system yet known. The origins of the current world system are traced to four starting points, all of which developed initially with little or no input from any of the other areas. Each of the four areas began as groups of unranked societies, became chiefly societies, then became interstate systems, before developing imperial systems. West Asia (Levant/Fertile Crescent) emerged first, achieving chiefdoms by the sixth millennium BCE, an interstate system by 3700 BCE and empires possibly by the second half of the fourth millennium but certainly by the second half of the third millennium BCE. Next in line was East Asia with chiefdoms by the beginning of the fifth millennium BCE, states early in the second millennium and empires later in the same millennium. Mesoamerica (primarily focused on Mexico) had chiefs by the middle of the second millennium BCE and states by the first half of the first millennium CE. A South American point of origin centred on what is now Peru had chiefdoms and states by the first millennium BCE and one or more empires some time later by the mid-point of the second millennium CE.

All other parts of the world are viewed as less than pristine developments. That is, developments elsewhere were imitative, entailed coercive conquests from one of the points of origin or never quite achieved parallel levels of complexity prior to being absorbed by a more complex world system.

Within this context, globalization is seen as episodes of significant and relatively rapid increases in size and the degree of connectivity within each existing world system. Endogenous globalization takes place within a specific region, and each of the four regions has experienced several instances of this type of globalization. Exogenous globalization involves increasing significantly the connections between separate world systems. Cioffi-Revilla sees only two cases. The first one was built around the Silk Road and helped integrate East and West Asia/Europe increasingly after 200 BCE. The second one forcibly destroyed the autonomy of the two American systems by subordinating them after 1500 CE to the world system that now encompassed the eastern hemisphere. Thus, after 1500, the four original regions had become one world system subject to intermittent bouts of endogenous globalization.

Cioffi-Revilla's model suggests a strong description of what has transpired that is based on his reading of what evidence is currently available. He is the first to point out that many of the details of the processes associated with these developments are still unknown or not fully understood.

New information continues to emerge, sometimes putting what details are thought to be known in jeopardy. For instance, archaeologists have pushed back the timing of the origins of all four of these regions in recent years and may continue to do so. The model needs a great deal of elaboration and may require revision somewhere down the road. But Cioffi-Revilla's point is that a historically based understanding of social evolution – however flawed by ambiguities and errors based on current knowledge – is a better place to begin social science analyses than the more typical complete denial of a past or its relevance to understanding contemporary problems. World system change has been going on for millennia. We do not help ourselves much by limiting studies of problems to a few recent years of changes – some of which have their own origins thousands of years ago.

Christopher Chase-Dunn and Tom Hall (1997) have earlier advanced a complex of theoretical and conceptual arguments for analysing long-term changes. One of their arguments is that there are four types of systems that need to be distinguished in explaining change. One focuses on the exchange of bulk goods – commodities that are both heavy, and therefore more difficult to transport over long distances at an early point, and relatively low in profit. Another emphasizes the exchange of lighter weight, high-profit, prestige and luxury goods. A third one is centred on military and political interactions – or basic international relations. Finally, a fourth one specializes in information and cultural interactions. Chase-Dunn and Hall argue that these systems do not necessarily overlap closely. You could have, for example, a very geographically restricted bulk goods system simultaneously with a widespread prestige goods system of exchange. Military and political relations are also likely to be more circumscribed than are economic interactions. But one of the reasons for examining these various types of systems is that they pulsate – they expand and contract but, generally, tend to expand over time.

Systemic expansion is very much akin to globalization. Tom Hall's chapter looks in particular at incorporation processes. Incorporation involves processes that lead to the absorption of new areas and peoples by existing world systems. The questions revolve around how these processes work, what sorts of a priori developments are conducive to successful incorporation and what differences does incorporation make for the areas and peoples that are swallowed? Much more work needs to be done on these processes, but one of Hall's points is that not much contact needs to be made in order to accelerate social changes across adjacent systemic zones (the fuzzy boundaries between systems). Secondly, processes of change cannot be studied exclusively locally, nor can they be studied only from the perspective of the larger system. It is the interaction between local and systemic context that will provide the biggest analytical pay-off.

Whereas Cioffi-Revilla's model stresses the similarities in political development sequences in his four initially autonomous regions, Christopher Chase-Dunn, Daniel Pasciuti, Alexis Alvarez and Tom Hall pursue a more specific instance of systemic incorporation in their chapter. They focus on developmental dissimilarities within south-western Asia in which a large number of important institutions and strategies first appeared (sedentary villages, farming, chiefdoms, cities, writing, states, empires). South-western Asia was also characterized by two core areas in Mesopotamia and Egypt. Connected by trade in prestige goods as early as the late fourth millennium BCE, the two cores did not fully merge (from a military–political systemic perspective) before around 1500 BCE, thanks in large part to the conquest of Egypt by the Hyksos who moved into the Nile Delta from the Palestine–Syrian area.

Chase-Dunn and his associates contend that the Hyksos-driven merger of the hitherto separate political–military subsystems is an instance of semi-peripheral groups acting as catalysts and main agents of systemic-scale transformations.[6] Semi-peripheral status (differentiating core and periphery in terms of relative population densities with cores having greater densities than peripheries and semi-peripheries falling somewhere in between) is conducive to innovation that can be used to improve the relative status of the innovators. As a consequence, semi-peripheral groups have, on occasion, conquered weakened states that were once too strong to take on. In the process, they create larger, better connected systems encompassing at a minimum the area from which they originally came as well as the newly conquered area.[7]

Yet, what the Chase-Dunn *et al.* team really wishes to examine is whether the timing of major development processes in the two ends of south-western Asia was synchronous. Did Mesopotamians and Egyptians expand their cities and political systems in sync with one another? One reason for suspecting such a possibility is an earlier finding that East and West Asian developments in the rise and fall of states and city growth were correlated in timing between 600 BCE and 1500 CE. This process, termed 'entraining' and possibly linked to trading interactions, could have important implications for our understanding of how distant regions become more closely connected. But first we have to map the timing of developments to see what happened where and when before we can apply this knowledge to explaining the complexities of globalization in particular and development in general.

However, no evidence of synchronized city growth and political expansion for the 2800–400 BCE period is forthcoming. Development did not proceed at the same pace in Egypt and Mesopotamia, nor was the nature of developments similar, perhaps thanks in part to differences in ecology and geopolitics. While both areas were focused on river systems, control of the primary agrarian area was more feasibly achieved in Egypt by controlling movement on the Nile than was possible by attempting to control movements on the Tigris and Euphrates. Then, too, Mesopotamia was more vulnerable to attacks by adjacent rivals (initially Elam and nomads from the hills and desert) than was Egypt. The Hyksos penetration of Egypt was more the exception to the rule of the ancient pattern of Egyptian predominance over Palestinian and Libyan nomads to the east and west of the Nile.

Thus, we have a case of ancient 'endogenous globalization' in one region that deserves further explanation as to what the drivers of scaling up were. The Hyksos element is overt, supporting the Chase-Dunn *et al.* suggestion that nomads and semi-peripheral groups were key links in ancient forms of integration. Climate change, and especially the effects of climate change on nomadic–core interactions and city/imperial growth, is another possibility that deserves closer examination. Trade-based entraining, however, does not appear to provide much of a handle on mid-second millennium globalization in Asia.

Frank and Thompson also look at one world system, but their focus is on Afro-Eurasia during the early Iron Age (1200 BCE to 200 CE). Their specific question centres on the synchronization and distribution of economic waves of prosperity and depression. Frank (1993) has argued that a single world system began to emerge in Bronze Age south-west Asia and came to encompass Asia, Europe and North Africa. Of course, it is one thing to assert the early development of a single and fairly widespread world system and quite another to assess the accuracy of such an assertion. Frank's argument was that one way to test the assertion was to examine the tendency for different parts of Afro-Eurasia to experience economic expansions and contractions at roughly the same time. A third part of Frank's (1993) argument was the construction of a concrete schedule of economic fluctuations encompassing the Bronze and early Iron Ages.

In the chapter found in this volume, Frank and Thompson follow up an earlier Bronze Age study (4000–1200 BCE) with a look at the early Iron Age.[8] The empirical question is whether a more comprehensive examination of archaeological and historical sources on economic fluctuations produces evidence that corresponds to Frank's (1993) predicted schedule of economic cycles. A second empirical question, assuming that some generalization is possible, is precisely where the general cycles seem to apply. Both the Bronze Age and the early Iron Age findings are similar. It is possible to construct a general schedule of economic fortunes for Afro-Eurasia that, however, does not always correspond to what had been predicted earlier. Moreover, it is fairly rare for the general cycles to fit all parts of the Old World equally well. Periods of overlapping economic fortunes were most likely to be felt near the shifting core areas of Afro-Eurasia – and less likely to be similar as one moved further away from the more active zones of production and consumption. There is a longitudinal pattern, however, of increasingly widespread and intensive economic contractions to be experienced at roughly the same time. So, evidence of increasing interdependence in general, but it was not necessarily uniform, persistent or characterized by high levels of integration.

Historical globalization in the ancient Old World – in this chapter identified as growing interdependence and increased awareness of its implications – was marked by uneven advances and regressions influenced by a variety of factors, including climate change, technology change, trade, conflict, disease and political–military concentration/deconcentration. Contemporary globalization processes do not necessarily work much differently. If the evidence does not fully support an extremely early, pan-Afro-Eurasian world system, its gradual expansion can be tracked empirically. So, too, can the continuities and discontinuities of early globalizations processes.

While Frank and Thompson were looking mainly for continuities, Sing Chew's chapter examines discontinuities almost exclusively. Chew's main interest is the 'dark ages' – periods of systemic crisis in which normal processes have encountered obstacles that lead to long breakdowns of the systems in question. More specifically, Chew examines several long, half-millennium in duration periods in global history: 2200–1700 BCE, 1200–700 BCE and 400–900 CE. In each case, processes of globalization were halted by persistent periods of distress. Chew notes that it is important to understand these dark ages because they show that global history is not simply a tale of perpetual network expansion. Major ruptures occur, and it may well be that these punctuations are the catalysts for evolutionary change.

Historically, dark ages have often been attributed to imperial corruption and/or marauding barbarians. Both elements may well be present, but their causal force is unimpressive to Chew. He stresses instead ecological imbalances brought on by intensive exploitation of natural resources. Resource depletion leads to a breakdown in normal processes of societal interaction. Resource depeletion also requires an indefinite and variable time for recovery, which may or may not be assisted by technological innovation and the discovery of new areas and resources to exploit. In the interim, however, one can expect a closely connected syndrome of economic slowdowns, political breakdowns, social upheavals and war, deurbanization, migration, demographic losses, ecological degradation, tectonic shifts and climate deterioration. Part of the process of clawing one's way out of these systemic crises may also involve ideological/cultural shifts and major forms of political/societal reorganization. Dark ages, therefore, constitute major opportunities for systemic transformation. By studying them more intensely as general phenomena, we may be better off analytically than in attempting to examine 'normal' developments of expansion and contraction.

Joachim Rennstich is also interested in adaptive behaviour, but his focus is on circumvention processes. Blockages, often land based, occur periodically to the expansion of world trade. Historically, new maritime-based networks have been developed to go around these blockages. In the process of doing so, trade has become an increasingly globalized phenomenon. Examples include the Phoenicians early in the first millennium BCE, Italian city states in the thirteenth and fourteenth centuries CE, as well as Dutch endeavours in the sixteenth century CE.

The crux of these circumventions has been to reorganize existing network nodes or to develop entirely new nodes and systems. One way in which these new or reorganized networks are manifested is the emergence or expansion of world cities, often connected to maritime port services, which constitute major nodes in these trade systems. While these maritime responses to continental blockages have taken place on a number of historical occasions, Rennstich also contends that an evolutionary shift has taken place in the circumvention process – one brought on by the emergence of an information network society. Given the nature of the flow of digital information, one still has networks and major nodes in the networks, but the emphasis need no longer be placed on maritime innovation. At the same time, the earlier maritime network innovations have established a strategic foundation for building increasingly complex systemic structures that an information technology-based economy continues in many respects. Global history repeats itself in some respects while mutating into new forms of societal interaction.

Like all the other chapters in this volume, Dennis Flynn and Arturo Giraldez reject the notion that globalization is a novel and recent phenomena. Their point, however, is that true globalization began only after 1571. Globalization could only take place when all populated continents were in sustained interaction through global trade. Thus, prior to 1571, greater connectiveness was achieved throughout the Old World – as earlier chapters emphasize – but two-thirds of the globe (most of the Atlantic, the Americas and most of the Pacific) remained pretty much outside Old World networks. In 1571, however, Manila was established as a Spanish entrepôt connecting eastern Eurasia to the Americas.

Flynn and Giraldez elaborate their interpretation with a discussion of the global economic causal forces at work. The Manila entrepôt was set up in part to deliver large quantities of American silver to China, where the price of silver had boomed as the result of an increasing reliance on silver as a monetary medium within the huge and rich Chinese domestic economy. It took several generations (to about 1640) for the Chinese price of silver to move down to the world price standard. This silver boom process was repeated in the first half of the eighteenth century due in part to one of the consequences of the first boom. American food crops were introduced into the Chinese diet encouraging rapid population increase and increased economic demand on the part of Chinese consumers. Thus, we have an instance of a complex case of globalization processes and consequences that feed back into subsequent globalization complexity and worldwide reorganization.

Last, but certainly not least, Patrick K. O'Brien's chapter focuses at length on another set of globalization consequences. One of the outcomes of increased European commercial successes was the colonial takeover of a good proportion of the globe. O'Brien's main question is whether these colonies discouraged the prospects for nineteenth- and twentieth-century economic growth in the Third World. His basic answer is no. Colonization seemed to have little to do with whose economy expanded thanks to an explosion in contemporary trade volumes.

To pursue this conclusion, O'Brien divides the non-European world into three zones. Zone 1 encompasses areas that were populated largely by white European settlers (such as North America, parts of South America, Australia, New Zealand and South Africa). Zone 2 takes in the immediate geographical periphery of western Europe (Russia to the Balkans). Zone 3 is the Third World remainder – parts of which were controlled by European governors and parts of which were not. The questions then are which zones profited most from the explosion of trade-induced economic growth between 1815 and 1948 (after which colonization was pretty much on the wane), and can one discriminate within zone 3 between colonized and autonomous territories?

O'Brien's answer, in brief, is that zone 3 remained relatively marginal to global economic expansion throughout the post-1815 era. Zone 3 was never much diversified in terms of the raw materials it supplied to the world economy. Other than oil, which did not come on line much before the mid-twentieth century, zone 3 supplied relatively inexpensive food and organic materials that, for the most part, Europe was not dependent upon because it could obtain most of its own raw materials closer to home.

To make matters worse, zone 3 was least favoured in terms of European investment and migration. Zone 1 fared much better in these spheres of activity. As a consequence, the poorest regions of Asia, Africa and South America remained poor and committed to relatively inefficient subsistence agrarian production (throughout at least the 1815–1948 period). Their economic problems were made even more severe by the geopolitical shocks of the major power fighting of 1914–45, the first-world tendency to develop technological substitutes for their raw material exports and the widespread decline in death rates resulting from improved health practices.

Within this context, zone 3 colonies and autonomous areas fared equally well or poorly. What mattered more than colonial identity were such factors as resource endowments, distance from European markets and infrastructure for delivering interior commodities to ports for global distribution. The thrust of a globalizing world economy simply left zone 3 on the margins, without anyone deliberately planning to marginalize a substantial proportion of the world's population.

Conclusion

So, do our multiple chapters resolve the relationships between globalization and global history? No. Do they specify precisely how contemporary globalization is informed by past instances of intensified interconnectivity? Again, the answer is no. Both questions will take quite some time to sort out and, even then, there will be considerable differences of opinion as to how best to go about accounting for change in the past, present and future. Our chapters merely represent a sampling of tentative suggestions – some of which are conflicting while others have yet to be fully elaborated – about how we might go about unravelling globalization phenomena and constructing global histories. Many more studies will be needed to specify further the historical processes of global (and globalizing) network construction and intensification. We have no doubt they will be forthcoming.

This book, and our scholarly endeavour, is dedicated therefore to a new attempt to comprehend the world in its entirety, using historical enquiry to illuminate the processes transforming our own world circumstances. In our present era, we face the danger of a reversion to power politics and the naked pursuit of power and domination, leading to a self-fulfilling prophecy of a so-called 'clash of civilizations'. The rekindling of ancient enmities in many parts of the world and the inflaming of new rivalries based on the pursuit of wealth or power will inevitably fuel a new phase of global conflicts, unleashing a perhaps unending spiral of violence and counterviolence, fear and securitization. It is our belief that scholars of global history and globalization can indeed make a positive contribution to challenging this danger of division and conflict inherent in the present conjuncture in global history and answer this challenge by offering analysis and insight that encourages a nascent global culture based upon greater mutual understanding, tolerance and cooperation.

Globalization is ultimately not about a set of predetermined historical outcomes, already set in motion by the 'laws' of nature or history. Our common global history remains therefore open, and it is up to all of us to help shape its outcomes. In the rich tapestry that is our common global history, it will be by finally embracing the positive potential of 'globalizations' and 'globality' and the acceptance of a 'humanocentric' understanding of the world (as opposed to an egocentric approach or the dominant conventional 'Eurocentric' perspective, or alternative centrisms in reaction to it) that we will eventually come to see all human history as our own and, by doing so, comprehend the future as one common destiny. Perhaps this is the final meaning of both globalization and global history – that these two concepts, and their mutual relationship in theory and real practice, represent the forging of collective human consciousness. If this is the case, such construction of a global knowledge may in turn contribute to the emergence and evolution of new forms of collective human will, which we sincerely hope will contribute to a global culture based on collective responsibilities for the welfare, peace, prosperity, security and dignity of all human beings, no matter where they may live on this planet.

Notes

1 Obviously, not all local activity is equally likely to influence global patterns. But then some local activity is also likely to be more resistant to global influences than activity elsewhere.

2 See in particular Denemark *et al.* (2000) and Thompson (2000). This volume, in part, represents work by the 'World Historical Systems Theory Group' of the International Studies Association, founded in 1989 and composed of scholars from many disciplines, all concerned with long-term historical processes, patterns and analysis of change and/or continuity in these activities.

3 For a pioneering work on this topic written four decades ago, see McNeill (1963).

4 See Jerry Bentley's chapter in this volume.

5 See Roland Robertson and David Inglis' chapter in this volume.
6 Was it also an earlier manifestation of increased global consciousness that preceded the Graeco-Roman phenomenon by a millennium and a half?
7 Cioffi-Revilla would presumably consider the Hyksos-led integration of southwestern Asia as endogenous globalization. Yet it possesses all the trappings of his exogenous globalization processes.
8 The Bronze Age study can be found in Frank and Thompson (2005).

References

Chase-Dunn, Christopher and Thomas D. Hall, eds. 1997. *Rise and Demise: Comparing World-Systems*. Boulder, CO: Westview Press.

Denemark, Robert A., Jonathan Friedman, Barry K. Gills and George Modelski, eds. 2000. *World System History: the Social Science of Long-term Change*. London: Routledge.

Frank, Andre Gunder. 1993. 'The Bronze Age world system and its cycles'. *Current Anthropology* 34: 383–413.

Frank, Andre Gunder and William R. Thompson. 2005. 'Bronze Age economic expansion and contraction revisited'. *Journal of World History* 16 (2): 115–72.

McNeill, William H. 1963. *The Rise of the West*. Chicago, IL: University of Chicago Press.

Thompson, William R. 2000. 'Comparing approaches to the social science history of the world system', in Robert A. Denemark, Jonathan Friedman, Barry K. Gills and George Modelski, eds. *World System History: the Social Science of Long-term Change*. London: Routledge.

2 Globalizing history and historicizing globalization

Jerry H. Bentley

The globalization of history and historicization of globalization are two unfinished intellectual projects. Indeed, they are barely under way. There are reasons why it has taken historians and others so long to recognize the need to globalize history and historicize globalization. These reasons have to do with the context in which professional historical scholarship developed. Yet, to the extent that historical scholarship makes claims to understand the world and its development through time, both projects are necessary and essential.

During the past 150 years of professional historical scholarship, historians have proved to be quite adept at historicizing all manner of social and cultural constructions. They have historicized political institutions, social structures, cultural traditions, religious beliefs, technological innovations and even human emotions. They have brought penetrating historical analysis to bear not only on political and social elites, but also on the experiences of various constituencies formerly without history, such as women, workers, peasants, minorities, slaves and other oppressed peoples. Ironically, however, with a few notable exceptions (such as Novick 1988; Duara 1995), historians have not done a very good job of historicizing professional historical scholarship itself. If some plucky scholar were to undertake a historical sociology of the historical profession, let me mention two findings, apart from the social, racial, gender and other associations of professional historians, that might emerge from the study.

First, looking at the immediate political environment, this putative historical sociologist might point out that professional historical scholarship emerged at a time of intense nationalism and energetic state-building projects in Europe. In view of this context, it is not surprising that professional historians devoted attention to states, and particularly to national states – their creation, their institutions, constitutions, cultural traditions, collective experiences, relations with neighbours and sometimes their decline and collapse. Historians lavished attention on national states, which they construed as discrete and internally coherent communities, rather than the many other social, cultural, religious, ethnic or racial groupings that they might have taken as units of analysis. The decision to focus attention on states was quite deliberate. Leopold von Ranke once referred to states as 'spiritual substances . . . thoughts of God' (Ranke 1973: 119), and Peter Novick aptly characterized Ranke's approach to the past as one of 'pantheistic state-worship' (Novick 1988: 27). In effect, the early professional historians provided national communities with genealogies that legitimized and naturalized their existence (Duara 1995). In return for this welcome notice, national states rewarded professional historians and subsidized their work by supporting universities, establishing professorial chairs in history, maintaining archives that facilitated the study of national communities, funding the publication of historical documents, underwriting research on national histories and mandating the study of national histories in school curricula. Already by the mid-nineteenth century, historians and states had worked out close symbiotic relationships based on strong mutual interests – a pattern that continues to the present day. As a result, professional historical scholarship emerged and developed as an intellectual artifact of the national state era of world history: in the absence of national states, professional historical scholarship as we know it is almost inconceivable.

Second, looking beyond Europe to take the larger global context into consideration, our historical sociologist might also point out that professional historical scholarship emerged at a time when European and Euro-American peoples dominated most of the world's lands and peoples. Thus, alongside the construction of national states, the twin and intricately intertwined processes of industrialization and imperialism figured prominently as context for the emergence of professional historical scholarship. Industry not only transformed Europe, but also brought unprecedented military and economic strength to European and Euro-American peoples, enabling them to conquer distant lands, exploit their resources and subject their peoples to colonial rule. For the emergence of professional historical scholarship, the particular significance of industry and empire is that they encouraged scholars to construe Europe as the site of genuine historical development. Georg Wilhelm Friedrich Hegel, Karl Marx and Leopold von Ranke dissented from one another on many fundamental issues, yet they were nevertheless in remarkable agreement in viewing Europe (including the Mediterranean basin) as the dynamic core of world history, while regarding Africa, the pre-Columbian Americas and even Asian lands as sinks of lethargy and stagnation, untouched by conscious or meaningful historical development. In Hegel's pronouncements, for example, the Mediterranean basin was 'the centre of World-History', but East Asia was 'severed from the process of general historical development, and has no share in it', while Africa was 'the land of childhood, which lying beyond the day of self-conscious history, is enveloped in the dark mantle of Night' (Hegel 1956: 79–102). These views, which corresponded closely with those of European imperialists (Adas 1989), laid the foundation for a convenient though ideologically charged division of scholarly labour that persisted well into the twentieth century: Europe and recently

Europeanized lands in the Americas became the subjects of proper historical analysis, while Asian lands became the provinces of orientalists, and sub-Saharan Africa, the pre-Columbian Americas, Oceania and the tropical world all fell to the tender mercies of the anthropologists.

This sketchy historical sociology helps to explain two characteristics of professional historical scholarship: first, its gravitation towards national states as the default and almost natural frameworks of historical analysis, and second, its assumption that European experience is the touchstone for the understanding of world history. On the basis of observations similar to these, some early and perhaps overexuberant exponents of post-modern critiques drew the inference that historical scholarship amounts to little or nothing more than a discourse that reflects and legitimizes the modern capitalist society from which it emerged. This view has faded recently, receding before more nuanced analyses that recognize historians' entanglements in society while holding open the possibility that reflexive scholarship is still capable of yielding meaningful constructions of the past. To the extent, however, that historical scholarship is indeed more than discourse or ideology – to the extent that it has the potential to break free of enthralment to the nation and European modernity and to broker some valid understanding of the world and its development through time – I would argue the need to globalize history and historicize globalization.

Thus far, scholars have moved more in the direction of globalizing history than of historicizing globalization. More precisely, although they have not by any means entirely globalized historical analysis, they have generated a great deal of knowledge about the world's various lands, peoples and societies. At least since the time of *Homo erectus*, if not before, all peoples have experienced some need to know about a larger world beyond their own societies that was a source of foods, tools, resources, spouses and opportunities for exchange. Since remote antiquity, migrants, merchants, explorers, soldiers, administrators, diplomats, missionaries, pilgrims and other travellers have ventured forth from their own societies and returned with information and lore about distant lands. More recently, a half-century of professional area studies scholarship has generated a huge library of knowledge about every corner of the world.

Whether in the form of premodern travel accounts or early modern ethnography or contemporary area studies, knowledge about the larger world has always been highly problematic. Quite apart from epistemological issues and problems of cross-cultural communication, in most if not all cases, some kind of interest has driven or informed or conditioned the production of knowledge about the larger world. The nature of the interests has varied over time and space but, speaking in general terms, I would suggest that the interests of empire, business and mission have been especially prominent in promoting the production of knowledge about the larger world. In other words, efforts to collect, compile and organize information about foreign lands and peoples has commonly reflected the needs of imperialists seeking knowledge that would enhance security and help them administer subject peoples, or the interests of businessmen seeking knowledge that would promote commerce and the exploitation of resources and opportunities, or the concerns of missionaries seeking knowledge that would aid their quest for converts. These interests are of course not mutually exclusive: on the contrary, they have overlapped and reinforced one another in multifarious ways. It is conceivable that some few individuals have ventured into the larger world and produced knowledge about foreign lands and peoples out of pure, disinterested curiosity, but the records of travel and foreign description known to me all emerged from some kind of context saturated with interests such as those just mentioned.

The problems that afflict knowledge serving imperial interests are well known and widely appreciated from a generation of scholarship since the publication of *Orientalism* by Edward W. Said (1978). Said and many others have clearly exposed the distortions that masqueraded as reliable and proven knowledge about Asian and African societies while serving to justify European and Euro-American colonial rule in modern times. Yet the production of knowledge shaped by imperial interests is by no means an exclusively European and Euro-American affair, nor did it first emerge in modern times. On the contrary, similar knowledge has flourished routinely in contexts of imperial expansion. China, for example, has been a perennial source of 'orientalist' knowledge. Following the central Asian campaigns of the general Meng Tian in 215 BCE, Chinese scholars elaborated a large body of thought about the nomadic Xiongnu people, culminating in the careful historical and ethnographic descriptions of the court historian Sima Qian. While reflecting very different perspectives on the best way of dealing with the Xiongnu, this body of knowledge consistently sought understanding of the Xiongnu in the interests of frontier management and control of nomadic peoples (Di Cosmo 2002). During the Tang dynasty, Chinese interest in foreign lands extended to south-east Asia as well as central Asia (Schafer 1963, 1967). During the eighteenth century, Qing scholars also turned their attention to peoples of the south-west, relying on the same techniques of precise cartography and close-up ethnography that served European colonizers so well as they produced knowledge to support imperial expansion in early modern times (Hostetler 2001). In the nineteenth and twentieth centuries, a variety of Confucian, Christian and Communist interests informed Chinese scholarship on ethnic minorities (Harrell 1995).

Knowledge influenced by imperial interests has not necessarily been totally invalid or dismissible as hopelessly corrupt. Alongside distortion and misunderstanding, Chinese knowledge about the Xiongnu sometimes offered genuine insight into the nature of nomadic society, particularly in the sensitive work of Sima Qian. Yet there is no mistaking the fact that Sima Qian turned his attention to the Xiongnu because he sought knowledge that would be useful in the context of Chinese expansion into central Asia and clashes with nomadic peoples. Similarly, the Greek historian Herodotus provided valuable accounts and often generous descriptions of foreign peoples and their ways. Yet his magnanimous and open-minded work was not an expression of innocent, disinterested curiosity about the larger world. Rather, it was an enquiry undertaken in the context of a considerable Greek political and commercial presence in the Mediterranean basin that raised serious security problems when Greek interests clashed with those of the mighty Persian empire.

The interests of business have been no less influential for purposes of both promoting and colouring the production of knowledge. Like imperialist projects, business ventures call for serviceable knowledge about foreign lands, peoples and resources. Efforts to develop this knowledge trace back to antiquity, as many peoples collected information about individual specific lands where they had active business interests. In premodern times, the most systematic efforts to compile an organized body of knowledge about the world were those of Muslim merchants and geographers who, after the eighth century CE, ventured throughout most of the eastern hemisphere assembling information about peoples and products from south-east Asia to sub-Saharan Africa. Indeed, records of Muslim merchants and geographers rank as the most important historical sources for some lands in post-classical times (Tibbetts 1971; Levtzion and Hopkins 1981; Al-Muqaddasi 1994). Although not necessarily inclined towards conquest and control of foreign peoples, merchants and business agents have routinely sought profits. This fundamental condition of their project led them to observe closely the world of natural resources, the economic realm of products and services and the male-dominated public sphere of trade, finance and power. They paid less attention, however, to the private spheres of custom, family and spirituality, except insofar as these issues were relevant to their pursuit of profit. Thus, like knowledge produced under imperial influences, business-oriented studies offered a sometimes useful but very partial perspective on foreign lands and peoples.

Quite apart from its bias towards practical utility and the realization of profits, knowledge prompted by business interests has often reinforced knowledge serving imperial interests, and particularly so since early modern times. Whether trade followed the flag or the flag followed trade, imperial and business interests have largely converged since the formation of European colonial and commercial concerns in the sixteenth century. Not surprisingly, European exploration and expansion generated a vast library of reportage on the world beyond Europe. Both at the time of their original publication and sometimes also in later editions, such as those published since 1846 by the Hakluyt Society, these works may well have offered accurate and pertinent information about the larger world but, in doing so, they also 'validated and justified European exploration and commercial exploitation of the resources of overseas areas of the world' (Bridges and Hair 1996: 236).

Like imperialists and merchants, missionaries have a strong interest in knowing the larger world, the better in their cases to communicate their messages and win converts. Missionary interests certainly prompted the ad hoc study of individual foreign lands and peoples in premodern times. Buddhist missionaries appear to have paid close attention to Chinese values and interests, as they translated technical Buddhist terms into language familiar to Chinese audiences, and Sufis have a reputation for adapting Muslim teachings to cultural traditions that embraced very different values. During the eras of the crusades and Mongol empires, Christian European missionaries closely observed Muslim societies in Spain and Palestine and nomadic societies in central Asia as well as Hindu and Buddhist societies in India, China and other lands, all with an eye towards casting their messages in the most effective terms. Less enduring faiths such as Mithraism and Manichaeism also flourished for a season at least partly because of useful understanding of potential converts and their cultural traditions (Bentley 1993). While recognizing that missionary interests have prompted the targeted study of individual foreign societies for centuries, I am unaware of any large-scale, systematic efforts comparable to the work of Muslim geographers before the sixteenth century.

After the sixteenth century, however, European exploration and expansion created a framework favouring the production of knowledge about the larger world that was supremely useful for missionary purposes. Rarely, of course, have large-scale missionary projects been purely spiritual affairs, unentangled with more worldly interests. On the contrary, the interests of empire or business or both have commonly travelled in missionaries' baggage and influenced the knowledge that they have generated. In the case of state-sponsored Christian European missionaries after the sixteenth century, the interests of both empire and business were on conspicuous display. This does not necessarily mean that missionaries' knowledge is worthless or unreliable. Like studies prompted by imperialist or business interests, knowledge inspired by missionary zeal had the potential to open doors to sympathetic understanding of foreign cultural traditions. To mention only one example, this point is clear from the work of the Spanish Franciscan Bernardino de Sahagún, who went to Mexico in 1529 to convert Indian souls to Christianity. Sahagún took pains to master the Nahuatl language, elicit information about the various peoples of the Aztec empire and record their history and literature. He paid close and respectful attention to his informants – and he did so at some risk to his own safety and reputation. He offered an often sympathetic account of the indigenous peoples of Mexico, and his various writings remain by far the most important textual sources on Aztec society (Sahagún 1950–82; Edmonson 1974; Klor de Alva *et al.* 1988). Yet, even while acknowledging that Sahagún and other missionaries have sometimes developed respectable knowledge and offered unusual insight into foreign cultural traditions, it is also clear that their effort to understand other peoples was to some greater or lesser extent a tool serving the interests of their own societies.

As recent critiques have made abundantly clear, this general observation holds true not only for premodern and early modern efforts to produce knowledge about the larger world, but also for professional area studies of the past half-century (Rafael 1994; Palat 1996; Lewis and Wigen 1997; Wallerstein 1997; Cumings 1998). It is true enough that individual area studies scholars have not often seen themselves as the agents or collaborators of empire, business or mission – and indeed, for the most part, their writings have had limited practical application for those purposes. It is also true that area studies emerged as a distinctively North American way of developing and organizing knowledge that differed considerably from the efforts of earlier imperialists, businessmen and missionaries to understand the larger world. Area studies found a home mostly in universities, not in government ministries, business offices or missionary headquarters. With massive infusions of aid from government and private sources after the Second World War, area studies quickly became a professional academic venture closely associated with the established disciplines of knowledge, not a practical venture geared towards the control of subject lands, the exploitation of foreign resources, trade with distant peoples or the conversion of foreign souls.

Nevertheless, the massive political and financial infrastructures supporting area studies demonstrate eloquently that perceived national interests stand behind this gargantuan project to produce knowledge about the larger world. Indeed, professional area studies scholarship, as it has developed since the Second World War, has represented a distinctive and very particular expression of the very general need that all societies have to understand the world around them. It has fostered expertise in world languages, and it has generated libraries of information about foreign lands and peoples. In spite of recent critiques, there is no question in my mind that area studies scholarship has generated more knowledge and better knowledge than any earlier project to understand the larger world. In some cases, I would argue further that area studies scholarship has pointed beyond the development of basic information and the production of reliable knowledge to the formulation of understanding, insight and even wisdom about the larger world. As the principal rubric under which contemporary peoples organize scholarly knowledge about the larger world, however, area studies scholarship inevitably and inescapably reflects the various political, military, economic, commercial and cultural interests that prompt peoples to seek knowledge and understanding of the world beyond their own societies.

Perfectly disinterested knowledge about the larger world is a noble dream akin to the notion of total objectivity. Nevertheless, even when tainted by worldly interests, knowledge produced under the sign(s) of empire, business, mission or area studies has transmitted some quantum of reliable information that is useful for some purposes of understanding the larger world. It has admittedly also imparted some quantum of rubbish, and the purposes it has served have not always been particularly noble. Yet, historical area studies scholarship has outstanding potential to yield insight into the world and its development through time. Realizing this potential, however, requires scholarly efforts that elude what Ian Buruma recently called 'the traps of mimicry, pedantry, [and] prejudice' that have ensnared so many students of the larger world (Buruma 2002). What method(s) or scholarly convention(s) might enable historians and other scholars to avoid these traps?

The short answer is that there is no simple answer to this question. Granting that contemporary scholars mostly reject the blatant ethnocentrism that sometimes informed scholarship of earlier generations, it is not necessarily a simple matter to escape the gravitational field of Eurocentrism, which is certainly one of the more prominent snares awaiting scholars dealing with the larger world. Some scholars even wear their Eurocentrism proudly on their sleeves like some badge of honour (Landes 1998). Yet, even if it is possible to avoid crude formulations, more subtle forms of Eurocentrism are difficult to recognize and reject. Samir Amin (1989) and Arif Dirlik (1999) have both argued powerfully that Eurocentrism is not an attitude that is alterable at will so much as a perspective on the world rooted in the political economy of global capitalism, while Dipesh Chakrabarty (2000) has charged that, because of its collusion with the national state and European modernity, academic history itself is a thoroughly Eurocentric project. How is it possible to unthink perspectives on the world that have conditioned the foundations of professional historical scholarship itself?

In the absence of some scholarly Archimedean point offering unfiltered access to the larger world, it seems that all historical scholarship will inevitably reflect the perspectives of the historians who produce it. In this case, perhaps the most pertinent question is how to make a virtue of this necessity, particularly when dealing with the world beyond oneself and one's own society?

Two main alternative strategies have emerged to deal with this problem in historical scholarship. One approach, which has taken several different and distinctive forms, involves a turn to the local. Jean-François Lyotard made the argument for focusing on the local in perhaps the most general terms. Following the logic of his famous pronouncement that the defining characteristic of the post-modern age is 'incredulity toward metanarratives', Lyotard insisted that the only meaningful narratives were local narratives (Lyotard 1984, 1989). Steven Feierman advanced a compatible argument in historical rather than philosophical terms when he held that European categories cannot adequately account for African experience, which he maintained was comprehensible only in African terms (Feierman 1993, 1995). While it certainly embarrassed Eurocentric visions of the global past, this post-modern rejection of metanarratives, grand narratives, master narratives and any other kind of narrative larger than the local had its own political and ideological purposes, in that it served as a convenient foundation for identity politics in search of a useable past.

The best works valorizing identity present spirited and cogent challenges to Eurocentric history. Dipesh Chakrabarty's essays, for example, argue powerfully and persuasively for the recognition of alternative modernities. In an analysis that is quite compatible with Feierman's argument about European categories and African experience, Chakrabarty insists on the recognition of patterns that European constructs cannot accommodate, such as Indian 'work' that revolves around and is thoroughly saturated with religious rituals and practices, and so passes well beyond materialist Marxist conceptions of labour. He also calls eloquently for recognition of subaltern pasts that are radically different for academic historians who cannot accept the gods, miracles and supernatural beliefs that permeated subaltern consciousness, existence and practice. Alongside critical observations and prescriptive advice, Chakrabarty also explores modes of Bengali life that demonstrate their differences from European experience and, hence, the inadequacy of European categories to subsume them. Discussions of literary imagination, social practices and family ideals all enable him to argue powerfully that the liberal–rational mode of European modernity is only one (provincial) way of organizing life in modern times. There are different modes of reason, and there is a need to tell different stories of these different reasons rather than permit one privileged mode of rationality to stand as critic and judge for all the diverse ways of being human (Chakrabarty 2000).

So far, so good: Chakrabarty's focus on Bengali experience effectively challenges Eurocentric history and contributes to the globalization of history by putting new perspectives on the agenda. It is conceivable that other scholars might draw on the experiences of other lands and peoples to similar effect. But the strategy of turning attention to the local has its costs. Fernando Coronil has articulated the problem succinctly and pointedly: 'This current, directed against metanarratives of history, produces disjointed mininarratives which reinforce dominant worldviews; reacting against determinisms, it presents free-floating events; refusing to fix identity in structural categories, it essentializes identity through difference; resisting the location of power in structures or institutions, it diffuses it throughout society and ultimately dissolves it. Ironically, this popular trend leaves us facing a world of disjointed elements at a time when the globalization of space – marked by integrative and exclusionary processes – makes it intellectually compelling and politically indispensable to understand how parts and whole hang together' (Coronil 1992: 99–100). Quite apart from his contemporary political concerns – and Coronil is by no means the only scholar to argue recently that post-modern and post-colonial scholarship undermines historically grounded political action (Ahmad 1992; Sarup 1993; Dirlik 1997) – Coronil's critique points out that, all too often, the turn to the local involves a refusal to engage analytically with large-scale processes that profoundly influence the development of both individual societies and the larger world, not to mention the conditions and the quality of life in all corners of the world. Local narratives might be essential for the purpose of constructing alternatives to Eurocentric visions of the past, but by themselves they are both insufficient and inadequate for realizing that purpose.

In and of itself, of course, the production of local narratives does not necessarily entail denial of large-scale processes, although the rejection of large-scale narratives clearly discourages efforts to deal with them. Even while making it clear that his own principal interest is the imagination of a 'radically heterogeneous' world, for example, Chakrabarty also explicitly recognizes 'the demonstrable and documentable permeability of cultures and languages' (Chakrabarty 2000: 46, 83). But he does not pursue this acknowledgement to an analysis of cross-cultural interactions. His points about difference between European and Bengali experience are persuasive enough but, in delineating distinctive features of Bengali identity, he overlooks the question of how European and Indian historical actors influenced one another? What were the connecting points, as it were, that make it possible to recognize the 'permeability of cultures and languages', and how did they help to transmit influence in multiple directions, in order to shape the lives and experiences of all peoples involved? When questions such as these come onto the agenda, it becomes necessary to devise analytical categories and chronological frameworks that are larger than those of the individual societies and historical agents under consideration. It would not be necessary to resort to universalizing European constructs such as those Chakrabarty rejects and impose them unthinkingly on all the rest of the world but, whatever form they take, there is a genuine need for larger analytical categories and chronological frameworks for purposes of dealing with issues hinted at but left unexplored by scholarship taking the local turn.

This point directs attention towards the second main strategy for dealing responsibly with the larger world, which in fact refers to the second term in my title, namely the effort to historicize globalization. While the strategy of going local effectively undermines some of the assumptions of Eurocentric history, the strategy of going global by historicizing globalization offers opportunities to decentre Europe by situating European experience in the larger context of world history (thereby, incidentally, contributing from a different angle to Chakrabarty's project of provincializing Europe).

The historicization of globalization is not an unproblematic project. On the contrary, it is fraught with logical, epistemological, moral and other kinds of difficulties. This is clear from the kinds of problems that have bedevilled world history, which is the closest scholarly analogue to the effort to historicize globalization. Some efforts at world history have assimilated all too readily with familiar Eurocentric conceptions, for example, as scholars have adopted both the analytical categories (nation, tribe, culture, civilization and the like) and the social theory (especially Marxist and Weberian) that were characteristic cultural productions of European modernity. In some formulations, world history has reproduced teleologies that make European modernity the reference point of the global past. In other cases, it has overlooked differences both within and between societies through the flattening and homogenization of peoples – hence, the turn to the local and calls for the recognition of heterogeneity such as those of Lyotard, Feierman and Chakrabarty. At its worst, world history has served ideological functions by constructing visions of the global past in which Europe and its outposts figure as sites of dynamism and progress, while other regions become little more than sinks of stagnation and regression.

In spite of all the problems and potential pitfalls, the historicization of globalization is a necessary and indispensable project for purposes of constructing realistic and meaningful visions of the world and its development through time. The turn to the local and the valorization of heterogeneity has important but limited value for this purpose. At some point, it becomes essential to explore the context of heterogeneity and also the links between communities that are supposedly discrete and ostensibly coherent. What might the project of historicizing globalization contribute to the construction of meaning about the global past?

In an era of incredulity towards metanarratives, it might seem pointless to seek a unified vision of the global past. Yet this challenge has emboldened macrotheorists from Marx and Weber, to Spengler and Toynbee, to Michael Mann and Jared Diamond to seek the key to world history. While conceding that the theorists have articulated some useful insights, historians and other scholars alike have mostly judged their efforts unsuccessful, at least insofar as they claim to explain all of world history. All the macrotheories collapse on empirical grounds and, in oversimplifying the world's diversity, they grotesquely distort the experiences of many peoples. Moreover, most of them also depend heavily on some strain of exceptionalist thought or discredited metanarrative.

Thus, it is clear that no single narrative or metanarrative or macrotheory will accommodate all the multiplicity and variety of world history, which calls with particular insistence for a vision of the past that recognizes both heterogeneity and the systems that link heterogeneous peoples, a vision that can account for both fragmentation and integration on multiple levels – local, regional, national, continental, hemispheric, oceanic, global and perhaps others as well. Responding to this need, world historians such as William H. McNeill (1963), Philip D. Curtin (1984), Alfred W. Crosby (1986) and others have focused their analyses on historical interactions and exchanges between peoples and societies. At the same time, however, they have portrayed messy worlds and resisted temptations to reduce the diversity of historical experience to overly simple principles.

My own view is that there are indeed some larger human stories, or at least contexts, that can serve as useful frameworks for analysing the global past and historicizing globalization. More specifically, the global stories of rising human population, expanding technological capacity and increasing interaction between peoples of different societies have profoundly shaped the experiences of almost all human societies and, furthermore, have worked collectively like a triple helix to reinforce one another with powerful effects throughout history (Bentley 2003; see also Goudsblom *et al.* 1989; Sherratt 1995; McNeill and McNeill 2003; Christian 2004). This approach to the global past, which I think of as the study of 'historical globalization', does not authorize rigid theoretical positions or teleological narratives, but rather emphasizes shifting patterns of cross-cultural connections, relationships, networks, interactions and exchanges. This approach maintains that the world has never been the site of discrete, unconnected communities, that cross-cultural interactions and exchanges have taken place since the earliest days of human existence on planet earth, that Europe has not always been a unique or privileged site of dynamism and progress, that identities have always been multiple and malleable, subject to minor tweaking or radical change as individuals and communities have adjusted their self-conceptions to the circumstances of their existence.

It is certainly a challenge to construct coherent and meaningful global stories from the many, diverse, complicated local histories of rising population, expanding technological capacity and increasing cross-cultural interaction. My own narrative would argue neither that globalization is a phenomenon of the past few decades (or the past few hundred years) nor that it is an age-old historical constant. Rather it would historicize globalization by recognizing that human beings (including *Homo erectus* as well as *Homo sapiens*) have ventured well beyond their own communities for different reasons and with different effects for almost two million years. In doing so, they have populated all habitable regions of the earth, constructed thousands of heterogeneous social and cultural traditions, built vast networks of trade and exchange, found ways to exploit or dominate one another, carried biological species across their own naturally established boundary lines into new territories and swapped or appropriated techniques, ideas and religious beliefs. These processes, known in historians' vocabularies by the shorthand terms of migration, social development, trade, imperialism, biological exchange and cultural diffusion, have profoundly influenced the development of individual societies, including the construction of identities recognized by some scholars as radically heterogeneous, as well as the development of the world as a whole. It is of course not the case that most or even many individual human beings directly participated in large-scale globalizing processes before recent times – by engaging in a war of imperial expansion, for example, or by travelling to distant lands as a merchant, by dying from a disease introduced from afar or by converting to a foreign religious faith. Nevertheless, globalizing processes of cross-cultural interaction have profoundly influenced the development of almost all societies and, by defining, shaping or transforming the conditions of existence, they have at least indirectly touched the lives of almost all human beings who have walked the earth.

The historicization of globalization does not represent a cure-all, either for historical scholarship or for the more general effort to understand the larger world. It has little to say about the experiences or historical dynamics of individual communities, except insofar as they have participated in large-scale historical processes. Another consideration is that, by taking long-term perspectives, this vision of the past could easily obscure the messiness and contingency of world history, even if it brings some large-scale processes into clearer focus. Moreover, this approach clearly reflects modern cultural perspectives and might well seem meaningless to anyone situated beyond the horizon of modernity.

Granting that it raises new problems, the effort to historicize globalization might nevertheless enable historians to address some other significant issues. Most importantly, in my view, it offers a framework permitting historians to move beyond the issues that have been the principal concerns of professional historical scholarship from Leopold von Ranke to the present – cultural distinctions, exclusive identities, local knowledge and the experiences of individual societies (most of them in fact construed as national communities) – by making a place on historians' agenda for large-scale processes that connect the world's many ostensibly distinct and discrete societies. At the same time, the effort to historicize globalization also has good potential to facilitate the construction of alternatives to received Eurocentric visions of world history. The strategy of going local is not the only way to challenge Eurocentrism and indeed, for some purposes, it is not even a particularly good way to do so. Global and comparative analyses are also necessary and are in some ways more effective correctives to Eurocentric historical myths (see Wong 1997; Frank 1998; Brook and Blue 1999; Pomeranz 2000).

In combination, the efforts to globalize history and historicize globalization are essential for purposes of clearly understanding the world and its development through time. While recognizing that national states and local communities have always figured as crucial contexts of all peoples' historical experiences, these twin projects make it possible to bring historical focus also to large-scale, globalizing processes that have touched many peoples and profoundly influenced the development of individual societies as well as the world as a whole. Networks of cross-cultural interaction, communication and exchange, after all, are defining contexts of human experience just as surely as are the myriad national states and local communities that scholars have conventionally taken as the default categories of historical analysis. The challenge for those working to globalize history and historicize globalization is to find paths leading beyond notions that the world is a site divided into national spaces, beyond assumptions that European modernity is the appropriate standard for the measurement of all the world's societies, beyond the various political, economic and cultural interests that have tinted but also tainted efforts to produce knowledge about the larger world and beyond temptations to take refuge in the individual histories of local communities as the only knowable subjects of history.

References

Adas, Michael. 1989. *Machines as the Measure of Men: Science, Technology, and Ideologies of Western Dominance*. Ithaca: Cornell University Press.

Ahmad, Aijaz. 1992. *In Theory: Class, Nation, Literatures*. London: Verso.

Al-Muqaddasi. 1994. *The Best Divisions for Knowledge of the Regions*, trans. by B.A. Collins. Reading: Garnet Publishing.

Amin, Samir. 1989. *Eurocentrism*, trans. by Russell Moore. New York: Monthly Review Press.

Bentley, Jerry H. 1993. *Old World Encounters: Cross-Cultural Contacts and Exchanges in Pre-Modern Times*. New York: Oxford University Press.

Bentley, Jerry H. 2003. 'World history and grand narrative' in Eckhardt Fuchs and Benedikt Stuchtey, eds. *Writing World History, 1800–2000*. Oxford: Oxford University Press.

Bridges, R.C. and P.E.H. Hair. 1996. 'The Hakluyt Society and world history' in R.C. Bridges and P.E.H. Hair, eds. *Compassing the Vaste Globe of the Earth: Studies in the History of the Hakluyt Society, 1846–1996*. London: Hakluyt Society, pp. 225–39.

Brook, Timothy and Gregory Blue, eds. 1999. *China and Historical Capitalism: Genealogies of Sinological Knowledge*. Cambridge: Cambridge University Press.

Buruma, Ian. 2002. 'Making a fetish of mystery'. *New York Review of Books* (15 August 2002): 42.

Chakrabarty, Dipesh. 2000. *Provincializing Europe: Postcolonial Thought and Historical Difference*. Princeton: Princeton University Press.

Christian, David. 2004. *Maps of Time: An Introduction to Big History*. Berkeley: University of California Press.

Coronil, Fernando. 1992. 'Can postcoloniality be decolonized? Imperial banality and postcolonial power'. *Public Culture* 5: 89–108.

Crosby, Alfred W. 1986. *Ecological Imperialism: The Biological Expansion of Europe, 900–1900*. Cambridge: Cambridge University Press.

Cumings, Bruce. 1998. 'Boundary displacement: area studies and international studies during and after the Cold War', in Christopher Simpson, ed. *Universities and Empire: Money and Politics in the Social Sciences during the Cold War*. New York: Free Press, pp. 159–88.

Curtin, Philip D. 1984. *Cross-Cultural Trade in World History*. Cambridge: Cambridge University Press.

Di Cosmo, Nicola. 2002. *Ancient China and Its Enemies: The Rise of Nomadic Power in East Asian History*. Cambridge: Cambridge University Press.

Dirlik, Arif. 1997. *The Postcolonial Aura*. Boulder: Westview.

Dirlik, Arif. 1999. 'Is there history after Eurocentrism? Globalism, postcolonialism, and the disavowal of history'. *Cultural Critique* 42: 1–34.

Duara, Prasenjit. 1995. *Rescuing History from the Nation: Questioning Narratives of Modern China*. Chicago: University of Chicago Press.

Edmonson, Munro S., ed. 1974. *Sixteenth-Century Mexico: The Work of Sahagún*. Albuquerque: University of New Mexico Press.

Feierman, Steven. 1993. 'African histories and the dissolution of world history' in Robert H. Bates, V.Y. Mudimbe and Jean O'Barr, eds. *Africa and the Disciplines: The Contributions of Research in Africa to the Social Sciences and Humanities*. Chicago: University of Chicago Press, pp. 167–212.

Feierman, Steven. 1995. 'Africa in history: the end of universal narratives' in Gyan Prakash, ed. *After Colonialism: Imperial Histories and Postcolonial Displacements*. Princeton: Princeton University Press, pp. 40–65.

Frank, Andre Gunder. 1998. *ReOrient: Global Economy in the Asian Age*. Berkeley: University of California Press.

Goudsblom, Johan, E.L. Jones and Stephen Mennell. 1989. *Human History and Social Process*. Exeter: University of Exeter Press.

Harrell, Stevan, ed. 1995. *Cultural Encounters on China's Ethnic Frontiers*. Seattle: University of Washington Press.

Hegel, Georg Wilhelm Friedrich. 1956. *The Philosophy of History*, trans. by J. Sibree. New York: Dover.

Hostetler, Laura. 2001. *Qing Colonial Enterprise: Ethnography and Cartography in Early Modern China*. Chicago: University of Chicago Press.

Klor de Alva, Jorge, H.B. Nicholson and Eloise Qiñones Keber, eds. 1988. *The Work of Bernardino de Sahagún: Pioneer Ethnographer of Sixteenth-Century Aztec Mexico*. Albany, NY: SUNY Press.

Landes, David S. 1998. *The Wealth and Poverty of Nations: Why Some Are So Rich and Some So Poor*. New York: Norton.

Levtzion, Nehemia, and J.F.P. Hopkins, trans. and eds. 1981. *Corpus of Early Arabic Sources for West African History*. Cambridge: Cambridge University Press.

Lewis, Martin W. and Kären E. Wigen. 1997. *The Myth of Continents: A Critique of Metageography*. Berkeley: University of California Press.

Lyotard, Jean-François.1984. *The Postmodern Condition: A Report on Knowledge*, trans. by G. Bennington and B. Massumi. Minneapolis: University of Minnesota Press.

Lyotard, Jean-François. 1989. 'Universal history and cultural differences' in Andrew Benjamin, ed. *The Lyotard Reader*. Oxford: Oxford University Press, pp. 314–23.

McNeill, J.R., and William H. McNeill. 2003. *The Human Web: A Bird's-Eye View of World History*. New York: Norton.

McNeill, William H. 1963. *The Rise of the West: A History of the Human Community*. Chicago: University of Chicago Press.

Novick, Peter. 1988. *That Noble Dream: The 'Objectivity Question' and the American Historical Profession*. Cambridge: Cambridge University Press.

Palat, Ravi Arvind. 1996. 'Fragmented visions: excavating the future of area studies in a post-American world'. *Review* 19: 269–315.

Pomeranz, Kenneth. 2000. *The Great Divergence: China, Europe, and the Making of the Modern World Economy*. Princeton: Princeton University Press.

Rafael, Vicente L. 1994. 'The cultures of area studies in the United States'. *Social Text* 12: 91–111.

Ranke, Leopold von. 1973. *The Theory and Practice of History*, ed. by Georg G. Iggers and Konrad von Moltke. Indianapolis: Bobbs-Merrill.

Sahagún, Bernardino de. 1950–82. *Florentine Codex: General History of the Things of New Spain*, 13 vols., trans. by Arthur J.O. Anderson and Charles E. Dibble. Salt Lake City: University of Utah Press.

Said, Edward W. 1978. *Orientalism*. New York: Vintage.

Sarup, Madan. 1993. *An Introductory Guide to Post-structuralism and Postmodernism*, 2nd edn. Athens: University of Georgia Press.

Schafer, Edward H. 1963. *The Golden Peaches of Samarkand: A Study of T'ang Exotics*. Berkeley: University of California Press.

Schafer, Edward H. 1967. *The Vermilion Bird: T'ang Images of the South*. Berkeley: University of California Press.

Sherratt, Andrew. 1995. 'Reviving the grand narrative: archaeology and long-term change'. *Journal of European Archaeology* 3: 1–32.

Tibbetts, G.R. 1971. *Arab Navigation in the Indian Ocean before the Coming of the Portuguese*. London: Oxford University Press.

Wallerstein, Immanuel. 1997. 'The unintended consequences of Cold War area studies', in *The Cold War and the University: Toward an Intellectual History of the Postwar Years*. New York: Free Press, pp. 195–231.

Wong, R. Bin. 1997. *China Transformed: Historical Change and the Limits of European Experience*. Ithaca, NY: Cornell University Press.

3 The global *animus*

In the tracks of world consciousness

Roland Robertson and David Inglis

Introduction

Ideas about taking the 'world as a whole' seem at first glance to be quintessentially modern in nature. Relatively recent developments, such as mankind's exploration of space and landing on the moon, can be seen as stimulating ideas as to 'globality', that is forms of consciousness that regard the earth as 'one place' (Beck 2000). In this sort of imaginary, all the planet's geographical areas are seen to be intimately interconnected with each other in one way or another, all its various life-forms are seen (as in James Lovelock's Gaia hypothesis and in ecological thinking) to be mutually interdependent, and all its human populations are regarded not as divided between each other but as parts of the overall entity called 'humankind'. If 'globalization' is defined as involving both 'the compression of the world and the intensification of consciousness of the world as a whole' (Robertson 1992: 8; Robertson and Inglis forthcoming: passim), then it would seem to be the case that, if the latter is purely a phenomenon of modernity, then so too must be 'globalization' itself.

One might object that 'consciousness of the world as a whole' can be empirically demonstrated to precede the emergence of modernity. The aptly named 'world religions' have for millennia often involved claims as to the nature of existence that are held to be true at all times, in all places and for all people (Robertson 1994). Yet, this sort of 'religious' thinking is not synonymous with (more) 'secular' ideas as to the world being not just 'one place', but a place that is characterized by increasing compression, interconnection and interdependence between its component parts. These seem to be purely 'modern' phenomena. Thus, it would seem plausible to contend that the genesis of 'world consciousness' should be located in the explorations and conquests of diverse parts of the world by Europeans over the last 500 years, for example in terms of conceptualizations of the 'world as whole' that were expressed in, and augmented through, developments in global cartography (e.g. Crone 1966). In this sense, then, one might say that ideas of 'globality' are clearly cultural expressions of the rise of the geo-economic–political order produced by Western modernity. In his review of such issues, Scholte (2000: 62, 65) has argued that, while 'global consciousness began to tease secular minds half a millennium ago . . . [it] touched few minds [before the nineteenth century] . . . Even for that small minority, globality was usually a passing rather than a central thought'.

This chapter takes a different tack with respect to the historical emergence of issues of 'global consciousness' and 'globality'. We will set out the main contours of what we take to be a particularly well-developed set of premodern 'global' sensibilities, namely what we call the *global animus* (or global 'spirit') that characterized much ancient Greek and Roman thought. Many thinkers of the period from the reign of Alexander the Great in the late fourth century BC through to the height of Roman power in the second century AD identified and reflected upon what they took to be the increasingly interconnected nature of all parts of the known world. In this Greek and Roman literature, we find what often seem strikingly 'modern' sentiments as to matters such as a 'global' division of labour, migrations and diasporas that occur among all nations and across the whole face of the earth, and the concomitant necessity of finding ways of representing the world 'taken as one place' in textual terms. This sense of worldwide interconnectedness was primarily secular and empirical rather than speculative and theological in nature, and appears so frequently in certain surviving texts that it should be seen not as a tangential theme at this period but as a central preoccupation of many authors of the time. We will seek to demonstrate that the Graeco-Roman world produced forms of thinking that reflected upon what was taken to be the increasingly interconnected and unified nature of that world itself. Graeco-Roman civilization may therefore be seen as having engaged in what is often taken to be an essentially modern mental activity, namely a reflexive self-interrogation of its own 'globalizing' tendencies.

We will first examine how certain Greek intellectuals from the fourth century BC onwards developed new ways of thinking about the nature of the 'world as a whole', ideas that were later taken on by their Roman counterparts. Most importantly, a novel type of historiography was developed that was intended to be able to grasp the increasingly interconnected nature of the whole world. We will then move on to consider how contemporary thinkers understood the Roman empire as an entity that was 'worldwide' in scope. We will consider here how Roman imperial conditions were seen to have revolutionized travel and geographical movement across the face of the earth. Finally, we will consider how the city of Rome itself was often thought to be a truly 'world-city', in that it drew to it people from all parts of the world and contained within it goods and other phenomena from every conceivable region of the earth. We will conclude by arguing that the existence of the Greek and Roman 'global *animus*' illustrates that forms of global consciousness and 'globality' are not developments solely confined to modernity, as has often been thought.[1]

Thinking the world

In order to understand Roman conceptions of 'global' matters, it is necessary to trace the history of these ways of thinking back to their antecedents in Greek thought of the preceding centuries. From the fourth century BC onwards, Greek thought was characterized by two opposing understandings of a person's social and political affiliations. On the one hand, one could see oneself first and foremost as the citizen of the particular city-state, such as Athens or Sparta, in which one lived, one's loyalties being firmly oriented to the *polis* of one's birth. On the other hand, one could regard oneself as not being limited by any parochial affiliations to the place of one's birth. On this viewpoint, one should see oneself literally as a 'cosmopolitan', a citizen of 'the whole world' (*oikoumene*), whose loyalties lay not with particular groups of people but with all humankind. For this view, the universal 'brotherhood of man' had much more claims on one's loyalties than any particular socio-political entity.

Such a viewpoint was particularly associated with certain philosophical schools of thought. One of the founding figures of the Cynic school, Diogenes, 'declared himself *a-polis* (without a city), *a-oikos* (homeless) and *kosmopolites* (a citizen of the universe)' (Goulet-Cazé 2000: 329). Similar sentiments were voiced by Stoic thinkers such as Zeno, who regarded all humanity, regardless of creed or race, as part of a single brotherhood entity (Baldry 1965; Farrington 2001). The subsequent spread of these ideas first among Greek and then, at a later date, Roman elite groups was greatly aided by the social, political and cultural conditions of the eastern Mediterranean area from the later fourth century BC onwards. Cosmopolitan ideas were both products of, and responses to, the new situation opened up by Alexander the Great's conquests in the East, which had taken his Macedonian army as far afield as India. In this Hellenistic age of Greek colonization of the east, Greeks more and more tended to see themselves as part of a general Hellenic universe, rather than primarily as citizens of particular city-states, as had their ancestors of the classical age of the *polis* in the fifth and early fourth centuries BC. Cynic and Stoic doctrines of cosmopolitanism reflected the loosening ties of the city-state on the imaginations of educated people.

From this set of dispositions that were common currency in the Greek intellectual universe of the third and second centuries BC emerged new, less philosophical and more empirically oriented, ways of conceiving of the extent and shape of the 'whole world'. The most notable development in this regard was the genre of 'universal historiography' (*katholou ton praxeon istoria*). This was a means of historiographical writing that sought to narrate the history of the 'whole world' from a cosmopolitan perspective that was not rooted in local and parochial prejudices. As Mortley (1996: 1) notes, as espoused by Greek historians of the period, 'universal history was a genre for its time. It provided a view of history which was capable of giving an account of the entire new world opened up by the conquests of Alexander, of incorporating the experiences of the *barbaroi* ["barbarians"] as something less than exotic, and of providing the reader with a sense of unity within diversity'. The important point here from our point of view is that this style of historiography explicitly sought not only to tell the history of the 'whole world' as the Greeks saw it, but also to provide a narrative that explicated in secular and empirical terms how different parts of the world were increasingly interconnected with each other, in the first instance as a result of the conquests of Alexander. This way of thinking emphasized intricate webs of connection between geographically diverse locales, stressing that the entire world should be taken 'as a whole'. For example, the first-century BC historian Diodorus of Sicily (1968: 17) intended his history as a delineation of the 'affairs of the entire world . . . considered as if they were the affairs of some single city'.

Such Hellenistic developments in political science and historiography as to the increasingly integrated nature of the world greatly appealed to Roman elites in a period – from the second century BC onwards – when Roman power seemed to be spreading inexorably to all four corners of the earth. The central figure who demonstrated the importance to the Romans of 'universal historiography' and its emphasis on the interconnectedness of all places was the Greek statesman and historian Polybius, an Achaean who was resident in Rome between the years 167 and 150 BC (for a detailed discussion, see Inglis and Robertson 2004). His version of 'universal historiography' sought to grapple with what he saw as the pre-eminent political fact of his day, namely that the Romans had 'succeeded in less than fifty-three years [from 220 BC to 167 BC] in bringing under their rule almost the whole of the inhabited world (*oikoumene*), an achievement which is without parallel in human history' (Polybius 1979: 41). This was an unparalleled achievement because even the Macedonians under Alexander only came to dominate the eastern parts of the inhabited world. According to Polybius, the Romans, on the other hand, had 'brought not just mere portions of the world under their rule, . . . [but] have left an empire which far surpasses any that exists today or is likely to succeed it' (Polybius 1979: 42). Given that the Romans had conquered directly, or had brought into indirect submission, most of the world, this has led to a situation of complex inter-relations between hitherto unconnected peoples, events and places. Polybius' (1979: 43) account of such developments is contained in a nutshell in the following passage:

> . . . in earlier times the world's history had consisted, so to speak, of a series of unrelated episodes, the origins and results of each being as widely separated as their localities, but from this point [the 140th Olympiad – 220–216 BC] onwards, history becomes an organic whole [*somatoeides*]: the affairs of Italy and Africa are connected with [*symplekesthai*] those of Asia and of Greece, and all events bear a relationship and contribute to a single end.

In this and other passages, Polybius designates the world under Roman hegemony as *somatoeides* or 'organic whole'. The very nature of historical reality itself, with all the affairs of all the parts of the world inter-related in increasingly complicated ways, is an organic whole, greater than the sum of its parts. For Polybius, historical reality was characterized in his day by homogeneity and unity, rather than heterogeneity and dispersal. He felt that his task was to find a manner of historiographical composition that could represent this state of affairs. It is universal historiography's capacity to grasp the 'organic whole' that makes it, in Polybius' eyes, the *only* genre that will in the present day be up to the task of representing the 'whole world'. In particular, monographs, accounts of one particular place such as a city-state, just cannot grasp the complex relationships now operative between that place and multiple other places. As Sacks (1981: 110) summarizes Polybius' viewpoint, 'the universal [historiographical] form can reveal the structure of the unity of the *oikoumene*, whereas the monographic form cannot'. The particular feature of Polybius' 'universal historiography' is that it operates by self-consciously 'weaving together the various strands of history into a single tapestry' (Sacks 1981: 117; also Walbank 1972, 1985). Polybius repeatedly tells the reader of his works that he is 'weaving together' (*symplokein*) the separate histories of the different parts of the world into a whole. This narrational device helps him to emphasize the increasing links between Rome and the rest of the world, and thus to display the overall current historical state of *somatoeides* in the *oikoumene* (Sacks 1981: 119; Walbank 1985: 320).[2]

The never-ending empire

The work of Polybius figures in Roman understandings of the world from the late second century BC onwards, in much the same way as the writings of Alexis de Tocqueville do in the historically later case of the United States: each foreign observer's vision of their socio-political conditions is taken on by, and becomes part of, the national self-understanding of the national group that he analysed. Polybius' notion that Rome was, both historiographically and politically, the centre of the world not only flattered the Roman political elite's sense of self-importance, it also seemed to reflect actual political conditions of the day, as Roman dominion stretched ever further to all points of the compass, not just to the east but to the north and west too (Momigliano 1975). Later Roman historians, philosophers and politicians tended to be very familiar with Polybius' writings, and this helped ingrain in the Roman elite's collective consciousness the sense that the whole world – or at least most of the parts of it that mattered – was under their rule, and that geographical areas that had previously been separated from each other were now all interconnected, primarily through the means of the Roman *imperium*.

The Latin translation of the Greek word *oikoumene*, meaning the 'whole world', was *orbis terrarum* (Nicolet 1991). Throughout the later Republican period – first century BC – and on into the first two centuries of Empire, the perception of the world held by the Roman political class and by other members of the elite was that the *orbis terrarum* was increasingly a thoroughly Roman entity, and that its various component parts had been brought into intercourse with each other through the means of Roman conquest and administration. From the first century AD onwards, the emperor was known by the Greek term *agathos daimon tes oikoumenes*, the 'guiding spirit of the whole world', and Rome was viewed as the true 'centre of the earth' (Voegelin 1974: 132).[3] In order to display such ideas in pictorial form, the first of the Roman emperors, Augustus, had a gigantic map of the world put up on permanent display in the Campus Martius in the centre of the city. 'The map showed Rome as the physical centre of the world. Standing at the mid-point between the frozen North and the burning South, between the violent barbarians of the West and the spineless barbarians of the East, Rome seemed the geometrical site of every kind of balance, the legitimate queen of the world' (Dupont 1994: 80).[4]

The second century AD Greek orator Aelius Aristides (1953: 906) claimed, in his eulogistic address to the people of Rome, that the world – or at least a very large part of it – had been rendered like the 'backyard' of the 'house' that was the city of Rome:

> Homer said 'Earth common of all' and you have made it come true. You have measured and recorded the land of the entire civilized world; you have spanned the rivers with all kinds of bridges and hewn highways through the mountains and filled the barren stretches with posting stations; you have accustomed all areas to a settled and orderly way of life.

Echoing the Stoic theme of Diodorus mentioned above, that the whole world was to be seen as if it were one city, Aristides (1953: 906) added that the Romans had 'organized the whole civilized world as it were into one family'. While clearly this greatly idealizes the *realpolitik* of Roman hegemony, the phrase nonetheless indicates how, at the period of the zenith of Roman power, it was possible to represent the world as being in important ways an organic whole, as Polybius had argued at the time of the very start of the rise of Roman *imperium*.

One of the effects of the expansion of the *pax Romana* throughout the Mediterranean area and then beyond it in all directions was the perception held by many authors of the period that one could travel throughout the world without let or hindrance. Travel throughout the *orbis terrarum* was made possible by a combination of good roads and Roman policing of them, such that 'now indeed it is possible for [anyone] . . . to travel wherever he will, easily, just as if passing through [his own country]' (Aristides 1953: 906). A similar theme of unfettered mobility throughout space, but this time from the pen of an earlier author and concerning the Roman securing of the seaways of the Mediterranean, is shown in the following extract from the play *Medea* written by Seneca the Younger. Given that, in his day, the entire stretch of *mare nostrum*, from Cadiz in the west to Tyre in the east, was under Roman sway, the pirates who had previously plagued the shipping lanes having been brought to heel by the Roman navy, Seneca (1917: 259, 261) has the Chorus compare times past with times present:

> Now in our time, the deep has ceased to provoke resistance and submits to our will; no famous Argo, under the protection of the goddess Athena and with princes to man its oars, is at sea; instead, any little craft now wanders at will upon the deep. All bounds have been removed, cities have set their walls in new lands, and the world, now passable throughout, has left nothing where it once had place: the Indian drinks of the cold Araxes, the Persians quaff the waters of the Elbe and the Rhine.

The sense we are given here is not only that the sea routes have become safe to travel on throughout the Mediterranean, and that travel on them is now a matter of course rather than a matter for great effort and trepidation, but also that the effect of Roman power has been to create conditions characterized by migrations and geographical fluidity and mobility. In the past, one would not have found Persians in Germany or Indians in Armenia, but the Roman polity, by allowing the free passage of people within its territories, had created a context of considerable migratory flux. From this point of view, the empire was a mechanism for the movement not only of goods (as we will see below) but of people, creating novel configurations of persons and places.

Given all this, Seneca (1889: 328) further reflected on the central Stoic theme of the 'cosmopolitan' nature of humanity: 'in all cases it is clear that nothing remains in the same place in which it was born: the movement of the human race is perpetual'. Looking around him, he concluded, in a less philosophical and more empirical vein, that the contemporary world was for the most part populated by people who had been displaced, either voluntarily or not, from their places of birth, such that the main feature of the *orbis terrarum* in his day was the scattering of different ethnic and cultural groups all across the globe, making the latter a mosaic of migrations and diasporas:

> . . . whole tribes and nations have changed their abodes. What is the meaning of Greek cities in the midst of barbarous districts? Or of the Macedonian language existing among the Indians and the Persians? Scythia and all that region which swarms with wild and uncivilized tribes boasts nevertheless Achaean [Greek] cities along the shores of the Black Sea. Neither the rigours of eternal winter, nor the character of men as savage as the climate, has prevented people migrating thither. There is a mass of Athenians in Asia Minor. Miletus has sent out into various parts of the world citizens enough to populate seventy-five cities. That whole [southern] coast of Italy . . . is a part of what once was 'Greater Greece'. Asia claims the Tuscans as her own: there are Tyrians living in Africa,

> Carthaginians in Spain; Greeks have pushed in among the Gauls, and Gauls among the Greeks.
>
> (Seneca 1889: 328)

From this state of affairs, which he believed had been much accentuated in his own time by the rise of Roman imperial power, he concluded that 'you will scarcely find any land which is still in the hands of its original inhabitants – all peoples have become confused and intermingled' (Seneca 1889: 330). The analogies with accounts in our own day of the migratory movements across the world in view of 'globalizing' processes need hardly be stressed. Just as the young diplomat or business executive today is faced with a wide set of possibilities as to where in the world s/he might be posted to, so too was the ambitious young soldier and government bureaucrat of the Roman world confronted with a diverse range of possible locales to be assigned to. Statius (2003: 343), in the latter part of the first century AD, asks of a young friend:

> To which countries, to which of Caesar's lands are you posted? Will you breast the Northern rivers and the choppy Rhine waters, or sweat in the hot acres of Libya? Will you set Pannonian mountains trembling . . .? Will the Danube be your lodging? . . . Or will you tread the sand of Solyma, and the captured palm-groves of Idume . . . [will you visit] the wild Araxes . . . [or] the moors of Caledonia[?]

A similar note as to the vast range of geographical possibilities open to the young and ambitious is sounded by the satirist Petronius (1996: 158):

> Youth, leave your seat and seek another shore
> For you a grander prospect is in store.
> Take heart; the distant Danube will hear tell
> Of you, and the cold North wind as well,
> With Egypt's calms, from East to West, all lands!

Rome as world city

As is clear from the above, the Roman imaginary could envisage the vast spaces of the *orbis terrarum* as offering practically unlimited scope for the peregrinations of the traveller. However, if one sought experience of the entire world, for ancient thinkers one did not need actually to travel around its different parts. All these were present in Rome itself, which was viewed as *caput orbis*, 'the capital of the world' (Dalby 2000: 20). The two main poles of the Romans' mental universe were the city of Rome and the wider world. As a result, the proclamations of the emperor's will were delivered *urbi et orbi* (Dupont 1994: 76). The phrase demonstrates that, for the Roman mind, *urbs* (the city) and *orbis* (the whole world) were very closely connected. While it was thought that Rome was mistress of the world, it was also the case that the city was in a sense felt to *be* the world. The implication of this situation is that the idea of 'world city' (Sassen 1991) is not a purely modern invention.

We can see this in the fact that the theme of the 'city-as-world' was a dominant one in Roman ideas of the first and second centuries AD (Spengler 1991 [1918]: 246). As Aristides put it in his eulogy of the greatness of Rome, 'what another city is to its own boundaries and territory, this city [Rome] is to the boundaries and territory of the entire civilized world, as if the latter were a country district and she [Rome] had been appointed its governing town' (Aristides 1953: 901). Writing in the first century AD, the Greek author Athenaeus (1927: 87, 89) expressed sentiments that had become quite common in the literature of the time. Rome is 'an *epitome* of the whole world . . . one may see at a glance people from all the cities of the world settled there . . . I would need more than one whole day to enumerate all the cities represented in Rome . . . Even entire nations are settled there *en masse*, like the Cappadocians, the Scythians, the Pontians and more besides. All these live in Rome, representatives of the entire population of the world'.

People from all the regions that Romans had conquered, and from lands beyond the Roman frontiers too, were present in the city: 'This city receives those who flow in from all the earth', as Aristides (1953: 901) put it. The eighteenth-century American essayist James Wilson (1967 [1790]: 581) phrased a similar point in this way: 'it might be said, not that the Romans extended themselves over the whole globe, but that the inhabitants of the globe poured themselves upon the Romans'.

Once again, the texts of Seneca provide a fascinating insight into how Roman elites felt about this state of affairs. Seneca (1889: 325–6) argued not only that the Roman world as a whole was characterized by migrations and diasporas, but that this situation was exemplified in a highly condensed fashion in Rome itself:

> Look . . . on these vast crowds, for whom all the countless roofs of Rome can scarcely find shelter: the greater part of those crowds have lost their native land: they have flocked hither . . . from all parts of the world. Some have been brought by ambition, some by the exigencies of public office, some by being entrusted with embassies, some by luxury which seeks a convenient spot, rich in vices, for its exercise, some by their wish for a liberal education, others by a wish to see the public shows. Some have been led hither by friendship, some by industry, which finds here a wide field for the display of its powers. Some have brought their beauty for sale, some their eloquence: people of every kind assemble themselves together in Rome, which sets a high price both upon virtues and vices. Bid them all to be summoned to answer to their names, and ask each one from what home he or she has come: you will find that the greater part of them have left their own abodes, and journeyed to a city which, though great and beauteous beyond all others, is nevertheless not their own. This city . . . may be said to be the common property of all peoples . . .

In the first century AD, the population of Rome was roughly one million people, densely packed into an area less than 8 miles square (Carcopino 1991: 33; de Souza 2002: 51). As a result, the streets were characterized by extreme bustle, if not to say chaos, populated as they were by people from all parts of the Roman world and sometimes beyond (Carcopino 1991: 69). While Roman philosophy of the period was increasingly heavily influenced by cosmopolitan Stoic doctrines as to the 'brotherhood of all men', at a more everyday level, the presence of 'foreigners' in the city could be a source of much irritation, if not disgust, to more conservative Roman citizens (Mazzolani 1970; Grant 1987: 182–4). For them, as the poet Lucan (1962: 398) put it, Rome was *mundi faeces repletam* – filled with the dregs of the whole world.

Yet the presence of foreign goods, manners and, to some extent, people was a source of much pleasure for most Romans, many of whom, by the second century AD, were themselves the descendants of people originating from outside Italy. One of the great attractions in Rome, for both locals and visitors alike, was the Colosseum, which Martial (1993: 13) called the greatest of all the wonders of the world, far exceeding other such spectacular monuments as the hanging gardens of Babylon and the pyramids of Egypt. Such a wondrous locale was felt by Roman writers to draw its audiences from all parts of the known world. In this vein, Martial (1993: 15) enquired rhetorically of the emperor:

> What race is so remote, so barbarous, Caesar, that no spectator from it is in your city? The farmer of Rhodope has come . . . so too the Sarmatian and he who drinks Nile's stream, and he on whom beats the wave of farthest Tethys [i.e. the Briton]. The Arab has sped hither, the Sabaeans too and the Cilicians . . . Sygambrians have come . . . and Ethiopians also . . . Diverse sounds the speech of the peoples, and yet it is one, when you are called true father of the fatherland.

Not only the audiences of the Colosseum, but those participating more actively in its entertainments were seen by contemporary authors to be drawn from all parts of the world. These included the gladiators who fought to the death for the amusement of the crowds. These were drawn from all parts of the empire and beyond, such that one might see a Gaul fighting a Thracian, or a Spaniard locked in mortal combat with a Numidian. Drawn from almost every part of the world the Romans knew, including its most farflung peripheries, the 'international' nature of the martial displays of the arena meant that, for the spectator witnessing the intense drama of combat *mano a mano*, for 'a fleeting instant the edges of the world would meet at its centre, immediately to be hurled back, separated by blood, to the far ends of the universe' (Dupont 1994: 89).[4]

One interesting index of the 'global' reach of Roman power is the presence in the city of every conceivable sort of animal, originally captured or reared within far-off lands (Renaghan 1998). One might see in the Colosseum, engaged either in bloody slaughters or in more genteel circus-like displays, hippopotami from Nubia, lions from Mesopotamia, elephants from north Africa, giraffes from east Africa, crocodiles from Egypt, bears from Spain and Scotland and tigers from Hyrcania (Toynbee 1973; Scullard 1974; Carcopino 1991: 261; Dalby 2000: 177). Elephants and other creatures were familiar sights as parts of street-troupe entertainments. Exotic sorts of pets from far-off climes were also in vogue for those who could afford them. Giraffes, for example, became a *sine qua non* of a rich family's well-stocked private menagerie (Renaghan 1998).

The case of the importation of animals into Rome from many different parts of the globe illustrates vividly the dense networks of trade that characterized the Roman world, with the city of Rome at their centre. But trade was not limited to lands within the imperial borders. By the first century AD, Rome had fairly extensive trading links with India, Malaysia and even China, the parts of the *oikoumene* that were known, albeit dimly, by the Romans but to which their political power did not extend (Sitwell 1984; Casson 1994; Curtin 1998). Although such trade was generally operated by Indian and Parthian middlemen, rather than by direct contact between Rome and the Far East, nonetheless there was a steady movement of goods, both more mundane and more luxurious, from east to west and from west to east. Chinese silk was particularly popular as a material for elegant clothing among Roman women (Charlesworth 1924). As commodities from the east came into the Roman world, so too did Roman coinage move out, prompting Pliny the Elder to estimate that the vast sum of 'one hundred million *sestertii* go from Rome to India, China and Arabia every year' (Dalby 2000: 194).

The panoply of foreign goods that regularly arrived in Rome, primarily by sea but also to some extent by land, prompted Aristides (1953: 896) to represent Rome as the one place on earth

> . . . where the commerce of all mankind has its common exchange and all the produce of the earth its common market. Whatever the seasons make grow and whatever countries and rivers and lakes and arts of Hellenes and non-Hellenes produce are brought from every land and sea, so that if one would look at all these things, he must needs behold them either by visiting the whole civilized world or by coming to this city. For whatever is grown and made among each people cannot fail to be here at all times and in abundance . . . the city appears a kind of giant emporium of the world.

The phrase 'emporium of the world' is telling here, in that it allows us to reflect on the similarities between the Roman sense of the international panoply of goods available in Rome and the modern conception of world fairs and expositions offering up to the viewer a huge variety of the wares of the world, phenomena that we tend to think of in connection with 'globalizing' processes of the nineteenth and twentieth centuries.

Given the apparent abundance in Rome of every sort of item one could possibly dream of, it was inevitable that moralists would condemn what they saw as unnecessary indulgence and excessive self-gratification. Culinary fashion among the upper classes was pithily characterized by Petronius (1996: 89) in this way: 'Far-out and foreign win/What's out-of-bounds is in'. In like fashion, Seneca (1889: 334–5) castigated 'those whose luxury transcends the bounds of an empire which is already perilously wide'. From this point of view, epicures and gastronomes had gone too far, in both geographical and gustatory terms, in search of exquisite sweetmeats from every conceivable part of the world (Miller 1969). Seneca (1889) went on to deride those who would only eat shellfish if they knew it came 'from the unknown shore of the farthest sea', that is to say Britain, one of the ends of the earth in his day. Such finicky epicures demanded that there be brought:

> . . . from all regions everything, known or unknown, to tempt their fastidious palate: food, which their stomach, worn out with delicacies, can scarcely retain, is brought from the most distant ocean . . . they do not even deign to digest the banquets which they ransack the globe to obtain . . . they wander through all countries, cross the seas and excite at a great cost the hunger which they might allay at a small one.

Here, we have a critique of the ancient equivalent of today's trendy and exoticized 'global fusion cuisine', in favour of 'good, old, traditional' ingredients and recipes. Just as French gourmands and traditional English trenchermen today decry the mixing and matching of culinary cultures and the creation of hybrid dishes based on ingredients from different national larders, so too did Roman authors find much to criticize in new forms of eating that seemed to them to be overdone in terms of quaint, unfamiliar ingredients from far afield, and bizarre mixings of flavours and textures from across the world. The ancient material as to tastes in food and other goods indicates that disputes as to the value of cultural fusions and hybrids is not necessarily confined to modernity.

Conclusion

In this chapter, we have argued that ideas and attitudes that are in many ways closely analogous to modern notions of 'globality' – where the world is taken 'as a whole', where all parts of the globe are seen to be increasingly interconnected and where individual experience is connected to worldwide forces and processes – were relatively common sentiments among Graeco-Roman social elites from the Hellenistic period onwards through to the height of Roman imperial power in the first two centuries after Christ. Such 'global' ways of thinking were not just speculative, philosophical and theological in form, but informed Graeco-Roman conceptualizations of empirical social, political, economic, geographical and historical reality. A high level of conscious awareness of the increasingly interconnected nature of the world taken 'as a whole' can indeed be seen as a characteristic feature of much Graeco-Roman thinking of the period. As a result, there are strong empirical grounds for making the claim that a particular version of a 'global' sensibility was well developed in the Graeco-Roman world some 2,000 years ago and more. Consequently, modern scholars should revise their opinions that 'global' outlooks, perceptions and dispositions are mostly or wholly the products of Western modernity in the last 500 years or so.

Our review of a selection of the extant ancient literature suggests that the Greeks and Romans of some two millennia ago were more than aware of how their world was changing in the direction of increasing geophysical, economic, political, social and cultural compression and interdependence of hitherto unrelated peoples and places. If our account is compelling, then its implication is this: our ancient ancestors were, in their own particular fashions, in many ways as conscious of living in a 'globalizing' world as we are today. From their sense of Rome as a truly 'world city' through to their perception that the very nature of the human sciences would have to be recast so as to be able fully to grasp the ever greater importance of processes that occurred at a worldwide level, we can see that the ancient 'global *animus*' was a spirit very alive to the nature of phenomena that were seen to be truly earth spanning in scope and importance. If this is so, then we in the present day urgently need to revise our beliefs as to our own apparently unique capacities to grasp the global level in human affairs.

Notes

1 Given limitations on space, we can only provide here an ideal typical model of Graeco-Roman thought in this direction, with all the necessary simplifications and methodological dilemmas such an approach entails. A more detailed version of our argument, which avoids these potential problems, will appear in Robertson and Inglis (forthcoming).

2 There are, of course, many problems with Polybius' account of universal historiography. For a discussion, see Inglis and Robertson (2004).

3 Given that the Romans of the first and second centuries AD were aware of a huge landmass to the north and east that was not under their control, it is clear that they themselves knew that the rhetoric used to describe the 'worldwide' extent of their dominions was exaggerated. Nonetheless, in the early days of empire, it was thought that the spread of Roman power was inexorable and that it would indeed eventually spread out to fill the whole inhabited world, all the way from Gibraltar in the west to a dimly perceived China in the east.

4 Imperial claims to power are often dressed up in terms that stress the allegedly 'global' reach of the empire in question. For example, the Mughal emperors styled themselves as 'lords of the universe' (Pagden 2002: 42). What distinguishes the Graeco-Roman conception of the *somatoeides oikoumene* from these ideas is that: (1) we find a stress on the interconnectedness of all parts of the world in authors such as Seneca who have no particular or specific interest in glorifying the emperor or ruling elites; and (2) the Graeco-Roman claims are generally empirically oriented (i.e. they purport to describe mundane reality in relatively pragmatic ways) rather than directly intended as eulogy or propaganda. Out of

the authors we have examined, the most explicitly eulogistic is Aristides, whose pronouncements as a result have to be treated with some caution. Nonetheless, the other authors whose words we present are not generally intending their writings for propagandistic purposes, and should be seen as expressing in many ways the common intellectual currency of educated elites of their day.

References

Aristides, Aelius. 1953. 'Roman oration' in James H. Oliver, 'The ruling power: a study of the Roman Empire in the second century after Christ through the Roman oration of Aelius Aristides'. *Transactions of the American Philosophical Society* New Series, 43 (I): 873–999.

Athenaeus. 1927. *The Deipnosophists*, Vol. I. London: William Heinemann.

Baldry, H.C. 1965. *The Unity of Mankind in Greek Thought.* Cambridge: Cambridge University Press.

Beck, Ulrich. 2000. *What Is Globalization?* Cambridge: Polity.

Carcopino, Jerome. 1991. *Everyday Life in Ancient Rome.* Harmondsworth: Penguin.

Casson, Lionel. 1994. *Travel in the Ancient World.* Baltimore: Johns Hopkins University Press.

Charlesworth, M.P. 1924. *Trade Routes and Commerce of the Roman Empire.* Cambridge: Cambridge University Press.

Crone, Gerald Roe. 1966. *Maps and Their Makers: An Introduction to the History of Cartography.* London: Hutchinson.

Curtin, Philip D. 1998. *Cross-Cultural Trade in World History.* Cambridge: Cambridge University Press.

Dalby, Andrew. 2000. *Empire of Pleasures: Luxury and Indulgence in the Roman World.* London: Routledge.

de Souza, Philip. 2002. *Seafaring and Civilization: Maritime Perspectives on World Trade.* London: Profile.

Diodorus of Sicily. 1968. *Diodorus of Sicily, In Twelve Volumes*, trans. by C.H. Oldfather. Cambridge, MA: Harvard University Press.

Dupont, Florence. 1994. *Everyday Life in Ancient Rome.* Oxford: Blackwell.

Farrington, Benjamin. 2001. 'Diodorus Siculus: universal historian' in *Head and Hand in Ancient Greece.* Nottingham: Spokesman Press.

Goulet-Cazé, Marie-Odile. 2000. *A Guide to Greek Thought: Major Figures and Trends.* Cambridge, MA: Belknap/Harvard University Press, pp. 321–35.

Grant, Michael. 1987. *The World of Rome.* London: Meridian.

Hardie, Philip R. 1986. *Virgil's Aeneid: Cosmos and Imperium.* Oxford: Clarendon Press.

Inglis, David and Robertson, Roland. 2004. 'Beyond the gates of the *polis*: reworking the classical roots of classical sociology'. *Journal of Classical Sociology* 4 (2): 165–86.

Lucan. 1962. *The Civil War (Pharsalia)*, Books I–X, ed. and trans. by J.D. Duff. London: William Heinemann.

Martial. 1993. 'On the Spectacles' in *Epigrams*, Vol. I. Cambridge, MA: Harvard University Press.

Mazzolani, Lidia Storoni. 1970. *The Idea of the City in Roman Thought: from Walled City to Spiritual Commonwealth.* London: Hollis and Carter.

Miller, J. Innes. 1969. *The Spice Trade of the Roman Empire.* Oxford: Clarendon Press.

Momigliano, Arnoldo. 1975. *Alien Wisdom: the Limits of Hellenization.* Cambridge: Cambridge University Press.

Mortley, Raoul. 1996. *The Idea of Universal History from Hellenistic Philosophy to Early Christian Historiography*. Lewiston: Edwin Mellen.

Nicolet, Claude. 1991. *Space, Geography and Politics in the Early Roman Empire*. Ann Arbor: University of Michigan Press.

Pagden, Anthony. 2002. *Peoples and Empires*. London: Phoenix.

Petronius. 1996. *Satyrica*, ed. and trans. by R. Bracht Branham and Daniel Kinney. London: Everyman/J.M. Dent.

Polybius. 1979. *The Rise of the Roman Empire*, ed. and trans. by F.W. Walbank. Harmondsworth: Penguin.

Renaghan, Janeen. 1998. 'Savage fashion: animals and attitude in Ancient Rome'. *Zoogoer* July/August (weblink http://nationalzoo.si.edu/Publications/ZooGoer/1998/4/savagefashion.cfm; last accessed 27/9/05).

Robertson, Roland. 1992. *Globalization: Social Theory and Global Culture*. London: Sage.

——. 1994. 'Religion and the global field'. *Social Compass* 41 (1): 121–35.

Robertson, Roland and David Inglis. Forthcoming. *Globalization and Social Theory: Redefining Social Science*. Milton Keynes: Open University Press.

Sacks, Kenneth J. 1981. *Polybius on the Writing of History*. Berkeley: University of California Press.

Sassen, Saskia. 1991. *The Global City: London, New York and Tokyo*. Princeton, NJ: Princeton University Press.

Scholte, Jan Aart. 2000. *Globalization: A Critical Introduction*. Basingstoke: Palgrave.

Scullard, H.H. 1974. *The Elephant in the Greek and Roman World*. London: Thames and Hudson.

Seneca. 1889. 'Consolatio Ad Helvia/Addressed to His Mother Helvia: Of Consolation', in *L. Annaeus Seneca: Minor Dialogues*, trans. by Aubrey Stewart. London: George Bell and Sons.

——. 1917. 'Medea' in *Seneca's Tragedies*, Vol. I, trans. by Frank Justus Miller. London: William Heinemann.

Sitwell, N.H.H. 1984. *The World the Romans Knew*. London: Hamish Hamilton.

Spengler, Oswald. 1991 [1918]. *The Decline of the West: An Abridged Edition*, Helmut Werner, ed. Oxford: Oxford University Press.

Statius. 2003. *Silvae*. Cambridge, MA: Harvard University Press.

Toynbee, J.M.C. 1973. *Animals in Roman Life and Art*. London: Thames and Hudson.

Voegelin, Eric. 1974. *Order and History*, Vol. 4, *The Ecumenic Age*. Baton Rouge: Louisiana State University Press.

Walbank, F.W. 1972. *Polybius*. Berkeley: University of California Press.

——. 1985. '*Symploke: Its Roles in Polybius' Histories*' in *Selected Papers: Studies in Greek and Roman History and Historiography*. Cambridge: Cambridge University Press

Wilson, James. 1967 [1790]. 'Lectures on law: citizens and aliens' in *The Works of James Wilson*, Vol. II, Robert Green McCloskey, ed. Cambridge, MA: Harvard University Press.

4 Civilizing processes and international societies[1]

Andrew Linklater

Proponents of the English School approach to international relations – Herbert Butterfield and Martin Wight in particular – maintained that all historical international societies emerged in regions with distinctive patterns of civilization. Conceptions of moral or religious unity made societies of states possible; perceptions of civilizational identity including a sense of superiority over outlying areas facilitated the development of a political vocabulary that enabled separate communities to associate in an anarchic society. The theme has arisen in discussions of Hellenic international society (Wight: ch. 1) and is a recurrent dimension of analyses of Western colonialism and its place within the development of the modern states-system (O' Hagan 2002). Its significance for the modern world is illustrated by the fact that Western political elites invented 'the standard of civilization' more than a century ago to justify the subjugation of non-Western peoples and to detail the social and political changes their subjects would have to undergo before they could become equal members of international society (Gong 1984). In more recent times, the struggle against Fascism, the Western policy of the 'containment' of the Soviet threat and the 'war against terrorism' have all been described as a conflict between civilization and evil or barbarism. In the post-bipolar world, a new standard of civilization has emerged in response to human rights violations. Concerns about regimes that sponsor international terrorist organizations and fears that 'weapons of mass destruction' will fall into the hands of terrorist groups have intensified this trend.

References to the civilized world have fallen into disrepute in intellectual circles since the end of the Second World War. Barbarism in Europe was one reason for that; another was the belief among radical observers that the language of civilization was integral to the sense of ingrained Western superiority that frustrated legitimate aspirations for self-determination in the non-European world. Stark contrasts between the civilized world and backward peoples have been replaced – at least in part – by the idea of a multiplicity of civilizations, none more valid and valuable than the rest. However, ideas about civilization, civility and civilizing processes survive in the academic study of society and politics, and play an important role in analysing patterns of interaction within international societies of states.

Illustrating the theme, Butterfield (1953: ch. 7) argued that every international society has to be understood in conjunction with 'the whole civilizing process' that underpins it. In his approach, civilization referred to 'patterns of behaviour which emerge over time through the experience of people who are capable of empathy with others and capable of denying themselves short-term gains for the long-term goal of maintaining ordered relations' (quoted in Sharp 2001: 11; see also Sharp 2003). Checks on egotistical behaviour and curbs on aggressive impulses and threatening behaviour are core elements of the civilizing process according to this definition. Similar themes are evident in Adam Watson's observation that the 'diplomatic dialogue' in international societies is 'a civilized process based on awareness and respect for other people's point of view; and a civilizing one also, because the continuous exchange of ideas, and the attempts to find mutually acceptable solutions to conflicts of interest, increase that awareness and respect' (Watson 1982: 20). Robert Jackson's claim that modern international society has displayed remarkable success in developing principles of 'civility' that promote 'mutual intelligibility, recognition, communication, and interaction between people of different civilizations' rephrases the more general theme (Jackson 2000: 408).

Jackson prefers 'civility' to 'civilization' because the latter term is often associated with some discredited notion of a hierarchy of peoples, and many post-structuralist and post-colonial thinkers would probably agree that the notion of civilizing processes and practices is best removed from the vocabulary of politics entirely. Leaving aside Jackson's position on the idea of civilization, it is possible for analysts of societies of states to claim that they do not pass judgement on the respective merits of different societies when they use such terminology, but rather endeavour to understand how notions of civilization have shaped the evolution of societies of states. They can argue that they use the concept of civilization to capture dispositions that are fundamental to the existence of an international society – the willingness to preserve constraints on violence, to forgo short-term national advantages for the sake of maintaining international order and to display some degree of empathy towards other members of this unique form of world political organization.

To take such an approach is to come close to more general trends in historical studies of Western modernity and in comparative sociology. References to civility are by no means unusual in studies of the control of violence, physical gestures and polite conversation (see Bremmer and Roodenburg 1991; Burke 1993; Burke *et al.* 2000). But they are especially central to Norbert Elias's study of the civilizing process in modern Europe between the fifteenth century and the late twentieth century, which is a standard reference point in this literature. Elias used 'the civilizing process' in a non-evaluative way to describe changes in the management of aggressive impulses, bodily control and in levels of emotional identification within European national societies over five centuries. As this list indicates, there are parallels between Elias's study of the civilizing process within modern states and English School conceptions of civility in international societies. Both draw attention to how political order – domestic and international – depends on internalized constraints on violence and empathy between persons as against the fear of external compulsion. But the differences between the approaches are substantial. Members of the English School have devoted little attention to changes within nation states (and specifically to how far, or whether, there are causal connections between civility in international relations and the civilizing process as Elias defined it). Although he was unusual among sociologists of his generation in recognizing the influence of global political processes on societal development, Elias did not analyse civilizing processes in international relations. Indeed, his typically Hobbesian interpretation of world politics led him to deny that there was a global civilizing process and to add that one was unlikely to develop in the absence of a worldwide monopoly of power. Despite these differences, Elias's account of Western modernity can contribute to the English School analysis of international society and specifically to the 'sociology of states-systems' developed by Martin Wight. This chapter describes the empirical research directions that emerge from linking their ideas.

This chapter begins by offering a brief description of Elias's conception of the civilizing process, noting in particular its primary function of controlling the harm the members of any society can do to one another in the course of satisfying their most basic physical and other needs. Particular stress will be placed on his belief in the existence of long-term processes of change in modern Europe, in which social tolerance of public acts of violence was reduced. A second task is to summarize Elias's comments about the relative lack of a global civilizing process, which reflects growing levels of repugnance to violent behaviour evident within European states, but it is important to note here his remarks about whether globalization may promote the widening of emotional identification and greater levels of sympathy between the members of different nation states. Building on this point, a third goal is to consider parallels between Elias's analyses of changing orientations to public acts of cruelty and recent works that discuss cruelty and compassion in world affairs. A fourth task is to summarize Wight's notion of a comparative sociology of states-systems. A fifth is to explain how Elias's study of the civilizing process can contribute to its advancement. What can be derived from his perspective is an approach to states-systems that examines evidence of any long-term trends regarding dominant emotional responses to cruelty and suffering. Elias's claims about the lowering of the threshold of repugnance towards violent conduct within modern Western states invite the question of whether the modern states-system is unusual in making unnecessary suffering a key ethical and political problem for humanity as a whole. Establishing whether it is different from its predecessors in this respect is a task for future sociological research. Some pointers to possible directions are suggested in a classification of the forms of harm that separate societies would have to be reducing or eradicating before a global civilizing process could be said to exist. This chapter offers the tentative conclusion that various global norms that outlaw 'serious bodily and mental harm' distinguish the modern states-system from its precursors and provide some encouragement for the Enlightenment hope that more radical advances beyond earlier international societies remain possible.

The civilizing process

It is important to consider whether the analysis of the civilizing process relies on a progressivist interpretation of the last five centuries of European history. Admittedly, it is hard not to conclude that Elias believed that significant advances had occurred in the modern era. However, he stressed that his account of the civilizing process was not designed as a 'slur' on other societies. Indeed, one of his central claims is that modern European societies are not alone in undergoing a civilizing process. What Elias meant by this statement is that all societies must address the problem of how their members can satisfy their elementary needs without 'destroying, frustrating, demeaning or in other ways harming each other time and time again' in the process (Elias 1996: 31). All of them face the permanent challenge of socializing their members into shared understandings about the need to observe constraints on physical violence, and all must equip their inhabitants with necessary skills in adapting their behaviour to the legitimate needs of other social actors. The point is that the argument that Europe witnessed the development of a civilizing process does not depend on 'ethnocentric value-judgments' that 'we are good' while 'they are bad' (Elias and Dunning 1986: 133–4).

The question of what distinguishes the modern civilizing process from parallel phenomena in other societies immediately arises. In response, Elias (2001a: 48) observed that it is rarely realized that levels of personal security are higher in modern European societies than they were in the Middle Ages or antiquity – and higher than in many other phases of human history. In the course of explaining this difference, Elias analysed the internal pacification of European societies, the development over five centuries of closer emotional identification within national populations and, crucially, the evolution of forms of self-restraint in tandem with growing repugnance towards violence.

The account of the civilizing process begins with the fact that the 1500s saw the rise of the modern state with a monopoly control of the instruments of violence and the supreme power of taxation. In this era, state structures began to amass considerable powers with which to check violent impulses. The rising levels of personal security that accompanied domestic pacification allowed the emergence of higher levels of social and economic interdependence than had existed in the Middle Ages. In a related development, 'self-control' and 'internal' checks on aggressive inclinations grew in importance; personal security came to depend less on external constraints and the fear of coercion and more on the control of the emotions (Elias 1978: 155). The tendency 'to identify more readily with other people . . . regardless of social origins' emerged alongside the growth of internalized controls on aggressive tendencies (Elias 1996: 34). Crucially, attitudes to cruelty and suffering changed fundamentally over the centuries that were Elias's main object of analysis. Public execution and judicial torture were eradicated from the main European societies; cruelty to children and animals emerged as a matter of public concern. Changing emotional responses to public displays of violence and to cruelty found expression in the fact that anything distasteful or disgusting – including animal slaughter and dying – was increasingly hidden 'behind the scenes' (Fletcher 1997: 21; Elias 2000: 102, 2001b: 15).[2] The formation of the modern conscience is illustrated by such changing attitudes towards violent acts to other persons and animals in Western societies (Elias 1996: 335, 2000: 161ff; Fletcher 1997: 19).

Elias's distinctive analysis of long-term patterns of change encompassing not only social and political structures (sociogenetic processes) but also the organization of individuals' emotional lives (psychogenetic processes) may seem to reflect the obsolescent progressivism of the nineteenth-century philosophies of history. Perhaps he did believe that 'overall humanity was in fact progressing';[3] however, Elias stressed that civilizing tendencies are 'always linked to counter-trends', which may eventually gain the 'upper hand' (see van Krieken 1998: 69–70). The progressivist temperament of the nineteenth and twentieth centuries led most Europeans to adopt the erroneous view that terrible cruelty belonged to their violent past or was typical of the uncivilized remainder of the world. Nazi rule revealed the scale of the modernist delusion. The extermination camps could not be accommodated within modern political thought by depicting them as a regression to a more barbaric past; in large part, they relied on the modern achievement of bureaucratic rule, which administered genocide without involving the population as a whole in the direct use of violence. The point, for Elias, was that the civilizing process had simultaneously checked aggressive inclinations and created new possibilities for political violence and domination. Debates have arisen as to whether Nazi genocide demonstrated that Germany had not followed the dominant Western and northern European pattern of development, or suggested that 'such an outbreak of savagery and barbarism' as occurred under Nazism 'might stem directly from tendencies inherent in the structure of modern industrial societies' (Elias 1996: 303; Fletcher 1997: 158ff, 168ff). We cannot enter into this discussion here. Suffice it to note that any progressivist tendencies that permeated Elias's sociological investigations were quickly counterbalanced by the claim that the 'civilization of which I speak is never completed and always endangered' (Elias 1996: 173).

A global civilizing process?

To what extent has the civilizing process that Elias identified in the relations between states and citizens, men and women, parents and children, and in the treatment of non-human species influenced relations between independent political communities? To what extent is the economic and technological integration of the human race contributing to a global civilizing process in which the populations of different communities identify more closely with one another? Are emotional responses to human suffering changing with the result that growing numbers of human beings believe they have moral and political responsibilities to other peoples which earlier generations did not feel to the same extent?

Elias did not subject such questions to detailed enquiry; nor did he neglect relations between states. He maintained that it was impossible to understand the civilizing process in modern Europe without taking account of international politics or considering long-term patterns of change affecting humanity as a whole. Unsurprisingly, then, his writings lament sociology's neglect of international relations (Elias 1978: 168, 1991: 138ff, 1996: 179). His conception of relations between states is encapsulated in the comment that the 'vicious circle' of 'mutual distrust between human groups', and the 'unbridled use of violence' when leaders 'expected an advantage and were not afraid of retaliation', has been almost 'normal throughout the ages' (Elias 1996: 137–8). The absence of a stable monopoly of power, which was the key to the pacification of modern societies, meant that international relations mainly revolved around a series of 'elimination contests' precipitated by the 'double-bind process', or the security dilemma as it is known in international relations (Elias 1978: 30, 1996: 176–7). Mennell (1990: 364) maintains that Elias believed that violent conflict between the remaining great powers was the dominant feature in the history of international relations.

There is an interesting parallel between Elias's Hobbesian approach to world politics and the long-term developmental tendencies in all states-systems described by Wight (1977: ch. 1). But, despite this point of convergence, the fact is that most members of the English School would protest that Elias's approach leans too far in the direction of Hobbes and overlooks the peculiar features of anarchical societies including the complex legal and moral mechanisms that constrain the use of force, notwithstanding the absence of global political institutions that have a monopoly control of the instruments of violence. According to this approach, what is missing from Elias's perspective is the realization that elaborate civilizing processes are evident in the relations between national monopolies of power which recognize no higher political authority. Members of the English School of international relations disagree about whether the modern society of states – or any society of states – can do more than establish basic principles of coexistence, but some (including Bull, Dunne, Vincent and Wheeler) have argued that the modern society of states has made some progress in promoting respect for human rights and can make further advances in this area by weaving new principles of humanitarian intervention into the constitution of international society. The upshot of these remarks is that all societies of states contain at least some civilizing processes that are not as easily enforced as national equivalents but clearly influence the behaviour of sovereign states.

Despite his Hobbesian predilections, Elias advanced several intriguing observations about the greater sensitivity to human suffering – and the higher level of emotional identification between the members of different societies – which exists in the modern states-system. The contrast is with antiquity and the Middle Ages. 'The ancient Greeks', he argued, 'who are so often held up to us as models of civilized behaviour, considered it quite a matter of course to commit acts of mass destruction, not quite identical to those of the National Socialists but, nevertheless, similar to them in several respects' (Elias 1996: 445). In the Greek world, 'the level of "moral" repugnance against what we now call "genocide" and, more generally, the level of internalized inhibitions against physical violence, were decidedly lower, the feelings of guilt or shame associated with such inhibitions decidedly weaker, than they are in the relatively developed nation-states of the twentieth century' (Elias and Dunning 1986: 145). The interconnectedness between domestic levels of violence and the tolerance for the use of force in world politics is highlighted in his account. Greater acceptance of force in international affairs mirrored violence in everyday life within city-states;[4] exactly the same linkage between force within and between communities was thought to exist in the Middle Ages.[5]

In the more pacified conditions of modern Europe, the main threat to the civilizing process stemmed from the international struggle for power and security – from outside rather than from inside the state. The two world wars had revealed how quickly 'the sensitivity towards killing, towards dying people and death' can evaporate when mass publics confront growing insecurity (Elias 2001b: 51). However, widespread revulsion towards Nazi atrocities demonstrated that changing orientations towards cruelty and suffering within modern states exercised some influence on world politics even in the most violent of times.

At least this example of a global civilizing process cannot be easily reversed if Elias's analysis is broadly correct (Fletcher 1997: 24). Whether globalization will deepen ethical commitments to the eradication of human suffering is a central question for Elias – indeed the central issue at stake in studying the growing interdependence of the human species (Elias 1987: llxxii; Mennell 1998: 101). It is important to pause at this stage to note that Elias (1996: 460) did not see the civilizing simply in terms of the 'the non-violent coexistence of humans' but maintained that more 'positive characteristics' are involved. Like Butterfield or Watson, whose comments on international societies were cited earlier, Elias (1996: 109) believed 'the extent and depth of . . . people's mutual identification with each other and, accordingly, the depth and extent of their ability to empathize and capacity to feel for and sympathize with other people in their relationships with them' are 'central criteria of a civilizing process'. Globalization raised the question of whether cosmopolitan forms of emotional identification might yet rival 'elimination contests' in determining the future course of world politics. At the very least, globalization had made more people more aware than ever before that much of humanity lives 'on the verge of starvation' (Elias 1996: 26). While 'relatively little is done' to solve the problem, the 'feeling of responsibility which people have for each other' had probably 'increased' (Elias 1996: 26).

However, greater connectedness being human beings could give rise to a still more powerful 'decivilizing counter thrust' in which groups reacted aggressively to the encroachment of alien values and to the insecurities attending greater interdependence (Elias 1995: 36, 2001a: 222). The 'immense process of integration' that the species has been undergoing might therefore give way to a 'dominant disintegration process' (Elias 2001a: 218). Turning to recent global events, perhaps the most important question raised by '9/11', the appeal to 'civilization' in response to 'decivilizing' counterthrusts, and the use of military force to deal with real and imagined security threats, is whether the dominant process will strengthen or weaken global norms on the importance of reducing unnecessary suffering (see Linklater 2002a).

Cruelty and compassion in world politics

The remainder of this chapter draws on Elias's ideas about changing emotional responses to cruelty and suffering in order to provide new directions for the sociology of states-systems. Prior to doing that, some comments are needed about how far this approach accepts the main body of Elias's argument or borrows selectively from it. Strong support for his account of the civilizing process can be found in the criminological literature, which suggests that the historical record indicates a substantial reduction in violent crime in Europe around the seventeenth and eighteenth centuries, a trend that may have come to an end (Johnson and Monkkonen 1996; Garland 2001: ch. 1). Support for Elias's thesis about Western modernity can be found in Spierenburg (1991) and Sznaider (2001: 4), who describes 'the campaigns of compassion' in the nineteenth century that spearheaded the struggle to abolish slavery and torture, to promote prison and hospital reform, to improve the lives of children and to abolish cruelty towards animals. Sznaider (2001: 9, 81) maintains that Foucault's account of modernity, which portrays ostensibly humanitarian developments as new forms of discipline and control, underestimated the importance of social struggles to eliminate the 'unjustifiable affliction of pain'. This is not the occasion to assess these apparently competing interpretations of Western modernity, although it should be emphasized that Elias and Foucault presented narratives that are complementary in many ways – for example, by arguing that modern societies no longer use public acts of violence for punitive purposes, that they rely on high levels of self-monitoring and self-control, that they place the distasteful behind the scenes (behind the prison and asylum walls according to Foucault) and that their 'civilizing' traits do not lay 'decivilizing processes' to rest.[6]

A related issue is whether Elias was correct that tolerance of the use of force was greater in Hellenic international society than in the modern states-system. The claim that 'annihilation was rare and usually exemplary' because the Greeks recognized the value of exacting tribute from defeated enemies calls Elias's position into question (Shipley 1995). Placed alongside interpretations of Elias's portrayal of the Middle Ages (see Rosenwein 1998), recent scholarly writings suggest that Fletcher (1997: 19), van Krieken (1998: 131) and others are correct to argue that more extensive empirical research is needed to decide whether or not Elias's account of European modernity and its international relations is broadly right. Whatever the final verdict, the fact is that Elias's writings raise important questions about cruelty, suffering and emotional identification that provide new directions for international relations, which has devoted insufficient attention to connections between intrastate and interstate violence and civility.[7]

Not that those themes have been wholly neglected in the study of International Relations. Several recent works lend implicit support to the proposition that movement in the direction of delegitimizing violence, physical domination and the deliberate infliction of suffering within nation states has clear counterparts in international relations. Crawford (2002: 387ff) analyses how, especially over the last two centuries, moral thinkers and religious reformers 'harnessed the emotions of embarrassment and shame' to persuade Western peoples to show compassion towards the victims of slavery, colonial domination and forced labour. Rae (2002) analyses how the growth of the universal human rights culture underpins feelings of repugnance towards 'pathological homogenisation' – the process in which states aim for nationally unified populations by persecuting or expelling religious, ethnic and other minorities. Thomas (2001) has traced the revival of the 'bombing norm' since 1945, which explains why Western democratic populations have become increasingly sensitive to unnecessary civilian suffering in war. The development of international criminal law since the Nuremberg and Tokyo war crimes trials is a further example of the global civilizing process.

Analysing changing attitudes to colonial domination, human rights violations and excessive military force is a promising way of building bridges between Elias's analysis of the sociogenetic and psychogenetic dimensions of the civilizing process and similar developmental patterns in international relations – more specifically, it is a way of tracking the rise and fall of cosmopolitan emotions. The discussion inevitably leads to how far modern cultures have embraced a cosmopolitan ethic based on 'our universal susceptibility to pain and cruelty' (Rorty 1989: ch. 9; Ignatieff 1998: 149). Here, one must recognize the transformative role of war photography and what Sontag (2003: 42) has described as the recent shift from 'positive images of the warrior's trade' to 'images of the sufferings endured in war', one that reflects the movement from religious exaltations of suffering to secular views that 'suffering . . . is a mistake or an accident or a crime. Something to be fixed. Something to be refused' (Sontag 2003: 88). The central question is how these ethical sensibilities can be translated into political action in the face of temptations to ignore suffering because of compassion fatigue, to consume images of suffering as the disengaged voyeur or to derive perverse satisfaction from observing the misery of other peoples (Taylor 1998; Cohen 2001; Campbell 2003). There is then no shortage of literature on the scope of emotional identification in contemporary global politics, which provides a starting point for comparisons between the modern world and earlier historical eras and takes its lead from Elias's sociological enquiries. But there is no intellectual tradition of enquiry that provides a comparative analysis of levels of cruelty and compassion in different states-systems, no systematic examination of long-term trends with respect to global civilizing processes in these unusual forms of world political organization and little methodical analysis of whether cosmopolitan responses to human suffering are stronger in the modern society of states than they were in earlier times.

The sociology of states-systems

The idea of 'a comparative study' or 'sociology of states-systems' was discussed in Wight's posthumously published paper called *De Systematibus Civitatum* (Wight 1977: 22, 33). As Dunne (1998: 124ff) has explained, Wight and his colleagues in the British Committee on the Theory of International Politics during the 1960s wrote several papers on the 'historic states-systems' of Ancient Greece, China in the Spring and Autumn and Warring States period and the modern world, but their planned volume on the sociology of states-systems did not appear. Hedley Bull rightly argues that the project that Wight and others were developing represented a move beyond 'those studies of states-systems which view them as determined purely by mechanical factors such as the number of states in the system, their relative size, the political configuration in which they stand, the state of military technology' to one that concentrated on 'the norms and values that animate the system, and the institutions in which they are expressed' (Bull 1977: 17). Wight focused on norms, values and institutions to understand how independent political communities created international order in the absence of an overarching monopoly of power.

De Systematibus Civitatum encapsulates Wight's views about the moral and political foundations of order in the Ancient Chinese, Hellenic–Hellenistic and modern systems of states. The essay notes the part that 'messengers, conferences and congresses, a diplomatic language and trade' played in all three systems (Bull 1977: 16). It asks if similar patterns of international thought (realism with its stress on inevitable competition and conflict; rationalism with its interest in the element of society in world politics; and revolutionism with its belief in the possibility of a universal community of humankind) are common to all three states-systems.[8] The paper also advances the proposition that all systems of states display similar long-term patterns of development: the gradual destruction of smaller powers in the course of the competition for security and power, followed by the struggle between the few remaining great powers to dominate the system, and the terminal phase, in which one state finally succeeds in replacing a multiactor system with a form of imperial power. A parallel with Elias's observation about the probable, if not inevitable, outcome of 'elimination contests' in international relations has already been noted.

There is a second parallel in that the English School and Elias both deal with what is the scope of emotional identification in world affairs (see also De

Swaan 1995). For Wight, this theme is evident in his question of how far notions of a universal community of humankind have influenced world politics in all historical epochs whether by fostering transnational schisms within international society, by providing the rationale for imperial expansion or by encouraging political actors to work for global justice and perpetual peace. In this context, Wight remarks on levels of 'moral sensitiveness' in different societies of states and offers a comparison of the modern and Hellenistic systems that concurs with Elias's findings. Perhaps, Wight (1966: 126) argues, 'modern Europe has acquired a moral sensitiveness, and an awareness of the complexities, denied to simpler civilizations. The Greeks and Romans gave small thought to political ethics, still less to international ethics'. Wight's point is that the Ancient Greek city-states had little compunction in using force and observed few moral restraints on the conduct of war.

Two different themes are present in Wight's claim that ideas about the solidarity of the Hellenes and the unity of the human race certainly existed in Ancient Greece but were too hesitant to check egotism in foreign policy. The first is contained in the observation that 'no Greek Vitoria or Grotius' emerged in the ancient world to reflect on the normative foundations of international society or to defend the equivalent of modern notions of the equal sovereignty of states, the principle of non-intervention and so forth; the second is that the modern ethical conviction that certain violent acts of state can so shock the conscience of humankind as to demand external intervention had no counterpart in the Ancient World – there was no Greek equivalent to the modern international law of war or to the universal culture of human rights. The distinction between these themes is important for the study of global civilizing processes. The sociology of states developed by Wight, Butterfield and others was primarily concerned with the first of them – that is, with the norms, values and institutions that preserve order between states. Their principal aim was to understand the level of moral and political sensitiveness that linked the representatives of national governments in a diplomatic culture. Turning to the second theme, it is clear that members of the English School did not neglect the ways in which cosmopolitan ethical principles have influenced the foreign policy behaviour of national governments. The bias towards the analysis of international order can be explained by the fact that the English School believe that international societies are fragile arrangements that are permanently at risk of being weakened by the struggle for security and power; they are not so certain to survive that the central political question is how to refashion them in accordance with cosmopolitan moral commitments.

As noted earlier, Elias's remarks on world politics share many of the same assumptions – and yet the extent to which the members of different societies identify with each other is more central to his writings. The reason for this is that Elias was as concerned with the psychogenetic as with the sociogenetic dimensions of the civilizing process. His main ambition was to explain how the modern conscience and modern personality structures developed alongside the restructuring of public life in early modern Europe. Elias's interest in the changing nature of emotional identification within European societies led him to reflect on the extent to which forms of cosmopolitan identification had developed – or were developing – in global politics. This dimension emerges as a central area of sociological enquiry despite the fact that cosmopolitan identities cannot eradicate decivilizing processes and may only delay the violent collapse of the society of states. Elias's remarks on whether globalization is widening the scope of emotional identification revealed no great optimism then about the possibility of cosmopolitan trajectories of development.

A distinctive sociology of states-systems is suggested by these themes, a sociology that is concerned with the expansion and contraction of the boundaries of moral and political community (Linklater 1990), with the nature of political loyalties and the structure of human emotions. Whether or not his judgement was correct, Elias's claim that the level of moral repugnance towards genocide was lower in Ancient Greece than in modern Europe raises crucial questions for a comparative sociology of states-systems. Attitudes to cruelty and the extent to which compassion towards suffering have influenced the relations between states are important matters for a sociology of global civilizing processes with the following two purposes: to understand whether or how far 'anxiety for the well-being of humankind' (Hegel's phrase quoted in Elias 1996: 262) has developed in all states-systems; and to consider whether or not the modern states-system is unusually committed to the ethical view that its constituent parts should regard unnecessary suffering as a moral problem which all societies, individually and collectively, should attempt to solve (see Linklater 2002b).

Harm and international relations

Analysing levels of 'moral sensitiveness' to harm is one way of taking the sociology of states-systems forward. This direction is suggested by Elias's claim that civilizing processes deal with the question of how human beings can satisfy their basic needs without 'destroying, frustrating, demeaning or in other ways harming each other' in the process (Elias 1996: 31). Building on earlier work in this area (Linklater 2002b), it is necessary to distinguish between different types of harm in world politics. The following two groups of types of harm have been developed in the light of Elias's distinction between dimensions of the civilizing process that have the negative function of checking aggressive impulses and dimensions of that process that have the more positive role of promoting the 'capacity to feel for and sympathize with' others.

The first set includes three forms of harm where human beings deliberately set out to injure others. They are:

- Deliberate harm that governments and/or societies do to the members of other communities. Examples include attempts to maximize the suffering of combatants and non-combatants during military conflict whether through deliberate acts of violence against civilians or through cruelty to prisoners of war; deliberate attempts to cause hardship and suffering by imposing economic costs on other peoples; and racist and xenophobic representations of other cultures that are designed to degrade them and cause emotional pain.

- Deliberate harm that governments do to their own citizens, for example by torturing them or otherwise abusing their human rights. Controlling the use of force has been the central problem for societies of states. The modern society of states is almost certainly unique in that the harm that governments do their own citizens has become a moral and legal problem for the world as a whole especially since the end of the Second World War (although the enforcement of global norms is clearly selective). Another way of making this point is to claim that the modern society of states appears to be unique in developing cosmopolitan harm conventions (conventions that are designed to prevent harm to the individual members of humanity) in addition to international harm conventions (conventions that are designed to limit the violence that states do to each other). The upshot is the erosion of the 'Westphalian' principle that governments are not answerable to the international community for the ways they treat their subjects or citizens.
- Deliberate harm that non-state actors do to the members of different societies. Examples include violence caused by international terrorist organizations and by transnational criminal organizations that engage in the traffic of women and children for the purpose of 'sexual slavery' or that trade in illicit drugs. How societies of states have dealt with private international violence which challenges the state's monopoly of power and moral or legal authority is one central question here, as is the matter of how far they have gone in developing conventions that are intended to protect individuals everywhere (as in the notion that the pirate or slave trader is an enemy of humankind – *hostis humani generis*).

The next four forms of harm shift from deliberate attempts to cause mental and/or physical injury to:

- Unintended harm where, for example, a government or business enterprise unknowingly damages the physical environment of another society. (International law, especially since the Stockholm Conference on the Environment in 1972, has addressed this problem by creating national obligations to avoid harming the environment of neighbouring states and the global commons.)
- Negligence where, for example, a state or business enterprise knowingly submits others to the risk of harm. The failure to ensure that those involved in hazardous industries have adequate health and safety

provision is a case in point. (The need to reduce or eliminate this form of harm became more prominent as a result of the 1984 Bhopal incident.)

- Harm through unjust enrichment where, for example, members of affluent societies benefit unfairly from protectionist strategies, from export subsidies, from the vulnerability of foreign producers who may have to sell their products cheaply on the world market and from the rules of global commerce, which favour the powerful and disadvantage the weak.
- Harm through acts of omission where, for example, a person or community fails to take measures to alleviate the suffering of others in circumstances where there is no, or little, cost to itself. This is the most complex and controversial of the forms of harm described above. Legal systems take different positions on the extent to which the failure to rescue is punishable. As Feinberg (1984) explains, the Anglo-American legal tradition is in general more lenient of 'Bad Samaritanism' than is its continental European counterpart. Moreover, some philosophers deny that the failure to rescue constitutes harm; others argue that inaction in the face of human suffering, assuming the possibility of humanitarian assistance without great personal cost, harms others by indicating that the question of whether they survive does not matter to them. Here, harm is psychological rather than physical; or harm arises because inaction prolongs suffering. There is no consensus in world politics that the failure to intervene to prevent genocide causes harm; and there are no laws that make 'Bad Samaritanism' a punishable offence.

The extent to which a global civilizing process has developed in any states-system – the extent to which a 'global conscience' emerged and influenced the course of world affairs – can be determined by how far the majority of states (or the dominant states) recognized and dealt with these forms of harm. Here, it is only possible to identify questions that warrant further research. How far have all societies of states developed moral conventions designed to protect military personnel and civilian populations from unnecessary suffering in war? To what extent has the sense of a common moral responsibility to protect individuals from violence perpetrated by their governments developed in all or most societies of states? How far have measures to protect all human beings from the violent behaviour of pirates, mercenaries and similar groups appeared in all international societies? To what extent have the members of different states-systems acted to reduce or eliminate unintended harm and the adverse effects of negligent behaviour? To what extent have they sought to protect all human beings from unjust enrichment or from the consequences of acts of omission? At stake in all these questions is the issue of how far human suffering was treated with indifference, how far cruelty dominated relations between independent political communities, and how far compassion and sympathy influenced the pattern of events. The issue is how far moral concerns with human security led to the development of cosmopolitan harm conventions. Such questions are central to a comparative sociology of states-systems that explores how far a global commitment to preventing violence, to extending emotional identification across state borders and to promoting compassion developed in different historical eras.

The modern society of states in comparative context

What would such a comparative approach reveal about the modern society of states? Would it uncover significant differences in the extent to which cruelty and compassion influence international relations? What would it reveal in the way of a global counterpart to the civilizing process described by Elias? What evidence might it discover for the claim that 'things that were once permitted are now forbidden'?[9] The words of the French historian, Lucien Febvre, should be remembered here. Having questioned the portrayal of the peoples of the Middle Ages as 'childlike', Febvre (Burke 1973: 18) proceeded to ask if there is 'any reason to think that at certain periods in history tendencies towards one pattern predominated in frequency and violence over tendencies towards the opposite pattern – more cruelty than pity, more hate than love?'. Febvre (Burke 1973: 24) observed that 'we have no history of pity, or of cruelty', which provides a satisfactory answer to this question.

If Elias is broadly right that a civilizing process took place in modern Europe between the fifteenth and twentieth centuries, then it seems reasonable to suppose that its prohibitions of violence have had some influence on the conduct of international affairs. Elias concedes as much when he claims that the transition from peace to war is more exacting for the citizens of modern states than it was for the subjects of medieval kingdoms or principalities five centuries ago. Then, the 'social prohibitions' on violence were much weaker (Elias 1987: 80–1, 1996: 210). Certainly, there is no shortage of views that the modern society of states has undergone a global civilizing process in recent decades. Such approaches suggest – examples and counterexamples will be identified in a moment – that encouraging long-term trends in the modern society of states have emerged in recent decades. The modern society of states may or may not represent an advance beyond other international systems, but at least that much can be claimed for it.

The most familiar illustration of this theme is the democratic peace theory, which argues that the members of the liberal world have eradicated war from their relations with each other; another example can be found in analyses of the European Union, which regard it as a successful regional 'security community' or as a 'civilian power' committed to eliminating the use of force not only in Europe but in the rest of the world (Linklater 2005). For some, the contemporary society of states has witnessed important advances in 'meeting behaviour', which 'pacifies the struggle for power, prestige and wealth . . . at continental and global levels' (van Vree 1999: ch. 8). Liberals will argue that significant changes in moral attitudes have occurred since the end of the Second World War (Ignatieff 1998), and can cite the development of the universal human rights culture and the growth of international criminal law as examples. Pointing to the Nuremberg and Tokyo war crimes trials, but also referring to greater moral concern about global economic inequalities, Bull (2000: 220–1) argued that an 'extension of our capacity to empathize with sections of humanity that are geographically and culturally distant from us' has taken place 'at least in the advanced countries'. The rise of popular movements calling for global efforts to deal with global warming and climate change, media attention to the plight of the vulnerable as expressed in concerns about child labour and sweatshop industries, and in support for fair trade and for ethical investment, can be regarded as evidence of the development of a 'global conscience', which makes the powerful unwilling to look on impassively while the weak suffer. Perhaps these developments can be harnessed to support the claim that modern states may be 'consciously working out, for the first time, a set of transcultural values and ethical standards' (Watson 1987: 152) that are concerned with reducing cruelty and suffering and with widening emotional identification in world affairs.

Criticisms of this position include the realist or neo-realist claim – which finds support in Elias's writings – that aggressive impulses will finally overwhelm any civilizing processes; that the existence of a global civilizing process is wholly dependent on the existence of a balance of military power – which has lost its constraining role in the last few years (Dunne 2003); that compassionate feelings aroused by visual representations of human suffering are superficial and superimposed on emotional indifference which results from overexposure to the world's ills (Tester 1998); and that the impression of advancing civilization masks the existence of new forms of barbarism and new potentialities for violence (Mestrovic 1993; Gray 2002). Such arguments maintain that there is no reason to think that the citizens of modern liberal–democratic states are more compassionate towards distant strangers than their predecessors were in other epochs. They suggest that there is little evidence for the view that more cosmopolitan 'personality structures' and emotions have developed in the liberal world over the last few decades. The notion of a long-term global civilizing trend is a chimera.

Conclusions

Norbert Elias's analysis of changing emotional responses to cruelty and violence suggests directions for a sociology of states-systems that builds on Wight's pioneering essays on this subject. The account of the civilizing process was designed to understand long-term patterns of change in modern European states rather than to explain the relations between them. Indeed, Elias usually portrayed international relations as unchanging, as governed by logics of power and control. Members of the English School would be right to stress his failure to recognize that states form an international society with its own distinctive civilizing processes. To understand that process, Wight and others argued, it is necessary to consider how ethical visions of a universal community of humankind have had a civilizing effect on relations between states. There is a parallel here with Elias's underdeveloped focus on how the lower tolerance of violence within societies has influenced their external relations. The key question is how far the widening of emotional identification within national communities can be regarded as the prelude to the widening of emotional identification between states; it is how far a global conscience is forming around repugnance towards cruelty within all societies and in the conduct of international relations, and around feelings of compassion for the suffering in distant places; and it is whether globalization may yet promote the development of levels of cosmopolitan identification that have been rare in international history. Whether the modern society of states is developing, or seems likely to acquire, unusually powerful ethical commitments to reducing human suffering is unclear – unsurprisingly because analysing the place of cruelty and compassion in the civilizing processes of different international societies is uncharted territory. Casting light on these dimmer areas of the human experience of world politics is the task for a novel approach to the historical sociology of international politics.

Notes

1 This paper is a revised version of my article 'Norbert Elias, the civilizing process and international relations' published in *International Politics* 41(1) 2004: 3–35.

2 Garland (1990: 223) argues that the repugnant moves behind the scenes rather than disappears; in consequence, its reappearance in the public domain can never be discounted.

3 Elias (1996: 25) argued that the 'power gradient' decreased during the twentieth century in relations between men and women, parents and children, the European societies and the former colonies and, 'with qualifications', in the relations between rulers and the ruled. Illustrative of his position is the claim that, as a result of the civilizing process, most of the inhabitants of European societies 'no longer regard it as a Sunday entertainment to see people hanged, quartered, broken on the wheel. . .. As compared with antiquity, our identification with other people, our sharing in their suffering and death, has increased' (Elias 2001b: 2–3). His belief that 'the scope of identification' is wider in modern Europe than it was in the Middle Ages – this is the main contrast in Elias's writings – is assessed critically by, for example, Evans (1997) and Rosenwein (1998).

4 Elias (1996: 51) maintains that in 'all warrior societies (including, for example, ancient Athens), proving oneself in physical combat against other people, being victorious over them, and if necessary murdering them, played an integral part in establishing a man's standing. The present-day military tradition seeks to limit training in the use of physical violence as far as possible to violence against people who do not belong to one's own state-society'.

5 See the following in Elias (1998a: 192–3): 'The threshold of sensibility among people in antiquity – like those of Europeans in the Middle Ages and the early modern period – was quite different from that of the present day, particularly in relation to the use of physical violence. People assumed that they were violent to each other, they were attuned to it'. Elias (1998b: 22–3, 2000: 162–4) contains the following: 'The wars of the seventeenth century were cruel in a somewhat different sense to those of today. The army had, as far as possible, to feed itself when on foreign soil. Plunder and rapine were not merely permitted, but were

demanded by military technique. To torment the subjugated inhabitants of occupied territories. . . was, as well as a means of satisfying lust, a deliberate means of collecting war contributions and bringing to light concealed treasure. Soldiers were supposed to behave like robbers. It was a banditry exacted and organized by the army commanders'.

6 Thomas (1984) describes how bourgeois attitudes towards animal cruelty in the nineteenth century simultaneously challenged the cruelty of the aristocracy and sought to eliminate in top-down fashion the barbaric practices of the proletariat. His observation invites the comment that an account of Western modernity may need to draw on arguments from both Elias and Foucault.

7 Examples include the extent to which manuals governing diplomatic conduct influenced the manners books that Elias relied on in his study of the civilizing process (see Bremmer and Roodenburg 1991: ch. 7), the extent to which war is one of the main 'schools of crime' and how far peace is the precondition of civility within national societies (Johnson and Monkkonen 1996: chs 2 and 4).

8 Wilkinson (2000: 60) maintains that there have been 28 states-systems in human history.

9 Quoted in Elias (1998b: 235). The comment is derived from Caxton's late fifteenth-century *Book of Curtesye* (Elias 19998b: 273).

References

Bremmer, J. and H. Roodenburg, eds. 1991. *A Cultural History of Gestures*. Cambridge: Polity.

Bull, H. 1977. 'Martin Wight and the study of international relations', in M. Wight, ed. *Systems of States*. Leicester: University of Leicester Press.

Bull, H. 2000. 'Justice in international relations', in K. Alderson and A. Hurrell, eds. *Hedley Bull on International Relations*. London: Macmillan.

Burke, P., ed. 1973. *A New Kind of History from the Writing of Lucien Febvre*. London: Routledge and Kegan Paul.

Burke, P. 1993. *The Art of Conversation*. Cambridge: Polity.

Burke, P., B. Harrison and P. Slack, eds. 2000. *Civil Histories: Essays for Sir Keith Thomas*. Oxford: Oxford University Press.

Butterfield, H. 1953. *Christianity, Diplomacy and War*. London: Epworth Press.

Campbell, D. 2003. 'Cultural governance and pictorial resistance: reflections on the imaging of war'. *Review of International Studies* 29 (Special Issue): 57–73.

Cohen, S. 2001. *States of Denial: Knowing about Atrocities and Suffering*. Cambridge: Polity Press.

Crawford, N.C. 2002. *Argument and Change in World Politics: Ethics, Decolonization and Humanitarian Intervention*. Cambridge: Cambridge University Press.

De Swaan, A. 1995. 'Widening circles of identification: emotional concerns in sociogenetic perspective'. *Theory, Culture and Society* 12 (2): 25–39.

Dunne, T. 1998. *Inventing International Society*. London: Macmillan.

Dunne, T. 2003. 'Society and hierarchy in international relations'. *International Relations* 17: 303–20.

Elias, N. 1978. *What is Sociology?* New York: Columbia University Press.

Elias, N. 1987. *Involvement and Detachment*. Oxford: Basil Blackwell.

Elias, N. 1991. *The Symbol Theory*. London: Sage.

Elias, N. 1995. 'Technization and civilization'. *Theory, Culture and Society* 12:18–41.

Elias, N. 1996. *The Germans*. Cambridge: Polity Press.

Elias, N. 1998a. 'The civilizing of parents', in J. Goudsblom and S. Mennell, eds. *The Norbert Elias Reader*. Oxford: Basil Blackwell.

Elias, N. 1998b. 'Informalization and the civilizing process', in J. Goudsblom and S. Mennell, eds. *The Norbert Elias Reader*. Oxford: Basil Blackwell.

Elias, N. 2000. *The Civilizing Process: Sociogenetic and Psychogenetic Investigations*. Oxford: Basil Blackwell.

Elias, N. 2001a. *The Society of Individuals*. London: Continuum.

Elias, N. 2001b. *The Loneliness of the Dying*. London: Continuum.

Elias, N. and E. Dunning. 1986. *Quest for Excitement: Sport and Leisure in the Civilizing Process*. Oxford: Blackwell.

Evans, R. 1997. *Rituals of Retribution: Capital Punishment in Germany, 1600–1987*. Harmondsworth: Penguin.

Feinberg, J. 1984. *Harm to Others: The Moral Limits of the Criminal Law*. Oxford: Oxford University Press.

Fletcher, J. 1997. *Violence and Civilisation: An Introduction to the Work of Norbert Elias*. Cambridge: Polity Press.

Garland, D. 1990. *Punishment and Modern Society: A Study in Social Theory*. Oxford: Clarendon Press.

Garland, D. 2001. *The Culture of Control: Crime and Social Order in Contemporary Society*. Oxford: Oxford University Press.

Gong, G. 1984. *The Standard of Civilization in International Society*. Oxford: Clarendon Press.

Gray, J. 2002. *Straw Dogs: Thoughts on Humans and other Animals*. London: Granta Publications.

Ignatieff, M. 1998. *The Warrior's Honour: Ethnic War and the Modern Conscience*. London: Chatto and Windus.

Jackson, R. 2000. *The Global Covenant: Human Conduct in a World of States*. Oxford: Oxford University Press.

Johnson, E.A. and E.H. Monkkonen, eds. 1996. *The Civilization of Violence: Violence in Town and Country since the Middle Ages*. Chicago: University of Illinois Press.

Linklater, A. 1990. *Beyond Realism and Marxism: Critical Theory and International Relations*. London: Macmillan.

Linklater, A. 2002a. 'Unnecessary suffering', in K. Booth and T. Dunne, eds. *Worlds in Collision: Terror and the Future of Global Order*. London: Palgrave.

Linklater, A. 2002b. 'The problem of harm in world politics: implications for the sociology of states-systems'. *International Affairs* 78 (2): 319–38.

Linklater, A. 2005. 'A European civilizing process', in C. Hill and M. Smith, eds. *The International Relations of the European Union*. Oxford: Oxford University Press.

Mennell, S. 1990. 'The globalization of human society as a very long-term social process: Elias's theory'. *Theory, Culture and Society* 7: 359–71.

Mennell, S. 1998. *Norbert Elias: An Introduction*. Dublin: University College Dublin Press.

Mestrovic, S.G. 1993. *The Barbarian Temperament: Toward a Postmodern Critical Theory*. London: Routledge.

O'Hagan, C. 2002. *Conceptualising the West in International Relations: From Spengler to Said*. Basingstoke: Palgrave.

Rae, H. 2002. *State Identities and the Homogenisation of Peoples*. Cambridge: Cambridge University Press.

Rorty, R. 1989. *Contingency, Irony and Solidarity*. Cambridge: Cambridge University Press.

Rosenwein, B.H., ed. 1998. *Anger's Past: The Social Uses of an Emotion in the Middle Ages*. London: Cornell University Press.

Sharp, P. 2001. 'The English School, Herbert Butterfield and Diplomacy', paper presented to the International Studies Association Annual Conference, New Orleans.

Sharp, P. 2003. 'Herbert Butterfield, the English School and the civilizing virtues of diplomacy'. *International Affair* 79 (4): 855–78.

Shipley, G. 1995. 'The limits of war', in J. Rich and G. Shipley, eds. *War and Society in the Greek World*. London: Routledge.

Sontag, S. 2003. *Regarding the Pain of Others*. London: Hamish Hamilton.

Spierenburg, P. 1991. *The Broken Spell: A Cultural and Anthropological History of Preindustrial Europe*. Brunswick, NJ: Rutgers University Press.

Sznaider, N. 2001. *The Compassionate Society: Care and Cruelty in Modern Society*. Oxford: Rowman and Littlefield.

Taylor, J. 1998. *Body Horror: Photojournalism, Catastrophe and War*. Manchester: Manchester University Press.

Tester, K. 1998. 'Bored and blasé: television, the emotions and Georg Simmel', in G. Bendelow and S.J. Williams, eds. *Emotions in Social Life: Critical Themes and Contemporary Issues*. London: Routledge.

Thomas, K. 1984. *Man and the Natural World: Changing Attitudes in England, 1500–1800*. Harmondsworth: Penguin.

Thomas, W. 2001. *The Ethics of Destruction: Norms and Force in International Relations*. London: Cornell University Press.

van Krieken, R. 1998. *Norbert Elias*. London: Routledge.

van Vree, W. 1999. *Meetings, Manners and Civilization: The Development of Modern Meeting Behaviour*. London: Leicester University Press.

Watson, A. 1982. *Diplomacy: The Dialogue Between States*. London: Methuen.

Watson, A. 1987. 'Hedley Bull, states systems and international societies'. *Review of International Studies* 13: 147–53.

Wight, M. 1966. 'Western values in international relations', in M. Wight and H. Butterfield, eds. *Diplomatic Investigations: Essays in the Theory of International Politics*. London: George Allen and Unwin.

Wight, M. 1977. *Systems of States*. Leicester: University of Leicester Press.

Wilkinson, D. 2000. 'Civilisations, world systems and hegemonies', in R.A. Denemark, J. Friedman, B.K. Gills and G. Modelski, eds. *World System Theory: The Social Science of Long-Term Change*. London: Routledge.

5 Globalizations

The first ten, hundred, five thousand and million years

David Wilkinson

Premises and contexts now in vogue for discussions of globalization (short term, present tense, futurist, policy oriented, narrowly focused, voluntaristic, purposive) should be supplemented and, to some extent, supplanted by others. Briefly, globalization should be seen as a nested set of processes, including very long-term processes, with deep historical and biological roots, on a wide functional scale, largely driven rather than chosen, towards the uncertain ends characteristic of complex systems.

This examination of globalization draws substantively upon the previous work of the author in empirical research on world systems and civilizations (see e.g. Wilkinson 2002) mindful of the context being developed by other workers on large-scale systems (e.g. Gills and Frank 1992; Frank and Gills 1993; Cioffi-Revilla and Landman 1999; Chase Dunn *et al.* 2000; Cioffi-Revilla 2000; Denemark *et al.* 2000; Thompson 2002; Hui 2005). Procedurally, it adopts the research programme of complex systems analysis (a.k.a. 'social physics' and 'homeokinetics'), developed by A.S. Iberall and associates in pioneering the study of complex systems from the 1970s (Iberall 1972, 1974; Soodak and Iberall 1978; Iberall *et al.* 1993), a programme with whose civilizational applications readers may be familiar (Iberall 1995; Iberall and Wilkinson 1991, 1993; Iberall *et al.* 2000).

Dynamic empirical systems analysis, examining change over time in real (vs. mathematical) systems, requires us to decide what are the shortest and longest process times of concern. This involves a generalized form of spectroscopy. Spectroscopy originates as the resolution of compound wave phenomena (e.g. sunlight, noises) into their simpler components, which are differentiated as a range of frequencies. Homeokinetics' more generalized spectroscopy investigates compound processes by discriminating their component subprocesses according to their timescales (Wilkinson and Iberall 1986; Iberall and Wilkinson 1987). The spectroscopic strategy is to seek out cycles (or parts of cycles) at all timescales in a system in which they can be discovered. The enumeration typically begins by defining an end-product, itself perhaps a system state or process, and then gathering into a coherent description all the competing, neutral and cooperating processes that produce the end-product (Iberall 2001).

What is the relevant end-product in this present enquiry? Globalization in the most general sense should signify an enlargement of some system, entity or process, in its spatial scale, to or towards some limits imposed by Earth's dimensions. For current purposes, it is convenient to limit application of the term to human social processes, or human-driven ecological processes, although there may be occasions when an even broader view is desirable. The initial 'local' scale need not be specified and might be as small as a village or hand, or as large as a 'civilization' or subglobal 'world system' (for these terms and their empirical referents, see e.g. Wilkinson 1995).

Given this general sense of the term, there should be no difficulty in raising the question: which such human or human-driven processes have in the past expanded from local to global scope, or are doing so now? The usual timescale in which 'globalization' is considered is at minimum post-Cold War, at maximum post-Second World War. Several answers to the question will be voiced immediately by politician activists of various stripes who focus on this timescale (see, for example, the useful survey by Brawley 2003). In the mostly narrow concept in vogue, globalization means the adoption on the world scale of policies and practices of politically unimpeded flow of money and goods across the borders of states in the world system much as these commodities flow across the borders of states in the US federal system. Contemporary 'anti-globalists' will also cite, and object to, world banking (loans made available on more or less onerous terms by loan agencies with global reach), world marketing and branding (McDonald's everywhere, even in France), world investing (permitting rapid 'capital flight' when local economies produce fear or panic), worldwide production (permitting 'runaway production' and 'job exporting'), worldwide media reach (promoting 'cosmopolitanism') and worldwide corporate mobility (permitting 'tax havens' for fleeing headquarters).

A composite nightmare of the anti-globalists might depict a world of six billion social clones all living in suburban houses, speaking Valley English, drinking coffee at Starbucks, eating burgers at McDonald's, shopping at Wal-Mart, voting the straight Republocrat ticket – in short, a universal Los Angeles filled with interchangeable Californians burning Iraqi oil in the gas tanks of Japanese cars as they drive to Ethiopian restaurants where they will drink Australian wines named after French grape-growing regions as they prepare to jet to Tokyo, perhaps to protest about globalization.

Yet it is only the Sleep of Reason which (as for Goya) brings forth this dream of monsters; persons fully awake can cheerfully dismiss it to the Land of Nod on sound homeokinetic principles. Far from being a novelty, the diffusing of ethnicity by mixing and remixing has necessarily permeated the human ecumene at least since its occupation 40,000 ybp or before (Iberall and Wilkinson 1984a). If cultural homogeneity were an available stable state, it would have been attained long ago. It is not. On the contrary, polyculturality, with continuous remixing at longer and larger scales, is a uniform and probably an obligatory feature for the start-up and maintenance of civilizations (Iberall and Wilkinson 1985, 1993).

Anti-global activists have been slower to recognize several other scaled-up processes which, however, certainly involve globalization (as noted, for example, by Naim 2003). The globalization of diasporas is clearly a phenomenon of historical importance. Refugees from war, revolution, drought and other disasters now flee not only locally (once the only option) but 'to the ends of the earth'. A globalizing world job market challenges and mocks localistic anti-immigration laws.

A globalization of identity seems to be in early development, as world individuals begin to count their own increasing 'hyphenations' – the 'Cablinasian' identity of Tiger Woods is an early attempt to recognize the merging of once segregated identities. The globalization of criminal enterprise has a remarkable significance, currently underappreciated because of the bad habit of treating illegal production and trade as non-existent when official production and trade statistics are compiled. The relentless pressure of global consumers for recreational and/or addictive drugs, the absence of equally profitable cash crop exports in, for example, Afghanistan and Bolivia and the inability of localistic anti-smuggling laws to impede the mass consumption of these commodities suggest that such enterprise will continue to evolve by a sort of natural selection. Drug syndicates are already well implicated in the local wars and politics of several producer and transit states, and there seems to be no evident barrier to cartel entry even into the more placid politician rental market of the wealthier consumer states, where they have an incentive to organize the market, corrupt the police, suppress small-scale competitors and finance the foes of legalization after the manner of the classic Baptist Bootlegger. Issues of branding and product standardization and quality control will doubtless arise. Can global cartel meetings in neutral Davos or Las Vegas be far away?

The globalization of political movements as a process has been under way, or perhaps one should say restarted, since the French Revolution began the export of liberal democracy by force and propaganda. Liberalism, socialism, fascism, Communism, Green environmentalism, Islamism all broadened their reach and their ambitions from their localized beginnings. It would be premature to suggest that we have reached a final 'run-off election', in which liberal capitalist democracy faces an Islamist coalition in a competition to reorganize global politics into a new 'world order' with or without the enthusiastic consent of those thus restructured, but there is certainly more than just a whiff of that prospect in the air at the moment.

It is in the context of the globalization of political movements that it might be noted more explicitly how so-called 'anti-globalization' political work is being done, not on local scales but on a global scale, by long-distance air travellers and Internet workers, so that the anti-globalization movement itself is part of a process of the globalization of political movements. This is more than mere historical irony. We may be witnessing the inception of a global and cosmopolitan 'opposition party'. Those who opposed the Hamiltonian federalization of the American confederal constitution on local autonomy grounds then united at the federal level, first in opposition, but eventually as the governing party, later first opposing the Lincolnian centralization of the federal constitution, then perfecting and administering it to their taste. If the evolution of US Democrats from Jefferson to Jackson, Wilson, F. Roosevelt, Johnson and Clinton is imitated among global politicians, we can perhaps foresee that the greatest future expansion of global rule-making and standardization will come at the hands of anti-globalist-run world organizations.

These three under-recognized globalizations – of diasporas, crime and politicians – are emphasized here not for immediate study, although they can all usefully be examined in the globalization context, but rather in preparation for the next argument – that the temporal scale of globalization concepts needs to be drastically stretched. Once we recognize that other processes than those usually considered under the 'globalization' rubric are in fact also spreading in the world's space, we are more prepared to ask: are there perhaps yet more social processes that have in the past extended themselves spatially and have some significance for the current globalization?

As soon as the question is asked, it will be perceived that the answer must be in the affirmative.

Globalization of warfare. The very names First World War and Second World War indicate that a highly significant process, the systemic war production process, had reached global scope well before the term 'globalization' is usually applied. And world-scale warfare was not an abrupt change; even in the seventeenth century War of the Grand Alliance (1689–97), French and British fought in America and India.

Globalization of world politics. As regards world politics in general, who would doubt that the United Nations, and before it the League, incorporates the 'globalization' of a diplomatic process scaled up from the European power balancing of the eighteenth and nineteenth centuries?

Indeed, that once Eurocentric process could arguably be dated as having been globalized as early as the Boxer rising in Manchu China in 1900, when a multinational force from America, Austria, Britain (and British India), France, Germany, Italy, Japan and Russia intervened. The mere fact that current history tends to disapprove of this intervention, while approving of other, more recent peace-keeping forces and enforcement actions (some involving a not too different dramatis personae) does not alter this event's claim to be a landmark of the globalization of multinational intervention. Once again, this was a scaling up of a more localized process; a European precedent was provided when the Congress of Vienna responded to the Hundred Days of Napoleon I.

And if we examine diplomacy that did not involve multinational force, the Berlin Conference of 1884–5, attended by Germany, Austria–Hungary, Belgium, Denmark, Spain, the United States, France, Great Britain, Italy, Holland, Portugal, Russia, Sweden, Norway and Turkey, which agreed upon rules for the occupation of the coast of Africa and the obligations of 'spheres of influence', has a reasonable claim to have initiated the globalization of territorial reallocation. In this, it was a prologue to Versailles 1919 and the Second World War conferences, which were also a scaling up (in ambition, effectiveness or both) of the settlements of Tordesillas, Westphalia, Utrecht and Vienna.

The scaling up of European war and diplomacy to encompass the entire globe is the consequence of yet another globalization which needs recognition, with an even longer timescale and of direct interest to civilizationists: the globalization of civilizations/world systems. This tale has been told previously at some length (Wilkinson 1987); suffice it to say here that two localized civilizations/world systems, one from the Nile Valley, the other from Mesopotamia, expanded, collided and fused *c.* 1500 BC into one 'central' system which continued its expansion, engulfing other world systems as it encountered them and entraining their processes to its own until, in the period between the Opium Wars and the First World War, it so engulfed the last such autonomous systems remaining, the Far Eastern and Japanese, and organized the globe around its then mostly European core states, prominently present in the Berlin conference, the Peking expedition, the League and the UN.

The globalization of world systems, the expansion of a diplomatic–political–military structure, is paralleled by the globalization of the world economy (*oikumene*). This globalization, in particular, has been attended to by A.G. Frank, Barry Gills and others (e.g. Gills and Frank 1992; Frank and Gills 1993; Denemark *et al.* 2000); its relation to the globalization of world systems, and especially of the Central system, has also been charted (Wilkinson 1992, 1993). Perhaps the most interesting feature of the expansion in space of the world economy over time is its tendency to precede, to inspire, perhaps even to constrain the expansion of world politics and the intensification of political organization. In this context, Hord's conclusion, based on study of the growth of connectivity over the millennia, that '[t]he world is going to be united' (2001: 50) is fully consistent with past data on globalization processes.

The globalization of both world systems and the world economy takes us at least to a 5,000-year timescale. This is also a sort of dream timescale, a scale of the expansion of political fantasy. I mentioned Napoleon earlier and will now mention him again in the context of the globalization of world imperialism. In a merely territorial and demographic sense, it was Victorian Britain, from whose second (post-American) empire an enormous number of independent states have now been devolved, which created the closest approximation (thus far) to a world empire of the globe. But if we consider vision and will-to-power, the closest approximation (thus far) to a world empire deliberately aspired to arguably belongs rather to Napoleon than to, say, Hitler or Stalin, let alone Louis XIV, Philip II, Suleiman the Magnificent, Pope Boniface VIII, Julius Caesar, Alexander, Kublai Khan or the Ummayad Caliph Suleiman, to name some other persons with ambitions of limitless scope.

But, once we begin to examine the realm of globalization of imperialist ambitions and visions, it is clear that our temporal scope must be as large as that of world systems research. The various dynasties whose history is collected as that of 'China' had monarchs who aspired, and claimed, to bring divine order to 'all under heaven', at least from the Chou/Zhou *c.* 1100 BC. And as early as about the twenty-third century BC, Naram-Sin of Akkad was (at least in his own inscriptions 'King of the World' (and God into the bargain)); he may not have been the first such dreamer. The scale of operations of the earliest world state globalizers was, by today's standards, modest – Naram-Sin, based in the territory of today's Iraq, got no further than today's Turkey – but the existence of global ambitions, even on the part of those who had no sense of the 'round earth' (for which Naram-Sin substituted the 'four quarters'), seems not just a historical fact but also the indication of a persistent drive. There has existed a will to expand, to and beyond whatever limits were recognized, and it has been manifested repeatedly, with significant effect. Conceived as a distinct form of internal pressure, that boundless 'will-to-power' belongs in our understanding of globalization phenomena, some of which it may still drive as before – Nietzsche would surely think so.

So there exists a 5,000-year timescale for globalization as a process, and one not much shorter for globalization as a goal, with both retaining contemporary relevance. Yet 5,000 years is not the longest scale with which we must deal in order to comprehend contemporary globalization. There currently exists a consensus (in the admittedly dynamic field of palaeoanthropology) that human prehistory saw at least one first '*out* of Africa' and probably two. In this burst or bursts, a once highly localized primate – whether best adapted to savannah, lakeshore or rainforest life is not clear – in a relatively short time outdistanced its primate cousins and invaded virtually every land niche from which it could conceivably extract nutrition sufficient for survival and reproduction, learning to devour and digest organisms from algae to zebras, from termites to whales, and becoming thereby the closest empirical approximation to the meaning of 'omnivore' – eater of everything – other than perhaps a black hole, or time itself. The globalization of the human species is a genuine event, the prerequisite of all other globalizations, and a mystery and a marvel as well. How was it accomplished? How did first *Homo erectus*, probably followed in breakout by *Homo sapiens sapiens*, outrun even the rat and the cockroach in the occupation of the land surface?

The relevant long timescale is certainly associated with that of fire using, which made a variety of new ecological niches (places and foodstuffs) available via campfire and cookery. Fire may even have been the first trade commodity, 300,000 to 1.5 million years ago (Ofek 2001).

Part of the explanation of the breakout remains entirely germane to the discussion of globalization in the very short term, and in the very constricted sense currently in vogue. The initial species-globalization process was identified in the 1980s as a diffusive one (Iberall and Wilkinson 1984b). The diffusion process was driven by a very small, steadily secularly maintained rate of growth of the entire human population (despite spatially and temporally localized reversals, i.e. population collapses), labelled, ironically, the 'Malthusian constant' (Iberall and Wilkinson 1984a). The irony in the name lies in the fact that Thomas Malthus was concerned with the precariousness of population growth, whereas it is now clear (as would not have been the case in 1799) that a long-term 'geometric' (i.e. exponential) rate of growth has been somehow sustained or restored over a many tens of thousands of years timescale. Malthus feared an imminent general population crash and preached self-restraint; instead, there has been a gradually increasing crush (the exponent in the exponential growth is very small).

The 'crush' is of central importance to the comprehension of globalized social processes. Very early indeed, the expanding human population ran into a container – the round earth, with its world ocean that could he colonized across but not in or on. An expansion that had previously maintained an essentially constant population density (Iberall and Wilkinson 1984b) nonetheless continued, but thereafter had repeatedly to adapt to increasing density. This was (and is) managed demographically by nucleating condensation (Iberall and Wilkinson 1985), by the creation of small very high-density areas – villages, towns, cities, metropolises, megalopolises – within a generally lower density 'countryside', technologically by a continual process of innovation, and economically by the well-known ever-increasing division of labour and the somewhat more disputed hierarchical layering of command-control by states, markets, monopolies and cartels.

This entire process is often termed economic 'growth' or 'development'. Complex system processes – energy flows, matter flows, action flows, for living systems demographic flows, for modern humans economic value-in-exchange flows – are bound in common and codependent (Iberall *et al.* 2000). While there has been some genuine increment of per capita well-being as a result of production growth (probably better measured by increase in human life expectancy than by the more elusive concept of increased 'real income'), basically value-in-exchange per capita has merely been near conserved, and human bionumber massively increased, probably by about six orders of magnitude, from an initial breeding pool of say 10,000 (Iberall and Wilkinson 1984a, 1984b, 1985, 1987).

The longest-term globalization process has then had as its chief function the management of the increase in the packing density and, consequently, the increase in 'social pressure' of a steadily more numerous human species within an essentially closed container. In some sense, the shorter term globalization processes seem to be subservient to the longer process: they provide a widening of the division of labour and of command and control, which allows the simultaneous survival of more and more humans.

As long as global population continues to increase, along with density and social pressure, it seems inevitable that other globalization processes, to the extent that they contribute to the slow increase in total global economic production (by increasing the division of labour and consolidation of management), will also continue. Even illegal immigration, and earning a marginal living from illegal drugs, are to be seen, in homeokinetic terms, as global system adaptations to parochial anti-globalist oppositions that have failed to comprehend the long-term demographic meaning of the processes whose local intrusions they hope to exclude.

Anti-globalization movements will merely serve to rechannel or at best ameliorate the globalization process, of which they are themselves a part, unless the demographic basis of contemporary globalization is directly addressed: human institutions are adapting in a large variety of ways, on an ever larger spatial scale, as they have had to do for a very long time, to a persistently increasing size and density of the human population, which persistently renders previous social adaptations obsolete. Although some of the multiform processes of globalization may be locally delayed or impeded, others will promptly substitute: humanity remains generally innovative and not resigned to be pushed over the brink. There is no basis upon which to expect a general reversal of globalization without a previous decline in population and density, such as so far has proved local or temporary or both.

No serious politician has as yet endorsed a programme of recovery of local autonomy through conscious planning for local population decline. Localist demographic politics, where it exists, usually dictates a precisely opposite strategy, with the arguments pitting pronatalist nativists against liberal advocates of immigration. Even China's one-child policy (much resisted) is not intended to disconnect China from the global system; quite the reverse, in fact. The global 'proletarian tide' of refugees from war, ecological disaster, brilliant central economic planning and mere resource exhaustion poverty would in any case doubtless restore any localized density reduction produced by self-restraint: Western Europe knows this already; Japan may discover it soon.

What is the long-term future of long-term globalization? Physical processes generally reach limits. Malthus may be redeemed at last: the world economy–ecology may finally adapt to population pressure by initiating a long cycle of global famines, epidemics and diasporas such as that reported locally for Ethiopia (Pankhurst 1986). Another possibility is of course a step-level crash, as with the Black Plague, perhaps as a result of a general failure of high-tech food production systems adapted to one climatic regime when another such regime is suddenly superimposed, or via a single epidemic (cf. AIDS in Africa). A third alternative requires limitless faith in human ingenuity: Fremlin's gremlins (Fremlin 1964). Sixty quadrillion human beings, stacked 2,000 stories high and all living at the margin, is sufficiently implausible; but humanity has already swollen by six levels of magnitude without self-annihilation, and another level or two at least might be aspired to by the true optimist.

Or of course we may discover that globalization is an inherently self-limiting process, and history may indeed decelerate to a happy ending. Complex living systems in general tend to conserve bionumber, i.e. maintain a roughly steady population (Iberall and McCulloch 1969). General material prosperity may lead to general reproductive self-restraint. Human demographic history seems to have proceeded somewhat differently: there always seems somewhere to be a 'proletariat' in the original Roman sense, a class of people with no property but their progeny, whose 'poverty in the midst of plenty' makes the incentives of prosperity meaningless for them. There is no warrant for anticipating an end to all the globalizations unless the problem of the marginalized populations is successfully addressed.

But is this possible? Homeokinetic social physics expects us to find any complex system within a nested hierarchy of complex systems above and below, each maintaining itself at its proper timescale (Wilkinson and Iberall 1986). For instance, among social insects, the colonies (e.g. beehives) appear to be super-organisms that behave collectively even while their individual members decide, communicate and remember. At what level is rationality to be expected? Social insects have multiple levels of self-identity – individual, genome, colony – which cooperate and compete in maximizing their respective organismal, infraorganismal and supraorganismal interests (Queller and Strassman 2002). In the human case, one could imagine that the superorganism is following a selfish strategy of increasing its survival chances by maximizing its total size, while motivating its equally selfish 'cells' (individuals) with a relatively small gain in their duration and metabolic well-being, and its selfish genomes with a higher than expected reproductiveness. The superorganism's strategy is not necessarily in the average interest of the individuals within the superorganism.

Some general findings of homeokinetics may be germane here. Humans can intermittently use rational study to govern decision-making. If a number of hierarchical levels compete for interest maximization, decision-making at each level can be only weak rationality. Accordingly, a superorganism does not necessarily seek its own best interest in the most rational manner. There must exist connections between levels, which involve communication. 'People are entitled to seek dialogues with systems other than members of our species' (Iberall 2000). Yet how can the bee communicate with the beehive?

In the absence of such communication, the social pressures stemming from a small net positive rate of change in earth's human population are likely to go on driving social reconfiguration as they have since the occupation of the human ecumene. By trade, diaspora and command-control adaptations, some at least of the short-term globalization processes must be expected to continue, with of course associated social costs and unremitting struggles to shift those costs. The question of which social reconfigurations might accommodate a small continual net population increase, with some balancing of the interests of individuals, classes (especially the marginalized), the species and its genomes, will provide a great deal of food for thought for students of globalization broadly comprehended.

References

Brawley, Mark R. 2003. *The Politics of Globalization*. Peterborough, ON, Canada: Broadview Press.

Chase-Dunn, Christopher, Susan Manning and Thomas O. Hall. 2000. 'Rise and fall: East–West synchronicity and Indic exceptionalism reexamined'. *Social Science History* 24: 727–54.

Cioffi-Revilla, Claudia. 2000. 'War and warfare: scales of conflict in long-range analysis', in R.A. Denemark *et al.*, eds. *World System History*. London: Routledge, pp. 253–72.

Cioffi-Revilla, Claudio and Todd Landman. 1999. 'Evolution of Maya polities in the ancient Mesoamerican system'. *International Studies Quarterly* 43: 559–98.

Denemark, Robert A., Jonathan Friedman, Barry K. Gills and George Modelski, eds. 2000. *World System History: The Social Science of Long-Term Change*. London: Routledge.

Frank, Andre Gunder and Barry Gills, eds. 1993. *The World System*. London: Routledge.

Fremlin, J.H. 1964. 'How many people can the world support?' *New Scientist* 415: 285–7.

Gills, B. and A.G. Frank. 1992. 'World system cycles, crises, and hegemonial shifts 1700 BC to 1700 AD'. *Review* (Fernand Braudel Institute) 15 (4): 621–87.

Hord, John K. 2001. 'The comparability of ancient and modern civilizations'. *Comparative Civilizations Review* 44: 7–54.

Hui, Victoria Tin-bor. 2005. *War and State Formation in Ancient China and Early Modern Europe*. Cambridge: Cambridge University Press.

Iberall, Arthur S. 1972. *Towards a General Science of Viable Systems*. New York: McGraw-Hill.

Iberall, Arthur S. 1974. 'On a thermodynamic theory of history'. *General Systems* 19: 201.

Iberall, Arthur S. 1995. 'On a characteristic 500-year process – time in culture civilizations'. *Comparative Civilizations Review* 32:146–62.

Iberall, Arthur S. 2000. 'What makes Sammy-Samantha and other mammals run? A first round of closure'. *Ecological Psychology* 12 (2): 109–39.

Iberall, Arthur S. 2001. 'The physics, chemical physics, and biological physics of the origin of life on earth'. *Ecological Psychology* 13 (4): 315–27.

Iberall, Arthur S. and W. McCulloch. 1969. 'The organizing principle of complex living systems'. *Journal of Basic Engineering* 91: 290–4.

Iberall, Arthur S. and David Wilkinson. 1984a. 'Human sociogeophysics phase II: diffusion of ethnicity by remixing'. *GeoJournal* 9 (4): 387–91.

Iberall, Arthur S. and David Wilkinson. 1984b. 'Human sociogeophysics phase I: explaining the macroscopic patterns of man on earth'. *GeoJournal* 8 (2): 171–9.

Iberall, Arthur S. and David Wilkinson. 1985. 'Human sociogeophysics phase II (continued): criticality in the diffusion of ethnicity produces civil society'. *GeoJournal* 11 (2):153–8.

Iberall, Arthur S. and David Wilkinson. 1987. 'Dynamic foundations of complex systems', in George Modelski, ed. *Exploring Long Cycles*. Boulder, CO: Lynne Reinner, pp. 16–55.

Iberall, Arthur S. and David Wilkinson. 1991. 'A physical tutorial'. *Comparative Civilizations Review* 24: 84–96.

Iberall, Arthur S. and David Wilkinson. 1993. '"Polycultures" and "culture-civilizations": forms and processes in the evolution of civilizations'. *Comparative Civilizations Review* 28: 73–9.

Iberall, Arthur S., David Wilkinson and Douglas White. 1993. *Foundations for Social and Biological Evolution*. Laguna Hills, CA: Cri-de-Coeur.

Iberall, Arthur S., Frank Hassler, Harry Soodak and David Wilkinson. 2000. 'Invitation to an enterprise: from physics to world history to the study of civilizations'. *Comparative Civilizations Review* 42: 4–22.

Naim, Moises. 2003. 'The five wars of globalization'. *Foreign Policy* 134: 29–36.

Ofek, Haim. 2001. *Second Nature: Economic Origins of Human Evolution*. Cambridge: Cambridge University Press.

Pankhurst, Richard. 1986. *The History of Famine and Epidemics in Ethiopia Prior to the Twentieth Century*. Addis Ababa: Relief and Rehabilitation Commission.

Queller, David C. and Joan B. Strassman. 2002. 'The many selves of social insects'. *Science* 296: 311–13.

Soodak, Harry and Arthur Iberall. 1978. 'Homeokinetics: a physical science for complex systems'. *Science* 201: 579–82.

Thompson, William R. 2002. 'Testing a cyclical instability theory in the ancient Near East'. *Comparative Civilizations Review* 46: 34–78.

Wilkinson, David. 1987. 'Central civilization'. *Comparative Civilizations Review* 17: 31–59.

Wilkinson, David. 1992. 'Cities, civilizations and oikumenes'. *Comparative Civilizations Review* 27: 51–87.

Wilkinson, David. 1993. 'Cities, civilizations and oikumenes II', *Comparative Civilizations Review* 28: 41–72.

Wilkinson, David. 1995. 'Civilizations are world systems', in Stephen K. Sanderson, ed. *Civilizations and World System*. Palo Alto: Altamira, pp. 248–60.

Wilkinson, David. 2002. 'Civilizations as networks: trade, war, diplomacy, and command control'. *Complexity* 8 (1): 82–6.

Wilkinson, David, and Arthur S. Iberall. 1986. 'From systems physics to world politics: invitation to an enterprise', in Margaret P. Karns, ed. *Persistent Patterns and Emergent Structures in a Waning Century*. New York: Praeger, pp. 35–71.

6 The Big Collapse

A brief cosmology of globalization[1]

Claudio Cioffi-Revilla

The globalized world system in which we live today – the first and only that is truly global in an absolute sense from a world historical perspective – is a complex spatio-temporal interaction network that began in multiple and politically special regions of the earth, at different times in history, under diverse cultural and environmental conditions, and has since been collapsing into a single highly interconnected structure with increasingly dense interaction networks. This is diametrically opposed to the long-term evolution of the physical universe, which presumably began in one place, at one time, and has since been expanding with overall decreasing density – the so-called Big Bang model. This chapter examines the process of globalization in world system history as a complex and punctuated process of long-term collapse resulting in the modern global world system with unprecedented and increasing network density. The analysis upon which this Big Collapse model is based draws on new data from the Long-Range Analysis of War (LORANOW) Project and related computational methods.

This chapter contains four sections. I begin by discussing background on the long-range paradigm for understanding globalization, a model that I call the 'Big Collapse'. The second section contains the main ideas and empirical foundations on the multiple origins and globalization phases of world systems leading to the model of the Big Collapse. In the third section, I discuss selected salient features of the Big Collapse model, subject to space constraints. The last section provides a summary.

Introduction/background

Understanding the long-term evolution of the world system and human cultures is one of the big unresolved puzzles in social science (Smithsonian Science Commission 2002), because new knowledge in this area has implications for understanding and evaluating the present and future prospects of humankind, not just the ancient past. For example, whether or not we evolve towards a spacefaring civilization (Zubrin 1999) depends, *inter alia*, on our ability to overcome potentially catastrophic processes such as environmental change and large-scale conflict. Deep scientific knowledge about earlier world systems – from which our present system evolved over the millennia – will prove crucial.

The old paradigm on the evolution of the world system – still held by most social scientists today, except for a few anthropological archaeologists and epigraphers – is based on a modernist view of history that eschews the significance of antiquity, particularly early antiquity and late prehistory. For instance, mainstream political science today is largely dominated by the Westphalian paradigm of the modern nation states system, even as it accepts some non-state actors within a global system (neo-Westphalian version). Sociology and economics are similarly modernistic in their dismissal of the ancient past, with a few exceptions (e.g. Frank and Gills 1993; Chase-Dunn and Hall 1997; Zaccagnini 2003). However, the modern Westphalian system that has evolved since 1648 CE is only the most recent configuration in a long and complex political process dating back many thousands of years ($\sim 10^3$), not just hundreds ($\sim 10^2$).

The Westphalian paradigm needs to be re-examined and replaced, not salvaged, because we face a disturbing critical anomaly in contemporary social science: the ascertained empirical age of the world system is now known to be much older, by several orders of magnitude, than the much shorter temporal scope of the dominant paradigm and extant theories of international relations, world politics and universal history. This contradiction – between the known facts and current explanations – will not go away; it can only grow more acute as archaeology and epigraphy increase the quality and quantity of relevant empirical data while other social sciences cling to their current modernist focus, ignoring the ancient record. Political science, in particular, seems decades behind in facing and solving this scientific problem, which holds the answers to problems of conflict, cooperation and global change in this age of instability.[2]

The Big Collapse

In this section, I present the 'Big Collapse' model, which describes the multiple origins of social complexity in a diverse array of world systems in late prehistory and early antiquity, and how those independent and pristine world systems evolved and eventually merged into the present global world system. The claim is that the Big Collapse model is both descriptive and explanatory, in the sense of Lave and March (1993), as I discuss in a later section.

The world system is a complex spatio-temporal structure, as illustrated by the long-range model illustrated in Figure 6.1. Specifically, the contemporary world system in which we live today is the direct descendant of a long evolution of earlier systems that began in four distinct regions of the prehistoric world approximately 10,000 years ago (10 Kya). The contemporary world system derives from four earlier world systems, much in the same way as a river is produced by lower scale streams that flow into a common basin.[3]

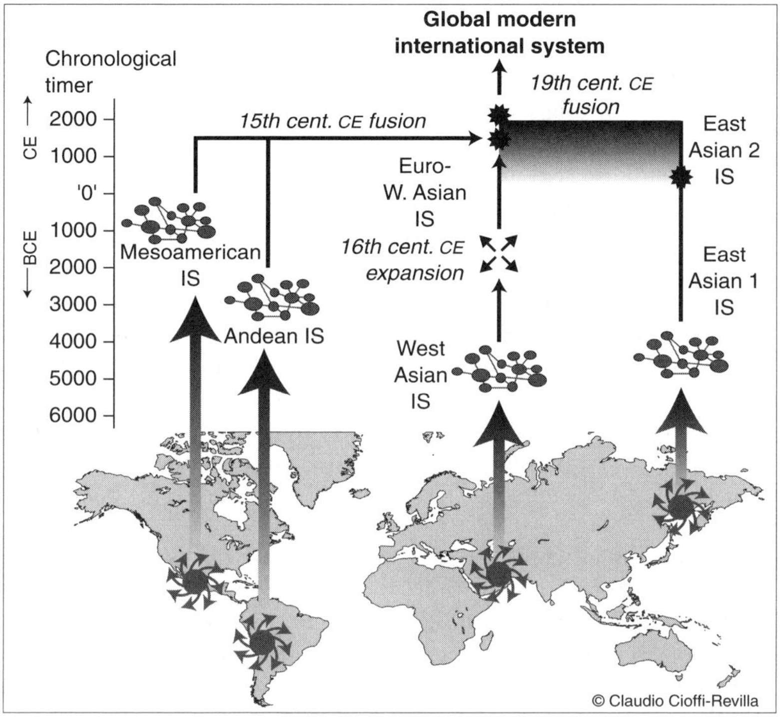

Figure 6.1 Multigenic model of origins and long-term evolution of social complexity. The Big Collapse explains how the four original world systems eventually compacted into a single modern world system. Based on Cioffi-Revilla (1999, 2000).

In order to explain the Big Collapse model better, I shall separate issues of world system origins from those of globalizations, because each has distinct attributes. Although the emphasis here is on globalizations, the question of origins of world systems – or *politogenics* – remains foundational. In the next subsection, I provide a comprehensive overview based on the *Handbook of Polities of the Ancient World*, which has been a work-in-progress since the late 1990s.[4] The Big Collapse is a large-scale process that comprises both dynamics of the river basin.

Origins and globalizations

Four and only four origins

Our contemporary world system evolved directly from four and only four earlier and original world systems that emerged in late prehistory and early antiquity. Each of these 'pristine' or 'primary' world systems emerged thousands of years ago in specific regions of West Asia, East Asia, South America and Mesoamerica. The four original world systems were centred in, and extended well beyond, regional constellations of polities clustered in contemporary Iraq, China, Peru and Mexico. The four original world systems are important in world history because, thousands of years ago, these regions set the stage for the Big Collapse that produced the world in which we live today.

These four unique regions spawned original world systems in the context of universal human history. Elsewhere, i.e. outside these specific regions of space and time, human societies either did not produce significantly complex or specialized institutions of government at the state level, or did so by secondary processes of imitation, conquest, diffusion or other non-inventive solution. For example, in North America, societies at Cahokia (Missouri), Chaco (New Mexico) or Moundville (Alabama) certainly produced powerful chiefdom-level polities, but not states or a fully connected, long-range political interaction network.[5] Similarly, states did not emerge in Europe until well after a world system had already formed and expanded from West Asia, although many European societies produced chiefdom-level polities during the Iron Age.

As a class of social complexity, a world system can be chiefly, stately or imperial, depending on composition.[6] By convention, a chiefly system consists of one or more chiefdoms and may potentially represent the first phase of a world system. An interstate system contains one or more states. An imperial system contains one or more empires, and always evolves from an earlier state-level world system.

Four – and only four – original world systems gave rise to our contemporary global world system, in spite of the great cultural and geographic diversity in human history and cultural evolution during late prehistory and early antiquity.

West Asia

In chronological order, the first and arguably most influential world system – on the most global scale – originated in West Asia soon after 8,000 years ago (8 Kya) or by the middle of the sixth millennium BCE (Cioffi-Revilla 2000–01).[7] Early polities centred at Jericho, Catal Hüyük and other Neolithic sites in the Levantine Fertile Crescent are among the oldest extant manifestations of governmental complexity, or individual chiefdom-level polities.

Although the Pre-pottery Neolithic-B (PPNB) polity of Jericho (7500 BCE; Kenyon 1979) once stood in relatively temporal isolation from the earliest West Asian chiefdoms of the 'Ubaid period (5500–4000 BCE), archaeological investigations have uncovered other pre-'Ubaid polities chronologically situated between PPNB-Jericho and 'Ubaid. Umm Dabaghiya (Iraq) and Ain Ghazal (Jordan) are two examples. Therefore, it is quite possible that the antiquity of the West Asian system may be pushed back to *c.* 7000 BCE or almost 2,000 years earlier than the current dating.

Based on the evidence currently available, the West Asian world system formed between *c*. 5800 and 4000 BCE, or 'Ubaid period, and consisted exclusively of chiefdom-level polities (ranked societies) involved in trade, warfare and other regional interaction relations. Eridu, Ur, Uruk, Kish, Umma and Haggi Muhammad were among the most important chiefdoms in Lower Mesopotamia, with Susa (Shush in Persian), Boneh Fazili, Choga Mish and Farukhabad to the east and Brak, Gawra, Hacilar, Gian Hasan and Mersin to the north and north-west.

The first true interstate system formed in Lower Mesopotamia by *c*. 3700 BCE (Middle Uruk period as a *terminus ante quem*). Although the exact complete composition of this pristine interstate system is still unknown, some of the most important states were Uruk and its neighbours in Lower Mesopotamia (Rothman 2001), Mish, Susa and Fanduweh in the eastern regions (present-day Iran) and a number of Anatolian states to the north-west (present-day Turkey).

The first empire in the West Asian world system emerged relatively soon after the formation of the first states. However, its identity remains unclear pending the availability of further raw data from dirt archaeology. The traditional view – based on extant iconography and epigraphy – holds that the polity of Akkad consolidated the first empire by *c*. 2334 BCE, under Sargon (Sharrun-kin) the Great (Liverani 1988; Postgate 1994: 44). However, the polity of Uruk underwent such an expansion in the fourth millennium BCE (Algaze 1993) that it is difficult to imagine it as a mere state and not an empire proper (Cioffi-Revilla 2000); from a political science , the Uruk polity of the Late Uruk period (3500–3100 BCE) was very probably an empire, surrounded by other state polities.[8] Politically, a state-level organization – as opposed to an empire – would have been insufficient to maintain government over the vast territory and diverse populations of the Uruk polity.

Overall, between 7500 BCE (Jericho) and 1500 BCE, the West Asian world system underwent an extraordinary long-term transformation through a sequence of well-marked political phase transitions (punctuated equilibria): from a disconnected region of simple and isolated societies (pre-pottery Neolithic period) to a network of chiefdoms, to a highly interconnected and interdependent network of politically complex polities at stately and imperial levels. In fact, the Amarna period of the second millennium BCE is well known as an epoch of superpower politics in the West Asian world system, with Egypt, Assyria and Hatti as the core actors of a multipolar system. By 1500 BCE, the West Asian world system had developed all the international features of today's world (trade, diplomacy, warfare, migration, anthropogenic environmental change), except for some obvious recent developments such as international organizations and modern technologies.

East Asia

The second original world system emerged in East Asia after *c*. 7 Kya, approximately 1,000 years after the formation of the West Asian world system in the Fertile Crescent. Based on the evidence currently available, the East Asian system emerged pristine (*ex nihilo*), not by any known process of diffusion from the West Asian. This hypothesis might change, as new archaeological and epigraphic investigations uncover previously unknown links between West and East Asia; but for now (as I have in all previous work), I continue to assume politico-military separation between the two Asian world systems.

Whereas the traditional Chinese paradigm (Han ideology) – based largely on epigraphy and Confucian culture – has been to view the origins of this system as centred solely in the Yellow River basin (this belief has now been proved to be a misconception), today archaeological investigations are documenting the origins of the East Asian world system in a multitude of regions across China, not just in the traditional Han homeland. Future investigation will no doubt enrich the database and show a multicultural spectrum of societies at the dawn of East Asian history, perhaps a more diverse social landscape than the spectrum of societies that generated the earlier West Asian system 1,000 years earlier.

The first East Asian world system probably formed over a large area during the Early Banpo to Yangshao and Dawenkow periods (*c*. 5000–3000 BCE), among chiefdom-level polities such as Banpo, Chengzi, Jiangzhai, Dawenkou, Daxi, Hutougou and other Hongshan chiefdoms (4500–3000 BCE). During the subsequent Longshan period (3000–2000 BCE), the East Asian world system already consisted of numerous chiefdoms scattered across a vast area in virtually all regions of present-day China – not just the north. The Erlitou period (*c*. 2000–1500 BCE) and the early Shang period (1900–1700 BCE) witnessed the emergence of the first interstate system in East Asia (Liu and Chen 2003), with a core area comprising the polities of Xia (capital at Erlitou) and Shang (capital at Xiaqiyuan), as well as other states that emerged soon after nearby. Traditionally, this is when the Xia dynasty is supposed to have ruled, but today the evidence for these polities is established by anthropological and dirt archaeology, not by epigraphy alone (Liu 1996; Chang 1999; Loewe and Shaughnessy 1999). In addition to the state of Shang and the state of Xia, other states also formed, probably at Panlongcheng (Hubei) and Suixian (Wuhan), although the complete system composition is still unknown (Bagley 1999; Shellach 1994, 1999). Chiefdoms were still numerous by this period as well.

According to Chinese tradition, the first empire of China was Qin (221–207 BCE) but – as in the case of the West Asian world system for the dispute between Akkad and Uruk – the best extant empirical evidence points to the Shang polity of between 1500 and 1350 BCE as the first empire in the East Asian world system. For example, Panlongcheng was contemporary with the Shang empire state while the capital was at Zhengzhou (Henan), 450 km to the north. Bronzes of exact Erligang style also suggest a Shang polity of imperial level extending south to the Yanzi valley area. The East Asian world system is also remarkable for having spawned – in Inner Asia – the largest territorial empire ever: the Mongol empire (thirteenth century CE).

South America

The third oldest world system emerged in South America after 5 Kya, or the Late Preceramic period, *c.* 2500–1800 BCE, and was centred in present-day Peru. A well-known characteristic of this world system is that it functioned for over 3,000 years without a written language, which remains a puzzle from a political science perspective. Another remarkable feature of the South American world system that was centred around the Andean civilizations is the highly constrained natural environment in which it emerged and evolved for thousands of years, specifically its north–south linear form, in contrast to the more diversified natural environments of the other three original world systems.

The first phase of the South American world system emerged with the formation of interacting chiefly polities up and down the Peruvian coastal regions irrigated by numerous mountain valleys and river basins draining from the Andes: Aspero (Supe river drainage, 2700 BCE), El Paraíso (near Lima, 2000 BCE), La Galgada (Santa river basin, 2400–1900 BCE), Río Seco, Salinas de Chao and other polities.[9]

According to most Andean specialists, the first state in the South American world system – Moché or Mochica – emerged in the first centuries BCE from this landscape of warring chiefdoms (Moseley 1992). However, the material and cultural influence of the much earlier Chavín de Huántar polity (900–300 BCE; Burger 1995) may support an alternative hypothesis that Chavín – earlier than Moché – may have been the first state.

The first true interstate system in South America probably emerged after the fall of the Moché state (*c.* 600 CE, after the Middle Horizon), when two powerful contemporary states emerged – Wari in the north (centred in the Peruvian highlands) and Tiwanaku in the south (centred in northern Bolivia) – and competed for primacy. This was also the first bipolar system of the western hemisphere. Both Wari and Tiwanaku were extensive territorial states governed from large capitals and powerful provincial administrative centres.

After a period of decline, the Chimu state – with its capital at Chan Chan – emerged during the Late Intermediate period, 1000–1470 CE. Again, by convention, the Inka polity is designated as the first empire in this world system, but the territorial extent and likely cultural diversity of the Chimu polity also make it a plausible candidate for the first South American empire.

Be that as it may, the South American world system originated and evolved for approximately 4,000 years before merging with – having been absorbed by – the Eurasian world system, *c.* 1500 CE. In spite of local coastal navigation during the very long epoch from 3000 BCE to 1500 CE, at present, there is no evidence of significant contact between pre-Columbian South American polities and Mesoamerican polities that emerged north of the Isthmus of Panama. It is worth noting that, from a globalization perspective, such a gap is analogous to the lack of politico-military interaction between West and

East Asian prior to the emergence of the Silk Road in *c*. 200 BCE, a comparable period of thousands of years.

Mesoamerica

Last, but not least, the Mesoamerican world system is the youngest of the four original world systems, having formed only approximately 3,000 years ago, perhaps 3.5 Kya. Similar to the oldest systems in the Old World – the West Asian world system – the Mesoamerican world system also had a highly diversified set of cultural origins: Olmec, Zapotec, Maya and other major early Amerindian cultures that shared some common attributes but also differed in significant respects. Another commonality with both Old World primary systems – West Asia and East Asia – lies in the variety of ecotopes in which the Mesoamerican world system originated and subsequently evolved.

The earliest Mesoamerican system that formed was arguably among Olmec chiefdoms, such as those centred at La Venta, San Lorenzo and others nearby, but regional clusters of chiefly networks developed early in the Zapotec and Maya areas as well (Marcus 1992, 1998; Marcus and Flannery 1996; Blanton *et al*. 1999). In fact, prior to the emergence of a true interstate system, Mesoamerica was politically organized into chiefdom clusters or chiefly subsystems with somewhat weak links among clusters. Calakmul and El Mirador provide an example in the Maya area; San José Mogote and other Zapotec chiefdoms are another instance in the Oaxaca Valley.

The earliest Mesoamerican state probably formed in the Valley of Oaxaca – the Zapotec state, *c*. 400 BCE – and had its capital at Monte Albán (Marcus and Flannery 1996). On a much larger regional scale, the first interstate system of Mesoamerica was formed by no later than the Late Formative period, and consisted of the Zapotec state, the state of Teotihuacan to the north-west and the cluster of powerful Maya states to the south-east (Calakmul, Tikal, Copan; Marcus 1992; Cioffi-Revilla and Landman 1999). After *c*. 500 CE, the composition of this system included Tula in the Mexican central highlands, El Tajín in the Gulf of Mexico and the post-Classic Maya states in the Yucatán Peninsula. The polity of Teotihuacán may have been an empire during the period 200–600 CE, with colonial outposts as far south as Kaminaljuyú in present-day Guatemala City (reminiscent of Uruk's Tell Brak in the West Asian system) and possibly elsewhere.

Considered as an international network of powerful polities for at least 1,000 years prior to the European conquest in *c*. 1520 CE, the Mesoamerican world system may also have projected its power and influence to regions of North America, such as Chaco, Cahokia and the Mississippian and Ohio polities.

Although not as old as the other world systems, the Mesoamerican world system produced in its relatively shorter duration as much cultural variety in social complexity. Chiefdoms, states, empires, trade networks, warfare, diplomacy and other features of world systems are all observable in the extant Mesoamerican record.

In other regions of the ancient world besides the four original ones I have just discussed – notably in Africa, Europe, North America and Oceania – systems or networks of polities also developed. However, such systems were not pristine and protracted in terms of having produced original social complexity extending to large-scale imperial complexity. For example, the Indus Valley region gave rise to the polities of Harappa, Mohenjo-daro and others in the same region but, most probably, these polities were inspired by or at least influenced by the much earlier and powerful polities of West Asia, in Mesopotamia and the Levant. Similarly, the system of Egyptian polities in the Nile Valley was also influenced by earlier and more complex developments in Mesopotamia and the Levant. Both cases – the Indus Valley polities and the Nile Valley polities – were linked by trade networks (and possibly migration as well) to the pre-existing West Asian world system.

Having examined how each of the four primary world systems originated, I shall now turn to the globalization processes that eventually collapsed them all together into the one massive world system in which we live today.

Several globalizations

Globalization – defined as a significant and relatively rapid increase in the size (network diameter) and connectivity of a world system – is an ancient social phenomenon that began thousands of years ago, not a recent or unprecedented occurrence that is unique in modern history. In a certain sense, globalization began in conjunction with origins, because each of the four primary world systems began to globalize almost as soon as it had originated.

Two quantitatively and qualitatively distinct classes of globalization events are observable in world history. Endogenous globalization occurs as a process of growth or expansion that takes place within a given world region (e.g. the expansion of Uruk in Mesopotamia, Rome in the Mediterranean basin or Chaco in the American south-west), whereas exogenous globalization occurs between or among geographically distant world systems that had previously been disconnected from each other (e.g. the sixteenth-century CE merging of Eurasian, South American and Mesoamerican world systems). The primary difference between the two is spatial, not so much temporal, and a distinctive feature of exogenous globalization is that it yields a fewer number of resulting world systems – as the analysis that follows will highlight. Accordingly, the Big Collapse occurs primarily through exogenous globalization, although both types are important to recognize within the long-range context of world systems dynamics.

Type I: Endogenous globalization

The earliest globalization of an endogenous type occurred in the West Asian world system, when Mesopotamian and nearby polities formed the first large-scale interaction sphere during the Uruk period. By the late Uruk period, the polities of both lower and upper Mesopotamia, as well as numerous surrounding polities in present-day Iran, Syria, Turkey and the Levant, were connected for the first time by the largest network of trade, warfare and political interactions. This system was global because, at the time in which it formed, it included all known countries within the West Asian region, not just a subset. In other words, as far as the inhabitants (especially the governing elites) of the West Asian world system during the late Uruk period were concerned, 'The Whole World' did not contain any other countries or socially complex regions beyond those occupied by them – neither East Asia nor Europe, Africa or the Americas existed as far as they were concerned. Objectively, this was of course an erroneous misconception – especially with regard to East Asia, South America and selected sites in North America (e.g. Watson Break?) – but that is irrelevant. What matters is the fact that the late Uruk West Asian world system was global in the sense that it was far larger and more densely interconnected than any other previous network of polities in the same region.

Several subsequent endogenous globalizations took place in the West Asian system, such as when Akkad formed an empire-scale polity extending from the Mesopotamian core to the Mediterranean to the west under King Sargon I of Akkad, and later during the Ur III dynasty. Moreover, as I have already discussed in the section on West Asia above (see also Figure 6.1), around 1500 BCE, the West Asian world system underwent another major expansion that eventually linked it to a vast network of other polities in the Mediterranean basin and Europe – forming a Euro-West Asian world system with unprecedented size and social, political and economic complexity.

Similarly, each of the other three original world systems underwent several instances of endogenous globalization. In the East Asian world system, endogenous globalization events occurred, for instance, when the Shang polity extended south, and again when East Asian polities extended west to the Tarim basin. In the South American world system, the first case of endogenous globalization arguably occurred when the Chavín de Huántar polity gave rise to a spatially large interaction sphere, and certainly with the rise of Moché. The Wari–Tihuanaco period witnessed an even larger globalization expansion of the endogenous type. The Mesoamerican world system also underwent several endogenous globalizations, as when the Zapotec and Teotihuacán polities created a large interaction sphere of unprecedented scale, and later linked to Maya, Toltec and other polity systems. By the time of the European conquest, the Mesoamerican world system constituted a core that extended its globalizing influence to the American south-west and possibly also to the Mississippi and Ohio river basins.

In each of these instances of endogenous globalization, initially simpler and relatively weakly connected networks of polities gave rise to larger and more complex polity networks. In many cases, endogenous globalization occurred together with the rise and fall of empires, as large-scale networks of heterogeneous polities are a characteristic of imperial organizations. However, the converse is not true, as the rise of an empire is not a necessary condition for endogenous globalization to occur.

Type II: Exogenous globalization

As shown in the politogenic model in Figure 6.1, four separate and distinct politico-military world systems were evolving in parallel, i.e. each of these systems was oblivious of each other since the time that each had originated – around the end of the third century BCE. By this time, several episodes of endogenous globalization had occurred in world history, as I have just explained in the previous section. In contrast, there have been only two events of exogenous globalization in world history.

The first true episode of exogenous globalization began with the emergence of the Silk Road, which for the first time linked the already vast Euro-Afro-West Asian world system with the equally vast East Asian system, by 200 BCE (*terminus ante quem*). This new large-scale network of interacting polities was unprecedented, creating an Afro-Eurasian world system in the eastern hemisphere and unleashing a set of social and environmental transformations with aftershocks that are still reverberating in today's world system. The formation of the Silk Road and its subsequent development was by no means a linear or uniform process, because it experienced several phases of growth and decline (Frank and Gills 1993; Chase-Dunn and Hall 1997; Thompson 2001), but its significance cannot be overstated in terms of having caused the first truly massive collapse of world systems – in this case, the merging of the Euro-Afro-West Asian world system and the East Asian world system into a single eastern hemisphere world system. Thus, only three truly autonomous world systems remained after the rise of the Silk Road, from the initial four.

The second and last major exogenous globalization event occurred when the Euro-Afro-Asian (or eastern hemispheric) world system became linked by politico-military conquest and commercial expansion with the two separate world systems of the western hemisphere, around 500 years ago. This time, the fusion or catalytic event was the European conquest of the Americas, an event in important ways systemically analogous to the emergence of the Silk Road more than 1,000 years earlier. This time, the collapse was even greater than it had been with the emergence of the Euro-Afro-Asian world system (which collapsed two systems into one), because this time a single and truly world system emerged from the previous three that had existed in isolation.

After 1600 CE, the global world system has greatly increased its connectedness and further reduced its connectivity diameter – down to the 'small world' compact structure observable today – but no further exogenous globalization is possible.

Discussion

The model just presented contains a number of new features that merit highlighting. First, the Big Collapse model is based on multiple origins of social complexity, not on a single origin from which social complexity radiated. Although today the earlier simplistic discussionist idea of a single origin of social complexity has long been abandoned, the numerous and rich implications of the pleogenic model have yet to be worked out. The Big Collapse model can be seen as one such implication, as the modern global world system of today is the descendant of four primary world systems that emerged in late prehistory and early antiquity. The model would be false if social complexity had not originated in several earlier and independent world systems. Second, the Big Collapse model is founded on the best empirical evidence from both archaeology and epigraphy, which indicates that each pristine world system began at a different time in terms of absolute chronology.

Much remains to be done in the calibration of relative and absolute chronologies, especially from a comparative or cross-cultural perspective. For example, Mesopotamian chronology is still being adjusted by area specialists and comparative social scientists (Rothman 2001), and the situation for East China (Nivison 1982–83, 1983, 1997) and the Americas is also far from being definitive. However, the asynchronous origins and early dynamics of world systems as reflected in the Big Collapse model are not in question; the model does not depend on the kind of fine-tuning that occupies the attention of specialists in regional chronologies.

Third, according to the Big Collapse model, each pristine subsystem of the world system underwent a canonical sequence from unranked societies to chiefly polities, to state polities and, finally, to empire polities. I call this sequence canonical because it occurred repeatedly, albeit with local cultural variations that can only be established after a more complete survey of polities becomes available for each system. For example, by the third century BCE, i.e. just prior to the first major collapse by exogenous globalization induced by the Silk Road, all four world systems had experienced numerous empires, which had emerged from earlier states, which in turn had emerged from earlier chiefdoms, which – finally – had emerged from earlier unranked societies. Almost all the imperial instances are perhaps known for each world system, but not all the less complex polities (chiefdoms and states) have been identified.

Fourth, the world system is the largest complex adaptive system created by humans, in the same sense that astronomers and cosmologists speak of galaxy clusters as the largest scale structure in the physical universe. Although 'small' in a graph-theoretic sense (Milgram 1967; Travers and Milgram 1969; Newman *et al.* 2003), any world system – whether those of earlier epochs or the modern global system today – represents the limiting structure that humans are capable of constructing. No other human system has greater complexity, based on reductionist 'consilience' alone (Wilson 1998). For this reason, the Big Collapse model bears ontological resemblance to the Big Bang model – both concern the largest scale processes in their respective domains, world history and cosmology. And, like the Big Bang, the Big Collapse is also based on incomplete science, in this case the social science of world systems.

Fifth, the Big Collapse model is both descriptive and explanatory, in the sense of Lave and March (1993). The model describes exactly how the world system originated and subsequently evolved – obviously omitting many details that are not yet known. The model also explains a number of features of the contemporary world system. For example, it explains why today's world system continues to experience enduring conflicts of great antiquity, such as the Iran–Iraq conflict (started during the Sumero-Elamite phase, *c.* 4 Kya). It also explains why cultural tensions and other transnational stresses can be so intense and destabilizing today, in spite of unprecedented knowledge and capacity for problem-solving – because of the massive density that has been increasing at a faster than exponential rate since the last collapse of the sixteenth century CE. The model would also predict that global human society had better create new mechanisms for understanding and resolving emerging conflicts, or violence and destruction will eventually over-run global problem-solving capacity.

Conclusions

Where does the modern world system come from, and what does such long-range evolution imply for world system science and comparative social science? The Big Collapse is a model that highlights several significant scientific accomplishments and future needs. The Big Collapse model, and the multigenic theory on which it is based, provides the first comprehensive account of world systems origins and long-range evolution that is consistent with the best available empirical evidence and is based on a universal and comparative social science perspective. Numerous scholars have contributed to solving the puzzle of politogenesis and world system evolution. Invariably, however, an important part of the picture is omitted. The most common error of omission is arguably to ignore politogenesis in the two original world systems of the Americas, or even in East Asia, as if West Asia alone mattered. The model presented in this chapter is admittedly incomplete – major cases of endogenous globablization are still poorly understood – and will remain so until a more detailed empirical survey of most of the major polities in all world systems is available. Such a task should become a priority for world systems research and comparative social science, similar to the high priority assigned by astronomers to surveying the night sky – only such surveys, based on the best primary data available, can provide the foundations for developing and testing long-range spatio-temporal models of social complexity.

Notes

1 This chapter is dedicated to the memory of the late Gordon Wiley and K.C. Chang, both of whom patiently provided me with initial guidance and comments on the origins and long-range analysis of social complexity. The original cross-cultural data on which this chapter is based has also benefited from the advice of David Keightley, Li Liu, Joyce Marcus, Gideon Shellach and Henry Wright. I also thank a number of other social science colleagues and former students for comments and discussions, among them Clay Bowen, Kathy Cameron, Steve

Chan, Christopher Chase-Dunn, Linda Cordell, Carol and Mel Ember, Tom Hall, William Honeychurch, Mike Kanner, David Lai, Steve Lekson, Manus I. Midlarsky, David Nivinson, Keith Otterbein, Peter Peregrine, Colin Rendrew, Daniel Rogers, Jerry and Paula Sabloff, Payson Sheets, John Vasquez, Barbara Voorhies, David Wilkinson and the editors of this book.

2 Recent political science investigations on premodern world systems hold some promise (Cioff-Revilla 1996; Ferguson and Mansbach 1996; Kaufman 1997; Denemark *et al.* 2000; Midlarsky 2000; Thompson 2001; Wilkinson 2004).

3 However, a significant difference between the Big Collapse model and the river basin metaphor is that the former lacks any spatial gravitational potential gradient (the temporal dimension is highly autocorrelated), whereas such a gradient completely determines the dynamics of the river basin.

4 The *Handbook of Polities of the Ancient World* of the LORANOW Project is a database archive in four volumes, West Asia, East Asia, South America and Mesoamerica, corresponding to each of the four primary world systems discussed in this chapter. The LORANOW Project is funded by the Center for Social Complexity, George Mason University.

5 The case of the polity at Watson Break (Louisiana), dated at *c.* 3400 BC, remains enigmatic because of its early date (Saunders 1997). Thousands of years exist between the epoch of Watson Break and the rise of the classic Mississippian polities.

6 In addition, world systems and polity networks can be classified as pure or mixed, the latter composed of chiefdoms, states and empires *in varying proportions*. Empirically, all world systems are mixed – even today's world system (Stein and Rothman 1994).

7 See, for example, Liverani (1988), Postgate (1994), Hallo and Simpson (1997) and Rothman (2001).

8 I acknowledge and appreciate, but disagree with, Harvey Weiss's dissent on my claim that the Uruk polity of the Late Uruk period was an empire.

9 The monumental complex at the site of El Paraíso 'is the largest preceramic monument in the western hemisphere' (Moseley 1992: 119), built with more than 100,000 tons of quarried stone. See also Donnan (1985), Fung Pineda (1988), Wilson (1988) and Pozorski and Pozorski (1992).

References

Algaze, Guillermo. 1993. *The Uruk World System: The Dynamics of Early Mesopotamian Civilization*. Chicago: University of Chicago Press.

Bagley, Robert. 1999. 'Shang archaeology', in Michael Loewe and Edward L. Shaughnessy, eds. *The Cambridge History of Ancient China: From the Origins of Civilization to 221 BC.* Cambridge: Cambridge University Press.

Blanton, Richard E., Gary Feinman, Stephen A. Kowalewski and Linda M. Nicholas. 1999. *Ancient Oaxaca*. Cambridge: Cambridge University Press.

Burger, Richard L. 1995. *Chavín and the Origins of Andean Civilization*. London: Thames and Hudson.

Chang, Kwang-chih. 1999. 'China on the eve of the Historical Period', in Michael Loewe and Edward L. Shaughnessy, eds. *The Cambridge History of Ancient China: From the Origins of Civilization to 221 BC.* Cambridge: Cambridge University Press.

Chase-Dunn, Christopher and Thomas D. Hall, eds. 1997. *Rise and Demise: Comparing World-Systems*. Boulder, CO: Westview Press.

Cioffi-Revilla, Claudio. 1996. 'Origins and evolution of war and politics'. *International Studies Quarterly* 40(1): 1–22.

Cioffi-Revilla, Claudio. 1999. 'Origins and age of deterrence: comparative research on Old World and New World systems'. *Cross-Cultural Research: Journal of Comparative Social Science* 33(3): 239–64.

Cioffi-Revilla, Claudio. 2000. 'Ancient warfare: origins and systems', in Manus I. Midlarsky, ed. *Handbook of War Studies II*. Ann Arbor, MI: University of Michigan Press, pp. 59–89.

Cioffi-Revilla, Claudio. 2000–01. 'The First International System: Polity Data Set of the West Asian Macro Social System in Southern Mesopotamia, 6000–1500 BC'. Paper presented at the Annual Meeting of the International Studies Association, Chicago, March 2000. Revised and extended, presented at the Annual Meeting of the American Political Science Association, Washington, DC, September 2001, and American Schools of Oriental Research, Denver, CO, November 2001.

Cioffi-Revilla, Claudio and Todd Landman. 1999. 'Evolution of Maya polities in the Ancient Mesoamerican system'. *International Studies Quarterly* 43(4): 559–98.

Denemark, Robert A., Jonathan Friedman, Barry K. Gills and George Modelski, eds. 2000. *World System History: The Social Science of Long-Term Change*. London: Routledge.

Donnan, Charles, ed. 1985. *Early Ceremonial Architecture of the Andes*. Washington, DC: Dumbarton Oaks Research Library and Collection.

Frank, Andre Gunder and Barry K. Gills. 1993. *The World System: Five Hundred Years or Five Thousand?* New York: Routledge.

Ferguson, Yale H. and Richard W. Mansbach. 1996. *Polities: Authority, Identities, and Change*. Columbia, SC: University of South Carolina Press.

Fung Pineda, Rosa. 1988. 'The Late Preceramic and Initial Period', in Richard W. Keatinge, ed. *Peruvian Prehistory*. Cambridge: Cambridge University Press.

Hallo, William W. and W.K. Simpson. 1997. *The Ancient Near East: A History*. Fort Worth, TX: Harcourt Brace.

Kaufman, Stuart J. 1997. 'The fragmentation and consolidation of international systems'. *International Organization* 51(2): 173–208.

Kenyon, Kathleen. 1979. *Archaeology of the Holy Land*, 4th edn. New York: W.W. Norton.

Lave, Charles A. and James G. March. 1993. *An Introduction to Models in the Social Sciences*. Lanham, MD: University Press of America.

Liu, Li. 1996. 'Settlement patterns, chiefdom variability, and the development of early states in North China'. *Journal of Anthropological Archaeology* 15: 237–88.

Liu, Li and Xingcan Chen. 2003. *State Formation in Early China*. London: Duckworth Press.

Liverani, Mario. 1988. *Antico Oriente: Storia, Societa', Economia*. Rome: Editori Laterza.

Loewe, Michael and Edward L. Shaughnessy, eds. 1999. *The Cambridge History of Ancient China: From the Origins of Civilization to 221 BC*. Cambridge: Cambridge University Press.

Marcus, Joyce. 1992. 'Dynamic cycles of Mesoamerican states'. *National Geographic Research and Exploration* 8(4): 392–411.

Marcus, Joyce. 1998. 'The peaks and valleys of ancient states', in Gary M. Feinman and Joyce Marcus, eds. *Archaic States*. Santa Fe, NM: School of American Research Press.

Marcus, Joyce and Kent V. Flannery. 1996. *Zapotec Civilization: How Urban Society Evolved in Mexico's Oaxaca Valley*. London: Thames and Hudson.

Midlarsky, Manus I., ed. 2000. *Handbook of War Studies II*. Ann Arbor, MI: University of Michigan Press.

Milgram, Stanley. 1967. 'The small world problem'. *Psychology Today* May: 60–7.

Moseley, Michael E. 1992. *The Incas and their Ancestors: The Archaeology of Peru*. London: Thames and Hudson.

Newman, Mark E.J., Albert L. Barabasi and Duncan J. Watts, eds. 2003. *The Structure and Dynamics of Complex Networks*. Princeton, NJ: Princeton University Press.

Nivison, David S. 1982–83. '1040 as the date of the Chou Conquest'. *Early China* 8: 76–8.

Nivison, David S. 1983. 'The dates of Western Chou'. *Harvard Journal of Asiatic Studies* 43: 481–580.

Nivison, David S. 1997. 'The Riddle of the Bamboo Annals'. Paper presented at the Annual Meeting of the American Oriental Society, Western Branch, Boulder, CO, 10–12 October 1997.

Postgate, J. Nicholas. 1994. *Early Mesopotamia: Society and Economy at the Dawn of History*. New York: Routledge.

Pozorski, Shelia and Thomas Pozorski. 1992. 'Early civilization in the Casma Valley, Peru'. *Antiquity* 66: 845–70.

Rothman, Mitchell S., ed. 2001. *Uruk Mesopotamia and Its Neighbors: Cross-Cultural Interactions in the Era of State Formation*. Santa Fe, NM: School of American Research Press.

Saunders, Joe W., Rolfe D. Mandel, Roger T. Saucier, E. Thurman Allen, C. T. Hallmark, Jay K. Johnson, Edwin H. Jackson, Charles M. Allen, Gary L. Stringer, Douglas S. Frink, James K. Feathers, Stephen Williams, Kristen J. Gremillion, Malcolm F. Vidrine and Reca Jones. 1997. 'A mound complex in Louisiana at 5400–5000 years before the present'. *Science* 277: 1796–9.

Shellach, Gideon. 1994. 'Social complexity in North China during the Early Bronze Age: a comparative study of the Erlitou and Lower Xiajiadian cultures'. *Asian Perspectives* 33(1): 261–92.

Shellach, Gideon. 1999. *Leadership Strategies, Economic Activity, and Interregional Interaction: Social Complexity in Northeast China*. New York: Kluwer Academic, Plenum Publishers.

Smithsonian Science Commission. 2002. Report of The Smithsonian Institution Science Commission. Jeremy A. Sablo, chairman. Washington, DC, December 2002.

Stein, Gil and Mitchell S. Rothman, eds. 1994. *Chiefdoms and Early States in the Near East: The Organizational Dynamics of Complexity*. Monographs in World Archaeology, Vol. 18. Madison, WI: Prehistory Press.

Thompson, William R. 2001. *Evolutionary Interpretations of World Politics*. New York: Routledge.

Thompson, William R. 2001. 'Trade Pulsations, Collapse, and Reorientation in the Ancient World'. Paper presented at the Annual Meeting of the International Studies Association, Chicago, IL.

Travers, John and Stanley Milgram. 1969. 'An experimental study of the small world problem'. *Sociometry* 32: 425.

Wilkinson, David. 2004. 'Explaining the Pulsations in the Polarity Structure of the Far Eastern Civilization/World System: A Preliminary Inquiry'. Paper presented at the Third International Conference on Hierarchy and Power in the History of Civilizations, Moscow, Russia, 18–21 June 2004.

Wilson, David J. 1988. *Prehistoric Settlement Patterns in the Lower Santa Valley, Peru*. Washington, DC: Smithsonian Institution Press.
Wilson, Edward O. 1998. *Consilience : The Unity of Knowledge*. New York: Knopf.
Zaccagnini, Carlo. 2003. 'Mercanti e politica nel mondo antico'. *Saggi di storia antica* 21, Rome, Italy.
Zubrin, Robert. 1999. *Entering Space: Creating a Spacefaring Civilization*. New York: Tarcher/Putnam.

7 [Re]periphalization, [re]incorporation, frontiers and non-state societies

Continuities and discontinuities in globalization processes

Thomas D. Hall

Introduction

Too often discussions of political and dynamic cycles rooted in world-systems perspectives commit the common 'error' of thinking that reading Immanuel Wallerstein's *Modern World-System* (1974) is sufficient. In fact, the *Modern World-System* (1974) would be one of the worst places to start such a discussion, primarily because Wallerstein did not address such issues. Rather, one would be better equipped to read many of the recent works on such topics, and to follow through with the literature they cite (Kohl 1979, 1987a, 1987b, 1987c, 1992, 1994; Allen 1992; Frank and Gills 1993; Chase-Dunn and Hall 1997; Kardulias 1999; Cline 2000; Denemark 2000; Denemark *et al.* 2000; Peregrine 2000; Thompson 2000; Chew 2001; Hall 2002a). In all these writings, one would find many nuanced, critical and empirically grounded attempts to probe the limits of world-system models, including versions with and without the hyphen, and with or without the plural (Thompson 1983a, 1983b; Frank and Gills 1993).

Some recent work explores the utility of population ecology models for explaining cyclical processes and synchrony among cyclical processes in ancient world-systems (Chase-Dunn *et al.* 2003; Hall and Turchin 2003; Turchin and Hall 2003). A major insight from this work is that it takes relatively low levels of interaction, such as long-distance luxury trade, which Wallerstein explicitly eschewed (see Schneider 1977 for an early critique of his position, and those in Chase-Dunn and Hall 1997), to induce synchronization of cyclical processes in widely separated world-systems. I will argue later that this insight ramifies to the analysis of incorporation of new areas and/or peoples into expanding world-systems.

The overall argument has evolved somewhat as follows: many archaeologists have long noted the complex, if poorly understood, roles of intersocietal and/or inter-regional interactions in the shaping of local social processes, and hence on the materials that they leave for archaeologists to uncover (for a somewhat dated review, see Hall and Chase-Dunn 1993; more recent review in Kardulias 1999). Many archaeologists thought that world-system analysis as formulated by Immanuel Wallerstein might provide some insights and hints as to how to study such processes. That initial hope was dashed when many of the assumptions that Wallerstein quite reasonably made for study of the capitalist era (i.e. since *c.* 1450 CE) were either woefully inadequate or downright empirically wrong in precapitalist settings.

Others then tried to extend this analysis in different ways (this work is reviewed in detail in the articles in Denemark *et al.* 2000 and Kardulias 1999). Christopher Chase-Dunn and I (1997) developed our own account of world-system evolution (updated in Chase-Dunn and Hall 2000, 2002), in which we attempted to turn many of Wallerstein's problematic assumptions into empirical issues. This, as I see it, is the utility of assorted models derived from world-systems analysis: to raise theoretically grounded questions that are amenable to empirical investigation *and* to use the results of those empirical investigations to reformulate both theoretical analyses and their attendant concepts. Out of this rather large project involving many different scholars operating from several different approaches, I wish to address one problematic, but potentially very fruitful, subtopic: what are the processes leading to incorporation of new areas and peoples into a world-system and what are the consequences of the absorption of new peoples and/or new areas into a world-system for both the areas or peoples incorporated and the world-system that incorporates them? That is, what can we say about world-system incorporation?

I begin with a brief review of discussion of incorporation.

A capsule discussion of incorporation

Chase-Dunn and Hall (1997: 275) defined a world-system in the following general terms: 'intersocietal networks in which the interactions (trade, warfare, intermarriage, information, etc.) are important for the reproduction of the internal structures of the composite units and importantly affect changes that occur in these local structures'. This definition is necessarily abstract to fit all sorts of systems. Note well that this definition leaves as an empirical issue how many 'levels' (core, semi-periphery, periphery) a system has, and whether those levels are merely different (core–periphery differentiation) or have some form of hierarchical relationship (core–periphery hierarchy). I also note that an unfortunate legacy of Wallerstein's approach is the term 'world', which he uses to mean self-contained, not global or planetary. Wallerstein says, 'my "world-system" is not a system "in the world" or "of the world". It is a system "that is a world"' (Wallerstein 1993: 294).

Bounding world-systems is itself problematic. Chase-Dunn and Hall recognize four different types of networks that constitute a world-system. These are:

- a bulk goods network (BGN), a system of exchange of low value-to-weight goods;
- a political–military network (PMN) of regularized military or political interactions;

- a prestige or luxury goods network (PGN) of more or less regular exchange of high value-to-weight goods; and
- an information or cultural network (IN) of regularized exchanges of information.

In general, these networks are progressively larger, except in small islands or the twenty-first-century world-system (see Figure 7.1). The sharp lines in the diagram give a false sense of precision. Rather, one should readily imagine a contour map of the density of exchanges in these networks. The 'boundary' of any one network would be a region where there is a very steep fall off in exchange densities. Thus, boundaries are zones, not sharp lines. Single events are not part of these exchanges. Not that singular events are not sometimes very important. Rather, they are not part of a system. It is systemic – even if inchoate – exchanges that are important. I also note that the existence of various forms of cycles of exchange is, in fact, significant evidence that there is a system.

One of the dynamic properties of world-systems is that they all pulsate or expand and contract, with a net tendency to increase in size. When this happens, they engulf new territories and, at times, new peoples. I use the term 'incorporation' as a covering term for any process by which new areas or peoples become engulfed into an existing world-system (this discussion draws heavily on Hall 1987, 1989a; Chase-Dunn and Hall 1997: ch. 4; see also Carlson 2001, 2002; Hollis 2005). These can be different processes for each of the networks. Further, I conceptualize incorporation as a continuum that ranges from very weak to very strong. Figure 7.2 illustrates this conception and provides a concordance of parallel or analogous terms.

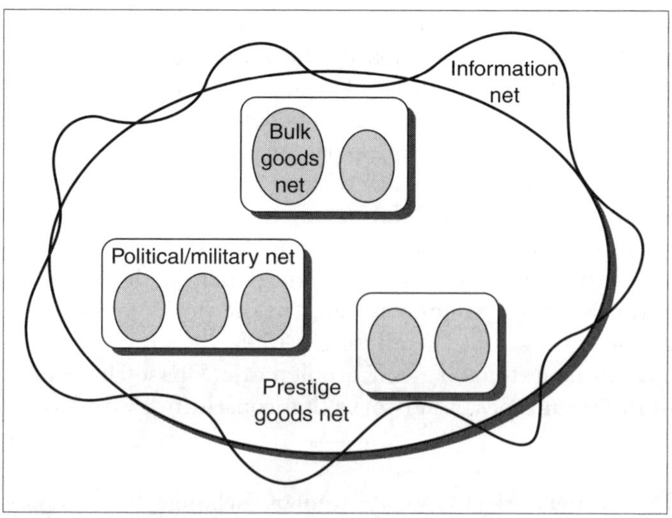

Figure 7.1 World system networks (from Chase-Dunn and Hall 1997: 54).

Wallerstein uses 'incorporation' to refer to processes towards the stronger pole of this range, in which areas become fully peripheralized or underdeveloped. In contrast, I have emphasized the weaker pole of the continuum. Here, too, the boundaries are fuzzy. My studies of European intrusions into what is now the southwestern United States show that even very mild forms of incorporation can have drastic effects on incorporated regions and peoples (see especially Hall 1989a for detailed examples). Following Sing Chew's work (2001) on ecological degradation, the ecological footprint of an urban area is quite large, extending into a large hinterland or, in my terms, regions that are only mildly incorporated. In both these sets of examples, the degree of incorporation occurs only along the prestige goods and/or information networks, typically at a low level.

Research reported in collections by Ferguson and Whitehead (1992a, 1992b) and Hill (1996) (although few of these writers use this term) demonstrates that the effects of even very mild incorporation can be quite dramatic, especially on non-state peoples. Finally, the recent work on synchrony among population, city size and empire size (see Chase-Dunn and Hall 1997; Chase-Dunn *et al.* 2000; Chase-Dunn and Manning 2002) shows that even low levels of incorporation can cause various cyclical processes to become synchronized. This further emphasizes the point that Jane Schneider made in 1977 that low levels of trade can have important systemic consequences beyond the level of goods exchanged.

Indeed, these zones of incorporation, or what many would call frontiers (see Hall 1998, 2000a, 2001a, 2002b), are regions where a small number of

Strength of incorporation	None	Weak	Moderate	Strong
Impact of core on periphery	None	Strong	Stronger	Strongest
Impact of periphery on core	None	Low	Moderate	Strong
		Names for types of peripheries		
Hall and Chase-Dunn and Hall	External arena	Contact	Marginal or region of refuge	Full-blown/ dependent
Wallerstein	None	External arena	Incorporation	Peripheralization
Arrighi	None	—— Nominal or formal ——		Effective or real
Sherratt		—— Margin ——		Periphery or structural interdependence
Frank and Gills		—— Hinterland ——		Periphery

Figure 7.2 The continuum of incorporation (from Chase-Dunn and Hall 1997: 63).

factors converge to give rise to a wide variety of processes of change, including genocide, ethnocide, culturicide, ethnogenesis, amalgamation, differentiation and so on. Furthermore, processes that first occur in newly incorporated regions may rebound back to more central areas to produce further changes there. By examining just a few factors such as:

- three types of world-systems (non-state, tributary, capitalist), multiplied by
- four types of system boundaries (BGN, PMN, PGN, IN), multiplied by
- at least several (say at least three) types of non-state groups (say bands, tribes and chiefdoms to take a familiar, if problematic, trinity), multiplied by
- at least four types of frontiers: buffer vs. barrier and/or internal vs. external, multiplied by
- at least four types of physical differences: steppe vs. sown and/or hill vs. valley

yields at least 576 potential different zones of incorporation. In short, incorporation is a covering term for an immense variety of processes.

There is yet one further complication to incorporation. What happens when one world-system either merges with or incorporates entirely a formerly autonomous world-system? Clearly, mergers can occur at some of the larger levels and not at others. It is in this sense that all of Afro-Eurasia constituted one world-system at the information and prestige good networks levels for at least two and a half millennia, and quite possibly much longer. This can give rise to zones that are contested between one or more world-systems. Such zones often have special and complex trajectories of development precisely because of their contested positions (see Berquist 1995; Allen 1997; Cline 2000).

Clearly, then, incorporation is a complex set of processes.

The implications of the analysis of incorporation in precapitalist contexts

As I noted, there are several sets of issues that have pushed the extension of the world-systems perspective into the precapitalist past. One is an attempt to raise questions about the modern, capitalist world-system that Wallerstein has discussed extensively. As with any evolutionary enquiry, such a question is not only historical: what happened? how? and why? But there also is an implied, here explicit, question: could it have happened differently? Third, what insights may we gain into the future possibilities from the examination of past processes (for one set of answers, see Boswell and Chase-Dunn 2000). These are all questions that inform the analysis of Chase-Dunn and Hall (1997).

One difference between that approach and those of Frank, Chew and several others is that we start at the onset of the Neolithic, approximately 12 millennia ago, whereas the others start some time after 3000 BCE or so, after states had already been developed. I argue that a key problem in precapitalist social evolution is the multiple origins of states. That there are multiple, independent origins of states strongly suggests that there are systematic processes at work. Early states were small, but grew quickly and incorporated new areas and peoples, and began to merge into larger systems quite some time ago. Thus, the issues of incorporation and merger loom large in social evolution (see Figure 7.3 or Wilkinson 1987, 1991, 1992, 1993, 1995, 2000; Chase-Dunn and Hall 1997: 203, 205). It also seems plausible to argue that there can be many forms of early tributary states, only some of which developed in any one region, and some of those came to dominate and displace others. Thus, the surviving states – the ones we actually know quite a bit about – are a rather limited sample of the possible. Given this unknown survival, it is all too easy to transform 'what happened' into 'what had to happen' and thereby blind ourselves both to other possibilities and to the contingencies that led to the success of the surviving forms.

Thus, it is useful to examine the origins of states, especially at the

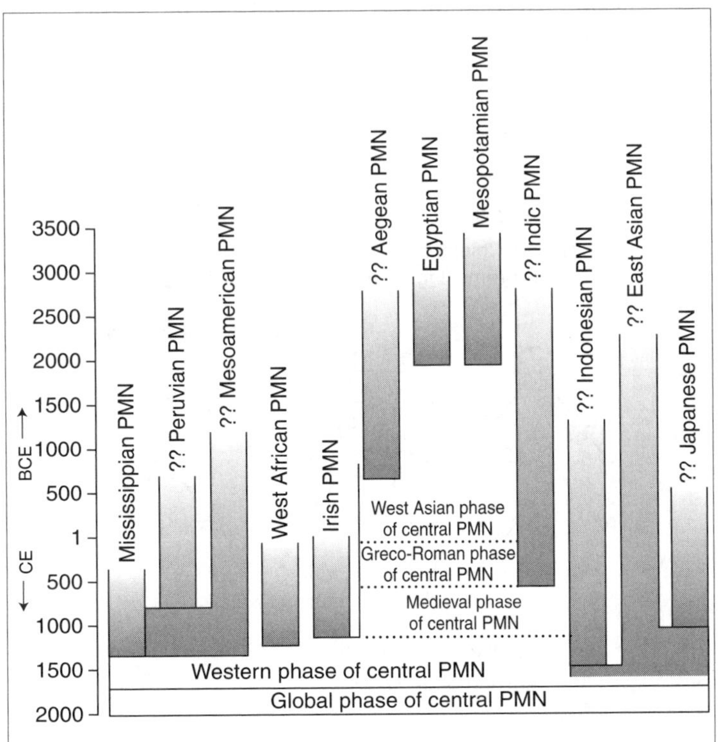

Figure 7.3 Mergers of early world-systems (Chase-Dunn and Hall 1997: 203, after Wilkinson 1987: 32).

chiefdom–state transitions (both these terms are problematic; I use them for short reference only). David Anderson (1994, 1996; see also Hall 2001b) shows that cycling from one to up to three hierarchical levels of political organization among chiefdoms is quite common (see Figure 7.4). Given this, eventually some paramount (three-level) chiefdoms avoid collapse by the invention of some form of state. Once this happens, the entire social field, or chiefdom-, now state-based, world-system is changed. I should note that this is not the only path to state origin. Sometimes, they emerge without chiefdom cycling, which appears to be the case for Cahokia (personal communication from Timothy Pauketat, June 2004; see also O'Brien 1992; Pauketat and Emerson 1997). States can then spread by imitation or, what is more likely, by interaction between the existing state and regional non-state societies.

The work of Ferguson and Whitehead (1992a, 1992b) on 'war in the tribal zone' shows that state formation also transforms the social space and developmental possibilities for non-state societies. Sometimes, these changes create conditions that favour the formation of chiefdoms or even secondary states; sometimes, they create conditions that favour collapse to primary chiefdoms or even band-level societies, but probably most often they create conditions for the formation of 'tribes'. Long ago Morton Fried (1967, 1975) argued that 'tribes' are a social form that almost always formed in reaction to states. Of particular interest in this region are those groups that took up some form of herding, and developed a symbiotic relationship with neighbouring states.

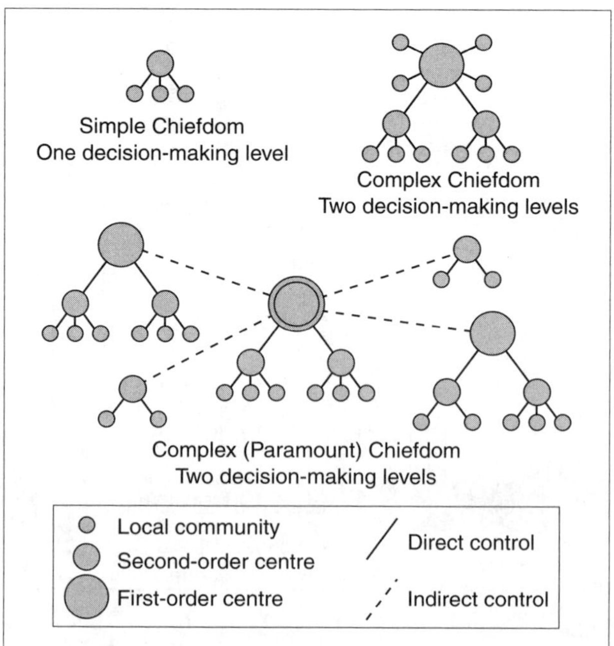

Figure 7.4 Cycling stages of chiefdoms (Anderson 1994: 9).

State elites nearly always perceive non-state peoples, and especially those who do not live in permanent settlements, as 'barbaric' or 'uncivilized', and impute a large variety of derogatory qualities to them. This perception is so common that quite often even original documents describing such groups can be suspect. At times, the equation of non-sedentary peoples with 'barbarity' is a thinly disguised rationalization for conquest. For a detailed example of this from historical times, see Fenelon and Defender-Wilson (2004), which documents how Lewis and Clark, on their famous exploration of the western United States, saw what their preconceptions told them to see among indigenous peoples.

Following the work of Barfield (1989, 1990, 1991, 1993, 2001; also Kradin 2002; Kradin *et al.* 2003), nomadic pastoralists and states typically co-evolve, with changes in one driving changes in the other. Furthermore, pastoralists, as one would expect, can become strong vectors for the spread of new ideas and technologies, especially after horses were domesticated, and especially for those technologies (e.g. iron making) that are readily portable. In the terminology I am using here, they are strong vehicles of further, if very mild or weak, incorporation of other non-state groups at considerable distance from state centres. Such processes have been poorly studied, both because archaeological and other evidence is difficult to locate and because most efforts have focused on states.

Still, significant work has been done. These topics are explored in a number of edited collections (Mathien and McGuire 1986; Spielman 1991; Schortman and Urban 1992; Anderson 1994; Peregrine and Feinman 1996; Parkinson 2002). The Parkinson collection includes a number of insightful essays, including his introduction. Both David Anderson (1994) and Michael Galaty (2002) provide very useful examples of how to shuttle back and forth between archival evidence and archaeological evidence and yet avoid many of the pitfalls of the 'war in the tribal zone' effect, that is the transformative consequences of contact between state and non-state societies. Far more attention needs be devoted to such processes to understand how the relations between non-state societies and states shape the evolution of states.

Here, Tom Barfield's (1989) insight is salient: 'Central Asian nomads became more powerful in tandem with Chinese state strength. Contrary to the popular imagery nomads do not always, or even, often, cause state collapses' (for some contrary views, see chapters in Kradin *et al.* 2003). When they do cause a collapse, it is usually because they are either pushing on an already weakened state or those specific states are particularly fragile. Barfield (1990) notes how, in the eastern Mediterranean, irrigation systems were both vital and fragile, and hence a nomad invasion could be disastrous. Furthermore, in much of southwest Asia and north Africa (and one might add most of the northern Mediterranean littoral), herding zones were small, societies were more often transhumant than nomadic and, hence, often smaller than some of the very large Central Asian steppe confederacies. Still, as Lattimore (1962) noted long ago, 'civilization is often the mother of barbarism'.

Furthermore, such pastoralists often supplied vital goods to states. Meat and wool come immediately to mind. Beckwith (1991) shows that steppe nomads were a crucial source of horses to the Chinese, as well as a conduit for much of the silk trade. The point being that such interactions, part of world-system functioning, are vital to understanding both states and their surrounding non-state peripheries. Kradin (2002) argues that steppe confederacies formed their own special kind of world-systems that are important to understanding social evolutionary processes.

Many writers have indicated the vital roles played by steppe nomads in linking events in China and Rome (Teggart 1939; Khazanov 1983; Barfield 1989; Hall 1991; Frank 1992; Chase-Dunn and Hall 1997: ch. 8; Kradin 2002; Kradin *et al.* 2000, 2003). Frank has also argued for the centrality of central Asia. This is an instance in which the insights from population ecology are especially salient. The traffic in goods and raiding by pastoralists is clearly sufficiently strong to be a major mechanism, if not the sole mechanism, to bring the various dynamic cycles in East and West Afro-Eurasia into synchronization.

As noted, pioneering work on world-system merger and contested peripheries and semiperipheries has been done by Allen (1997), Berquist (1995) and Cline (2000). Given the relatively small size of early states, and the relatively small size of their attendant world-systems, mergers, absorptions and contested subregions must have been quite common. The 'trick' or 'art' here is to see such conditions in their larger contexts. Solely local study of zones of merger, incorporation or contestation is *not* possible. Many of the social processes and forces that shape local changes originate in, or are at least strongly shaped by, other, more central areas. As with study of frontiers in general (Hall 2000a, 2001a, 2002b), these are zones of intense, complex interaction between local conditions and the larger world-system context. *To neglect either* is to critically distort our understanding of local processes.

The rise of regional surveys and the use of GIS and other techniques offer potential to be able to conduct such studies. But first, we need to ask the questions, so that we know what to look for, and what formerly neglected or understudied evidence may prove vital to understanding incorporation, merger or contestation in both local and systemic change. Some of the relevant issues are what was the purpose of expansion (both manifest and latent to use an older terminology)? When a state seeks new territory or new resources, expulsion of the current occupants can actually be a 'success' for both: for the state, because it acquires the territory or resource; for the non-state peoples, because they maintain a considerable degree of autonomy. On the other hand, expulsion of current occupants is a failure for the state when its goal was to acquire new sources of labour, and a failure for those non-state peoples who did not want to move.

In other cases, some local populations may be able to exploit intersystem rivalries to maintain some degree of autonomy and possibly even develop their own growth. Meggido may be such a case (Cline 2000). Many of the maritime trading states are others. Galaty (2002) speculates that early Illyrians benefited from their interactions with colonizing Greeks. There are also innumerable instances of such development on the fringes of the Roman Empire (Randers-Pehrson 1983; Wallace-Hadrill 1985; Wells 1992, 1999a, 1999b), including the story about how Artemis, in 9 CE, succeeded in slaughtering three Roman legions on the Germanic frontier.

In northern New Spain (now south-western United States), Apachean groups were first almost crushed, then survived as their position shifted from that of contested and attacked peripheral people, while Comanches shifted in the opposite direction from favoured border neighbours to crushed group. In both cases, the shift had little to do with Apache or Comanche actions, but a great deal to do with their frontier positions: either on a more-or-less static frontier or in zones that were either between two expanding states or between regions of the same state (for more details, see Hall 1986, 1989a, 1998, 2000b; or Brooks 2002; Hämäläinen 1998).

In all these cases, these frontier, peripheral groups played important roles in shaping interstate, and sometimes intersystem, dynamics.

Satisficing and optimizing strategies

There is a broader significance for social evolution to world-systems expansion and incorporation processes. Here, I wish to draw on the insightful work by Rein Taagepera (1978a, 1978b, 1979) on empire size. He shows that, while empire growth is steady, if volatile and sporadic, it exhibits relatively clear increases in average size (see Figure 7.5). This suggests, to me at least, that such jumps mark new social inventions, what Michael Mann has called techniques of power (Mann 1986). Furthermore, as noted earlier in this chapter, multiple variations of a new social form are typical, as with states. This suggests that first 'inventions' of social forms often follow a satisficing process, that is the first one found that works is pursued. As more variants appear, different forms come into competition and an optimizing process begins. It is interesting that, in Taagepera's diagram (1978a: 120) (see also Figure 7.5), the first such jump or shift falls in the middle of the so-called axial age, corresponding to the development of the major world religions. The next jump overlaps with the development of mercantile–capitalist empires. It is also interesting that, in his phase 2, the largest empire is the Mongol Empire, an early form of a very large world-system.

Why the Mongol Empire did not last for a long period is a complex problem. In brief, there is the Chinese proverb that 'one may conquer from horseback, but not rule from there'. However, there was an inherent instability in steppe pastoralist states and/or world-systems. The processes of succession of rulership, typically via military contest along lateral (brothers) and lineal (father to son[s]) lines, makes succession particularly problematic and the state inherently unstable. The problem, however, is not that Mongols could not devise a more stable system. Rather, in the volatile steppe environment,

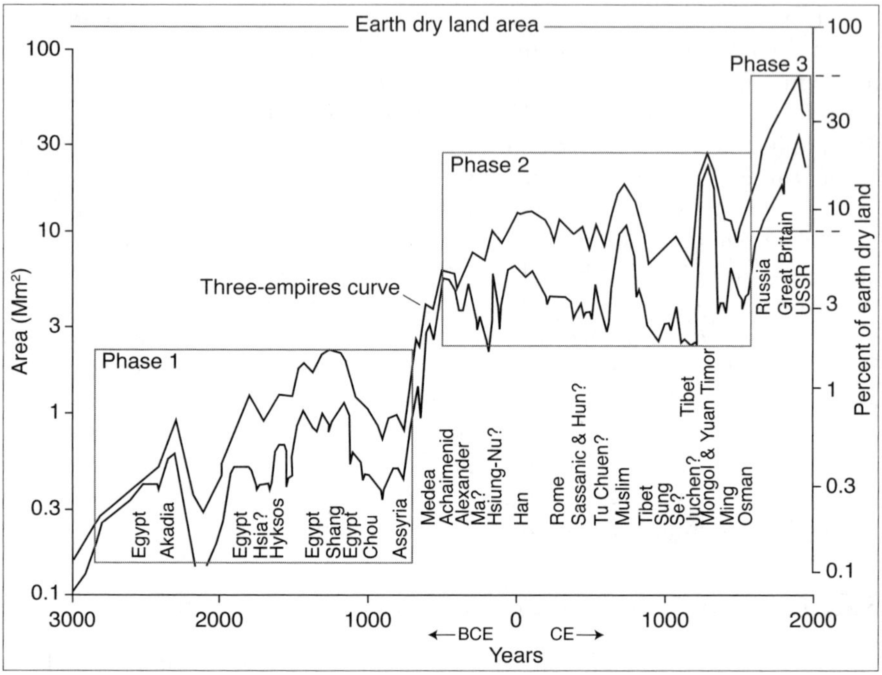

Figure 7.5 Empires sizes from Taagepera (1978a: 120).

such a means of success served multiple goals: emergence of a strong, skilled leader; elimination of most potential rivals; and a temporary adjustment in human and herd populations.

If Taagepera's data could be extended back in time and could include various chiefdoms, the diagram would, no doubt, show an even larger break at the invention of the state. Certainly David Anderson's (1994, 1996) summary of chiefdom cycling supports such a claim. Indeed, a logical extension of his analysis is that states are social inventions that prevent the collapse of paramount chieftaincies. He argues that, where there are any sort of reliable data, it appears that chiefdoms cycle for millennia before states are invented – unless, of course, there is contact with already existing states, which greatly alters the entire process.

It is here that the synchronicity and incorporation arguments can be melded usefully. With both pulsations of world-systems and the rise and fall of chiefdoms and states, there are a large number of cyclical processes at work in various systems. As Turchin and Hall (2003) argue, there is, on the one hand, a significant difference between stable oscillations and unstable or chaotic cycles. Yet, on the other hand, for durations of only a few cycles, the difference is not crucial. Furthermore, given that some cycles, such as the succession cycle that Turchin (2003a) has labelled the Khaldun cycle, are of the order of 300 years, a few cycles easily span a millennium. Also, given that relatively small factors can bring these cycles into synchrony (see Turchin and Hall 2003; Figure 7.6), the role of weak contacts at the prestige goods net or information net can have profound impacts on trajectories of change. This, in itself, is not news. Jerry Bentley, among many others, has made that argument (1993). Rather, the 'news' is the discovery of how and why such seemingly low levels of contact and exchange can have such large impacts, with some suggestive indications of what the mechanisms might be.

Also buried in this is why interactions with non-state societies, especially pastoralists, but others who can convey goods or ideas, are so important. Not all changes originate in states, even in state-based tributary or capitalist world-systems.

There is one further insight worth exploring briefly. Peter Turchin (2003b) argues that synchronizing or interacting cycles among predator–prey populations can give rise to periods of very rapid evolution. They can also transform stable oscillations into chaotic oscillations, or the reverse. Extending this logic from animal populations to populations of human societies [as Turchin (2003a) does] is fraught with problems, yet still suggestive and informative. It suggests, among other things, that such synchronizing of cycles via minimal contacts (or even other mechanisms) may accelerate processes of social change, and also helps to explain why patterns such as those uncovered by Taagepera occur.

Concluding remarks

One important lesson from any form of world-system analysis is that change cannot be studied either solely locally or solely from the larger system. It is the local–contextual interaction that is critical. Within such interactions, two areas have been relatively neglected, although they have been receiving more attention lately. First is the impact of peripheries or hinterlands on cores – too often, the assumption has been that change proceeds from the core to periphery. That is not even true for the contemporary world-system;

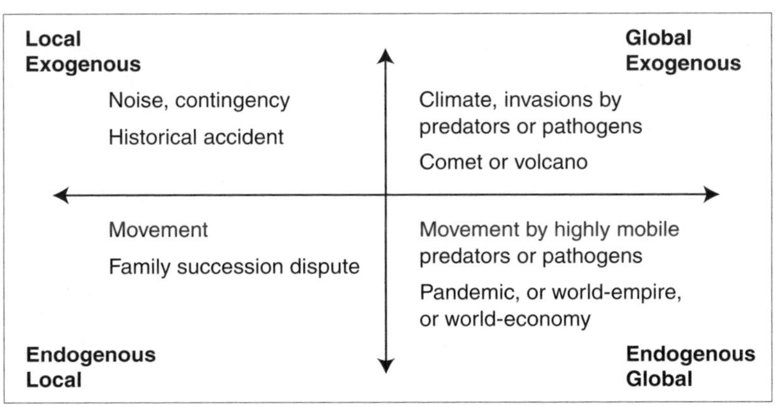

Figure 7.6 Mechanisms of synchrony (from Turchin and Hall 2003).

witness the FTAA talks collapse in Miami due to the reluctance of peripheral and semi-peripheral states to go along. Phil Kohl (1987b) long ago pointed out that, in ancient world-systems, raw materials were sometimes kept in the periphery and workers moved to them, rather than the reverse, which is more common in the modern world-system. Second, peripheral regions are often the best, and at times the only, place to study some social processes (Hall 1989b). Certainly, this is often the case for ethnogenesis, and especially for processes of incorporation and merger.

Another is the need for more detailed studies of incorporation, especially in its weaker forms, and especially at the prestige goods and the information nets. There is much to be learned from examining how these processes work in detail and how they shape long-term social change. Of special concern should be the complex roles of pastoral nomads as agents of social change. The effects of expanding world-systems on weakly incorporated areas or peoples – the 'war in the tribal zone' effect (Ferguson and Whitehead 1992a, 1992b) – point to the need to rethink all evolutionary sequences, especially the many multilinear ones. Finally, while there are clearly long-term, structural processes that shape social evolution, individual actions and actors cannot be ignored. It is often in these zones of weak effects that the roles of individual humans, states or non-state groups have their greatest impacts.

References

Allen, Mitchell. 1992. 'The mechanisms of underdevelopment: an Ancient Mesopotamian example'. *Review* 15 (3): 453–76.

——. 1997. *Contested peripheries: Philistia in the Neo-Assyrian world-system*. Unpublished PhD dissertation, Interdepartmental Archaeology Program, UCLA.

Anderson, David. G. 1994. *The Savannah River Chiefdoms: Political Change in the Late Prehistoric Southeast*. Tuscaloosa: University of Alabama Press.

——. 1996. 'Fluctuations between simple and complex chiefdoms: cycling in the Late Prehistoric Southwest', in J.F. Scarry, ed. *Political Structures and Change in the Prehistoric Southeastern United States*. Gainesville, FL: University Press of Florida, pp. 231–52.

Barfield, Thomas J. 1989. *The Perilous Frontier*. London: Blackwell.

——. 1990. 'Tribe and state relations: the inner Asian perspective', in Philip S. Khoury and Josephe Kostiner, eds. *Tribe and State Formation in the Middle East*. Berkeley: University of California Press, pp. 153–82.

——. 1991. 'Inner Asia and cycles of power in China's Imperial dynastic history', in Gary Seaman and Daniel Marks, eds. *Rulers from the Steppe: State Formation on the Eurasian Periphery*. Los Angeles, CA: Ethnographics Press, Center for Visual Anthropology, University of Southern California, pp. 21–62.

——. 1993. *The Nomadic Alternative*. Englewood Cliffs, NJ: Prentice-Hall.

——. 2001. 'The shadow empires: imperial state formation along the Chinese-nomad frontier', in Susan E. Alcock, Terence N. D'Altroy, Kathleen D. Morrision and Carla Sinopoli, eds. *Empires: Perspectives from Archaeology and History*. Cambridge: Cambridge University Press, pp. 11–41.

Beckwith, I. Christopher. 1991. 'The impact of the horse and silk trade on the economies of T'ang China and the Uighur Empire'. *Journal of the Economic and Social History of the Orient* 34 (2): 183–98.

Bentley, Jerry H. 1993. *Old World Encounters: Cross-Cultural Contacts and Exchanges in Pre-Modern Times*. Oxford: Oxford University Press.

Berquist, Jon L. 1995. 'The shifting frontier: the Achaemenid Empire's treatment of western colonies'. *Journal of World-Systems Research* 1 (17) (unpaginated ejournal http://jwsr.ucr.edu/index.php).

Boswell, Terry and Christopher Chase-Dunn. 2000. *The Spiral of Capitalism and Socialism: The Decline of State Socialism and the Future of the World-System*. Boulder, CO: Lynne-Rienner.

Brooks, James F. 2002. *Captives and Cousins: Slavery, Kinship, and Community in the Southwest Borderlands*. Chapel Hill, NC: University of North Carolina Press.

Carlson, Jon D. 2001. 'Broadening and deepening: systemic expansion, incorporation and the zone of ignorance'. *Journal of World-Systems Research* 7 (2): 225–63 (ejournal http://jwsr.ucr.edu/index.php).

——. 2002. 'The 'otter-man' empires: the Pacific fur trade, incorporation and the zone of ignorance'. *Journal of World-Systems Research* 8 (3): 389–442 (ejournal http://jwsr.ucr.edu/index.php).

Chase-Dunn, Christopher and Thomas D. Hall. 1997. *Rise and Demise: Comparing World-Systems*. Boulder, CO: Westview Press.

——. 2000. 'Comparing world-systems to explain social evolution', in Robert Denemark, Jonathan Friedman, Barry K. Gills and George Modelski, eds. *World System History: The Social Science of Long-Term Change*. London: Routledge, pp. 86–111.

——. 2002. 'Paradigms bridged: institutional materialism and world-systemic evolution', in Sing C. Chew and J. David Knottnerus, eds. *Structure, Culture, and History: Recent Issues in Social Theory*. Lanham, MD: Rowman and Littlefield, pp. 197–216.

Chase-Dunn, Christopher and E. Susan Manning. 2002. 'City systems and world-systems: four millennia of city growth and decline'. *Cross-Cultural Research* 36 (4): 379–98.

Chase-Dunn, Christopher, Susan Manning and Thomas D. Hall. 2000. 'Rise and fall: east–west synchronicity and Indic exceptionalism reexamined'. *Social Science History* 24 (4): 727–54.

Chase-Dunn, Christopher, Thomas D. Hall and Peter Turchin. 2003. Three Thousand Years of Urbanization, Empire Formation and Climate Change. Paper presented at the conference on World System History and Global Environmental Change, Human Ecology Division, Lund University, Sweden, 19–22 September (http://www.humecol.lu.se/woshglec/).

Chew, Sing C. 2001. *World Ecological Degradation: Accumulation, Urbanization, and Deforestation 3000 BC–AD 2000*. Walnut Creek, CA: Altamira Press.

Cline, Eric. 2000. '"Contested peripheries" in world systems theory: Megiddo and Jezreel Valley as a test case'. *Journal of World-Systems Research* 6 (1): 8–17 (ejournal: http://jwsr.ucr.edu/index.php).

Denemark, Robert A. 2000. 'Cumulation and direction in world system history', in Robert A. Denemark, Jonathan Friedman, Barry K. Gills and George Modelski, eds. *World System History: The Social Science of Long-Term Change*. London: Routledge, pp. 299–312.

Denemark, Jonathan Friedman, Barry K. Gills and George Modelski, eds. 2000. *World System History: The Social Science of Long-Term Change*. London: Routledge.

Fenelon, James V. and Mary Louise Defender-Wilson. 2004. 'Voyage of domination, purchase as Conaues, Skakawea for savagery: distorted icons from misrepresentation of the Lewis and Clark expedition'. *Wicazao sa Review* 19 (1): 85–104.

Ferguson, R. Brian and Neil L. Whitehead, eds. 1992a. *War in the Tribal Zone: Expanding States and Indigenous Warfare*. Santa Fe, NM: School of American Research Press.

——. 1992b. 'The Violent Edge of Empire', in R.B. Ferguson and N.L. Whitehead, eds. *War in the Tribal Zone*. Santa Fe, NM: School of American Research Press, pp. 1–30.

Frank, Andre Gunder. 1992. *The Centrality of Central Asia*. Comparative Asian Studies No. 8. Amsterdam: VU University Press for Center for Asian Studies Amsterdam (CASA).

Frank, Andre Gunder and Barry K. Gills, eds. 1993. *The World System: Five Hundred Years or Five Thousand?* London: Routledge.

Fried, Morton. 1967. *The Evolution of Political Society*. New York: Random House.

——. 1975. *The Notion of Tribe*. Menlo Park, CA: Cummings.

Galaty, Michael. 2002. 'Modeling the formation and evolution of an Illyrian tribal system: ethnographic and archaeological analogs', in William Parkinson, ed. *The Archaeology of Tribal Societies*. Archaeology Series 15. Ann Arbor, MI: International Monographs in Prehistory, pp. 109–22.

Hall, Thomas D. 1986. 'Incorporation in the world-system: toward a critique'. *American Sociological Review* 51 (June): 390–402.

——. 1987. 'Native Americans and incorporation: patterns and problems'. *American Indian Culture and Research Journal* 11 (2): 1–30.

——. 1989a. *Social Change in the Southwest, 1350–1880*. Lawrence, KS: University Press of Kansas.

——. 1989b. 'Is Historical Sociology of Peripheral Regions Peripheral?', in Michael T. Martin and Terry R. Kandal, eds. *Studies of Development and Change in the Modern World*. New York: Oxford University Press, pp. 349–72.

——. 1991. 'The role of nomads in core/periphery relations', in Christopher Chase-Dunn and Thomas D. Hall, eds. *Core/Periphery Relations in Precapitalist Worlds*. Boulder, CO: Westview Press, pp. 212–39.

——. 1998. 'The Rio de La Plata and the Greater Southwest: a view from world-system theory', in Donna Guy and Thomas Sheridan, eds. *Contested Ground: Comparative Frontiers on the Northern and Southern Edges of the Spanish Empire*. Tucson, AZ: University of Arizona Press, pp. 150–66.

——. 2000a. 'Frontiers, ethnogenesis, and world-systems: rethinking the theories', in Thomas D. Hall, ed. *A World-Systems Reader: New Perspectives on Gender, Urbanism, Cultures, Indigenous Peoples, and Ecology*. Lanham, MD: Rowman & Littlefield Press, pp. 237–70.

——, ed. 2000b. *A World-Systems Reader: New Perspectives on Gender, Urbanism, Cultures, Indigenous Peoples, and Ecology*. Lanham, MD: Rowman & Littlefield Press.

——. 2001a. 'Using comparative frontiers to explore world-systems analysis and international relations'. *International Studies Perspectives* 2 (3): 253–69.

——. 2001b. 'Chiefdoms, states, cycling, and world-systems evolution: a review essay'. *Journal of World-Systems Research* 7 (1): 91–100 (ejournal http://jwsr.ucr.edu/index.php).

——. 2002a. 'World-systems analysis and globalization: directions for the twenty-first century', in Betty A. Dobratz, Timothy Buzzell and Lisa K. Waldner, eds. *Theoretical Directions in Political Sociology for the 21st Century*. Research in Political Sociology, Vol. 11. Oxford: Elsevier Science, pp. 81–122.

——. 2002b. 'World-systems, frontiers, and ethnogenesis: incorporation and resistance to state expansion', in Gerhard Preyer and Mathias B s, eds. *Borderlines in a Globalized World: New Perspectives in a Sociology of the World-Systems*. Dordrecht: Kluwer Academic Publishers, pp. 35–66.

Hall, Thomas D. and Christopher Chase-Dunn. 1993. 'The world-systems perspective and archaeology: forward into the past'. *Journal of Archaeological Research* 1 (2): 121–43.

Hall, Thomas D. and Peter Turchin. 2003. Lessons from Population Ecology for World-Systems Analyses of Long-Distance Synchrony. Paper presented at the conference on World System History and Global Environmental Change, Human Ecology Division, Lund University, Sweden, 19–22 September 2003 (http://www.humecol.lu.se/woshglec/).

Hämäläinen, Pekka. 1998. 'The western Comanche trade center: rethinking the Plains Indian trade system'. *Western Historical Quarterly* 29 (4): 485–513.

Hill, Jonathan D., ed. 1996. *History, Power, and Identity: Ethnogenesis in the Americas, 1492–1992*. Iowa City: University of Iowa Press.

Hollis, Shirley. 2005. 'Contact, incorporation, and the North American southeast'. *Journal of World-Systems Research* 11 (1): 95–130.

Kardulias, P. Nick, ed. 1999. *Leadership, Production, and Exchange: World-Systems Theory in Practice*. Lanham, MD: Rowman & Littlefield.

Khazanov, Anatoly M. 1983. *Nomads and the Outside World*. Cambridge: Cambridge University Press (2nd edn 1994, Madison, WI: University of Wisconsin Press).

Kohl, Philip L. 1979. 'The "world economy" in West Asia in the third millenium BC', in M. Toddei, ed. *South Asian Archaeology 1977*. Naples: Instituto Universitario Orientale, pp. 55–85.

——. 1987a. 'The use and abuse of world systems theory: the case of the pristine West Asian state'. *Advances in Archaeological Method and Theory* 11: 1–35.

——. 1987b. 'The ancient economy, transferable technologies and the Bronze Age world-system: a view from the northeastern frontier of the Ancient Near East', in Michael Rowlands, Mogens Larsen and Kristian Kristiansen, eds. *Centre and Periphery in the Ancient World*. Cambridge: Cambridge University Press, pp. 13–24.

——. 1987c. 'State Formation: Useful concept or idée fixe?', in Thomas Patterson and Kristine Gailey, eds. *Power Relations and State Formation*. Washington, DC: American Anthropological Association, pp. 27–34.

——. 1992. 'The Transcaucasian "periphery" in the Bronze Age: a preliminary formulation', in Edward Schortman and Patricia Urban, eds. *Resources, Power, and Interregional Interaction*. New York: Plenum Press. pp. 117–37.

——. 1994. 'Comment on Edward Schortman and Patricia Urban's "Living on the edge: core/periphery relations in Ancient Southeast Mesoamerica"'. *Current Anthropology* 35 (4): 416–17.

Kradin, Nicholai. 2002. 'Nomadism, evolution and world-systems: pastoral societies in theories of historical development'. *Journal of World-Systems Research* 8 (3): 368–88 (ejournal http://jwsr.ucr.edu/index.php).

Kradin, Nikolay N., Andrey V. Korotayev, Dmitri M. Bondarenko, Victor de Munck and Paul K. Watson, eds. 2000. *Alternatives of Social Evolution*. Vladivostok: Institute of History, Archaeology and Ethnology, Far Eastern Branch of the Russian Academy of Sciences.

Kradin, Nikolay N., Dmitri M. Bondarenko and Thomas J. Barfield, eds. 2003. *Nomadic*

Pathways in Social Evolution. The Civilization Dimension Series, Vol. 5. Moscow: Russian Academy of Sciences, Center for Civilizational and Regional Studies.

Lattimore, Owen. 1962. 'La civilisation, mère de Barbarie?' *Annales ESC* 17 (1): 95–108 (cited in Wallerstein 1974: 98).

Mann, Michael 1986. *The Sources of Social Power: A History of Power from the Beginning to AD 1760*. Cambridge: Cambridge University Press.

Mathien, Frances Joan and Randall McGuire, eds. 1986. *Ripples in the Chichimec Sea: Consideration of Southwestern-Mesoamerican Interactions*. Carbondale, IL: Southern Illinois University Press.

O'Brien, Patricia. 1992. 'The "world-system" of Cahokia within the Middle Mississippi tradition'. *Review* 15 (3): 389–417.

Parkinson, William A., ed. 2002. *The Archaeology of Tribal Societies*. Archaeology Series 15. Ann Arbor, MI: International Monographs in Prehistory.

Pauketat, Timothy R. and Thomas E. Emerson. 1997. *Cahokia: Domination and Ideology in the Mississippian World*. Lincoln: University of Nebraska Press.

Peregrine, Peter N. 2000. 'Archaeology and world-systems theory', in Thomas D. Hall, ed. *A World-Systems Reader: New Perspectives on Gender, Urbanism, Cultures, Indigenous Peoples, and Ecology*. Lanham, MD: Rowman & Littlefield, pp. 59–68.

Peregrine, Peter N. and Gary M. Feinman, eds. 1996. *Pre-Columbian World-Systems*. Monographs in World Archaeology No. 26. Madison, WI: Prehistory Press.

Randers-Pehrson, Justine Davis. 1983. *Barbarians and Romans: The Birth Struggle of Europe, AD 400–700*. Norman, OK: University of Oklahoma Press.

Schneider, Jane. 1977. 'Was there a pre-capitalist world-system?' *Peasant Studies* 6 (1): 20–9.

Schortman, Edward M., and Patricia. A. Urban, eds. 1992. *Resources, Power, and Interregional Interaction*. New York: Plenum Press.

Spielman, Katherine A., ed. 1991. *Farmers, Hunters, and Colonists: Interaction Between the Southwest and the Southern Plains*. Tucson: University of Arizona Press.

Taagepera , Rein. 1978a. 'Size and duration of empires: growth–decline curves, 3000 to 600 BC'. *Social Science Research* 7 (1): 180–96.

——. 1978b. 'Size and duration of empires: growth–decline curves, 3000 to 600 BC'. *Social Science Research* 7 (2): 180–96.

——. 1979. 'Size and duration of empires: growth–decline curves, 600 BC to 600 AD'. *Social Science History* 3 (3–4): 115–38.

Teggart, Frederick. 1939. *Rome and China: A Study of Correlations in Historical Events*. Berkeley, CA: University of California Press.

Thompson, William R., ed. 1983a. *Contending Approaches to World System Analysis*. Beverly Hills, CA: Sage.

Thompson, William R. 1983b. 'Introduction: world system analysis with and without the hyphen', in William R. Thompson, ed. *Contending Approaches to World System Analysis*. Beverly Hills, CA: Sage. pp. 7–24.

——. 2000. 'Comparing approaches to the social science history of the world system', in Robert A. Denemark, Jonathan Friedman, Barry K. Gills and George Modelski, eds. *World System History: The Social Science of Long-Term Change*. London: Routledge, pp. 287–98.

Turchin, Peter. 2003a. *Historical Dynamics*. Princeton, NJ: Princeton University Press.

——. 2003b. 'Evolution in population dynamics'. *Nature* 424 (17): 257–8.

Turchin, Peter and Thomas D. Hall. 2003. 'Spatial synchrony among and within world-systems: insights from theoretical ecology'. *Journal of World-Systems Research* 9 (1): 37–64 (ejournal: http://jwsr.ucr.edu/index.php).

Wallace-Hadrill, J.M. 1985. *The Barbarian West, 400–1000*. New York: Barnes and Noble.

Wallerstein, Immanuel. 1974. *The Modern World-System: Capitalist Agriculture and the Origins of European World-Economy in the Sixteenth Century*. New York: Academic Press.

——. 1993. 'World system vs. world-systems', in A.G. Frank and B.K. Gills, eds. *The World System: Five Hundred Years or Five Thousand?* London: Routledge, pp. 291–6.

Wells, Peter S. 1992. 'Tradition, identity, and change beyond the Roman frontier', in Edward Schortman and Patricia Urban, eds. *Resources, Power, and Interregional Interaction*. New York: Plenum Press, pp. 175–88.

——. 1999a. 'Production within and beyond imperial boundaries: goods, exchange, and power in Roman Europe', in P. Nick Kardulias, ed. *World-Systems Theory in Practice*. Lanham, MD: Rowman & Littlefield, pp. 85–101.

——. 1999b. *The Barbarians Speak: How the Conquered Peoples Shaped Roman Europe*. Princeton: Princeton University Press.

Wilkinson, David. 1987. 'Central civilization'. *Comparative Civilization Review* 17: 31–59.

——. 1991. 'Core, peripheries, and civilizations', in C. Chase-Dunn and T.D. Hall, eds. *Core/Periphery Relations in Precapitalist Worlds*. Boulder, CO: Westview Press, pp. 113–66.

——. 1992. 'Cities, civilizations and oikumenes: I'. *Comparative Civilizations Review* 27 (Fall): 51–87.

——. 1993. 'Cities, civilizations and oikumenes: II'. *Comparative Civilizations Review* 28 (Spring): 41–72.

Wilkinson, David. 1995. 'Central civilization'. in Stephen K. Sanderson, ed. *Civilizations and World-Systems: Two Approaches to the Study of World-Historical Change*. Walnut Creek, CA: Altamira Press, pp. 32–60.

——. 2000. 'Civilizations, world systems and hegemonies', in Robert A. Denemark, Jonathan Friedman, Barry K. Gills and George Modelski, eds. *World System History: The Social Science of Long-Term Change*. London: Routledge, pp. 54–84.

8 Growth/decline phases and semi-peripheral development in the Ancient Mesopotamian and Egyptian world-systems[1]

Christopher Chase-Dunn, Daniel Pasciuti, Alexis Alvarez and Thomas D. Hall

Introduction

This paper presents an overview of the development of complex and hierarchical societies in ancient south-western Asia from a comparative world-systems perspective, and presents an analysis of the timing of urban and empire growth/decline cycles in Mesopotamia and Egypt to test the hypotheses that these two regions may have experienced waves of development synchronously. We also discuss how climate change may have influenced the patterns of development. In a nutshell, our argument is that there have been systemic relations among different peoples since at least the first human settlements by the Natufians some 12,000 years ago (Chase-Dunn and Hall 1997). The developmental logic of these intersocietal systems has changed over time as new techniques of power and institutions have emerged, but there are also broad continuities and similar patterns over millennia as world-systems became larger. This chapter utilizes the conceptual apparatus of the comparative world-systems perspective to examine the patterns of development in prehistoric and ancient western Asia. Thus, we speak of strong core polities and weaker and dependent peripheral societies, as well as societies in the middle, which we call semi-peripheral. And we bound systems by using interaction networks in which important, two-way and regular interaction links peoples with different cultures. This network approach to bounding world-systems is explicated in Chase-Dunn and Jorgenson (2003).

We contend that some of the peoples who were semi-peripheral in the ancient world-systems were the main agents that brought about the transformations of developmental logics. We also contend that the formation, differentiation and development of nomadic peoples in tandem with sedentary states and empires played a crucial role. Nomads were often the catalysts of systemic change in these early state-based world-systems. This chapter builds on studies by David Wilkinson (2000), William R. Thompson (2000) and Guillermo Algaze (1993, 2000).

Karl Butzer (1997) contends, with respect to Levantine development processes, that the existence of cycles is *prima facie* evidence of some sort of system. We have noted that all world-systems large and small exhibit cycles of expansion and contraction of trade networks, which we call pulsation. Furthermore, once chiefdoms emerge, another cycle appears, the rise and fall of large polities.

Following the work of David Wilkinson, we note that the Mesopotamian and Egyptian interstate systems merged around 1500 BCE to become a single larger system of states that we call the Central System. And about 1,500 years earlier, around 3000 BCE, long-distance prestige goods trade connected these two regions. As these mergers occurred, it might be expected that growth/decline phases in the two regions would become synchronous. Indeed, we have found an important instance of this kind of synchrony between east and west Asia that emerged around 500 BCE and lasted until around 1500 CE (Chase-Dunn *et al.* 2000; Chase-Dunn and Manning 2002).

One area worthy of further examination is the effects of climate change on patterns of social development. Brian Fagan (1999) contends that it was sudden climate changes and natural disasters that provoked humans to invent new forms of social organization. Bill Thompson has argued (2000: figure 1) that climate change may affect social systems in complex and, at times, contradictory ways.

Pulsation, rise and fall and semi-peripheral development in the south-western Asian system

In this chapter, we focus mainly on south-western Asia and the Mediterranean Levant. The time period under consideration is from the emergence of mesolithic sedentism (about 10,000 BCE) to the point at which the growing south-west Asian political/military network (PMN) became linked with the Egyptian PMN by the Hyksos conquest of Egypt (about 1500 BCE). We will examine the hypothesis of semi-peripheral transformative action in the context of a discussion of the processes of polity formation, technological change, the rise and fall of larger polities, the pulsation of interaction networks and the transformation of the very logic of social integration from kin-based normative regulation to state-based institutionalized coercion. The hypothesis of semi-peripheral development asserts that semi-peripheral regions in core–periphery hierarchies are fertile sites for innovation and the implementation of new institutions that sometimes allow societies in these regions to be upwardly mobile and/or to transform the scale (and sometimes the qualitative nature) of institutional structures. This is not simply the notion that core traits diffuse towards the periphery. It is rather the idea that semi-peripheral innovation enables upward mobility and occasionally transforms whole systems. Semi-peripheral actors have taken different forms in different systems. Semi-peripheral marcher chiefdoms and semi-peripheral marcher states conquer older core states to form a new core-wide polity. Semi-peripheral capitalist city-states exploit an opportunity to accumulate wealth based on trade and the production of commodities. And, in the modern world-system, it is semi-peripheral nation states that have risen to become the hegemonic within still multicentric cores. This notion is further explicated in Chase-Dunn and Hall (1997: ch. 5).

The hypothesis of semi-peripheral development presumes a cross-cultural conceptualization of core–periphery hierarchies in which more powerful societies importantly interact with less powerful ones. The idea of core–periphery hierarchy was originally developed to describe and account for the stratified relations of power and dependency among societies in the modern world-system. The comparative world-systems approach developed by Chase-Dunn and Hall (1997) distinguishes between *core–periphery differentiation*, in which there is important interaction among societies that have different degrees of population density, and *core–periphery hierarchy*, in which some societies are exercising domination or exploitation of other societies. It is not assumed that all world-systems have core–periphery relations. Rather, this is turned into a research question to be determined in each case.

The 8,500-year period from 10,000 BCE to 1500 BCE in western Asia witnessed a series of fundamental pristine transformations in the nature of human societies: the original Mesolithic emergence of sedentary diversified foraging (the first dwellers in permanent villages), the Neolithic invention and application of farming, the emergence of the first hierarchical chiefdoms, the first multitier settlement systems and, eventually, the first cities and states. The south-west Asian world-system developed the first relatively stable core–periphery hierarchy in which imperial core states exploited and dominated peripheral peoples. This region also witnessed the first instance of a core-wide empire resulting from the conquest of a set of older core states – the Akkadian Empire. As will be seen, our earlier characterization of this as an instance of a semi-peripheral marcher state erecting a pristine empire (Chase-Dunn and Hall 1997: 84–9) needs to be modified in some important respects.

What follows is an analytical narrative about the development of social complexity and hierarchy in prehistoric and ancient south-western Asia and the Levant. The rapid and dramatic emergence of states, cities and writing in the west Asian system in the fourth millennium BCE was built upon a set of prior developments that spread from the adjacent Levant over the previous 5,000 years. The metaphor of ecological succession is relevant for understanding the evolution of world-systems. Small plants breaking down rocks create soil. This produces what is necessary for larger plants and trees to grow. The analogue of soil is socially produced surplus and the institutional structures that allow human societies to become larger and more hierarchical. But, as with ecological succession, this is not a smooth upward accession from small to large. Regressions and collapses were frequent, and the areas in which the first breakthroughs occurred are most usually not the same locations in which later, larger scale developments emerged. It was a process of temporally and spatially uneven social development. The institutional soil first formed in the prehistoric Levant and then spread to ancient south-western Asia.

The hilly flanks

The Mesolithic invention of relatively permanent village life was made possible by a diversified foraging strategy that mixed the gathering of vegetable resources, fishing and hunting of small game. This developed in a context in which the villagers continued to cooperate and compete with more nomadic hunter-gatherers. The Natufian culture of the Levant is the earliest known example of Mesolithic sedentism based on diversified foraging – this developed around 9000 BCE (Moore 1982; Bar-Yosef and Belfer-Cohen 1991).[2] Sedentary foragers probably invented territorial boundaries as well as a more active intervention in the productive cycles of nature. In other regions, diversified foragers are know to have used fire to increase the growth of food-producing plants and grazing areas attractive to game. These activities have been termed 'protoagriculture' (Bean and Lawton 1976). A similar Mesolithic culture, dated to around 8650 BCE, has been found at Shanidar Cave and village sites in the Zagros Mountains on a tributary of the Tigris (Solecki and Solecki 1982).

In the smaller valleys in the hills adjacent to the prime gathering regions of the Natufian peoples, naturally occurring stands of grain were less productive. It is plausible that, when the nomads in these neighbouring regions tried to emulate the sedentary lifestyle of the mesolithic villagers, they found that those natural stands were quickly eaten up, and so they experimented with planting the seeds that they had gathered. The protohorticulture of the diversified foragers may have been transformed into true horticulture and the domestication of useful plants by the adjacent neighbours of the original sedentary foragers (Hayden 1981). The further archaeological study of the spread of diversified foraging and gardening will enable us to test this hypothesis. It may be that the first instance of semi-peripheral development was the emergence of a new productive technology (planting) in a region adjacent to one in which an earlier new departure had occurred (sedentism).

The techniques of gardening spread both west into the valley of the Nile and east towards Mesopotamia. Gardening increased the number of people that could be supported by a given area of land, making greater population density possible. Community sizes grew in rain-watered regions, and population growth led to the migration of farmers away from the original heartland of gardening. Horticultural techniques also diffused from group to group and were combined with the domestication of pigs, sheep and goats. This was the Neolithic 'revolution'. Still-nomadic hunter-gatherers traded with the Neolithic towns, and a new form of pastoral nomadism developed based on the herding of domesticated animals.

The simple model here is that technological development increased population density, and this facilitated the emergence of social hierarchies. There is evidence from the Chesapeake region of indigenous North America that migration of planters or *in situ* adoption of planting does not always immediately lead to greater complexity and hierarchy (Chase-Dunn and Hall

1999). It appears that the arrival of corn planting in the Chesapeake area allowed the 'mesolithic' diversified foragers living in rather large villages to redisperse into widely spread farmlets and to reduce the intensity of their trading and ritual symbolization of group identity and social hierarchy. So, technological change can, under some conditions, lead to deconcentration and less social hierarchy. This possibility needs to be kept in mind as we examine the spread of gardening across south-western Asia.

As villages eventually grew larger, trade networks did as well, and craft specialists began producing for export and importing raw materials. Trade networks probably expanded and contracted along different spatial dimensions, as was the case in other small-scale world-systems (Chase-Dunn and Mann 1998). It is known that obsidian (volcanic glass) was an important lithic material for the production of cutting tools and weapons in regions adjacent to the Levant and south-western Asia (Torrence 1986). Obsidian tools and debitage (waste materials that are byproducts of tool making) can be chemically fingerprinted so that the original quarries can be identified. And obsidian hydration rinds can be used as an indicator of the period in which the tool was formed. These techniques can be used to indicate the patterns of obsidian trade and procurement networks and how they changed over time. Similar methods are also available for some other lithic materials. These techniques have not been fully exploited for studying the emergence and pulsation of trading networks in the prehistoric Levant and south-western Asia.

Some regions began displaying mortuary practices that indicated the emergence of social stratification. In northern Mesopotamia, a degree of hierarchy is evident in the Hassuna/Samarra archaeological tradition from 6000 BCE to 5500 BCE. Precious minerals were traded over larger and larger regions, and regionally defined pottery styles developed. The Halafian archaeological tradition in northern Mesopotamia (5500–5000 BCE) had quite large villages, and some have argued that these were chiefdoms.

To the flood plain

According to Nissen (1988: ch. 3), the first three-tiered settlement system in south-west Asia emerged on the Susiana Plain (in what is now Iran adjacent to the Mesopotamian flood plain) in the Ubaid period (5500–4000 BCE). This would indicate the presence of complex chiefdoms, and Wright (1986) points to the importance of the existence of complex chiefdoms in a region as the necessary organizational prerequisite for the emergence of pristine states. In other words, first states do not emerge directly from egalitarian societies. Evidence from Uqair, Eridu and Ouelli shows that there were also Ubaid sites on the lower Mesopotamian flood plain that were as large as the sites on the Susiana Plain at this time. The Early Ubaid phase at Tell Ouelli shows remarkably complex architecture as early as anything on the Susiana Plain.

Thus, there was an inter-regional interaction system of chiefdoms based on a mix of rain-watered and small-scale irrigated agriculture.

In the next period (Uruk or Late Chalcolithic from 4000 to 3100 BCE), the first true city (Uruk) grew up on the flood plain of lower Mesopotamia, and other cities of similar large size soon emerged in adjacent locations. Surrounding these unprecedented large cities were smaller towns and villages that formed the first four-tiered settlement systems (Adams 1981). This was the original birth of 'civilization' understood as the combination of irrigated agriculture, writing, cities and states.[3] States also emerged somewhat later in the Uruk period on the Susiana Plain (Wright 1998), and these also developed four-tiered settlement systems (Flannery 1999a: 17). This was an instance of uneven development – the transition from an inter-regional interchiefdom system to an intercity-state system that emerged first in Mesopotamia and then spread to the adjacent Susiana plain.

A system of states: the temple and the palace

The main architectural feature of these new cities was the temple, and this structure has long been considered to be the primary institution of a theocratically organized political economy. Later evidence about Sumerian civilization shows that each city was represented by a god in the Sumerian pantheon, and the priests and populace were defined as the slaves of the city god – this justifying the accumulation of surplus product (Postgate 1992). Flannery (1999a) claims that even the earliest archaic states often also had palaces – residential buildings for the war-leader king. But, in Mesopotamia, most scholars think that palaces were a later development that emerged when competitive warfare among the city-states for the control of land and trade routes became more frequent. Congruent with this is evidence showing an implosion of population from surrounding towns and villages to live within the protected confines of walled cities (Adams 1981). Thus was the early 'peer polity' or 'early state module' (Renfrew 1986) of coevolving archaic states transformed into an intercity-state system of warring and allying states.

This transition from theocracy to the primacy of a warrior-king was an important development in the emergence of state-based modes of accumulation. The Sumerian cities erected their states – specialized institutions of regional control – over the tops of kin-based normative institutions (Zagarell 1986). Assemblies of lineage heads long continued to play an important role in the politics of Mesopotamia. But the structures of institutional coercion became ever more important for maintaining power and accumulating wealth. One interesting apparent difference between the emergences of archaic states in Mesopotamia and other instances of pristine state formation is the apparent absence of ritual human sacrifice. A powerful way to dramatize the power of a king is to bury a lot of other people with him when he dies. Except for the Early Dynastic III period in the royal cemetery at Ur, there is little evidence of human sacrifice in Mesopotamia. The temple economy required contributions of goods and labour time, including animal sacrifices that were consumed in religious feasts. But the sacrifice of humans in Mesopotamia was, as with modern states, mainly confined to killing in battle.

The story of the Uruk expansion is well known, although its exact nature remains controversial (Algaze 1993, 2000; Stein 1999). The emerging cities of Mesopotamia founded colonies and colonial enclaves within existing towns across a vast region in order to gain access to desired goods and to control trade routes (Algaze 1993, 2000). There is some disagreement as to the degree of direct control that these core city-states[4] were able to exercise over distant peripheral regions.

Archaeologist Gil Stein's (1999) confrontation of world-systems ideas with evidence was inspired by the work of Phil Kohl (1987a, 1992). What Stein has done is to go beyond Kohl to formulate testable alternative models of core–periphery relationships. His 'distance-parity' model is a major conceptual improvement over earlier work. And Stein's careful research at Hacinebe (on the Tigris in Turkey) has gone far to enlighten us about the true nature of Uruk trading stations in that part of the world.

Despite Stein's critical appraisal of the comparative world-systems approach, his work confirms what Chase-Dunn and Hall (1997) have argued, that core–periphery hierarchies in early state-based world-systems were limited in spatial scale and relatively unstable. Early states were not able to extract resources from distant peripheries because they were unable to project military power very far and did not have elaborated capitalistic mechanisms for facilitating unequal exchange.

Joyce Marcus' (1998) study of early states points out that the interstate system of Mesopotamia exhibited a cycle of 'rise and fall' in which the largest polities increase and then decrease in size, and that this phenomenon is also known in other cases of ancient state systems in the Andes and Mesoamerica. Indeed, all hierarchical world-systems exhibit a structurally similar cycle – from the 'cycling' of chiefdoms (Anderson 1994) to the rise and fall of great empires, and the rise and fall of hegemonic core states in the modern world-system.

Figure 8.1 graphs the territorial sizes of the largest states and empires in Mesopotamia from 3000 BCE to 1000 BCE as estimated by Taagepera (1978a, 1978b). The rise and fall phenomenon can clearly be seen. Also the great size of the Akkadian Empire (6.5 square megametres) was not equalled again until 800 BCE by the Neo-Assyrians, who then went on to create a state that ruled 14 square megametres in 650 BCE. This was a new level of political integration of territory more than twice the size of the Akkadian Empire. We also have data on the sizes of many of the largest cities in Mesopotamia. The Pearson's r correlation coefficient for the relationship between Mesopotamian largest city and empire sizes based on 13 time points from 2800 to 650 BCE is 0.59. This indicates that, as would be expected, large empires build large cities, and the processes that cause growth and decline phases affect both urbanization and empire formation.[5]

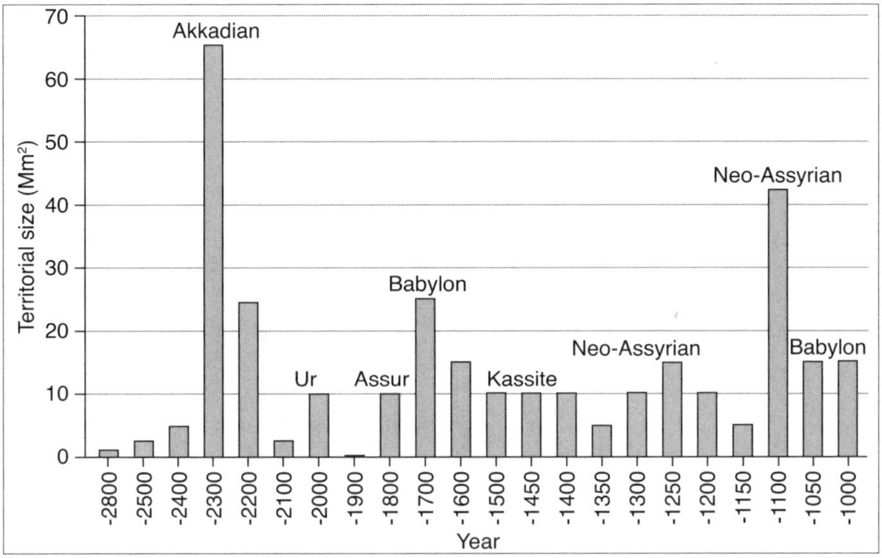

Figure 8.1 Territorial sizes of Mesopotamian states and empires (Taagepera 1978a, 1978b).

David Wilkinson (2000) has coded the power configuration sequence of the ancient south-west Asian state system from Early Dynastic II to the Kassite–Hurrain period. Wilkinson conceptualizes state systems in terms of a sequence of power configurations, and we have recoded these in terms of degrees of centralization of power:

6 universal state (one superpower, no great powers, no more than two local powers)
5 hegemony (either one superpower, no great powers, three or more local powers; or no superpowers, one great power, no more than one local power)
4 unipolar (all other configurations with one superpower)
3 bipolar (two great powers)
2 tripolar (three great powers)
1 multipolar (more than three great powers)
0 non-polar (no great powers)

It is reasonable to suppose that power configurations should be positively correlated over time with the territorial size of the largest empire. Figure 8.2 confirms this correlation for the ancient south-west Asian system.[6]

The Jemdet Nasr and Early Dynastic periods saw the further growth of cities in Mesopotamia and seven centuries of an intercity-state system with the rise and fall of hegemonic core states but no successful formation of a core-wide empire. This sequence is quite different from what happened in Egypt,

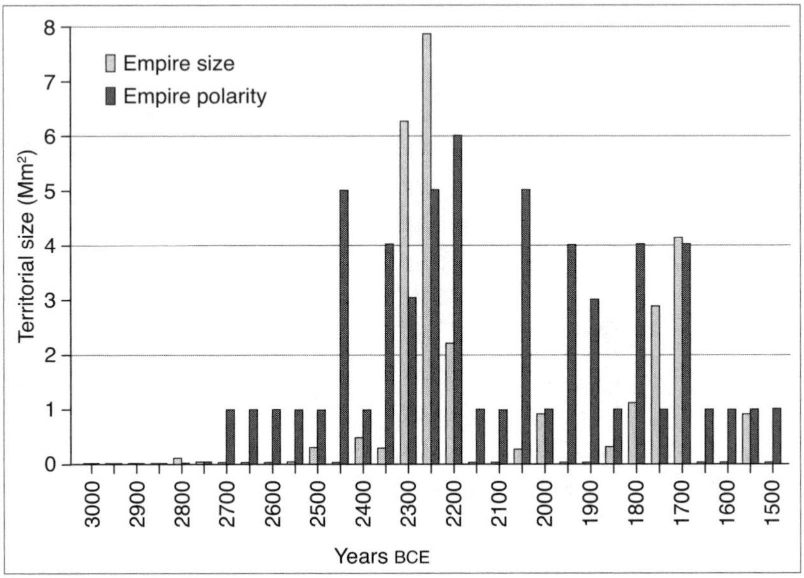

Figure 8.2 Power configurations and the territorial size of the largest empire.

where the emergence of monumental cities and large-scale agriculture led to much larger territorial states, and very soon to a core-wide empire (see Figure 8.4).[7] The explanations for these differences have long been alleged to be ecological, having to do with the differences in the communications and transportation possibilities in the two regions. Whereas the Nile is a single and quite navigable river both upstream and downstream, the Tigris and the Euphrates are much less navigable, and so communications and trade routes are more complex in Mesopotamia. In Egypt, a state can easily get effective control of the entire agricultural heartland by controlling movement on the Nile, whereas in Mesopotamia central control of flows of information and goods is much more difficult to gain (Mann 1986). Thus, the process of empire building took much longer in south-west Asia than it did in Egypt (see Figure 8.4).

This ecological explanation is now often disparaged by those who compare Mesopotamia and Egypt (e.g. Baines and Yoffee 1998) in favour of cultural differences that may have led to the differences in political organization. But it is equally plausible that the cultural differences were themselves consequences of ecological and political structures. In Egypt, the temple economy lasted far longer before it was transformed into a state led by a warrior-king because early empire formation along the Nile was not challenged by adjacent strong states. In Mesopotamia, each of the city-states needed constantly to defend its sovereignty from competing adjacent states. Many of the cultural differences between the two regions are due to these ecological and geopolitical differences.

Sargon

Although there were several efforts by powerful states to conquer the whole core region of Mesopotamia, this goal was not reached until the emergence of the Akkadian Empire in 2350 BCE. Chase-Dunn and Hall (1997: 84–9) presented a case for this first core-wide empire as an instance of a semi-peripheral marcher state conquest. This was based on the notion that the Akkadian-speaking conquerors were recently settled nomadic pastoralists in northern Mesopotamia who used elements of political organization and military technology stemming from their formerly peripheral origins to conquer the old core city-states and erect a larger empire. This portrayal is challenged by evidence that the Akkadian language had long been present in both northern and southern Mesopotamia and that Agade, the capital of the Akkadian Empire, was probably established *after* the Sargonic conquest rather than being a city populated by recently settled ex-nomads (Postgate 1992: 36). Although archaeologists have not yet firmly identified the location of Agade among the thousands of mudheaps (tells) in Iraq, it is thought that Agade was built in the northern part of the Mesopotamian region.

By the time of the Sargonic conquest, the characterization of northern Mesopotamia as semi-peripheral is problematic. The northern part of the alluvium was more heavily urbanized than the south (Adams 1981) in the Early Uruk period, but the situation reversed towards the end of the Uruk period with the exponential growth of Warka. The north may have had a greater concentration of Akkadian speakers (Postgate 1992: 38), but some of the northern cities (e.g. Kish) had long been among the contenders for hegemony in the intercity-state system of the Early Dynastic period. These particulars favour an interpretation of the Akkadian conquest that is based more on class and ethnic cleavages in Mesopotamia than on the core–periphery dimension (Yoffee 1991).

The Akkadian regime, called an 'upstart dynasty' by Postgate (1992), made the Akkadian language the official language of the state and, under Sargon's son Naram-sin (2291 BCE), imposed a standardized system of weights and measures across the Mesopotamian core. After the fall of the Akkadian dynasty, there was a period of disorder in which the Gutians (nomadic people from the Zagros Mountains) infiltrated the Mesopotamian core region and contended for power. The north–south dimension of conflict continued to be a cultural and geopolitical fault line. The Third Dynasty of Ur (2113 BCE) re-asserted southern dominance and Sumerian culture. David Wilkinson (1991) notes a pattern that he calls 'shuttling', in which centralized power shifted back and forth between two adjacent regions. This pattern of shuttling rise and fall, now increasingly composed of multicity states, characterizes what happened in south-western Asia throughout the rest of the period until the Babylonian Empire and the end of the period we are studying in this chapter. Subsequent Mesopotamian Empires until 1500 BCE were not larger than the Akkadian Empire had been (see Figure 8.1), and the location of the most powerful states shuttled back and forth between northern and southern Mesopotamia.

Core and periphery

The most serious incursions of peripheral tribes occurred during periods of political disorder in the core regions. There were probably both 'push' and 'pull' factors involved in this pattern of recurrent incursions. Disorder among the 'civilized' states made them vulnerable and encouraged interlopers. And nomadic pastoralists and hill tribes probably had their own organizational dynamics (Hall 1991: 2000). We know from other areas that nomadic pastoralists have their own cycles of centralization and decentralization (Barfield 1989). And climate changes affected both the abilities of the agrarian states to produce food and the abilities of the nomads to raise herds. Thompson (2000: Figure 3) indicates that there is a fairly good correspondence over time between the size of the largest Mesopotamian state and the Tigris/Euphrates river levels. This is encouraging for the hypothesis that climate change is related to rise and fall, and it may be an important factor in peripheral incursions.

The Amorite tribes were nomadic pastoralists coming from the deserts of the north-west. In order to prevent their incursions, the Ur III dynasty constructed a Great Wall of Mesopotamia right across the northern edge of the core region (Postgate 1992: 43). But there were also new invasions from the east by Elamites, and it was a combination of Amorite and Elamite incursions that led to the fall of the Third Dynasty of Ur. There followed the Isin–Larsa period in which small independent states each had an Amorite ruling house, and the Old Babylonian period that followed was a system of rather larger multicity states. The Amorite kings of Babylon, including the famous Hammurapi, expanded their empire until Babylon was itself conquered in 1595 BCE by a new group of nomadic invaders, the Hittites, led by Murcilis.

Merchant capitalism

During these developments, trade networks continued to expand, albeit unevenly. Periods of peace and empire allow trade to become more intense and goods to travel further. The commodification of goods and wealth had long been emerging within and between the states of Mesopotamia. Contracts of sale of lands and interest-bearing loans were known from the Early Dynastic period, and prices were clearly reflecting shortages in the Ur III period. In the Old Babylonian period, we find a clear instance of a phenomenon that became more frequent and widespread in the later commercializing tributary empire systems – the semi-peripheral capitalist city-state (Chase-Dunn and Hall 1997: 90–3).[8] This was the Old Assyrian merchant dynasty based in Assur on the upper Tigris, with its colonial enclaves of Assyrian merchants located in distant cities far up into Anatolia and beyond (Larsen 1987, 1992).

Assur was a merchant capitalist city-state with a farflung set of colonies in the midst of an interstate system in which most states were still pursuing a strategy of territorial expansion.

The capitalist city-state phenomenon is clearly a different kind of semi-peripheral development from that of the semi-peripheral marcher state. These states pursued a policy of profit-making rather than the acquisition of territory and the use of state power to tax and extract tribute. They emerged in the interstices between the territorial states in world economies in which wealth could be had by buying cheap and selling dear (merchant capitalism). One of their consequences was the expansion of trade networks because their commercial activities provided incentives for distant producers and accumulators to use surpluses for trade and to produce surpluses beyond local needs for this purpose. Thus, the capitalist city-states were agents of commodification and the expansion and intensification of a regional division of labour.

The Old Assyrian merchants, unlike most capitalist city-states, were not maritime specialists (as were, for example, the Phoenicians, Venice, Genoa, Malacca, etc.). But they did occupy a key transportation site that enabled them to tap into profit streams created by the exchange of eastern tin and Mesopotamian textiles for silver. Bronze was being produced in Anatolia using copper from the north and tin imported from the east, probably from regions that are now part of Afghanistan. The demand for tin was great, and the worshippers of Assur were able to insert themselves profitably into this trade by negotiating treaties with the other states in the region that allowed them access to markets at agreed taxation rates. They also organized and carried out the transportation of goods over long distances by means of donkey caravans, and they produced an effective structure of self-governance. This is an early instance of what Philip Curtin (1984) has called a 'trade diaspora', in which a single cultural group specializes in cross-cultural trade.[9]

Most of the evidence that we have about the Old Assyrian city-state and its colonies comes from the Kultepe tablets at Kanesh, an archive of business records and letters that show how the Old Assyrians organized and governed their business activities (Veenhof 1995). The records show that these were merchants trading on their own accounts for profit, not agents of states carrying out 'administered trade' akin to tribute exchanges. Although Karl Polanyi (1957) was wrong about the Old Assyrians in this regard, his larger perspective on the evolution of institutional modes of exchange remains an important contribution to our understanding of the qualitative differences between kin-based, state-based and market forms of integration. The conquest empire of the Hittites was certainly a case of the semi-peripheral marcher state strategy in which recently settled nomads overwhelmed an interstate system and created a new and larger empire.

The later history of Assur is also an interesting case that is relevant for our understanding of semi-peripheral development. The Old Assyrians were conquered by an Amorite sheik. Their later re-emergence as the Neo-Assyrian empire was a fascinating instance of a semi-peripheral capitalist city-state switching to the marcher state strategy of conquest,[10] and their success in this venture created an empire that was larger than any other that had been before it in south-western Asia (see Figure 8.1).

From peripherality to semi-peripherality

In the hinterlands, 'beyond the pale' dwelt those labelled 'barbarians', which might be glossed 'the not like us' peoples. What were their relations to sedentary peoples and how did they change? Much of this will be forever shrouded by the paucity of hard evidence. Hence, we are forced to use much later sedentary–nomad relations to gain insights into the first relations. Such ethnographic 'upstreaming' is always hazardous, the more so when its origins are the subject of investigation. Still, we can posit trading and raiding as two ways in which nomadic peoples can interact with sedentary peoples. Even when the nomadism is bipedal, nomads have immense advantages over sedentary peoples: they are fewer, they are mobile, more importantly, their resources are also mobile, they know their territory intimately, and their sedentary foes are, literally, sitting ducks. In fact, the only way raiding nomads can be subdued is to sedentarize them – something seldom if ever possible until the last few centuries.

On the other hand, we learn from Barfield's account that the popular image of nomads as destroyers is a gross exaggeration. Here one must distinguish between a city or village that is destroyed in a raid versus an entire empire which readily outlasts all such raids. Nomads cannot profit from either raiding or trading with a failing state because there will be little or nothing to raid or trade for! This is fundamentally what is behind Barfield's seemingly surprising finding that steppe confederacies were strong only when China was strong, and weak when it was weak. He does note, however, that things were often different in west Asia where states were smaller and weaker than China. While Bronze Age states were assuredly weaker, so were the various surrounding nomads.

Owen Lattimore (1967) cites a Chinese proverb to the effect that, while one can conquer from horseback, one cannot rule from there. Whether we are discussing mounted pastoralists, or prehorse nomads, the principle is the same: to maintain a conquest over sedentary peoples, nomads must cease being nomads. One of the major problems with ancient accounts of nomadic incursions is that it is often difficult to tell whether any particular instance was a relatively gradual process of in-migration with new language coming into dominance, or a military conquest that transformed the nomadic conquerors into a new dynasty.

The conventional approach, that nomads conquer weak states, may hold when nomads essentially overplay their hand of raiding to gain better terms of trade and then end up running the place, and ceasing to be nomads. This, of course, would be highly remarked in written records, whereas centuries of intermittent raids, which alternate with trade, would go unremarked.

But, other than accidentally overplaying their raiding, why would nomads conquer sedentary peoples? There may have been variants in western Asia of what William McNeill (1989) has called the steppe gradient. There was a tendency for steppe pastoralists in central Asia to move westward because the grasses are better towards the east, so strong nomadic confederations tended to emerge in the east, near China, displacing losing groups towards the west. There were probably localized versions of this phenomenon in western Asia.

This is one of the ways in which climate change, even relatively small climate change, can have strong effects. Slight shifts in rainfall patterns can change considerably the limits of useful rangeland for pastoralists. If any one group moves, all their neighbours, sedentary and nomadic, are affected. Here it is important to keep in mind the volatility of pastoral strategies. An abundance of grass in just a few seasons can lead to an explosion of herd sizes, unleashing quest for more pastures. The quest will intensify if the climate turns dryer and grasses become scarce. This, too, can unleash migrations and conquests, in which nomads seek to take over farmland for pastureland.

Here it is vital to see this as part of a larger system. Farmers and herders utilize different resources and different ecologies. Typically, but not always, land that is very suitable for pastoralism is not suitable for farming. This produces differentiation between farming and herding. Yet neither adaptation is wholly self-sufficient and this produces incentives for trade. But this type of differentiation readily turns into hierarchy, as sedentary populations far outnumber pastoral populations. By trading assorted 'surplus' goods, sedentary peoples encourage nomads to produce a surplus of meat and animal byproducts on land that is often not suitable for cultivation.

Most important for our argument about systemness and the entraining of processes across regions, nomads are often a key link who transmit changes in one region to distant regions. This, of course, was the argument of Frederick Teggart (1939) in Rome and China. For instance, one can imagine a state becoming weakened by a dynastic succession struggle. This could undercut the amount of surplus available for trade, especially with pesky barbarians. Those barbarians could then either step up raids to acquire what could no longer be obtained by trade, further weakening the state and undermining the legitimacy of the ruling elite. If this led to a collapse of the agrarian state, nomads might take over and run the state themselves. But, unless they had sufficient numbers, knowledge and organization, this outcome would be rare.[11] If nomadic peoples are frustrated in their interactions with existing states, they seek elsewhere for necessary goods and to sell off their surplus. This could start a gradient of clashes that would ramify far across intervening territories. If no alternatives were available, the nomadic society might itself experience a secondary collapse in reaction to the agrarian state collapse. This could actually open new territory to nomads from elsewhere looking for new pastures. Nomads can also facilitate or hinder long-distance trade between agrarian states. Small nomadic groups that raid trade caravans make long-distance trade risky and expensive. But a large nomadic confederation can agree to supply security to merchant caravans for a fee, making the risks and returns from trade venture much more calculable. Thus, we can expect some correlation of events between distant sedentary states and empires as a result of the transmission belts that nomadic groups constitute.

Egyptian and Mesopotamian synchrony?

As the Mesopotamian and Egyptian cores and their trade networks expanded, they came to have more and more direct and consequential connections with one another. Writing developed in Mesopotamia and Egypt at about the same time, and there may have been a diffusion of the idea of two-dimensional systems of symbolic codes (writing) in one direction or both. This would indicate that the information networks and the prestige goods networks were already connected. This raises the possibility that the cycles of rise and fall and the growth of cities may have become synchronized in the two core regions.

Research has demonstrated this phenomenon for the later cases of east and west Asia between 600 BCE and 1500 CE (Chase-Dunn *et al.* 2000; Chase-Dunn and Manning 2002). These were two distant core regions linked by a prestige goods network, but they had no direct political/military interaction. This synchronization of east and west Asian city growth/decline phases and the rise and fall of large states has been tested and retested and now begins to assume the status of a fact. It was a similar situation in some ways to the relationship between Mesopotamia and Egypt before 1500 BCE. Two separate agrarian core regions were trading prestige goods with one another, and much of the intervening territory was inhabited by nomadic pastoralists.

Regarding the hypothesis of Mesopotamian/Egyptian synchrony, Chase-Dunn and Hall (2000: 105) examined estimates of the population sizes of cities in Mesopotamia and Egypt based on data from Chandler (1987) and the territorial sizes of empires from Taagepera (1978a, 1978b). They found little support for the synchronization hypothesis. Table 8.1 replicates that earlier effort by supplementing the Chandler (1987) data with estimates from Modelski (2003) and with an improved method of detrending. The empire size data are from Taagepera (1978a, 1978b).

Although these data still contain the same reliability limitations as previous estimates of urban populations, Modelski's compendium represents the most complete and current compilation of urban populations. Modelski began with Chandler's compendium of urban populations and then expanded and improved the coverage using newer and more recent historical information. Using Modelski's data set, we have enlarged our data set for Egyptian and Mesopotamian cities from 7 to 23 time points in the Egyptian PMN and from 16 to 25 time points in Mesopotamia.

We tested the hypothesis of synchrony of growth and decline between Egyptian and Mesopotamian city sizes and empire sizes using the percentage change score. The change score methodology was used to rule out the long-

Table 8.1 Mesopotamian and Egyptian city and empire correlations based on percentage change scores for different time periods

Region	*Pearson's* r	*Significance level*	N	*Years* BCE
City-to-city correlations across PMNs				
Egypt–Mesopotamia	0.073	0.370	23	2800–400
Egypt–Mesopotamia	0.152	0.348	9	2800–1500
Egypt–Mesopotamia	0.177	0.264	15	1500–400
Empire-to-empire correlations across PMNs				
Egypt–Mesopotamia	–0.086	0.344	24	2800–400
Egypt–Mesopotamia	–0.140	0.350	10	2800–1500
Egypt–Mesopotamia	–0.049	0.432	15	1500–400

Notes
a Pearson's *r* significant at the 0.05 level.
b Pearson's *r* significant at the 0.01 level.

term secular increase in city and empire sizes. The synchrony hypothesis is about the phase relationships among medium-term growth/decline phases. A simple bivariate correlation between regions would necessarily be positive in part due to the long-term secular upward trend. In our earlier work, we detrended by calculating a partial correlation that controls for time. But this presumes that the long-term trend is linear, while observations of city and empire growth suggest a long-term accelerating increase. Detrending with percentage change scores does not presume the shape of the long-term trend. The percentage change score is calculated as follows: $\%\Delta = (T_2 - T_1/T_1)/N$, where N in the number of decades constituting interval T. The latter term is necessary because the intervals between measurement time points are not always of equal lengths.

None of the correlation coefficients in Table 8.1 are statistically significant, confirming our earlier finding of no support for the hypothesis of synchrony between Mesopotamia and Egypt. We examined three different time periods and found no synchrony for any of them. Figures 8.3 and 8.4 display the raw size data for the largest cities and the largest empires in Egypt and Mesopotamia.

The question of synchrony and the causes of rise and fall and urban growth/decline phases in early state systems will require further empirical examination. Both city and territorial size data sets need to be improved by correcting mistakes and adding data from recently published studies. Even though there is little indication of Mesopotamian/Egyptian inter-regional synchrony, it remains possible that climate change and interactions with peripheral nomads can explain the cyclical patterns in each that are revealed in Figures 8.3 and 8.4.

There is considerable support for cycles of rise and fall and sequences

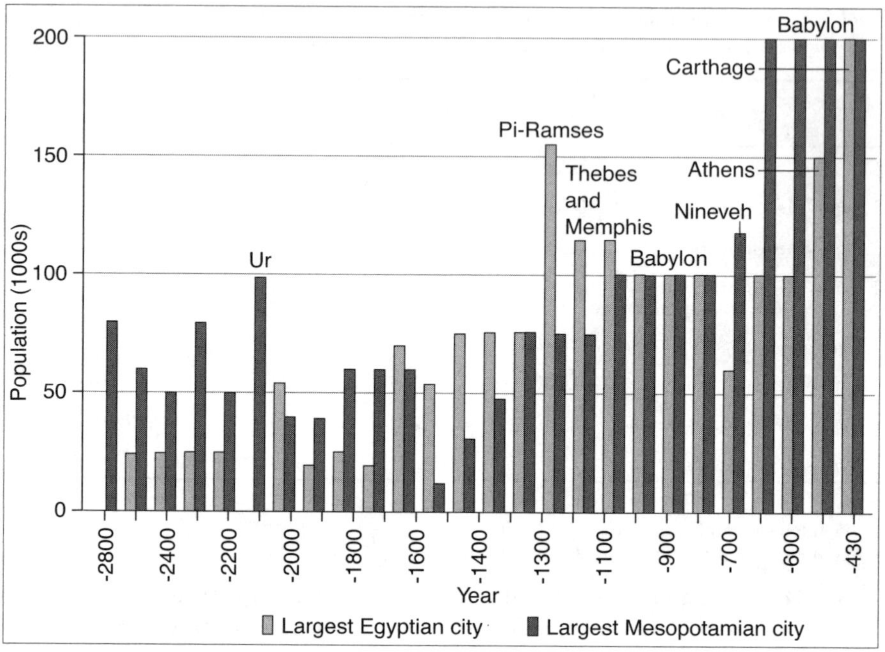

Figure 8.3 Largest cities in Egypt and Mesopotamia from 2800 BCE to 430 BCE.

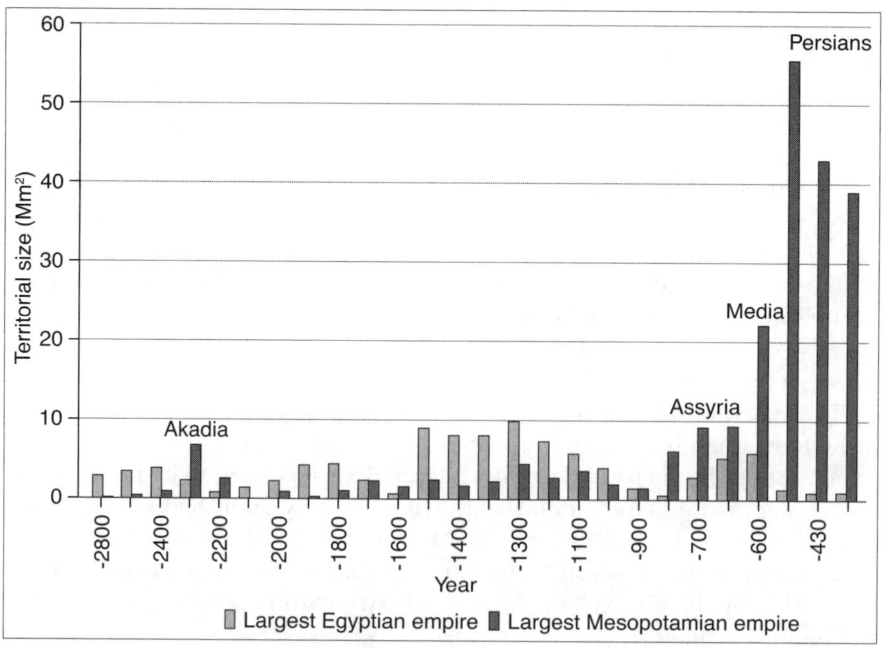

Figure 8.4 Largest empires in Egypt and Mesopotamia from 2800 BCE to 430 BCE.

of trade expansion and contraction in the Bronze Age and early Iron Age world-systems. The hypothesis of semi-peripheral development is confirmed for some instances of transformation, but not for others. We have presented a strong case for the importance of interactions with nomads and the likelihood that climate change has played an important role in the processes of uneven development in the prehistoric and early state-based world-systems.

Notes

1 An earlier version was presented at the All-UC Multicampus Research Unit in World History Conference, UCLA, 6–7 December 2003. Thanks to Guillermo Algaze, Claudio Cioffi, Jerry Cooper and Peter Peregrine for comments on an earlier version.

2 An apparently somewhat similar world-system of sedentary foragers existed in northern California until the gold rush of 1849 CE (Chase-Dunn and Mann 1998).

3 A state is understood here as a specialized administrative apparatus of regional control that is at least partially independent of kinship organization.

4 Flannery (1999a: 18) makes a big point that Lagash, one of the Mesopotamian states, has three cities as well as 20 towns and 40 villages, and so he contests the characterization of Mesopotamian states as city-states. Van de Mieroop (1999) makes the point that these states were city-states because political organization was physically and institutionally structured around the main city.

5 But this relationship does not hold in some other regional systems, including Egypt. See Chase-Dunn *et al.* (forthcoming).

6 Our study of the Indic interstate system (Chase-Dunn *et al.* 2000) found no correlation between power configurations and empire sizes in that region.

7 Although Egypt formed a core-wide empire early on, it continued to experience cycles of political centralization and decentralization just as other state systems do.

8 Dilmun, a maritime trading centre somewhere in the Persian Gulf (probably Bahrain or Oman) that engaged in the carrying trade between Mesopotamia and the Indus valley civilization, may have been an earlier example.

9 Gil Stein applies the concept of 'trade diaspora' in a somewhat different way to trading enclaves set up by the Uruk core state to supply itself with certain goods from a distant region. Curtin's original idea applied to culturally specialized trading ethnicities rather than to trade outposts of urbanized core societies.

10 Another instance of this kind of niche switching is the case of Hannibal. The Phoenicians had for centuries pursued the maritime capitalist city-state strategy in which they combined merchant capitalism with production capitalism by manufacturing profitable products for the carrying trade. Hannibal abandoned the trading strategy for the marcher state approach and he nearly succeeded in conquering Rome. The reticence of the Carthaginians, not fully convinced of the wisdom of territorial conquest, to support his venture in a crucial period was a main cause of its failure.

11 This is why nomadic conquests are short-lived and more lasting empires are erected by nomadic peoples who have settled down on the edges of core regions and acquired some of the organizational and cultural attributes of core power.

Bibliography

Adams, Robert McCormick. 1965. *Land Behind Baghdad: A History of Settlement on the Diyala Plains*. Chicago: University of Chicago Press.

——. 1966. *The Evolution of Urban Society: Early Mesopotamia and Prehispanic Mexico*. Chicago: Aldine.

——. 1981. *Heartland of Cities: Surveys of Ancient Settlement and Land Use on the Central Floodplain of the Euphrates*. Chicago: University of Chicago Press.

——. 1984. 'Mesopotamian social evolution: old outlooks, new goals', in Timothy Earle (ed.). *On the Evolution of Complex Societies: Essays in Honor of Harry Hoijer*. Malibu, CA: Undena Publications, pp. 79–129.

Adams, Robert McCormick and Hans Nissen. 1972. *The Uruk Countryside*. Chicago: University of Chicago Press.

Algaze, Guillermo. 1993. *The Uruk World System: The Dynamics of Expansion of Early Mesopotamian Civilization*. Chicago: University of Chicago Press.

——. 2000. 'The prehistory of imperialism: the case of Uruk period Mesopotamia', in M. Rothman, ed. *Uruk Mesopotamia and its Neighbors: Cross-cultural Interactions and their Consequences in the Era of State Formation*. Santa Fe: School of the Americas.

Al Khalifa, Shaikha Haya and Michael Rice, eds. 1986. *Bahrain through the Ages: the Archaeology*. London: Routledge.

Allen, Mitchell. 1992. 'The mechanisms of underdevelopment: an Ancient Mesopotamian example'. *Review* 15 (3): 453–76.

Anderson, David G. 1994. *The Savannah River Chiefdoms: Political Change in the Late Prehistoric Southeast*. Tuscaloosa: University of Alabama Press.

Baines, John and Norman Yoffee. 1998. 'Order, legitimacy and wealth in Ancient Egypt and Mesopotamia', in Gary M. Feinman and Joyce Marcus, eds. *Archaic States*. Santa Fe: School of American Research, pp. 199–260.

Bar-Yosef, Ofer and Anna Belfer-Cohen. 1991. 'From sedentary hunter-gatherers to territorial farmers in the Levant', in Susan A. Gregg, ed. *Between Bands and States*. Carbondale, IL: Center for Archaeological Investigations, Occasional Papers no. 9, pp. 181–202.

Barfield, Thomas J. 1989. *The Perilous Frontier*. Cambridge, MA: Blackwell.

Bean, Lowell John and Harry Lawton. 1976. 'Some explanations for the rise of cultural complexity in native California with comments on proto-agriculture and agriculture'. in L.J. Bean and Thomas C. Blackburn, eds. *Native Californians: A Theoretical Retrospective*. Socorro, NM: Ballena Press, pp. 19–48.

Bosworth, Andrew. 1995. 'World cities and world economic cycles', in Stephen Sanderson, ed. *Civilizations and World Systems*. Walnut Creek, CA: Altamira, pp. 206–28.

Butzer, Karl. 1995. 'Environmental change in the Near East and human impact on the land', in Jack M. Sasson John Baines, Gary Beckman and Karen S. Robinson, eds. *Civilizations of the Ancient Near East*, Vol. 1. New York: Scribners, pp. 123–51.

Butzer, Karl W. 1997. 'Sociopolitical discontinuity in the Near East C. 2200 BCE: scenarios from Palestine and Egypt', in H.N. Dalfes, G. Kulka and H. Wiess, eds. *Third Millennium BC Climate Change and Old World Collapse*. Berlin: Springer.

Chandler, Tertius. 1987. *Four Thousand Years of Urban Growth*. Lewiston, NY: Edwin Mellen Press.

Chase-Dunn, Christopher and Thomas D. Hall. 1997. *Rise and Demise: Comparing World-Systems*. Boulder, CO: Westview.

Chase-Dunn, C. and Thomas D. Hall. 1999. 'The Chesapeake World-system' (http://wsarch.ucr.edu/archive/papers/c-d&hall/asa99b/asa99b.htm).

Chase-Dunn, C. and Thomas D. Hall. 2000. 'Comparing world-systems to explain social evolution', in Robert Denemark, Jonathan Friedman, Barry Gills and George Modelski, eds. *World System History*. London: Routledge, pp. 85–111.

Chase-Dunn, Christopher and Andrew K. Jorgenson. 2003. 'Regions and interaction networks: an institutional materialist perspective'. *International Journal of Comparative Sociology* 44 (1): 433–50.

Chase-Dunn, Christopher and Kelly M. Mann. 1998. *The Wintu and their Neighbors: A Very Small World-system in Northern California*. Tucson, AZ: University of Arizona Press.

Chase-Dunn, Christopher and Susan Manning. 2002. 'City systems and world-systems: four millennia of city growth and decline'. *Cross-Cultural Research* 36 (4): 379–98.

Chase-Dunn, Christopher and Alice Willard. 1993. 'Systems of cities and world-systems: settlement size hierarchies and cycles of political centralization, 2000 BC–1988 AD'. A paper presented at the Annual Meeting of the International Studies Association, Acapulco, 24 March 1993. (http://irows.ucr.edu/papers/irows5/irows5.htm).

Chase-Dunn, Christopher, Susan Manning and Thomas D. Hall. 2000. 'Rise and fall: east–west synchronicity and Indic exceptionalism reexamined'. *Social Science History* 24 (4): 721–48.

Chase-Dunn, Christopher, Alexis Alvarez and Daniel Pasciuti. 2005. 'Size and power: urbanization and empire formation in world-systems', in C. Chase-Dunn and E.N. Anderson, eds. *The Evolution of World-Systems*. London: Palgrave, pp. 92–112.

Cioffi-Revilla, Claudio. 1991. 'The long-range analysis of war'. *Journal of Interdisciplinary History* 21: 603–29.

Collins, Randall. 1992. 'The geographical and economic world-systems of kinship-based and agrarian-coercive societies'. *Review* 15 (3): 373–88. Westport, CT: Greenwood Press.

Cooper, J.S. 1973. 'Sumerian and Akkadian in Sumer and Akkad', in G. Buccellati, ed. *Approaches to the Study of the Ancient Near East: A Volume of Studies Offered to Ignace J. Gelb. Orientalia* 42: 239–46.

Cooper, Jerrold S. 1983a. *The Curse of Agade*. Baltimore: Johns Hopkins University Press.

——. 1983b. 'Reconstructing history of ancient inscriptions: the Lagash–Umma border conflict'. *Sources from the Ancient Near East* 2 (1). Malibu, CA: Undena.

——. 1989. 'Writing'. *International Encyclopedia of Communications* 4: 321–31.

——. 1993. 'Paradigm and propaganda: the dynasty of Akkad in the 21st century', in M. Liverani, ed. *Akkad: The First World Empire*. Padua: Sargon, pp. 11–23.

Curtin, Philip D.1984. *Cross-cultural Trade in World History*. Cambridge: Cambridge University Press.

Diakonoff, Igor M. 1954. 'Sale of land in pre-Sargonic Sumer'. Papers presented by the Soviet delegation at the 23rd International Congress of Orientalists, Assyriology Section. Moscow: USSR Academy of Sciences.

——. 1969. 'Main features of the economy in the monarchies of Ancient Western Asia'. *Ecole Practique des Hautes Etudes-Sorbonne, Congres at Colloques* 10 (3): 13–32. Paris: Mouton.

——. 1973. 'The rise of the despotic state in Ancient Mesopotamia', in I.M. Diakonoff, ed.; G.M. Sergheyev, transl. *Ancient Mesopotamia*. Walluf bei Wiesbaden: Dr Martin Sandig, pp. 173–203.

——. 1974. *Structure of Society and State in Early Dynastic Sumer*. Monographs on The Ancient Near East 1 (3). Los Angeles: Udena Publications.

——. 1982. 'The structure of Near Eastern society before the middle of the 2nd millenium BC'. *Oikumene* 3: 7–100. Publishing House of the Hungarian Academy of Sciences.

Eckhardt, William .1992. *Civilizations, Empires and Wars: A Quantitative History of War*. Jefferson, NC: McFarland.

Ekholm, K. and J. Friedman. 1982. '"Capital" imperialism and exploitation in ancient world-systems'. *Review* 6 (1): 87–110.

Fagan, Brian. 1999. *Floods, Famines and Emperors: El Nino and the Fate of Civilizations*. New York: Basic Books.

Falkenstein, Adam. 1974. The Sumerian Temple City. Monographs on the Ancient Near East 1 (1). Los Angeles: Udena Publications.

Farber, Howard. 1978. 'A price and wage study for northern Babylonia during the Old Babylonian period'. *Journal of the Economic and Social History of the Orient* 21 (1):1–51.

Feinman, Gary M. and J. Marcus, eds. 1998. *Archaic States*. Santa Fe: School of American Research.

Flannery, Kent V. 1999a. 'The ground plans of archaic states', in G. Feinman and J. Marcus, eds. *Archaic States*. Santa Fe, NM: School of American Research, pp. 15–57.

——. 1999b. 'Process and agency in early state formation'. *Cambridge Archaeological Journal* 9 (1): 3–21.

Frank, Andre Gunder. 1993. 'The Bronze Age world system and its cycles'. *Current Anthropology* 34: 383–413.

Friedman, Jonathan and Michael J. Rowlands. 1977. 'Notes Towards an Epigenetic Model of the Evolution of 'Civilization"', in J. Friedman and M.J. Rowlands, eds. *The Evolution of Social Systems*. London: Duckworth, pp. 201–78.

Galvin, Kathleen F. 1987. 'Forms of finance and forms of production: the evolution of specialized livestock production in the Ancient Near East', in Elizabeth Brumfiel and Timothy K. Earle, eds. *Specialization, Exchange and Complex Societies*. Cambridge: Cambridge University Press, pp. 119–29.

Gibson, McGuire .1972. *The City and Area of Kish*. Miami: Field Research Projects.

Gills, Barry K .1995. 'Capital and power in the processes of world history', in Stephen Sanderson, ed. *Civilizations and World Systems*. Walnut Creek, CA: Altamira Press, pp. 136–62.

Hall, Thomas D. 1991. 'The role of nomads in core/periphery relations', in C. Chase-Dunn and T.D. Hall, eds. *Core/Periphery Relations in Precapitalist Worlds*. Boulder, CO: Westview, pp. 212–39.

——. 2000. 'Sedentary–nomad relations in prehistoric and Ancient Western Asia: questions and speculations'. Paper presented at the Annual Meeting of the International Studies Association, Los Angeles.

Hayden, Brian. 1981. 'Research and development in the Stone Age: technological transition among hunter-gatherers'. *Current Anthropology* 22 (5): 519–48.

Helms, Mary W. 1988. *Ulysses' Sail: An Ethnographic Odyssey of Power, Knowledge, and Geographical Distance*. Princeton: Princeton University Press.

——. 1992. 'Long-distance contacts, elite aspirations, and the age of discovery in cosmological context', in Edward Schortman and Patricia Urban, eds. *Resources, Power, and Interregional Interaction*. New York: Plenum Press, pp. 157–74.

Kardulias, P. Nick. 1999. 'Multiple levels in the Aegean Bronze Age world-system', in P. Nick Kardulias, ed. *World-Systems Theory in Practice*. Lanham, MD: Rowman and Littlefield, pp. 179–202.

Kenoyer, Jonathan M., ed. 1994. *From Sumer to Meluhha: Contributions to the Archaeology of South and West Asia in Memory of George F. Dales, Jr.* Wisconsin Archaeological Reports, vol. 3. Madison, WI: Department of Anthropology, University of Wisconsin.

Kenoyer, Jonathan M. 1998. *Ancient Cities of the Indus Valley Civilization*. Karachi: Oxford University Press.

Kohl, Phillip L. 1978. 'The balance of trade in southwestern Asia in the mid-third millennium BC'. *Current Anthropology* 19 (3): 463–92.

——. 1979. 'The "world economy" in West Asia in the third millennium BC', in M. Toddei, ed. *South Asian Archaeology 1977*. Naples: Instituto Universitario Orientale, pp. 55–85.

——. 1981. 'Materialist approaches in prehistory'. *Annual Review of Anthropology* 10: 89–118.

——. 1985. 'Symbolic cognitive archaeology: a new loss of innocence'. *Dialectical Anthropology* 9:105–17.

——. 1987a. 'The use and abuse of world systems theory: the case of the "pristine" West Asian state'. *Archeological Advances in Method and Theory* 11: 1–35.

——. 1987b. 'The ancient economy, transferable technologies and the Bronze Age world-system: a view from the northeastern frontier of the Ancient Near East', in Michael Rowlands, Mogens Larsen and Kristian Kristiansen, eds. *Centre and Periphery in the Ancient World*. Cambridge: Cambridge University Press, pp. 13–24.

——. 1988. 'State formation: useful concept or idée fixe?', in Christine W. Gaiely and Thomas C. Patterson, eds. *Power Relations and State Formation*. Washington, DC: American Anthropological Association, pp. 27–34.

——. 1992. 'The Transcaucasian "periphery" in the Bronze Age: a preliminary formulation', in Edward Schortman and Patrician Urban, eds. *Resources, Power, and Interregional Interaction*. New York: Plenum Press, pp. 117–37.

Kohl, Philip L. and Rita P. Wright. 1977. 'Stateless cities: the differentiation of societies in the Near Eastern Neolithic'. *Dialectical Anthropology* 2: 271–83.

Lamberg-Karlovsky, C.C. 1975. 'Third millennium modes of exchange and modes of production', in J.A. Sabloff and C.C. Lamberg-Karlovsky, eds. *Ancient Civilization and Trade*. Albuquerque: University of New Mexico Press, pp. 341–68.

Larsen, Mogens Trolle. 1976. *The Old Assyrian City-State and Its Colonies*. Copenhagen: Akadmisk Forlag.

——. 1987. 'Commercial networks in the Ancient Near East', in Michael Rowlands, Mogens Larsen and Kristian Kristiansen, eds. *Centre and Periphery in the Ancient World*. Cambridge: Cambridge University Press, pp. 47–56.

——. 1992. 'Commercial capitalism in a world system of the early second millennium BC'. Paper presented at the International Studies Association, Atlanta, GA.

Lattimore, Owen. 1967. *Inner Asian Frontiers of China*. Boston: Beacon.

Lerro, Bruce. 2000. *From Earth-Spirits to Sky-Gods*. Lanham, MD: Lexington Press.

McNeill, William H. 1963. *The Rise of the West*. Chicago: University of Chicago Press.

McNeill, William H. 1989. *Plagues and Peoples*. New York: Anchor.

Mann, Michael. 1986. *The Sources of Social Power: A History of Power from the Beginning to AD 1760*. Cambridge: Cambridge University Press.

Marcus, Joyce. 1999. 'The peaks and valleys of ancient states', in G. Feinman and J. Marcus, eds. *Archaic States*. Santa Fe, NM: School of American Research, pp. 59–94.

Marfoe, Leon. 1987. 'Cedar forest and silver mountain: social change and the development of long-distance trade in early Near Eastern societies', in M. Rowlands, Mogens Larsen and Kristian Kristiansen, eds. *Centre and Periphery in the Ancient World*. Cambridge: Cambridge University Press, pp. 25–35.

Midlarsky, Manus, I. 2000. 'The rise and decline of ancient civilizations: the case of Egypt'. Paper presented at the meetings of the International Studies Association, Los Angeles, March, 2000.

Modelski, George. 1997. 'Early world cities: extending the census to the fourth millennium'. Prepared for the Annual Meeting of the International Studies Association, Toronto, March, 1997.

——. 1999. 'Ancient world cities, 4000–1000 BC: centre/hinterland in the world system'. *Global Society* 13 (4): 383–92.

——. 2003. *World Cities: –3000 to 2000*. Washington, DC: Faros 2000.

Moore, Andrew M.T. 1982. 'The first farmers in the Levant', in Young, T. Cuyler, Jr, Philip E.L. Smith and Peder Mortensen, eds. *The Hilly Flanks and Beyond: Essays in the Prehistory of Southwestern Asia*. Presented to Robert J. Braidwood. Studies in Ancient Oriental Civilization, no. 36. Chicago: Oriental Institute of the University of Chicago, pp. 91–112.

Morner, N.-A. and W. Karlen, eds. 1984. *Climatic Changes on a Yearly to Millennial Basis*. Boston: D. Reidel.

Neumann, J. and S. Parpola. 1987. 'Climatic change and the eleventh-tenth century eclipse of Assyria and Babylonia'. *Journal of Near Eastern Studies* 46: 161–82.

Nissen, Hans J. 1988. *The Early History of the Ancient Near East, 9000–2000 BC*. Chicago: University of Chicago Press.

Oppenheim, A.L. 1957. 'A bird's-eye view of Mesopotamian economic history', in K. Polanyi, C.M. Arensberg and H.E. Pearson, eds. *Trade and Market in the Early Empires*. Chicago: Regnery, pp. 27–37.

——. 1969. 'Comment on Diakonoff's "Main Features of the Economy. . ."'. *Ecole Practique des Hautes Etudes--Sorbonne, Congres et Colloque* 10 (3): 33–40.

Polanyi, Karl. 1957. 'Marketless trading in Hammarabi's time', in K. Polanyi, C.M. Arensberg and H.E. Pearson, eds. *Trade and Market in the Early Empires*. Chicago: Regnery, pp. 12–26.

Polanyi, Karl, Conrad M. Arensberg and Harry W. Pearson, eds. 1957. *Trade and Market in the Early Empires*. Chicago: Regnery.

Postgate, J.N. 1992. *Early Mesopotamia: Society and Economy at the Dawn of History*. London: Routledge.

Redman, Charles L. 1978. *The Rise of Civilization: from Early Farmers to Urban Society in the Ancient Near East*. San Francisco: W.H. Freeman.

Renfrew, Colin R., ed. 1971. *The Explanation of Culture Change: Models in Prehistory*. Pittsburgh: University of Pittsburgh Press.

Renfrew, Colin R. 1975. 'Trade as action at a distance: questions of integration and communication', in J.A. Sabloff and C.C. Lamborg-Karlovsky, eds. *Ancient Civilization and Trade*. Albuquerque: University of New Mexico Press, pp. 3–59.

——. 1977. 'Alternative models for exchange and spatial distribution', in T.J. Earle and T. Ericson, eds. *Exchange Systems in Prehistory*. New York: Academic Press, pp. 71–90.

——. 1986. 'Introduction: peer polity interaction and socio-political change', in C. Renfrew and John F. Cherry, eds. *Peer Polity Interaction and Socio-political Change*. Cambridge: Cambridge University Press, pp. 1–18.

Renfrew, Colin R. and John F. Cherry, eds. 1986. *Peer Polity Interaction and Socio-political Change*. Cambridge: Cambridge University Press.

Rice, Michael. 1985. *Search for Paradise: an Introduction to the Archaeology of Bahrein and the Arabian Gulf, from Earliest times to the Death of Alexander the Great*. London: Longman.

Rowlands, Michael, Mogens Larsen and Kristian Kristiansen, eds. 1987. *Centre and Periphery in the Ancient World*. Cambridge: Cambridge University Press.

Runnels, Curtis and Tjeerd H. van Andel. 1988. 'Trade and the origins of agriculture in the eastern Mediterranean'. *Journal of Mediterranean Archaeology* 1 (1): 83–109.

Sahlins, Marshall. 1972. *Stone Age Economics*. New York: Aldine.

Schwartz, Glenn. 1988. 'Excavations at Karatut Mevkii and perspectives on the Uruk/Jemdet Nasr expansion'. *Akkadica* 56:1–41.

Seaman, Gary, ed. 1989. *Ecology and Empire: Nomads in the Cultural Evolution of the Old World*. Los Angeles: Ethnographics/USC, Center for Visual Anthropology, University of Southern California.

Schmandt-Besserat, Denise. 1992. *Before Writing: From Counting to Cuneiform*. Austin: University of Texas Press.

Snell, Daniel C. 1982. *Ledgers and Prices: Early Mesopotamian Merchant Accounts*. New Haven: Yale University Press.

Solecki, Rose L. and Ralph S. Solecki. 1982. 'Late Pleistocene/Early Holocene cultural traditions in the Zagros', in Young, T. Cuyler, Jr, Philip E.L. Smith and Peder Mortensen, eds. *The Hilly Flanks and Beyond: Essays in the Prehistory of Southwestern Asia*. Presented to Robert J. Braidwood. Studies in Ancient Oriental Civilization, no. 36. Chicago: Oriental Institute of the University of Chicago, pp. 123–40.

Stein, Gil J. 1999. *Rethinking World-Systems: Diasporas, Colonies and Interaction in Uruk Mesopotamia*. Tucson: University of Arizona Press.

Struve, V.V. 1973 [1933]. 'The Problem of the Genesis, Development and Disintegration of the Slave Societies in the Ancient Orient'. in I.M. Diakonoff, ed.; Inna Levit, transl. *Ancient Mesopotamia*. Walluf bei Wiesbaden: Dr Martin Sandig, pp. 17–69.

Taagepera, Rein. 1978a. 'Size and duration of empires: systematics of size'. *Social Science Research* 7: 108–27.

——. 1978b. 'Size and duration of empires: growth–decline curves, 3000 to 600 BC'. *Social Science Research* 7: 180–96.

Teggart, Frederick. 1939. *Rome and China*. Berkeley: University of California Press.

Thomas, H.L. 1982. 'Archaeological evidence for the migrations of the Indo-Europeans', in E.C. Polome, ed. *The Indo-Europeans in the Fourth and Third Millennia*. Ann Arbor: Karoma.

Thompson, William R. 2000. 'Climate, water, and center–hinterland conflict in the ancient world system'. Paper presented at the meetings of the International Studies Association, Los Angeles, March, 2000.

Torrence, Robin. 1986. *Production and Exchange of Stone Tools: Prehistoric Obsidian in the Aegean*. Cambridge: Cambridge University Press.

Van de Mieroop, Marc. 1999. *The Ancient Mesopotamian City*. New York: Oxford University Press.

Veenhof, Klass R. 1995. 'Kanesh: an Assyrian colony in Anatolia', in Jack M. Sasson

John Baines, Gary Beckman and Karen S. Robinson, eds. *Civilizations of the Ancient Near East*, Vol. 2. New York: Simon and Schuster, pp. 859–71.

Weiss, Harvey and Marie-Agnes Courty. 1993. 'The genesis and collapse of the Akkadian Empire: the accidental refraction of historical law', in Mario Liverani, ed. *Akkad: the First World Empire*. Padua: Sargon, pp. 131–55.

Weiss, Harvey, M.-A Courty, W. Wetterstron, F. Guichard, L. Senior and A. Curnow. 1993. 'The genesis and collapse of third millenium North Mesopotamian civilization'. *Science* 261: 995–1004.

Wilkinson, David. 1987. 'Central civilization'. *Comparative Civilizations Review* 17 (Fall): 31–59.

——. 1991. 'Cores, peripheries and civilizations', in C. Chase-Dunn and T.D. Hall, eds. *Core/Periphery Relations in Precapitalist Worlds*. Boulder, CO: Westview, pp. 113–66.

——. 1992. 'Cities, civilizations and oikumenes'. *Comparative Civilizations Review* 21 (Fall): 51–87 and Spring 1993: 41–72.

——. 2000. 'Problems in power configuration sequences: the southwest Asian macrosystems to 1500 BC'. Presented at the meeting of the International Studies Association, Los Angeles, February, 2000.

Wright, Henry T. 1986. 'The evolution of civilization', in David J. Meltzer, ed. *American Archaeology, Past and Future: A Celebration of the Society for American Archaeology, 1935–1985*. Washington, DC: Smithsonian Institutional Press, pp. 323–65.

——. 1998. 'Uruk states in southwestern Iran', in Gary Feinman and Joyce Marcus, eds. *Archaic States*. Santa Fe, NM: School of American Research, pp. 173–97.

Yoffee, Norman. 1991. 'The collapse of Ancient Mesopotamian states and civilization', in Norman Yoffee and George Cowgill, eds. *The Collapse of Ancient States and Civilizations*. Tucson: University of Arizona Press, pp. 44–68.

Young, T. Cuyler, Jr, Philip E.L. Smith and Peder Mortensen, eds. 1982. *The Hilly Flanks and Beyond: Essays in the Prehistory of Southwestern Asia*. Presented to Robert J. Braidwood. Studies in Ancient Oriental Civilization, no. 36. Chicago: Oriental Institute of the University of Chicago.

Zaccagnini, Carlo. 1987. 'Aspects of ceremonial exchange in the Near East during the late second millennium BC', in Michael Rowlands, Mogens Larsen and Kristian Kristiansen, eds. *Centre and Periphery in the Ancient World*. Cambridge: Cambridge University Press, pp. 57–65.

Zagarell, Allen. 1986. 'Trade, women, class and society in Ancient Western Asia'. *Current Anthropology* 27: 5: 415–30.

9 Early Iron Age economic expansion and contraction revisited

Andre Gunder Frank and William R. Thompson

We currently live in a planetary-wide world system. For many, this is something of a novelty. People of this persuasion view globalization as a wholly contemporary process that began only yesterday and seems overwhelming in its potential to disturb long-settled attitudes and expectations. For others, though, globalization is something less than novel. Under way for thousands of years, the contemporary manifestations of a very old process may contain novelty in pace and scope – but the basic substance of growing interdependence is relatively familiar.

Yet, even if one takes the less-than-novel stance on globalization, there are still many questions about the historical pattern of expanding interdependence. If true globalization required integrating the Americas with the Old World (to qualify as truly global), we can probably date the onset of this phase of interdependence somewhere between the Vikings, Christopher Columbus and the Spanish Manilla galleons. But what about the Old World of Afro-Eurasia which, for most of the time people have been around and for most of the people, was essentially coterminous with the known world? When did it become globalized or Afro-Eurasianized?[1] Here again opinions differ. Some might point to the nineteenth-century incorporation of China as the last piece in the mosaic, while others argue that China has merely been moving back towards the centre of the world system, after a brief stint – from a long-run view - of marginalization.

Another point of view is to stress the existence and expansion of an ancient world system dating back to at least 3500 BCE, if not before, that spread outwards from south-west Asia and ultimately encompassed the entire Old World. But when and at what rate of change did this occur? And how do we know it? The present analysis is the second part of a two-part re-examination of Andre Gunder Frank's 1993 interpretation of economic cycles in the ancient world system. The first part (Frank and Thompson 2005) focused exclusively on the Bronze Age to 1200 BCE. Picking up where that study left off, this paper will focus on the early Iron Age from 1200 BCE to 200 CE. The central questions continue to revolve around whether systematic evidence is available to support an Afro-Eurasian economic expansion/contraction periodization and, if so, how this might speak to the question of early Afro-Eurasian interdependence and world system status. After first summarizing the results pertaining to the Bronze Age, we will outline the assertions advanced previously about early Iron Age economic cycles and proceed to a systematic test of those assertions based on historical and archaeological literature references to the comings and goings of prosperity and depression.

The Bronze Age findings

Frank's (1993) arguments and periodization of the emergence of a singular world system were received with mixed support at the time of their publication. A sample of the response was published simultaneously so that there was little doubt about the range of views that were elicited by the claim that an initially south-west Asian-centred world system had emerged by the Bronze Age.[2] Moreover, it was possible to delineate cycles of economic expansion and contraction that were thought to hold across Afro-Eurasia and, because of their wide scale, to demonstrate the early existence of an ancient world system.

The objections to this type of work, based on the responses that were published, can be reduced to the following:

1 Little theoretical explication and justification was provided for the early emergence of an Afro-Eurasian system or the expectation that widespread synchronization in economic fluctuations occurred.
2 Geographical and transportation liabilities, among other factors, made it unlikely
3 that all actors in the system were in direct and sustained contact. Multiple systems are, therefore, more likely to have existed.
4 The data put forward in support of the economic fluctuation periodization were also used to generate the periodization. Other data on cities, warfare and migrations that might be related to economic growth as causes and effects were advanced inappropriately as straightforward indices of A and B phases.

It is not clear, however, that one needs an elaborate theory to assert that the origins of the present world system can be traced to south-western Asia in third or fourth millennium BCE. It is not as if world history between 4000 BCE and 2000 CE is entirely unknown. Various arguments have been put forward for the more or less continuous expansion of a world system from Bronze Age days. Rather than be forced to commit to a detailed exposition of whether and how some 6,000 years of history can be bridged, it does not seem unreasonable to explore hypotheses about the origins of the current system. Examining synchronization patterns is one way of looking at the claim of systemic continuity across time.

Ultimately, we will need theory to explain how the Afro-Eurasian system expanded. But we also need some sense of the rate and geographical pattern of expansion. This is the type of empirical analysis that can be undertaken prior to, or in conjunction with, developing a comprehensive explanation of why it happened the way it did. While it is admittedly difficult to explain phenomena in the absence of theory, it is also difficult to theorize in the absence of empirical information about the phenomena.

It is no more clear that all actors in a system need to be in direct and sustained contact to qualify as a system. If this were the case, a large number of actors in the contemporary system might be disqualified as members of the current world system. If Paraguay and Bangladesh have little interaction, are they to be considered outside the system that currently exists? Again, looking at synchronization patterns is one way to probe for the existence of multiple systems – as opposed to assuming that they must have existed given the obstacles to ancient interactions.

No one claims that the information advanced in support of the 1993 assertions were sufficient to the task.[3] At the same time, one must start somewhere. Theoretical generalizations are unlikely to generate periodizations of economic fluctuations. Some attention to empirical trends is inevitable. The real questions concern how many sources are needed and whether conceivably related information should be pressed into service simultaneously. There is no absolutely right answer to these questions. Ideally, we might utilize as many sources on economic growth fluctuations as are available. More realistically, however, the more appropriate question is whether information exists to cover the territory and time periods desired – and just how readily accessible this information is. Finite time and resource pressures inevitably lead to some compromise. Yet it is certainly possible to expand the number and variety of sources utilized in the 1993 examination. It is also desirable to avoid mixing in alternative types of information (such as urban expansion, wars and migrations) that might have something to do with economic growth and decline. That is, as long as there is sufficient historical literature information to generate a schedule of periods of economic expansion and contraction, the best practice is to maintain as much independence as possible between and among the various different indicators of turmoil and prosperity. That way, subsequent analyses can examine the relationships, if any, among economic growth, war, migrations and urban expansion.[4] Apparently, it was possible during the early Iron Age for intense conflict and economic growth to coexist – one example is the Chinese Warring States period.[5] Therefore, we would be wrong to assume that turmoil must always lead to economic decline or, for that matter, that economic growth must lead to peace, or vice versa.

In this spirit, we proceeded to re-examine the question of whether a Bronze Age world system was characterized by widespread and synchronized cycles of economic prosperity and depression. We relied exclusively on information culled from the historical and archaeological sources that chose to discuss economic fluctuations.[6] Based on this information, the goal was to code each 100-year segment for some 15 Afro-Eurasian regions between 4000 BCE and 1000 BCE as characterized generally by economic expansion or contraction.

We found general contraction phases for the periods of 4000–3800, 3200 to an unclear date, 2300–2050, 1750/1700–1600 and 1250–1000. Expansion phases included 3800–3200, 2700–2300, 2050 to various dates in different parts of the system and 1600–1250. This schedule did not conform perfectly to the earlier Frank dating scheme. The earlier outline only began in the third millennium, so we can say there was no disagreement about the fourth millennium. The same cannot be said about the third millennium. Frank's (1993) A and B phases began with 3000–2800 as expansionary whereas 2700–26/2500 was categorized as contracting. The updated version places 3000–2800 within a contraction phase beginning in 3200. Frank's earlier first contraction phase (2700–26/2500) and second expansion phase (2600–2400) both fit within the new 2700–2300 expansionary period.

In contrast, the treatment of the end of the third millennium is less subject to dispute. The 1993 schedule had a contracting phase between 24/2300 and 2000. The 2004 dating is 2300–2050. This high degree of overlap continues into the second millennium. The 1993 schedule had 2000–1800/1750 and 1600–1500–1200 as A phases and 1800–1750–1600 and 1200–1000 as B phases. The 2004 schedule assigns expansionary phases to the periods 2050–mixed dates (depending on region) and 1600–1250. Phases of contraction were assigned to the 1750/1700–1600 and 1250–1000 phases. Table 9.1 provides a summary of the 1993 and 2004 periodizations.

Nonetheless, these expansion and contraction phases were not always found to be Afro-Eurasian wide. The Bronze Age world system began as a fourth-millennium, Mesopotamian-centric network predicated on Sumerian attempts to acquire raw materials in and through Anatolia, Iran and Egypt. After the collapse or retrenchment of this first system, a third-millennium

Table 9.1 Frank (1993) versus Frank and Thompson (2005) on south-west Asian Bronze Age economic fluctuations

	Frank (1993)	*Frank and Thompson (2004)*
Contraction		4000?–3800
Expansion		3800–3200
Contraction		3200–?
Expansion	3000–2800	
Contraction	2700–26/2500	
Expansion	2600–2400	2700–2300
Contraction	24/2300–2000	2300–2050
Expansion	2000–1800/1750	2050–mixed
Contraction	1800/1750–1600–1500	1750–1700/1600
Expansion	1600/1500–1200	1600–1250
Contraction	1200–1000	1250–1000 (at least)

Source: Frank and Thompson (2005).

structure expanded to encompass Indus and Egyptian nodes, while retaining a relatively strong Mesopotamian node. Indus became the major intermediary between central Asia and south-western Asia via the Gulf and Dilmun. Anatolian Troy served as a conduit into central Europe and the Steppes. In the second millennium, the network structure shifted further west to focus on Egypt, the eastern Mediterranean, the Syro-Levantine trading cities and Mycenaean Greece. Indus faded away with the decline of the Harappan cities, while links to the western Mediterranean (Italy), central Europe and Nubia to the south of Egypt became stronger.

Economic synchronization appears to have been most evident in the areas most proximate to the shifting cores. The fourth millennium was Mesopotamian centred. The third millennium had a wider focus linking Indus to Mesopotamia, whereas the second millennium was focused primarily on the eastern Mediterranean littoral. Clearly, the Bronze Age system cannot be equated with the fullest extent of Afro-Eurasia at the outset. Rather, it moved unevenly, slowly and in fits and starts towards a more maximal territorial definition. Still, the major contractions that punctuated the structural shifts (coming at the end of the fourth, third and second millennia, as well as the less widely felt mid-third and mid-second millennia contractions) did tend to be increasingly manifested in most of the 15 Afro-Eurasian zones. The 2200–2100 BCE turmoil was registered in 11 out of 15 of the regions. The *c.* 1200 BCE turmoil was manifested nearly everywhere in some fashion. We read these propensities as evidence that the system was expanding in geographical scope and developing greater interconnectivity and vulnerability, at least to the end of the Bronze Age around 1200 BCE.[7]

What happened in the early Iron Age? Our earlier analysis stopped short of examining the first millennium BCE given time and resource limitations. We are now in a position to continue the examination through the second century in the first millennium CE. In general, our findings are not dissimilar to those pertaining to the Bronze Age. The empirical support for the 1993 periodization is mixed at best and needs a fair amount of revision. System-wide changes remain intermittent and much of the action continues to be western focused, as opposed to pan-Afro-Eurasian, until near the very end of the first millennium BCE.

Re-examining the Frank (1993) early Iron Age argument

Table 9.2 summarizes the Frank economic periodization of the early Iron Age world system. The left-hand column provides the dating while the right-hand column attempts to suggest briefly the reasons given in 1993 for why one period or another was thought to be expanding or contracting. The 1200–1000 BCE system-wide contraction was followed by a short period of economic expansion (1000–800 BCE) focused on Phoenician, Assyrian and possibly Chinese growth. Increased competition led to imperial collapse and commercial conflict in the Mediterranean up to the mid-point of the first millennium. A

Table 9.2 Frank's (1993) interpretation of the early Iron Age

A/B	*Timing*	*Indicators of expansion or contraction*
A	1000–800 BCE	Revitalization of Arabian spice route; Phoenician expansion in Mediterranean and Atlantic Europe; north–south exchange initiated in central Europe; Assyrian growth; possible urban revival in India; some Chinese integration under western Zhou
B	800–550 BCE	Assyrian collapse; increased competition in Mediterranean, western Asia and China; displacement of Phoenician trade in Aegean
A	600/500–450/400 BCE	Greek economic development; rise of Achaemenid empire and stabilization of western Asia; shift of world economy's centre of gravity from Syria/Levant to central Eurasia; expansion of Syrian caravan cities as terminus of Silk Road/Incense Road; reintegration of central Europe to Mediterranean
B	450–350 BCE	Economic crisis in Greece and Graeco-Persian relations; general economic contraction; Celtic attacks; revolts in the Persian Empire; Warring States period in China
A	350–250/200 BCE	Alexandrian expansion in western Asia; Mauryan expansion in India, Qin consolidation in China; increased western–Indian–Chinese trade
B	250/200–100/50 BCE	Egyptian and Greek economic decline but possibly localized phenomena given Roman and Chinese expansion
A	200/100 BCE–200 CE	Simultaneous rise of Han China, Kushan India, Parthian Iran, Axium in east Africa and Roman Empire

second A phase (600/500–450/400 BCE) was ushered in by Greek and Persian growth, only to be rent asunder by Graeco-Persian conflict, Celtic migrations in Europe and warring states in China. A third A phase (350–250/200 BCE) was brought about by Macedonian/Seleucid, Mauryan and Qin consolidations in the major urbanized portions of Eurasia. This third first-millennium A phase may have been interrupted by an equally short B phase (250/200–200/50 BCE) that was less than system-wide in scope. The first millennium BCE then ended in a strong upswing (200/100 BCE–200 CE) that encompassed successful empire building from China to the Mediterranean.

The basic question here is whether this interpretation is supported by the examination of additional sources that focus explicitly on discussions of the presence or absence of economic prosperity and depression? Table 9.3 focuses on 12 Afro-Eurasian regions over some 1,400 years, at 50-year intervals.[8] This structure (12 regions by 28 half-century intervals) creates 336 cells to code. Utilizing over 100 sources allowed all but 44 cells (about 13%) to be coded as contracting (economic depression/decline), expanding (economic growth and prosperity) or mixed.[9] The last category encompasses situations in which different parts of the region appear to have experienced different economic fortunes, or situations in which the 50-year periods were some combination of expansion and contraction, without either activity dominating for most of the 50-year interval. With about 87 per cent of the cells coded, 128 periods of contraction (38.1%) and 130 periods of expansion (38.7%) were discovered. The mixed category accounted for another 34 cells (10.1%).

The parts of Table 9.3 that are easiest to read are found at the top and the bottom. The first three centuries (1200–900 BCE) are fairly uniform in being designated as times of economic contraction. Egypt was a bit slower to succumb than the other regions at the outset of the *c.* 1200 Mediterranean collapse associated with the chaotic conditions associated with the Sea Peoples. The Phoenician Levantine cites were the first to emerge from this contraction phase. Several regions remained in contraction beyond the first 300 years of the early Iron Age: Greece to 850, Egypt to around 700, Iran possibly as late as 550 and the rise of the Achaeminids, Anatolia to 750 and India to about 600 BCE. Some relatively general propensity towards economic expansion occurred between about 750 and 550/500.

There was considerable divergence after the mid-millennium mark. Italy, Egypt, Palestine and Mesopotamia experienced mainly economic contraction to around 350/300 BCE. European (excluding Greece and Italy) contraction, for the most part, persisted to about 50 BCE. Greece remained primarily expansive through the Alexandrian attack on south-western Asia in the late fourth century and then experienced little growth thereafter. A number of Syro-Levantine cities appear to have retained some levels of prosperity, thanks to their intermediate position in east–west trade, to about 150 BCE. Carthage remained predominately expansive until its destruction at the hands of the Romans shortly after 150. India and China appear to have retained their tendencies towards economic growth several centuries into the first millennium CE.[10]

As recorded at the bottom of Table 9.3, there was a fairly strong and general shift back to economic expansion towards the very end of the first millennium BCE. Part of this movement is attributable to the Pax Romana established by the Roman Empire in what is referred to as the Augustan Age. Still, the new pan-Mediterranean prosperity largely bypassed Greece, Palestine (characterized by a series of revolts) and parts of Europe.[11] Whether or to what extent this same prosperity characterized Mesopotamia and Parthian Iran remains unclear after the transition to the first millennium CE. Indian and Chinese prosperity, as indicated previously, had begun much earlier and continued to at least 200 CE.

How might we translate this heterogeneous outcome into a schedule of A and B phases? The contraction phase that was initiated by the Mediterranean collapse around 1200 clearly persisted to about 850/750. An uneven period of expansion followed to about 550/500. The period of time between the Persian attack on Greece and Alexander's return of the favour does not lend itself readily to a singular generalization, although there is certainly

Table 9.3 Historical and archaeological evidence for economic expansion and contraction in the first millennium BCE early Iron Age

BCE	*Greece*	*Italy*	*Syria/Levant*	*Egypt*	*Palestine*
1200–1150	C	C	C	M	C
1150–1100	C	C	C	C	C
1100–1050	C	C	C	C	C
1050–1000	C	C	C-	C	C
1000–950	C	C	M	C	C
950–900	C	C		M	E?
900–850	C	M	E	C?	E?
850–800	E	E	E	C?	C
800–750	C	E	E	C?	E
750–700	E	E	E	C?	C
700–650	E	E	C	E	E?
650–600	E	E	E	E	E
600–550	E	E?	E	E	E?
550–500	E	C?	E	E	C
500–450	E	C	E	C	C
450–400	E	C	E	C	C
400–350	M	C	E	M	C
350–300	E	E	E	C?	C
300–250	C	C	E?	M?	E
250–200	C	C	E?	C	E
200–150	C	M	E?	C	E
150–100	M	M	C	C	C
100–50	C	M	M	C	C
50–0	C	E	M	M	M
0–50 CE	C	E	M	E	C?
50–100 CE	C	E	E	E	C
100–150 CE	C	E	E	E	C
150–200 CE	C	M	E	E	

more contraction than anything else. The post-Alexanderian Hellenistic era (roughly 300–150) was more expansive in Asia than in several European zones, which tended to continue contracting to the end or almost the end of the millennium. Yet, despite exceptions noted previously, the 50 BCE–200 CE period essentially resembled an A phase for a respectable portion of Afro-Eurasia.

Table 9.4 summarizes this new interpretation and juxtaposes it next to the Frank (1993) schedule. Considerable disagreement is manifested. No support for Frank's (1993) first A phase (1000–800) is found in the revised

Mesopotamia	*Iran*	*Anatolia*	*Other Europe*	*Carthage/ Africa*	*India*	*China*
C	C	C	C		C	
C	E?	C	C		C	
C	C	C	C		C	
C	C	C	C		C	
C	C	C	C		C	E
M	C	C	C		C	E
E	C	C	M?		C	
C	C	C	M?		C	
C		C	M?		C	C
E		E	E	E	C	C
M	C		E	E	C	
E	C	E	E	E	C	
M		E	E	E	E	
M	E	E	M	E	E	
C	E	C	M	E	E	
C		C	C	E	E	
C		E	C	E	E	E
C		E	C	C	E	E
E		M	C	E	E	E
E		E	C	E	E	E
E	M?		C	E	E	E
E	M?	M?	C	C	E	E
E	E?	C	M?	C	E	E
E	E?	E	E	M	E	E
		E	E	E	E	E
		E	M	E	E	E
		E	M	E	E	E
		E	M	E	E	E

schedule. Contraction persisted in most areas through the ninth century BCE. Similarly, Frank's next phase, an 800–550 B phase, is viewed as an A phase in the revised schedule. It should be noted that this revised A phase does overlap to some extent with Frank's (1993) 600/500–450/400 A phase. Moreover, there is more convergence on Frank's (1993) 450–350 B phase. Yet the revised schedule makes a distinction between what is essentially Europe and Asia after 300 BCE. Asian economic growth was noticeable after 300 whereas European growth was not. Only when we come to the end of the first millennium BCE is convergence recorded again thanks in part to Roman–Qin/Han

Table 9.4 A comparison of the 1993 and 2004 Early Iron Age economic periodicities

Phases	*Frank (1993) schedule*	*Revised schedule (2004)*
Contraction	1200–1000	1200–*c*.750
Expansion	1000–800	
Contraction	800–550	
Expansion	600/500–450/400	750–550/500
Contraction	450–350	500–300/50 (non-Asian Hellenistic areas including Greece to 50 BCE
Expansion	350–250/200	300–150 (Asian Hellenistic areas, India and China)
Contraction	250/200–100/50	
Expansion	200/100 BCE–200 CE	50 BCE–200 CE

– and imperial points in between – unification and pacification efforts. Even so, the revised ending A phase for the early Iron Age is much shorter than the 1993 interpretation.

How might one account for this brief and temporary divergence from what seems to be increasing interdependence? There is, of course, no guarantee that growing interdependence will prove to be a linear process. Steps forward, backwards and sideways seem to describe the path of Afro-Eurasian interdependence. Nor does some tendency towards synchronization, albeit highly uneven, necessarily connote interdependence. There is no moderate to strong trade linkage of China–India–the Mediterranean, after all, until towards the last centuries of the first millennium BCE when some semblance of the Silk Routes began to take shape across Eurasia and around India by sea. Thus, we should be slow to embrace the idea of an early and comprehensive, pan-Eurasian interconnectivity predicated on trade.

Instead, the historical pattern of Afro-Eurasian linkages is more a matter of early eastern probes from the west and, much later, western probes from the east.[12] South-west Asia reached to Afghanistan as long ago as 9–10,000 years through down-the-line trade in obsidian used as tools. Farmers from south-west Asia moved north into Europe. Several thousand years later, less sedentary groups from the central Europe/Russia/Black Sea region moved east towards China and later south into Iran and India. There were, no doubt, all sorts of indirect interactions between the east and west with the people that became the central Eurasian nomads as the principal agents. But south-west Asian–Indian interactions only became serious in the third millennium BCE and broke down in the second millennium BCE only to re-emerge in the first millennium. Chinese–Indian interactions appear to have become significant only in the second half of the first millennium BCE. Similarly, south-west Asian/Mediterranean interactions with China only began to attain significant levels in the last quarter of the first millennium BCE. We should be wary, therefore, of having very high and widespread interdependency expectations too early.

A second caveat involves a necessary qualification to the expectation that interdependence necessarily entails synchronization of economic fortunes. The first millennium BCE witnessed a serial commercial and colonial competition among Phoenicians, Etruscans, Greeks, Carthaginians and Romans. It was unlikely that all could prosper simultaneously and, even if that had been possible, they did not choose to develop absolute gains. Relative gains were more attractive. Thus, Phoenicians might do well at Greek expense. Or, alternatively, the Carthaginians were most likely to emerge as strong competitors only when the Phoenicians were under siege by Assyrians. Some dis-synchronization, therefore, is also paradoxical evidence of interdependence as long as some competitors benefit at the expense of others.[13]

These generalizations do not preclude intermittent pulsations of heightened interdependency throughout the first millennium BCE. For instance, early Phoenician–Israeli commercial interactions with India are indicated around the beginning of the first millennium BCE. Central Eurasian nomadic groups, most notably the Scythians in the west, moved against China and south-west Asia (their traces are found as far west as Egypt) in the 700s, and subsequently eastern Europe.[14] Persian (mid-500s) and Hellenistic (late 300s) reorganizations of south-west and parts of central Asia had reverberations in both India and China. In India, these reorganizations may have encouraged parallel reconcentrations of military–political power. They also led to restimulations of Indo-Hellenistic commercial interactions. In China, central Asian nomads fleeing Persian and later Alexandrian harassment moved east and intensified the nature of the 'barbarian' threat along the sedentary–nomadic frontier of China. Thus, the increased commercial interconnections among Rome, India and China after the second century BCE and throughout the second century CE on land and sea were not without precedent. They had simply occurred earlier in more fragmented and piecemeal ways.

As a consequence, we can say without qualification that Afro-Eurasia had become more interdependent in the first millennium BCE than it had been in earlier millennia if the emphasis is placed on a combination of the extent of the geographical scope encompassed by interdependency pulsations and the intensity or value of the flow of commodities exchanged.[15] The nature of the interdependency, however, still falls considerably short of persistent and high levels of integration throughout all Afro-Eurasia. The interconnections were still being formed. The interconnectivity also remained subject to breakdown as in the era that followed the second century CE and the collapse of imperial structures from the Mediterranean to the Pacific. Yet, even then, we should not overlook signs of a certain kind of interdependency related to military–political turmoil originating in the east (primarily Chinese–Xiongnu conflict) showing up in the south (India) and west (Rome). But that is primarily a different millennium and a different story.

If economic interdependency can only claim a piece of the explanation for the uneven propensities towards shared economic fluctuations across Afro-Eurasia in the first millennium, climate change and technological diffusion should also be given some credit as additional, likely culprits. The climate change question must be deferred to another paper on account of the limited state of our knowledge about Afro-Eurasian weather patterns of this time period. Suffice it to say that, at some point, we will probably find an important explanatory role for global climate change that influenced behaviour throughout the Old World – although not necessarily in exactly the same way everywhere.[16]

Technological diffusion, on the other hand, must also be given some credit for periods of economic expansion in the first millennium BCE. Although the labels of 'Bronze' and 'Iron' Ages no doubt exaggerate the extent to which life in these periods was influenced by the use of successively harder metals for tools and weapons, the return to economic growth in the Mediterranean area and enhanced Indian and Chinese agrarian productivity appear to be traceable in part to the lagged spread of iron and more effective ploughs from west to east across Eurasia.[17] Improved agricultural yields sustained more people, larger cities and greater volumes of trade.

By the end of the first millennium BCE, some decrease in turmoil as a result of political reorganization and strengthened imperial controls across Eurasia also facilitated growth. Thus, there were common denominators underlying phases of economic expansion other than economic interdependency. Conflict reverberations have been mentioned above (Assyrians suppressing Phoenician activities and therefore encouraging Carthaginian expansion, or central Asians fleeing the coercive expansion efforts of Persians, Greeks or Chinese). These reverberations were often unintended consequences of attempts to concentrate political and military power.[18] Assyrian, Achaeminid, Hellenistic (Macedonian and Seleucid), Roman, Mauryan, Parthian and Han imperial successes must also be given their due as agents of expanded interdependency. By pushing their frontiers in multiple directions, more people were forcibly brought into contact with one another for long periods of time. At the heights of imperial control, conditions within and between empires were also optimal for commercial expansion. Demand from imperial cities grew. Supply expanded as well in periods in which transaction costs (larger ships, better roads and fewer attacks on caravans and convoys) tended to be reduced.

Conclusion

There is no need to insist on complete unity at the outset in order to make a case for the early emergence and basic continuity of a world system that dates back to at least the fourth millennium BCE. Initially, it stretched from Afghanistan to Egypt with a strong focus on Mesopotamian south-west Asia. Gradually, it incorporated increasingly stronger links to Europe, more of north and north-eastern Africa and India. While the intensity of these linkages was subject to some flux – thanks mainly to bouts of economic and political turmoil – Afro-Eurasian linkages continued to expand, not unlike uneven attempts to blow up a balloon. A strong breath forces air into the balloon and its fundamental shape begins to appear. A weak grasp of the balloon airway allows some air to escape and the balloon partially collapses even though it still retains some of its earlier shape.[19] The next breath into the balloon may make a bigger balloon than the first breath did – or it may not. If one starts with a very large balloon, a number of efforts will be required to inflate it fully, and there is no reason to anticipate that each successive breath will yield a linear result.

Some evidence of economic periodicity was found in the Bronze Age, just as some evidence exists for the early Iron Age. In neither case does the evidence suggest early and uniform pan-Afro-Eurasian fluctuations in prosperity and depression. Areas closer to the most active economic zones were more likely to be affected by central economic fortunes than areas that were less proximate. Distance did matter. No doubt, there were multiple world systems in the Bronze and early Iron Age within Afro-Eurasia. By the end of the first millennium BCE, however, the boundaries of the more prominent systems had become increasingly blurred by expanded economic transactions and increased knowledge about the existence of other parts of the known world. The urbanized rim that almost encircled central Asia, stretching from the Mediterranean to China, was beginning to become more closely integrated than had ever been imagined as conceivable before. Unusually widespread economic prosperity for a time was one outcome of this achievement. With the advantage of hindsight, we know that Afro-Eurasia would not remain on an increasingly integrated trajectory after the second century CE without substantial deviation. But that is the basic globalization pattern – uneven advances and regressions fuelled and constrained by climate change, technological change, trade, conflict, disease and political–military concentration and deconcentrations. The point is that globalization is a very old pattern that began quite some time ago and continues today.[20]

Notes

1 The underlying assumption here is that globalization essentially means growing interdependence (and increased awareness of that condition). Hence, what is 'global' at any given time depends on the prevailing information base. For a long period of time, the Americas were *terra incognita* – at least to the people who remained in Afro-Eurasia, as opposed to those who crossed over the Bering Strait. Therefore, it does not seem inappropriate to equate the process of globalization with Afro-Eurasianization, at least prior to the time when Europeans stumbled on the Americas and Australia. Whether this interdependency process should be termed 'globalization' seems more of a semantic question than one of substance.

2 An emphasis on the emergence of an initially south-west Asian-centric has become more common since the early 1990s. Compare, among others, Frank and

Gills (1993), Chase-Dunn and Hall (1997), Modelski (2000), Wilkinson (2000) and McNeill and McNeill (2003).

3 The sources cited for the early Iron Age (if the 1200–1000 BCE B phase is included) encompass Sherratt (n.d.), Teggart (1939), Rostovtzeff (1941), Childe (1942), Jaspers (1949, 1955, 1957), Ghirshman (1954), Wang (1958) McNeill (1963, 1976), Coedes (1968), Gernet (1982), Kristiansen (1982, 1987, 1993), Franck and Brownstone (1986), Liverani (1987), Wilkinson (1987, 1992a, 1992b), Edens and Bawden (1988), Dietler (1989), Francis (1989, 1991), Glover (1991), James *et al.* (1991), Raman (1991), Sherratt and Sherratt (1991, 1993), Bosworth (1992), Chernykh (1992), Edens (1992), Frank (1992), Gills and Frank (1992) and Melko and Wilkinson (1992).

4 Still, there is nothing wrong with mixing indicators if that is what is available. The challenge is to go beyond the need to rely on information that is already readily available.

5 One argument is that the demands of warfare encouraged elites to maximize the exploitation of their land holdings.

6 Anyone familiar with the relevant literature will appreciate that discussions of ancient economic history are infrequent and only rarely accompanied by evidence. The nature of such a search requires wading through a considerable amount of political history to find a few sparse comments about the state of the economy. But, presumably, this imbalance of coverage mirrors the very limited information supplied in ancient original sources. At the same time, it is rarely clear precisely upon what sort of information an author bases his/her judgement that a given era was prosperous or depressed. All sorts of indicators – grave objects, the pace of urbanization, building, intense conflict, inscriptions, population growth, trade flows – are utilized (and probably in some not transparent mix). Unless there is disagreement in the literature, our culling activities are forced to take the author's assessments at face value. However, an irony in this type of analysis is that, when authors are highly self-conscious about the multiple interpretations possible from examining various indicators, the more difficult it is to arrive at a summary evaluation. An excellent case in point is Macmullen's (1988: 1–15) discussion of indicators on Roman economic decline. Our reliance on less substantiated or self-conscious evaluations suggests caution in viewing the culled evidence as carved in stone. Rather, it is merely a first cut (or should we say second cut) at attempting to encompass a very large and heterogeneous area and still arrive at impressions about the timing of fluctuations in economic fortunes.

7 The major outstanding question is the extent to which widespread problems were due to global climate shifts. To the extent that it can be demonstrated that they were, the argument for apparent interconnectivity in terms of interactions (as opposed to common fate) will have been lessened.

8 Murphy's law predicts that a more specific 50-year window (as opposed to the 100-year window used for the Bronze Age) will continue to have problems of fit because economic conditions are unlikely to move in accordance with annual calendars. But a 50-year window is preferable to a 100-year window in terms of specificity. Decadal coding might be possible for shorter time periods (that is, less than the 1,400 years examined here) and certain zones such as Rome, but such specificity would be more difficult to generate than one might think. Attempting to code large zones (e.g. India, China and so forth) is no more valid than it was in the Bronze Age. Very good arguments can be made for improving the geographical specificity as well as the temporal dimension. The problem is that the more specific information is often simply not available. In addition, some changes were made in the identities of the coded zones. The Bronze Age analysis included zones for the Gulf, Indus, Aegean/eastern Mediterranean, western

Mediterranean, central Europe, central Asia and the Steppe. In the early Iron Age analysis, the Gulf (see, for instance, Potts 1990; Ray 1994; Schippmann 2001), central Asia and the Steppe have been dropped because of the lack of much useful economic information for the first millennium BCE. Indus has been broadened to become India. The Aegean/eastern Mediterranean is equated with either Greece or Anatolia as most appropriate. The western Mediterranean and central Europe categories are merged to form an 'other Europe' category either because most of the information found did not discriminate between eastern and western Europe or because the information that was forthcoming on the two zones at the same time did not differ all that much. Finally, a case might be made for adding south-east Asia to the early Iron Age survey in terms of Indian contacts by mid-millennium and Chinese contacts towards the end of the first millennium. As in a number of the other areas, however, the quantity of information is low. South-east Asia's involvement in Afro-Eurasia, in any event, is probably greater in the first millennium CE and thereafter than in the first millennium BCE.

9 One hundred and ten sources yielded useful information (compared with 95 used for the Bronze Age). In both the Bronze and the early Iron Age cases, quite a few sources were examined that yielded no useful information on our prosperity/depression question. One of the ironies of the early Iron Age is that there are a number of 'black holes' concerning what happened in given areas. In a number of zones, archaeologists have apparently preferred to dig deeper than the first millennium BCE or not at all. A number of areas are also short on surviving written documents.

10 It seems most unlikely that China and India experienced unchecked economic growth for such long periods of time. The codings merely reflect what the sources suggest perhaps too loosely.

11 On the other hand, it did extend to the Gulf and Indian Ocean areas (see Ray 1994, 2003).

12 Of course, one might start even earlier with northern migrations from east Africa into south-west Asia. See, for instance, Clark (1997).

13 Therefore, some level of behavioural synchronization may be necessary to posit interdependency but it is never sufficient. Once synchronization is observed, the next question is whether it can be explained through interaction or is merely spurious. Similarly, then, dis-sychronization, if accompanied or brought about by interaction, can count towards interdependency as well.

14 Thereby initiating a pattern that would continue to be significant through the first half of the second millennium CE.

15 See Thompson (2004) for more discussion of the nature of this interdependency.

16 Fagan (1999, 2004), Chew (2001) and Thompson (2003) support this expectation. We need better data for more parts of Afro-Eurasia, though, before we can estimate how significant the climate factor might have been.

17 Iron tools were increasingly employed in the west after the 'Sea Peoples' interruption of normal activities, after the sixth century BCE in India and after the fourth century BCE in China.

18 The unintentional dimension should not be stressed too much. Many of these imperial efforts explicitly sought to conquer their known worlds. Increased resistance, geographical barriers and logistical constraints ensured that there were definite limits to early Iron Age expansion. At the same time, the increased nomadization of central Eurasia – a process that had begun in the second millennium BCE – must also be counted as a contributing factor to first millennium interdependencies across Eurasia.

19 A better analogy is probably an air mattress which has a more complex struc-

ture. Consequently, parts of the mattress are easier to fill with air than some other areas that resist 'integration' with the rest of the mattress interior. Either way, geography – the shape of the balloon or air mattress and the nature of Afro-Eurasian territory – provides a basic framework within which agents (air blowers) operate to exploit those ultimate limitations.

20 See, for instance, Chase-Dunn and Hall's (2000: 101) 'kissing coyote' rendition of the pulsations in interdependency or Modelski's (2000) very long alternating phases of concentration and dispersal.

Bibliography

Albright, W.F. 1975. 'Syria, the Philistines, and Phoenicia', in I.E.S. Edwards, C.J. Gadd, N.G.L. Hammond and E. Sollberger, eds. *The Cambridge Ancient History*, Vol. 2, Part 2: *History of the Middle East and the Aegean Region, c. 1380–1000 BC*, 3rd edn. Cambridge: Cambridge University Press.

Alfody, Geza. 2000. 'Spain', in Alan K. Bowman, Peter Garnsey and Dominic Rathbone, eds. *The Cambridge Ancient History*, Vol. 11: *The High Empire, AD 70–192*, 2nd edn. Cambridge: Cambridge University Press.

Allchin, Frank R. 1995a. 'Early cities and states beyond the Ganges valley', in Frank R. Allchin, ed. *The Archaeology of Early Historic South Asia: The Emergence of Cities and States.* Cambridge: Cambridge University Press.

Allchin, Frank R. 1995b. 'The emergence of cities and states: concluding synthesis', in Frank R. Allchin, ed. *The Archaeology of Early Historic South Asia: The Emergence of Cities and States.* Cambridge: Cambridge University Press.

Andreau, J. 2000. 'Commerce and finance', in Alan K. Bowman, Peter Garnsey and Dominic Rathbone, eds. *The Cambridge Ancient History*, Vol. 11: *The High Empire, AD 70–192*, 2nd edn. Cambridge: Cambridge University Press.

Ari-Yonah, Michael. 2001. 'The second temple (332 BC–70 AD) ', in Michael Ari-Yonah, ed. *A History of Israel and the Holy Land.* New York: Continuum.

Aubet, Maria E. 1996. *The Phoenicians and the West: Politics, Colonies and Trade*, transl. by Mary Turton. Cambridge: Cambridge University Press.

Balcer, Jack M. 1984. *Sparda by the Bitter Sea: Imperial Interaction in Western Anatolia.* Chico, CA: Scholars Press.

Bell, H. Idris. 1966. 'Egypt under the early principate', in S.A. Cook, F.E. Adcock and M.P. Charlesworth, eds. *The Cambridge Ancient History*, Vol. 10: *The Augustan Empire, 44 BC–AD 70.* Cambridge: Cambridge University Press.

Bintliff, John. 1984. 'Iron Age Europe, in the context of social evolution from the Bronze Age through to historic times', in John Bintliff, ed. *European Social Evolution: Archaelogical Perspectives.* Bradford: University of Bradford.

Blegen, Carl W. 1963. *Troy and the Trojans.* New York: Frederick A. Praeger.

Boardman, John. 1980. *The Greeks Overseas: Their Early Colonies and Trade.* London: Thames and Hudson.

Bosworth, Andrew. 1992. 'World cities and world systems: a test of A.G. Frank and B. Gills' "A" and "B" cycles'. Paper presented at the Canadian Association of Geographers' Conference, Vancouver, May 1992.

Bosworth, A.B. 1994. 'Alexander the Great, Part 2: Greece and the conquered territories', in D.M. Lewis, John Boardman, Simon Hornblower and M. Ostwald, eds. *The Cambridge Ancient History*, Vol. 6: *The Fourth Century BC*, 2nd edn. Cambridge: Cambridge University Press.

Bouzek, Jan. 1989. 'The Eastern Mediterranean and Central Europe: the beginning of the Iron Age', in Marie-Louise Stig-Sorensen and Roger Thomas, eds. *The Bronze Age and Iron Age Transition in Europe: Aspects of Continuity and Change in European Societies, c. 1200 to 500 BC.* Oxford: British Archaelogical Reports International Series.

Bouzek, Jan. 1997. *Greece, Anatolia and Europe: Cultural Interrelations During the Early Iron Age.* Goteborg, Sweden: Paul Astroms.

Brinkman, J.A. 1991. 'Babylonia in the shadow of Assyria (747–626 BC) ', in John Boardman, I.E.S. Edwards, N.G.L. Hammond, E. Sollberger with C.B.F. Walker, eds. *The Cambridge Ancient History*, Vol. 3: *The Assyrian and Babylonian Empires and Other States of the Near East, from the Eighth to the Sixth Centuries BC.* Cambridge: Cambridge University Press.

Cartledge, Paul. 1980. 'Iron Age Greece and the Eastern Mediterranean', in Andrew Sherratt, ed. *The Cambridge Encyclopedia of Archaeology.* New York: Cambridge University Press.

Chakrabarti, Dilip K. 1995. *The Archaeology of Ancient Indian Cities.* Delhi: Oxford University Press.

Chase-Dunn, Christopher and Tom Hall. 1997. *Rise and Demise: Comparing World-Systems.* Boulder, CO: Westview.

——. 2000 'Comparing world-systems to explain social evolution', in Robert A. Denemark, Jonathan Friedman, Barry K. Gills and George Modelski, eds. *World System History: The Social Science of Long-term Change.* London: Routledge.

Chernykh, E.N. 1992. *Ancient Metallurgy in the USSR: The Early Metal Age.* Cambridge: Cambridge University Press.

Chew, Sing. 2001. *World Ecological Degradation: Accumulation, Urbanization, and Deforestation, 3000 BC–AD 2000.* Walnut Creek, CA: Altamira.

Childe, V. Gordon. 1942. *What Happened in History.* London: Pelican Books.

Cho-Yun Hsu and Kathryn M. Linduff. 1988. *Western Chou Civilization.* New Haven, CT: Yale University Press.

Clark, Robert P. 1997. *The Global Imperative.* Boulder, CO: Westview.

Coedes, George. 1968. *The Indianized States of Southeast Asia*, ed. by Walter F. Vella, trans. by Sue B. Cowing. Honolulu: University Press of Hawaii.

Colledge, Malcolm A.R. 2000. 'Art and architecture', in Alan K. Bowman, Peter Garnsey and Dominic Rathbone, eds. *The Cambridge Ancient History*, Vol. 11: *The High Empire, AD 70–192*, 2nd edn. Cambridge: Cambridge University Press.

Collis, J. 1984. *The European Iron Age.* London: Barsford.

Cook, J.M. 1985. 'The rise of the Achaemenids and establishment of their empire', in Ilya Gershevitch, ed. *The Cambridge History of Iran*, Vol. 2: *The Median and Achaemenian Periods.* Cambridge: Cambridge University Press.

Cornell, T.J. 1989a. 'The recovery of Rome', in F.W. Walbank, A.E. Astin, M.W. Frederiksen, R.M. Ogilvie and A. Drummond, eds. *The Cambridge Ancient History*, Vol. 7, Part 2: *The Rise of Rome to 220 BC*, 2nd edn. Cambridge: Cambridge University Press.

Cornell, T.J. 1989b. 'The conquest of Italy', in F.W. Walbank, A.E. Astin, M.W. Frederiksen, R.M. Ogilvie and A. Drummond, eds. *The Cambridge Ancient History*, Vol. 7, Part 2: *The Rise of Rome to 220 BC*, 2nd edn. Cambridge: Cambridge University Press.

Cotterell, Arthur. 1981. *The First Emperor of China.* New York: Holt, Rinehart and Winston.

Dandemaev, Muhammad A. and Vladimir G. Lukonin. 1989. *The Culture and Social*

Institutions of Ancient Iran, trans. by Philip L. Kohl and D.J. Dadson. Cambridge: Cambridge University Press.

Dandamaev, M.A. 1991. 'Neo-Babylonian society and economy', in John Boardman, I.E.S. Edwards, N.G.L. Hammond, E. Sollberger with C.B.F. Walker, eds. *The Cambridge Ancient History*, Vol. 3: *The Assyrian and Babylonian Empires and Other States of the Near East, from the Eighth to the Sixth Centuries BC*. Cambridge: Cambridge University Press.

Desborough, V.R. d'A. 1972. *The Greek Dark Ages*. London: E. Benn.

Dietler, Michael. 1989. 'Greeks, Etruscans, and thirsty barbarians: early Iron Age interaction in the Rhone Basin of France', in Timothy C. Champion, ed. *Centre and Periphery: Comparative Studies in Archaeology*. London: Unwin Hyman.

Downey, Glanville. 1961. *A History of Antioch in Syria: from Seleucus to the Arab Conquest*. Princeton, NJ: Princeton University Press.

Drummond, A. 1989. 'Rome in the fifth century. I: The social and economic framework', in F.W. Walbank, A.E. Astin, M.W. Frederiksen, R.M. Ogilvie and A. Drummond, eds. *The Cambridge Ancient History*, Vol 7, Part 2: *The Rise of Rome to 220 BC*, 2nd edn. Cambridge: Cambridge University Press.

Eberhard, Wolfram. 1977. *A History of China*, rev. edn. Berkeley: University of California Press.

Edens, Christopher. 1992. 'The dynamics of trade in the Ancient Mesopotamian "world system"'. *American Anthropologist* 94: 118–39.

Edens, Christopher and Garth Bawden. 1988. 'History of Tayma and Hejazi trade during the first millennium BC'. *Journal of the Economic and Social History of the Orient* 32: 47–103.

Ellis, Peter B. 1990. *The Celtic Empire: The First Millennium of Celtic History, c. 1000 B –51 AD*. London: Guild Publishing.

Eph'al, I. 1988. 'Syria-Palestine under Achaemenid rule', in John Boardman, N.G.L. Hammond, D.M. Lewis and M. Ostwald, eds. *The Cambridge Ancient History*, Vol. 4: *Persia, Greece and the Western Mediterranean, c. 525 to 479 BC*, 2nd edn. Cambridge: Cambridge University Press.

Erdosy, George. 1988. *Urbanisation in Early Historic India*. Oxford: British Archaeological Research.

Erdosy, George. 1995. 'City states of north India and Pakistan at the time of the Buddha', in Frank R. Allchin, ed. *The Archaeology of Early Historic South Asia: The Emergence of Cities and States*. Cambridge: Cambridge University Press.

Fagan, Brian. 1999. *Flood, Famines, and Emperors: El Niño and the Fate of Civilizations*. New York: Basic Books.

——. 2004. *The Long Summer: How Climate Changed Civilization*. New York: Basic Books.

Francis, Peter. 1989. *Beads and the Bead Trade in Southeast Asia*. Lake Placid: Center for Bead Research.

Francis, Peter. 1991. 'Beadmaking at Arikamedu and beyond'. *World Archaeology* 23: 28–43.

Franck, Irene M. and David M. Brownstone. 1986. *The Silk Road: A History*. New York: Facts on File.

Frank, Andre G. 1992. *The Centrality of Central Asia*. Amsterdam: Center for Asian Studies.

Frank, Andre G. 1993. 'Bronze Age world system cycles'. *Current Anthropology* 34: 383–429.

Frank, Andre G. and Barry K. Gills, eds. 1993. *The World System: Five Hundred Years or Five Thousand?* London: Routledge.

Frank, Andre G. and William R. Thompson. 2005. 'Bronze Age economic expansion and contraction revisited'. *Journal of World History* 16: 115–72.

Fulford, Michael. 2000. 'Britain', in Alan K. Bowman, Peter Garnsey and Dominic Rathbone, eds. *The Cambridge Ancient History*, Vol. 11: *The High Empire, AD 70–192*, 2nd edn. Cambridge: Cambridge University Press.

Garsoian, Nina. 1997. 'The emergence of Armenia', in Richard G. Hovannisian, ed. *The Armenian People from Ancient to Modern Times*, Vol. 1: *The Dynastic Periods – From Antiquity to the Fourteenth Century*. New York: St Martin's Press.

Gernet, Jacques. 1982. *A History of Chinese Civilization*, trans. by J.R. Foster. Cambridge: Cambridge University Press.

Ghirshman, R. 1954. *Iran*. Harmondsworth: Pelican Books.

Gills, Barry K. and Andre G. Frank. 1992. 'World system cycles, crises, and hegemonial shifts, 1700 BC to 1700 AD'. *Review* 15: 621–87.

Glover, Ian C. 1991. 'The Southern Silk Road: archaeological evidence for early trade between India and Southeast Asia'. Paper presented to the UNESCO Silk Roads Maritime Route Seminar, Bangkok.

Goodman, Martin. 2000. 'Judaea', in Alan K. Bowman, Peter Garnsey and Dominic Rathbone, eds. *The Cambridge Ancient History*, Vol. 11: *The High Empire, AD 70–192*, 2nd edn. Cambridge: Cambridge University Press.

Grainger, John D. 1990. *The Cities of Seleukid Syria*. Oxford: Clarendon Press.

Grayson, A.K. 1991. 'Assyrian civilization', in John Boardman, I.E.S. Edwards, N.G.L. Hammond, E. Sollberger with C.B.F. Walker, eds. *The Cambridge Ancient History*, Vol. 3: *The Assyrian and Babylonian Empires and Other States of the Near East, from the Eighth to the Sixth Centuries BC*. Cambridge: Cambridge University Press.

Hall, William W. and William K. Simpson. 1998. *The Ancient Near East: A History*, 2nd edn. New York: Harcourt Brace.

Hammond, N.G.L. 1976. *Migrations and Invasions in Greece and Adjacent Areas*. Park Ridge, NJ: Noyes Press.

Harke, Heinrich. 1989. 'Transformation or collapse? Bronze Age to Iron Age settlement in west central Europe', in Marie-Louise Stig-Sorenson and Roger Thomas, eds. *The Bronze Age and Iron Age Transition in Europe: Aspects of Continuity and Change in European Societies, c. 1200 to 500 BC*. Oxford: British Archaeological Reports International Series.

Harris, W.V. 2000. 'Trade', in Alan K. Bowman, Peter Garnsey and Dominic Rathbone, eds. *The Cambridge Ancient History*, Vol. 11: *The High Empire, AD 70–192*, 2nd edn. Cambridge: Cambridge University Press.

Hayes, John H. and Sara R. Mandell. 1998. *The Jewish People in Classical Antiquity*. Louisville, KY: Westminster John Knox Press.

Hoddinott, R.F. 1981. *The Thracians*. London: Thames and Hudson.

James, P.J., I.J. Thorpe, N. Kokkinos, R. Morkot and J. Frankish. 1991. *Centuries of Darkness: A Challenge to the Conventional Chronology of Old World Archaeology*. London: Jonathan Cape.

James, T.G.H. 1991. 'Egypt: the twenty-fifth and twenty-sixth dynasties', in John Boardman, I.E.S. Edwards, N.G.L. Hammond, E. Sollberger with C.B.F. Walker, eds. *The Cambridge Ancient History*, Vol. 3: *The Assyrian and Babylonian Empires and Other States of the Near East, from the Eighth to the Sixth Centuries BC*. Cambridge: Cambridge University Press.

Jaspers, Karl. 1949. *The Perennial Scope of Philosophy*. New York: Philosophical Library.

Jaspers, Karl. 1955. *Reason and Existence: Five Lectures*. New York: Noonday Press.

Jaspers, Karl. 1957. *Die Grossen Philosophen*. Munchen: Piper.

Katzenstein, H. Jacob. 1973. *The History of Tyre*. Jerusalem: Shocken Institute for Jewish Research.

Kristiansen, Kristian. 1982. 'The formation of tribal systems in later European prehistory: northern Europe, 4000–500 BC', in C. Renfrew, M.J. Rowlands and B.A. Seagraves, eds. *Theory and Explanation in Archaeology*. New York: Academic Press.

Kristiansen, Kristian. 1987. 'Centre and periphery in Bronze Age Scandinavia', in Michael Rowlands, Mogens Larsen and Kristian Kristiansen, eds. *Centre and Periphery in the Ancient World*. Cambridge: Cambridge University Press.

Kristiansen, Kristian. 1993. 'The emergence of the European world system in the Bronze Age: divergence, convergence, and social evolution during the first and second millennium BC in Europe', in Kristian Kristiansen and Jorgen Jensen, eds. *Europe in the First Millennium BC*. Sheffield: Department of Archaeology, University of Sheffield .

Kristiansen, Kristian. 1998. *Europe Before History*. Cambridge: Cambridge University Press.

Kuhrt, Amelie. 1988. 'Babylon from Cyrus to Xerxes', in John Boardman, N.G.L. Hammond, D.M. Lewis and M. Ostwald, eds. *The Cambridge Ancient History*, Vol. 4: *Persia, Greece and the Western Mediterranean, c. 525 to 479 BC*. 2nd edn. Cambridge: Cambridge University Press.

Kuhrt, Amelie. 1995. *The Ancient Near East, c. 3000–330 BC*, Vol. 2. London: Routledge.

Kulke, Herman and Dietmar Rothermund. 1990. *A History of India*, rev. edn. London: Routledge.

Labat, Rene. 1975. 'Elam and Western Persia, c. 1200–1000 BC', in I.E.S. Edwards, C.J. Gadd, N.G.L. Hammond and E. Sollberger, eds. *The Cambridge Ancient History*, Vol. 2, Part 2: *History of the Middle East and the Aegean Region, c. 1380–1000 BC*. Cambridge: Cambridge University Press.

Lancel, Serge. 1997. *Carthage: A History*, trans. by Antonia Nevill. Malden, MA: Blackwell.

Levick, Barbara. 2000. 'Greece and Asia Minor', in Alan K. Bowman, Peter Garnsey and Dominic Rathbone, eds. *The Cambridge Ancient History*, Vol. 11: *The High Empire, AD 70–192*, 2nd edn. Cambridge: Cambridge University Press.

Levy, Jean-Philippe. 1967. *The Economic Life of the Ancient World*, trans. by John G. Biran. Chicago, IL: University of Chicago Press.

Liverani, Mario. 1987. 'The collapse of the Near Eastern regional system at the end of the Bronze Age: the case of Syria', in Michael Rowlands, Mogens Larsen and Kristian Kristiansen, eds. *Centre and Periphery in the Ancient World*. Cambridge: Cambridge University Press.

Li Xuegin. 1985. *Eastern Zhou and Qin Civilizations*, trans. by K.C. Chang. New Haven, CT: Yale University Press.

Lloyd, Alan B. 2000a. 'The Late Period (664–332 BC) ', in Ian Shaw, ed. *The Oxford History of Ancient Egypt*. Oxford: Oxford University Press.

Lloyd, Alan B. 2000b. 'The Ptolemaic Period (332–30 BC) ', in Ian Shaw, ed. *The Oxford History of Ancient Egypt*. Oxford: Oxford University Press.

Macmullen, Ramsay. 1988. *Corruption and the Decline of Rome*. New Haven, CT: Yale University Press.

McNeill, William. 1963. *The Rise of the West: A History of the Human Community*. Chicago, IL: University of Chicago Press.

McNeill, William.1976. *Plagues and Peoples*. New York: Anchor Doubleday.

McNeill, John R. and William McNeill. 2003. *The Human Web: A Bird's Eye View of World History*. New York: W.W. Norton.

Magie, David. 1950. *Roman Rule in Asia Minor: To the End of the Third Century After Christ*, Vol. 1: *Text*. Princeton, NJ: Princeton University Press.

Maier, F.G. 1994. 'Cyprus and Phoenicia', in D.M. Lewis, John Boardman, Simon Hornblower and M. Ostwald, eds. *The Cambridge Ancient History*, Vol. 6: *The Fourth Century BC*, 2nd edn. Cambridge: Cambridge University Press.

Markoe, Glenn E. 2000. *Phoenicians*. Berkeley: University of California Press.

Matthews, Victor H. 2002. *A Brief History of Ancient Israel*. Louisville, KY: Westminster John Knox Press.

Mazzoni, Stefania. 2000. 'Syria and the periodization of the Iron Age: a cross-cultural perspective', in Guy Bunnens, ed. *Essays on Syria in the Iron Age*. Sterling, VA: Peeters Press.

Melko, Matthew and David Wilkinson. 1992. 'General war and general peace: a comparative perspective'. Paper presented at the American Sociological Association Meetings, Pittsburgh, PA.

Mellink, M. 1991. 'The native kingdoms of Anatolia', in John Boardman, I.E.S. Edwards, N.G.L. Hammond, E. Sollberger with C.B.F. Walker, eds. *The Cambridge Ancient History*, Vol. 3: *The Assyrian and Babylonian Empires and Other States of the Near East, from the Eight to the Sixth Centuries BC.* Cambridge: Cambridge University Press.

Mitchell, Stephen. 1993. *Anatolia: Land, Men and Gods in Asia Minor*, Vol. 1: *The Celts in Anatolia and the Impact of Roman Rule*. Oxford: Clarendon Press.

Mitchell, T.C. 1991. 'Israel of Judah from the coming of Assyrian domination until the fall of Samaria, and the struggle for independence in Judah (c. 750–700 BC)', in John Boardman, I.E.S. Edwards, N.G.L. Hammond, E. Sollberger with C.B.F. Walker, eds. *The Cambridge Ancient History*, Vol. 3: *The Assyrian and Babylonian Empires and Other States of the Near East, from the Eighth to the Sixth Centuries BC*. Cambridge: Cambridge University Press.

Modelski, George. 2000. 'World system evolution', in Robert A. Denemark, Jonathan Friedman, Barry K. Gills and George Modelski, eds. *World System History: The Social Science of Long-term Change*. London: Routledge.

Nicolet, C. 1994. 'Economy and Society, 133–43 BC', in J.A. Crook, Andrew Lintott and Elizabeth Rawson, eds. *The Cambridge Ancient History*, Vol. 9: *The Last Age of the Roman Republic, 146–43 BC*, 2nd edn. Cambridge: Cambridge University Press.

O'Connor, David. 1980. 'Late Period Egypt and Nubia', in Andrew Sherratt, ed. *The Cambridge Encyclopedia of Archaeology*. New York: Cambridge University Press.

Oertel, F. 1966. 'The economic unification of the Mediterranean region: industry, trade and commerce', in S.A. Cook, F.E. Adcock and M.P. Charlesworth, eds. *The Cambridge Ancient History*, Vol. 10: *The Augustan Empire, 44 BC–AD 70.* Cambridge: Cambridge University Press.

Ogilvie, R.M. 1976. *Early Rome and the Etruscans*. Hassocks: Harvester Press.

Ostoja-Zagorski, Janusz. 1989. 'Changes in the economic and social structures in northern Poland at the transition from the Bronze Age to the Iron Age', in Marie L.S. Sorenson and Roger Thomas, eds, *The Bronze Age-Iron Age Transition in Europe, Part II.* Oxford: British Archaeological Reports.

Pallottino, Massimo.1991. *A History of Earliest Italy*, trans. by Martin Ryle and Kate Soper. Ann Arbor: University of Michigan Press.

Parr, Peter. 1980. 'The Levant in the early first millennium BC', in Andrew Sherratt, ed. *The Cambridge Encyclopedia of Archaeology*. New York: Cambridge University Press.

Picard, G.Ch. 1994. 'Carthage from the Battle of Himera to Agathocles' invasion (480–308 BC)', in D.M. Lewis, John Boardman, Simon Hornblower and M. Ostwald, eds. *The Cambridge Ancient History*, Vol. 6: *The Fourth Century BC*, 2nd edn. Cambridge: Cambridge University Press.

Potts, D.T. 1990. *The Arabian Gulf in Antiquity*, Vol. 2: *From Alexander the Great to the Coming of Islam*. Oxford: Clarendon Press.

Postgate, Nicholas. 1980. 'The Assyrian Empire', in Andrew Sherratt, ed. *The Cambridge Encyclopedia of Archaeology*. New York: Cambridge University Press.

Purcell, Nicholas. 1994. 'South Italy in the fourth century BC', in D.M. Lewis, John Boardman, Simon Hornblower and M. Ostwald, eds. *The Cambridge Ancient History*, Vol. 6: *The Fourth Century BC*, 2nd edn. Cambridge: Cambridge University Press.

Purcell, Nicholas. 2000. 'Rome and Italy', in Alan K. Bowman, Peter Garnsey and Dominic Rathbone, eds. *The Cambridge Ancient History*, Vol. 11: *The High Empire, AD 70–192*, 2nd edn. Cambridge: Cambridge University Press.

Raman, K.V. 1991. 'Roman contacts with Tamilnadu (southeastern India): recent findings'. Paper presented to the UNESCO Silk Roads Maritime Route Seminar, Bangkok.

Ray, Himarishu P. 1994. *The Winds of Change: Buddhism and the Maritime Links of Early South Asia*. Delhi: Oxford University Press.

Ray, Himarishu P. 2003. *The Archaeology of Seafaring in Ancient South Asia*. Cambridge: Cambridge University Press.

Ray, Niharranjan, B.D. Chattopadhyay, V.R. Mani and Ranabir Chakravarti, eds. 2000. *A Sourcebook of Indian Civilization*. Kolkata: Orient Longman.

Redford, Donald B. 1992. *Egypt, Canaan and Israel in Ancient Times*. Princeton, NJ: Princeton University Press.

Redgate, A.E. 1998. *The Armenians*. Malden, MA: Blackwell.

Reynolds, Joyce. 2000. 'Cyrenaica', in Alan K. Bowman, Peter Garnsey and Dominic Rathbone, eds. *The Cambridge Ancient History*, Vol. 11: *The High Empire, AD 70–192*, 2nd edn. Cambridge: Cambridge University Press.

Roebuck, Carl. 1966. *The World of Ancient Times*. New York: Charles Scribner's.

Rostovtzeff, M. 1941. *The Economic and Social History of the Hellenistic World*, Vol. 2. London: Oxford University Press.

Roux, Georges. 1980. *Ancient Iraq*, 2nd edn. New York: Penguin.

Ruger, C. 2000. 'Roman Germany', in Alan K. Bowman, Peter Garnsey and Dominic Rathbone, eds. *The Cambridge Ancient History*, Vol. 11: *The High Empire, AD 70–192*, 2nd edn. Cambridge: Cambridge University Press.

Sagg, H.W.F. 1984. *The Might That Was Assyria*. London: Sidgwick and Jackson.

Salles, Jean-Francois. 1987. 'The Arab-Persian Gulf under the Seleucids', in Amelie Kuhrt and Susan Sherwin-White, eds. *Hellenism in the East: The Introduction of Greek and Non-Greek Civilizations from Syria to Central Asia after Alexander*. Berkeley: University of California Press.

Sartre, Maurice. 2000. 'Syria and Arabia', in Alan K. Bowman, Peter Garnsey and Dominic Rathbone, eds. *The Cambridge Ancient History*, Vol. 11: *The High Empire, AD 70–192*, 2nd edn. Cambridge: Cambridge University Press.

Schippmann, Klaus. 2001. *Ancient South Arabia*. Princeton, NJ: Markus Weiner.

Sherratt, Andrew G. n.d. 'Core, periphery, and margin: perspectives on the Bronze Age', in C. Mathers and S. Stoddart, eds. *Development and Decline in the Bronze Age Mediterranean*. Sheffield: Sheffield Academic Press.

Sherratt, Andrew G. and Susan Sherratt. 1991. 'From Luxuries to Commodities: The nature of the Bronze Age trading system', in N.H. Gale, ed. *Bronze Age Trade in the Mediterranean*. Jonsered: Paul Astroms Forlag.

Sherratt, Andrew G. and Susan Sherratt. 1993. 'The growth of the Mediterranean economy in the early first millennium BC'. *World Archaeology* 24: 361–78.

Sinnigen, William G. and Charles A. Robinson, Jr. 1981. *Ancient History from Prehistoric Times to the Death of Justinian*, 3rd edn. New York: Macmillan.

Smith, Christopher J. 1996. *Early Rome and Latium: Economy and Society c. 1000 to 500 BC*. Oxford: Clarendon Press.

Snodgrass, A.M. 1971. *The Dark Age of Greece*. Edinburgh: Edinburgh University Press.

Snodgrass, A.M. 1980. *Archaic Greece: The Age of Experiment*. Berkeley: University of California Press.

Starr, Chester G. 1977. *The Economic and Social Growth of Early Greece, 800–500 BC*. New York: Oxford University Press.

Stolper, Matthew W. 1994. 'Mesopotamia, 482–330 BC', in D.M. Lewis, John Boardman, Simon Hornblower and M. Ostwald, eds. *The Cambridge Ancient History*, Vol. 6: *The Fourth Century BC*, 2nd edn. Cambridge: Cambridge University Press.

Tandy, David W. 1997. *Warriors into Traders: The Power of the Market in Early Greece*. Berkeley: University of California Press.

Taylor, John. 2000. 'The third intermediate period (1069–664 BC) ', in Ian Shaw, ed. *The Oxford History of Ancient Egypt*. Oxford: Oxford University Press.

Teggart, Frederick. 1939. *Rome and China: A Study of Correlations in Historical Events*. Berkeley: University of California Press.

Thomas, Carol G. and Craig Conant. 1999. *Citadel to City-State: The Transformation of Greece, 1200–700 BCE*. Bloomington: Indiana University Press.

Thompson, William R. 2003. 'Climate, water and political–economic crises in the Southwest Asian Bronze Age'. Paper presented at the World System History and Global Environmental Change Conference, Lund, Sweden, September 2003.

——. 2004. Eurasian C-Wave crises in the first millennium BCE', in Christopher Chase-Dunn and Eugene N. Anderson, eds. *The Historical Evolution of World-Systems*. New York: Palgrave-Macmillan.

Trump, D.H. 1980. *The Prehistory of the Mediterranean*. New Haven, CT: Yale University Press.

Tubb, Jonathan N. 1998. *Canaanites*. Norman, OK: University of Oklahoma Press.

Turner, E.G. 1984. 'Ptolemaic Egypt', in F.W. Walbank, A.E. Astin, M.W. Frederiksen and R.M. Ogilvie, eds. *The Cambridge Ancient History*, Vol. 7, Part 1: *The Hellenistic World*, 2nd edn. Cambridge: Cambridge University Press.

Van De Mieroop, Marc. 2004. *A History of the Ancient Near East ca. 3000–323 BC*. Malden, MA: Blackwell.

Van Dijk, Jacobus. 2000. 'The Amarna period and the later New Kingdom', in Ian Shaw, ed. *The Oxford History of Ancient Egypt*. Oxford: Oxford University Press.

Wang Gungwu. 1958. 'The Nanhai trade: a study of the early history of Chinese trade in the South China Sea'. *Journal of the Malaysian Branch of the Royal Asiatic Society* 31.

Warmington, B.H. 1993. *Carthage: A History*, rev. edn. New York: Barnes and Noble.

Watterson, Barbara. 1997. *The Egyptians*. Cambridge, MA: Blackwell.

Wells, Peter S. 1984. *Farms, Villages, and Cities: Commerce and Urban Origins in Late Prehistoric Europe*. Ithaca, NY: Cornell University Press.

Whittaker, C.R. 2000. 'Africa', in Alan K. Bowman, Peter Garnsey and Dominic Rathbone, eds. *The Cambridge Ancient History*, Vol. 11: *The High Empire, AD 70–192*, 2nd edn. Cambridge: Cambridge University Press.

Wilkes, J.J. 2000. 'The Danube Provinces', in Alan K. Bowman, Peter Garnsey and Dominic Rathbone, eds. *The Cambridge Ancient History*, Vol. 11: *The High Empire, AD 70–192*, 2nd edn. Cambridge: Cambridge University Press.

Wilkinson, David. 1987. 'Central Civilization'. *Comparative Civilizations Review* 17: 31–59.

Wilkinson, David. 1992a. 'Decline phases in civilizations, regions, and oikumene'. Paper presented at the Annual Meeting of the International Studies Association, Atlanta, GA, April 1992.

Wilkinson, David. 1992b. 'Cities, civilizations, and oikumenes, I'. *Comparative Civilizations Review* 27: 51–87.

Wilkinson, David. 2000. 'Civilizations, world systems and hegemonies', in Robert A. Denemark, Jonathan Friedman, Barry K. Gills and George Modelski, eds. *World System History: The Social Science of Long-term Change*. London: Routledge.

Ying-shih, Yu. 1967. *Trade and Expansion in Han China: A Study in the Structure of Sino-Barbarian Economic Relations*. Berkeley: University of California Press.

10 Dark ages

Ecological crisis phases and system transition

Sing C. Chew

System crisis

The basis for the reproduction of material life over world history has been the large-scale utilization of the resources of the natural environment. The recurring outcome of this process – based on the human communities' efforts to reproduce social life according to the social organizational patterns that have evolved – seems to be ecological degradation. Nonetheless, the motions of history also suggest periods of ecological recovery of the degraded areas, and the penetration of new areas for the extraction of fresh natural resources to sustain further world system evolution. Therefore, viewed from the perspective of *la longue durée*, ecological degradation and recovery appear to recur in phases.[1]

In my previous work (2001), I have shown that excessive ecological degradation leads to environmental collapse; and, along these lines, there are certain phases of environmental collapses that occur *mutatis mutandis* with civilization demises. This relationship between environmental collapses and civilization demises suggests that, when societal relations with the natural environment become excessive over time, a social system crisis is triggered.

Social (world) system crisis means that the continued evolution of the world system faces obstacles, and that necessary structural changes/adjustments have to be made for systems reproduction to continue. These crisis phases become the key periods for our understanding of the dynamics of world system evolution and transition (long-term social change). Over world history, these crisis moments are rare. When they do occur, these phases have a great impact in terms of geographic coverage, and they extend over a long period in terms of socio-economic and ecological recovery.

Conceptually, the factors and processes that triggered system crises over the last 5,000 years have not been worked out or well understood. That, however, has not prevented the identification of these system crises or B phases. With the plethora of positions on world system/s development, system crises or B phases have been proposed to cover different durations, and have different meanings for those working in this area (Wallerstein 1974, 1980; Frank 1993; Gills and Frank 1992; Modelski and Thompson 1996; Chase-Dunn and Hall 1997; Chew 2001).[2] According to each model, the duration of these downturn phases varies. Different durations ranging from 50 years to 1,000 years have been suggested.

Leaving this difference in duration aside for the moment, there are also different views of what is a B phase in relation to world system/s reproduction. For those who adhere to a continuing world system since 3000 BC such as Gills and Frank (1992), B phases represent the cyclical tendency or rhythms that a world system goes through as it expands. In other words, a B phase is a cyclical downturn of the world system within its rhythm of expansion and contraction – a structural process of the world system (Gills and Frank 2002: 159–60). They are recurrences of economic downturns. Along this reasoning, there is no notable difference between one B phase and another. They are all economic downturns with no distinguishing characteristics depicting a specific era (conjuncture) of the world system other than sharing similar tendencies such as hegemonic rivalries. There is no articulation of B phases as representing the point of system transformation/transition. Therefore, historical contingent circumstances/factors are not given much weight nor proffered to explain the genesis or resolution of system crisis and transitions.

Another view of a B phase is quite different. Wallerstein (1974, 1979, 1980), for example, understands B phases or *logistics* in another way. A specific B phase or logistic is not only signifying an economic crisis period (price fluctuations, etc.), it also demarcates specific characteristics of system transition, reorganization and consolidation depending on the particular B phase in question. For example, in his explication of the origin and evolution of the *modern* world system, the B phase between AD 1300 and AD 1450 has been analysed as a reorganization of the social structure ('the crisis of feudalism') in order to overcome the crisis conditions (Wallerstein 1980: 25), whereas the B phase between AD 1600 and AD 1750 is considered not as a 'crisis in the system' but as 'a period of consolidation' of social relations and structures with its respective specificities (Wallerstein 1980: 31). Thus, a specific B-phase crisis has certain triggers that trip the system crisis. In the case of the B phase between AD 1300 and AD 1450, the particular triggers for the 'crisis of feudalism' were a conjuncture of secular trends, immediate cyclical crisis and climatological decline.

The apparent differences in just two positions have implications for our understanding of the factors conditioning system crisis. If we consider a Wallersteinian B phase, we need to note that it has some commonalities such as cyclical economic contraction trends (price changes, production losses, etc.) with other recurrent B phases. In this case, Wallerstein's interpretation is similar to Gills and Frank's understanding of a B phase. However, for Wallerstein, a specific B phase is also different from other B phases, for it also has certain *contingent* particular characteristics (for example, breakdown of feudal social relations, climate changes) of the epoch in question that condition the system crisis. Hence, the specific conjuncture and its contingent socio-economic and political characteristics are included in an understanding of the precipitation and determination of the systems crisis and transition. Given this direction, for Wallerstein, the identification of common elements that condition system crises recurring over world history needs to be combined with the conjunctural elements in order to understand the crisis. The attempt, therefore, is to straddle nomothetic and idiographic methodologies for an explanation of system crisis and transition.

Between these two viewpoints of B phases, there are those that are closer or further away from the above two positions. Modelski and Thompson's contributions (Modelski and Thompson 1996, Modelski 2003) have suggested the recurrent nature of crisis and transitions over long cycles in the historical evolution of the world system. Agreeing with Gills and Frank on the dynamics of the world system since 3000 BC, the recurring crisis phases have been characterized by learning (technological, writing, information, etc.) innovations, political hegemonic struggles, population, urbanization, migrations, climate and warfare.[3] Unlike Gills and Frank (1992), Modelski and Thompson have identified both particular elements (technological innovation, information, writing, etc.) that underline a specific crisis phase and common elements such as de-urbanization, migration, population decreases that permeate every system crisis phase. Beyond the widely agreed element of negative economic trends defining a B phase, what we have are additional delineation of elements such as those that are specific (information, technological innovations and writing), and other common elements (de-urbanization, migration, climate and population decreases) that all form the matrix circumscribing system crisis and transition. System crises, therefore, are transition points of system adaptation and evolution.

This array of elements gets extended with the nomothetic approach taken by Chase-Dunn and Hall (1997) in accounting for system crisis/transformation. Although they have not periodized B phases as determining systems transition/transformation, they utilize a multiple and interactive model (population pressure, emigration, conflict, hierarchy, technological development, environmental degradation) to explain systems crisis/transition. If the crisis conditions are minor and a result of cyclical processes, then the transformation is incremental or developmental but, if it has great impact or is the result of an external disturbance, then the change is evolutionary, leading to new forms of socio-economic organization (Chase-Dunn and Hall 2002). Because of their assumption that transformation occurs when a change occurs in the mode of production, there is little reliance on analysing B phases or specific B phases to account for system crisis and transition.

For our purposes, B phases should refer only to periods of *systemic* crises of the world system. Their occurrences and the characteristic processes underlying these systemic crises prior to the modern era have not been fully noted or understood. We do have some indications from historical accounts of social, political and economic downturn periods, and preliminary identification of the characteristic processes depicting these phases. Besides the above preliminary starts to decipher recurrent patterns of social, economic and political characteristics underlying the crisis phases, there are very few idiographic efforts made to identify and explain the contingent factors, agents and conditions that might also have played a part in engendering each *specific* system crisis phase.[4] The latter task is even more challenging, especially in the light of the available archaeological evidence for the premodern period.

In view of the absences, our task is to sketch out a *theoretically generalized history* of system crisis or dark ages, and to impress on the reader that social system crises are ecological crises as well, and that they have ecological roots besides the anthropogenic ones that are so widely circulated. Our effort in this exercise is to move away from just a history understood and interpreted within a geospatial-dependent and time-contingent framework, and one that is focused on socio-economic and political dimensions only. The aim is to abstract a *theoretically generalized* account of the dynamics and structures of world system evolution, and those processes from the ecological sphere. In this regard, we need an understanding of system crisis and long-term social change that is theoretically generalizable along socio-economic and ecological dimensions. The end point would be a social science history of long-term change, i.e. a history of the evolution of the world system.

System crisis and ecology

Much scholarly attention is directed to analysing the anthropocentric processes such as capital accumulation, political hegemonic rivalries, technological changes or the lack thereof, trade system collapses, social–political unrest and border incursions to define the basis for system crisis. What perhaps needs more attention is the interaction between the world (social) system and the natural system to flesh out further the conditions for system crisis. Along such lines, various studies have intimated the relationship between climatological and ecological changes with human organizations and activities (see, for example, Ladurie 1971; Wallerstein 1974; Kristiansen 1998; Thompson 2000; Brown 2001; Chew 2001). Some such as Fernand Braudel (1972, 1981, 1982, 1984, 1989) have couched the social, political and economic factors in concert with the natural environment and the climatological patterns as determinants of long-term and large-scale transformations.[5] What needs to be explored in greater detail on a longer term basis are the impacts of climate and ecological changes on the generation of system crisis. After all, in the material reproduction of the world system, we rely on the natural system.

Given the above parameters, we need to *abstract historically* the several processes at work. Human-induced changes to the ecology and the climate in turn form barriers to the reproduction of the world system. The natural occurrences and shifts in terms of climate changes and natural disturbances, such as volcanicity, also condition the reproduction and evolution of the world system. Added to this equation are social and organizational factors (urbanization, accumulation, wars, technological innovations and population) that have an impact on system reproduction.

Most models that attempt to explain long-term system change concentrate overwhelmingly on anthropogenic causes. They have revolved around mapping the social, political and economic conditions to account for the basis of long-term and large-scale transformations. Such efforts have uncovered various factors and dimensions, such as the dynamics of capital accumulation, class relations, state actions, population and fertility levels and cultural values to explain long-term transformations (see, for example, Wolf 1982; Mann 1986; Abu-Lughod 1989; Goldstone 1991; Gills and Frank 1992; Wilkinson 1995). If we consider the parameters at work in engendering a system crisis as delineated in the previous paragraph, the explanation needs therefore to include natural environment and other non-social factors, for the latter forms the basis for the reproduction of the world system. Moving a further step forward, what needs also to be considered is the degree of weight these latter factors have in precipitating a system crisis. The answer cannot be sought theoretically but, rather, within a framework of historical structures and processes and via an analysis of the historical dynamics of nature–culture relations and climatological trends can we attempt to ascertain this.

System crisis: dark ages as a world system process

Towards a theoretically generalized history of dark ages[6]

System crises are moments when system reproduction experiences obstacles and difficulties. The historical dynamics of nature–culture relations exhibiting system crisis moments are revealed to us empirically in the form of what historians have described as dark ages. Over world history such dark ages i.e. prolonged periods of widespread social and economic distress lasting for centuries are rare. Between 3000 BC and AD 1000, there have been indications of only two such periods for north-western India, west Asia, the Mediterranean and Europe. V.R. Desborough, in *The Greek Dark Ages*, identified such a phase of distress for prehistoric Greece:

> during these generations the changes that came about are little short of fantastic. The craftsmen and artists seem to vanish almost without a trace: there is very little new stone construction of any sort, far less any massive edifices; the metal-worker's technique reverts to primitive, and the potter, except in early stages, loses his purpose and inspiration; and the art of writing is forgotten. But the outstanding feature is that by the end of the twelfth century the population appears to have dwindled to about one-tenth of what it had been little over a century before.

A.M. Snodgrass' characterizations of such a period in *The Dark Age of Greece* complements the conditions and extends it further to cover the collapse of trade and commerce across geographic boundaries beyond those of prehistoric Greece. Here is how he described it:

> the modern doctrine would hold that the following characteristics were present in the post-Mycenaean period: first, a fall in population that is certainly detectable and may have been devastating; secondly, a decline or loss of certain material skills; thirdly, a similar decline or loss in respect of some of the more elevated arts, of which the apparent loss of the art of writing is most striking to us, . . .; fourthly, a fall in living standards and perhaps in the sum of wealth; fifthly, a general severance of contacts, commercial and otherwise, with most peoples beyond the Aegean area and even with some of those within it.

In *Memory and the Mediterranean*, Fernand Braudel identified this type of disruption at the end of the twelfth century for the Mediterranean region:

> the move back into the past seems to have been most marked for Greece. Along with writing, the jewel amongst achievements, all the luxury arts vanished too: jewelry, mural paintings, engraved precious stones and seals, sculpted ivory and so on. Only pottery turned on the wheel seems to survive, with the last relic of the Mycenaean style vanishing during the eleventh century to be replaced by the first proto-geometrical ceramics. At the same time, all links with the Middle East seem to have been severed after the Dorian invasion and would only be restored much later when Greece and the Aegean in the full flush of expansion began to trade once more with the Syrian ports and Egypt, establishing outposts on the coast of Asia Minor.

These *anthropocentrically* inclined excerpts describe for us the social and economic conditions of the times. However, if we read Thascius Cyprianus' (cited in Toynbee 1939: 8) depiction of the dark age of another period, he gives us an account of the ecological and climatological conditions that have been not addressed by the previous scholars:

> This truth is proclaimed, even if we keep silence. . ., by the World itself, which testifies to its own decline by giving manifold concrete evidences of the process of decay. There is diminution in the winter rains that give nourishment to the seeds in the earth, and in the summer heats that ripen the harvests. The springs have less freshness and the autumns less fecundity. The mountains, disemboweled and worn out, yield a lower output of marble; the mines, exhausted, furnish a smaller stock of the precious metals: the veins are impoverished, and they shrink daily.

The above combination of excerpts provides a glimpse of what conditions were like socio-economically and ecologically during dark ages.

Given the rarity of occurrence of dark ages, these periods are interesting from a world system evolutionary viewpoint. Dark ages can disclose for us the transformative processes leading to change, and uncover the processes and structural changes leading to a reorganization of the world system. They present the extreme point of system limits and, as such, provide an opportunity for our understanding of the evolution and transformation of the world system.

From a growth and social progress model, the above descriptions of widespread distress indicate a significant crisis in social reproduction, whereby production/appropriation, exchange/distribution and consumption as interlocked processes were not maintaining comparable reproduction levels to the period prior to the phase of darkness.[7] Instead of growth and development, we see stagnation and devolution. Viewed from a long-term perspective, these distressed phases suggest that system transformation is not just a process that propels forward in a linear or geometric fashion, but one that is constituted by processes of evolution (growth) and devolution (stagnation) as the periods of dark ages reveal. The dynamics producing dark ages or crisis (devolution) in reproduction – assuming that the social reproduction processes have no priority of one over the other – should not be attributed to just *local* constraints hindering a region (such as prehistoric Greece) from reproducing itself within its social and ecological parameters. With the different levels and manner of interconnectedness of social formations in a world system, the roots of the crisis of reproduction are not solely limited to local or regional conditions, but to world systemic dimensions as well, depending on the state of evolution of the world system.[8] It involves, therefore, multiple levels of conditions and factors on a large geographic scale.[9]

Given the above, the constraints to system reproduction can arise as a result of different relations and interactions over time and space, and dark ages are the periods when these constraints manifest themselves. There are a variety of reasons and factors at different levels that could engender social reproduction constraints and, hence, crisis. For example, constraints can emerge as a consequence of a social formation's intensive relation with its ecological environment within and without, or they can be the result of the contradictions between and within social groups, or the outcome of the incommensurability of different functions of the social formation giving rise to contradictions (for example, a chosen social strategy that cannot be supported by the existing economy). Beyond this, reproduction limitations can also emerge as a result of unintended consequences from the social strategies chosen.

The numerous constraints and factors, such as contradictions between and within social groups or the incommensurability of different functions of the social formation giving rise to contradictions triggering crises of reproduction, identified have mostly been derived from social, political and economic roots. What is seldom discussed during these phases of dark ages is the social formation's relation with its ecological environment within and without. This neglect frames our perception that dark ages are characterized *only* by social, political and economic depressive conditions. They exhibit conditions of acute social, economic and political disruptions exhibited by trends such as economic slowdowns, structural social and political breakdowns, deurbanization, increased/reduced migration and population losses.[10] They do not reveal to us the scale of ecological degradation. If explanations of crisis sequences are limited only to socio-economic and political origins – dark ages are therefore not understood as periods circumscribed by ecological crisis and climatological changes – we will accordingly miss other factors and dimensions that might be determinative[11] or contingent in terms of explanatory power. Widening and deepening our gaze through the inclusion of the ecological landscape, the natural processes and the climatological cycles that circumscribe our material lives would compensate for the deficit. But such an adjustment would mean a different line of reasoning and presentation of historical data (from the ecological landscape) that will lead to an explanation for sequences (dark ages) in world history from a different angle from what has been proposed to date. It would stress that there are costs associated with the reproduction of socio-economic life, and the consequence has been a trajectory of numerous collisions with the natural environment as civilizations, empires, kingdoms and nation states seek to reproduce themselves (Ponting 1991; Chew 1999, 2001). The outcomes of such collisions have been natural resource depletion, loss of species diversity, polluted oceans and rivers, siltation, population losses due to flooding, etc. (Chew 1999, 2001; Hughes 2001). The end result is that, during these dark ages, we find ecological degradation on the world scale (Chew 1999, 2001).

Examining the dark ages in greater detail reveals that the culture–nature relations during such a period exhibit trends and tendencies that are significantly different from expansionary phases. The socio-economic patterns that emerged during these dark ages veered away from the usual intensive exploitation of nature that normally characterizes the trends and dynamics of human societal reproduction. During such phases of world history, all expansionary trends that are typical reproductive features of human communities display negative trajectories and tendencies, especially in the core areas of the world system.[12] Dark ages thus also represent ecological long phases reflecting the outcomes of the relations between culture and nature. We find several culture–nature trends and patterns that are subdued: fall in population levels, decline or loss in certain material skills, decay in the cultural aspects of life, fall in living standards and thus wealth and loss of trading contacts.[13]

Notwithstanding the visible impacts on socio-economic life as a consequence of the onset of the dark ages, these impacts do not extend necessarily and evenly across geospatial boundaries of the system. The articulations of the connections between and within regions during certain periods of world history reveal further the characteristic of culture–nature relations, especially those perpetrated by the dominant core for a certain period of time on the periphery of the world system. In this regard, ecological degradative shadows are cast by the dominant core over wide areas of the world system. These shadows are thus a consequence of core–periphery relations beyond those ecologically degradative effects that might be generated by the periphery itself. Depending on the systemic connections of the world economy at a particular point in time, and the level of intensity of the culture–nature relations experienced by a given region, the extent of impact of a dark age period is uneven. The state of crisis and/or transition appears to have its greatest impact on the regions of the world system that are considered the core/s of the system at the specific point in time. No doubt, this is related to the fact that it is in the core region/s where culture–nature relations are at their most heightened levels. This does not imply that the periphery does not experience any crisis-type conditions. The connections that the core has with the periphery via several economic and political processes ensure that at least some (if not all) crisis conditions will be felt. The extent, of course, is based on how incorporated the periphery is in the productive processes of the core/s.

To some extent, the crisis/transition also offers opportunities for some in the periphery to rearticulate themselves within the hierarchical matrix of the zonal production and reproduction processes. One would suspect that the conditions and impacts of the dark age occur in different phases for the core and the periphery/margins, and the simultaneity and synchronicity of these conditions are contingent on the connectivity of the world system at a particular point in time. As human history evolved and with the increasing systemic connectivity between regions and the development of new technologies, these long ecological swings of culture–nature relations (dark ages) are more systemic and have a greater impact when they occur.

Besides these devastating ecological outcomes, climatological changes are also associated with dark ages. Climatological changes and natural calamities when they occur during dark ages generate further challenges to social system reproduction. Their occurrences and impacts on social systems have been noted during periods of dark ages (see, for example, Weiss *et al.* 1993; Chew 1999; Keys 1999; Weiss 2000; Weiss and Bradley 2001). Higher than normal temperatures can generate salinization problems for agricultural cultivation, especially in areas where irrigation is used extensively. It could also lower harvest yields. The aridity that commonly occurs with high temperatures has often generated severe problems for pastoral herds that have led to nomadic migrations, thus causing further pressures on core centres.

Ecologically speaking, dark ages should be appreciated as periods for the restoration of the ecological balance that has been disrupted by centuries of intensive human exploitation of nature. Furthermore, if dark ages are prolonged crisis periods, crisis provides opportunities. In other words, crisis conditions, although perhaps restricting continuous unfettered expansion, provide the opportunities for the resolution of contradictions that have developed to such a state that inhibits the reproduction of the system. Thus, crisis enables the necessary adjustments to be made. It leads to pathways and processes that would mean system reorganization, and perhaps even transition. Given this, dark ages are systemic in nature, and their occurrence provides the opportunity for systemic reorganization, perhaps also engendering systemic transition followed by redistribution of resources, political power and economic concentration.

Dark ages therefore depict very specific moments in world history when system reproduction is in a state of crisis and/or transition. Resolution of the crisis requires an extended period of time (historically at least 900 years) as the length of occurrence of a specific dark age has revealed. Such an expanse of time (ecological time) provides the window of opportunity for the ecological balance to be restored in order to enable economic productive capacities to continue. Especially with resource depletion, the need arises for innovations in social organization and technology. If it is not possible for the ecological environment/balance and trade networks to be restored, new geographical areas of ecological assets have to be located and/or replacement of much depleted natural resources for production found. Furthermore, technological innovations could also occur to address the issue of depleted natural resources so that some level of economic production can continue. Besides this, it underlines further the different time duration for our understanding of the interaction between culture and the natural environment measured along ecological time compared with political and economic activities that are necessarily gauged along social time.

Related to the above developments, various social, political and economic processes come into play during such moments of systemic crisis and/or transition. They range from social upheavals (revolts, wars, etc.) and dislocations (such as migrations) to cultural/ideological shifts, along with political and social reorganizations, etc.

In certain circumstances, resolution of a system crisis might not necessarily lead to a system transition. In this case, the crisis is resolved because the ecological balance has been restored allowing for social reproduction on the extended scale to occur, and the state of the socio-economic organizations and political hegemonies in place have the capacity to meet the contingencies of the restored ecological balance. If, however, these conditions are not in place, a new set of organizing and learning principles will need to be engendered in order to meet the contingencies of the transformed terrain generated by the crisis conditions of the dark age. In such a context, qualitative changes ensue and a system transition occurs. In this regard, perhaps what have been identified as long economic cycles or *conjonctures* might not reveal the long-term trends of the world system, and thus might not be as valuable or insightful for our understanding of the long-term processes of the evolution of the world system. Instead, we suspect that perhaps these long ecological phases might be *the* system transition moments leading to structural changes of the system as a whole. What this means is that world history is not a flattened history accounting for networks of trading links and economic cycles of expansion and contraction with little or no distinguishing differences between periods, but one with ruptures through time leading to system reorganization and social evolutionary changes.

Hence, dark ages are important moments in world history for they provide opportunities for the ecological balance to be restored, political and economic opportunities for some peripheral groups to advance up the zonal power matrix, and for reconfiguration of the hierarchical division of political economic power of the world system at specific conjunctures of world history. The rarity of such occurrences in the last 5,000 years of world history suggests the resilience of the ecological landscape to human assault. Besides this, it underlines further the different time duration for our understanding of the interaction between culture and the natural environment measured along ecological time compared with political and economic activities that are necessarily gauged along social time.

Given the above discussion, we need to abstract theoretically generalizable structures and processes of dark ages in order to consider dark ages as a world system process that occurs in phases in world system evolution. In doing this, we offer a theoretically generalized account of system crises in the Bronze and Iron Ages. Owing to space limitations, I am not able to provide as much specific and contingent political, ecological and socio-economic detail to discuss the system crises during the Bronze and Iron Ages to buttress my argument further.

Culture–nature relations and ecological crisis: a brief overview 2200 BC to AD 900

Following the Neolithic Revolution, the urban revolution as a world historical process further framed the course of human history (see, for example, Childe 1950). One of the earliest signs of this urbanization process appeared in the riverine valleys of southern Mesopotamia, Egypt and north-western India over 5,000 years ago, and continued the transformation of the landscape by human communities that started with the advent of agriculture. The process of urbanization encompassed trade linkages and accumulation, cultural exchanges and a specialized and differentiated division of labour across the system. This type of architecture of physical structures, social institutions and commerce further heightened the hierarchical distribution of rewards within and between regions. Coupled with the population increases, the process of urbanization framed the level of extensive resources required to reproduce the system that emerged (Chew 2001).

Viewed from the perspective of the human community, underlying this world historical process was the expansion and efflorescence in the areas of production, trade, cultural transformation and the growth of cities. Trade, production and urbanization processes interacted with demographic increases to construct a human world of exuberance. Innovations in metallurgical processes and in the fabrication of commodities such as textiles established the search for and removal of natural resources and forests. In the Mesopotamian valleys, ziggurats, public buildings, canals, granaries and other facilities that depicted economic growth were erected coupled with extensive trading across the Arabian Sea and Red Sea to Egypt in the west and the Harappan civilization in the east (Chew 2001). In these last two centres, the levels of urbanization and human specialization (division of labour) were of the same scale. Temples, pyramids, grain storage areas and citadels were constructed from burnt bricks, granite and other materials that could be secured locally or imported.

Out of this urban and demographic transformation came the further development of a set of urbanized enclaves that specialized in resource extraction, trade exchanges and commodity production in a systemic context, initially extending from west Asia and eastern Mediterranean to north-western India (Chew 2001). Further expansion from the second millennium onwards brought Europe, central Asia and China into this expanding network of urbanization, commerce and trade exchanges.

Viewed from the perspective of nature, such world historical processes produced a continuous and degradative transformation of the landscape. Trees were removed for agriculture and to meet the energy and material needs of urbanizing communities. The valleys were excavated for canals to provide irrigation for crops and for the transportation of people and goods. Other lands were dug up for their natural resources and building materials. Such large-scale human activities as deforestation led to soil erosion in the mountains and hills, and the continuous impact of human activities further heightened the process. Rivers were dammed. In all, socio-economic activities along with wars were transforming the landscape with scars revealing the scale of such acts.

Notwithstanding periods of economic stagnation, such efflorescence of the human communities would ultimately lead to ecological distress. This emerged over very long periods of time. Coupled with these long phases of ecological crisis are climatological shifts and eruptions of natural processes that had a great impact on the social, political and economic landscape.

A *systemic* crisis or dark age began around 2200 BC initially affecting north-western India, the Gulf, Mesopotamia, Egypt and west Asia, and this had repercussions for the urbanized core areas such as Mesopotamia, Indus and Egypt. Following this, new power centres emerged in the Near East, northern Mesopotamia and the eastern Mediterranean. This systemic crisis continued until 700 BC, depending on the region, and affected the main areas of west Asia, Egypt, the eastern Mediterranean and central Europe (from 800 BC onwards). These periods of crisis were not only characterized by socio-economic distress, regime transitions and centre/hinterland conflicts but also riddled with population losses, deurbanization, natural resource depletion, environmental degradation and climatological changes. Negative ecological trends (such as deforestation) were observed from 2200 BC onwards (Chew 2001). Temperature increases and aridity pulsated from 2205 BC with warm periods and dryness alternating with cool conditions and moistness (Fairbridge *et al.* 1997: 603–6). Such ecological and climatological circumstances affected the reproduction capacities of some parts of the system, and reverberated throughout the system as the Bronze Age proceeded.

Recovery returned around 700 BC with social systems expanding and growing in complexity again. Expansion came first in the form of colonization by the Greeks in two phases. Between 775 and 675 BC, such expansion was for agricultural purposes, where the soils and lands of Greece, which were degraded after centuries of erosion and intensive cultivation, could no longer produce sufficient to meet the needs of the population. The excessive population mostly comprised poor peasants who were turned into tenant farmers (*hectemores*) with debts that were increasing, and were thus forced to swell the population of the cities. With the state of the degraded environment in Greece, with the exception of Boeotia, Attica and Sparta, where internal colonization was still possible with some fertile agricultural land left, expansion of the system came with migration to other arenas such as Italy, Sicily, southern France and west Asia. Growth in this case comes from a colonization process that was extensive in nature and a consequence of the ecological crisis of the dark age that had just ended. Following the success of the agricultural colonization strategies with surplus generation, a second round of colonization followed from 675 to 600 BC, mainly focusing on commercial activities. With this phase of colonization, trade routes were further fixed and strengthened. Wealth for the colonial cities was derived from agricultural exports, trade and production. Other growth poles of the system then were Egypt, Persia and Phoenicia and, as Braudel (2001: 225) puts it, the Mediterranean never became a 'Greek Lake'. With these different centres, no polity ever gained control of the Mediterranean.

It was only with the arrival of Rome that the Mediterranean became a Roman sea. The growing rise of Rome and the demise of Greece did not interrupt the continuous degradation of the environment (Chew 2001). Forests were removed in northern Africa, and Roman rule was established almost everywhere. Mines were dug in Spain, with cities, roads and production facilities established within the Roman empire. Crisis emerged again 700 years later, around AD 400, with similar trends and tendencies in terms of ecological and socio-economic variables to that of the dark ages that occurred during the Bronze Age. This time, the collapses were not in Mesopotamia, Harappa, Mycenaean Greece, Crete or the Hittite Empire, but were in the western portion of the Roman Empire and the system of the Iron Age.

Dark ages over world history 2200 BC to AD 900

Social historians and archaeologists have noted the various phases in world history in which dark ages have occurred. To them, these periods cover centuries, with perhaps the very earliest starting at 2200–1700 BC or what Barbara Bell (1971) has chronologized as the first dark age of ancient history. This downturn was followed by another period from 1200 BC to 700 BC, and another phase starting from AD 400 to AD 900.

Periodizing these dark age phases along a social time continuum, I would suggest that the first known crisis of the Bronze Age world system (there is an indication that there was an earlier crisis of the Bronze Age world system around 3800/3400 BC) started from 2200 BC onwards and continued to 1700 BC. The system crisis emerged again in 1200 BC and lasted until 700 BC, when it was finally resolved with the transition to the Iron Age. With the arrival of the Iron Age, system expansion continued through the early Iron Age. By AD 400, system crisis returned, resulting in another prolonged period of ecological and socio-economic distress that lasted until AD 900.

The extent of the impact of the dark age conditions in terms of geographical limits of the system is difficult to map completely, especially with the limited amount of available data to consider and our understanding of the level of connectivity of the system. Rather than being comprehensive in coverage, instead I will identify selectively the simultaneity and connectivity of the different areas of the world system that were affected by the dark age conditions. It should be realized that not all regions/zones of the world system were affected simultaneously during the same period. The effect was dependent on the state of connectivity between the regions of the system. A more comprehensive treatment will appear in the second volume of my book *World Ecological Degradation* (*Dark Ages: Ecological Stress and Systems Transformation*) (forthcoming, 2006).

The identified time periods for the dark ages were dated from archaeological finds and literary accounts of social, economic and political trends and activities. However, if we are to examine the pollen profiles of deforestation and reforestation, the periodization for the first dark age is much longer. In fact, in most cases, continuous from 2200 BC to 700 BC with no breaks indicating recovery after 1700 BC as the archaeological and literary accounts have indicated (see Table 10.1). Underneath the swell of socio-economic expansion starting after 1700 BC, the structural conditions of ecological distress continue and, through time, system crisis conditions emerge again at the social historical level until a system reorganization occurs to resolve the system crisis that arose from contradictions in culture–nature relations. This continuous period of uninterrupted ecological distress from 2200 BC to 700 BC means that natural or even human-induced regeneration takes longer and has its own rhythm even though an expansion has started at the level of the political economy with increasing social systems complexity noted.

If, as I have indicated, we conceive of dark ages as periods of ecological crises – besides being characterized commonly as having declining population, trade and economic disruptions, deurbanization and changes in political regimes by anthropologists, historians and archaeologists – we would expect to find some proxy indicators of ecological degradation such as deforestation levels, soil erosion and endangered species underlining these periods. Coupled with these ecological indicators, one would also expect to find climatological changes such as temperature, rainfall and natural disturbances punctuating these periods as well.

Besides natural processes of loss and regeneration, ecological degradation levels are outcomes of culture–nature relations. These relations are determined by the expansionary dynamics of the process of accumulation in the world system, urbanization processes and population levels. With *conjonctures* of economic expansion and other related processes, we would expect to find extreme signs of ecological degradation such as deforestation reflecting and following these economic expansionary phases. These *conjonctures* of economic expansion serve as markers identifying the periods of extreme exploitation of ecological resources. The scale and scope of ecological degradation is, of course, determined by the connectivity of the world system, as well as by the nature of core–periphery relations for the period in question. What this means is that ecological degradation can be quite overarching as a consequence of the relations between regions of the world system and the global division of labour existing during the particular period in question. Coupled with these dynamics of accumulation, urbanization and population circumscribing and underlining the pace of ecological degradation, conflicts and wars further exacerbate the degree of ecological degradation.

Deforestation

With its many uses, wood has been an important commodity in the reproduction of social life and the accumulation of capital since the Neolithic Revolution (Chew 2001). Over world history from at least 3000 BC onwards, the available forests have been exploited intensively to meet the needs of an evolving world system, starting from the core centres such as Egypt, Mesopotamia and Harappa (Perlin 1989; Chew 2001; Williams 2003). As such, deforestation was the order of the day. More than 4,500 years ago, we find the Mesopotamians and the Harappans deforesting their own hills and mountains, and conducting military campaigns and trade relations with their peripheries to seek a constant wood supply in order to reproduce their urbanization and accumulation processes. By no means were the Harappans and the Mesopotamians the exception, the Egyptians sought their wood in neighbouring areas of Lebanon and parts of the Syrian coast. For Europe, Kristiansen (1998: 281–92), reporting early third millennium BC pollen profiles for Thy, a region in north-western Denmark, has also alerted us to the extreme deforestation caused by extensive land use and animal husbandry. In fact, he has extended this deforestation level to most of north-western Europe for this time sequence.

With wood being an important element in the reproduction of the ancient economies, such levels of deforestation led to the collapse of social systems or to short reigns in Mesopotamia, north-western India, Egypt and Europe, and to realignments of communities and trading arrangements during the dark age period between 2200 BC and 1700 BC (Kristiansen 1998; Chew 2001). Approximately 500 years later, we find such ecologically degradative practices continuing in the eastern Mediterranean, such as in Crete and Mycenaean

Table 10.1 Arboreal pollen profiles – deforestation periods

Area		Phase 1	Phase 2	Phase 3	Phase 4
1	Belgium (Moerzeke)	3093 BC–2600 BC	2002 BC–1274 BC	AD 180–AD 544	
2	Bulgaria 1 (Besbog-2)		1730 BC–AD 1160		AD 1500–AD 1832
3	Bulgaria 2 (Mire Garvan)	3901 BC–2123 BC	1235 BC–AD 882		AD 1162–AD 1628
4	Byleorussia 1 (Dolgoe)	4800 BC–3850 BC	3400 BC–750 BC	AD 380–AD 1460	
5	Byleorussia 2 (Osvea)	3600 BC–330 BC			AD 1334–AD 1778
6	Finland 1 (Kirkkosaari)	3022 BC–AD 1537			
7	Finland 2 (Mukkavaara)	3618 BC–AD 1757			
8	Finland 3 (Hirvilampi)	4283 BC–3540 BC	2611 BC–696 BC	AD 389–AD 1040	
9	France (Le Marais St Boetien)	3520 BC–585 BC		AD 327–AD 936	
10	Germany 1 (Lake Constance)		2325 BC–270 BC	AD 290–AD 1500	
11	Germany 2 (Lake Steisslingen)		2175 BC–144 BC	AD 348–AD 1594	
12	Greece (Edessa)	3998 BC–2852 BC	1941 BC–292 BC		AD 1026–AD 1800
13	Greece 2		1641 BC–AD 1700		

14	Greenland (Lake 31)	2864 BC–2178 BC	1700 BC–121 BC		AD 1139–
15	Hungary (Lake Balaton SW)		2683 BC–816 BC	AD 381–AD 1296	
16	Ireland (Arts Lough)	3726 BC–1653 BC		AD 352–AD 1094	
17	Italy (Selle di Carnino)	4539 BC–3000 BC		AD 436–AD 1220	AD 1529–AD 1634
18	Latvia (Rudushskoe Lake)	3955 BC–1700 BC		627 BC–AD 837	AD 1300–
19	Norway (Grasvatn)	4064 BC–3032 BC	1612 BC–AD 323		AD 1097–AD 1700
20	Poland 1 (Bledowo Lake)	3633 BC–2518 BC		724 BC–AD 967	AD 1533–
21	Poland 3 (Kluki)	3803 BC–665 BC		AD 452–AD 884	AD 1000–AD 1573
22	Russia (Chabada Lake)	3800 BC–1737 BC	1400 BC–306 BC		AD 1405–
23	Spain 1 (Saldropo)		2202 BC–774 BC	AD 300–AD 948	AD 1266–
24	Spain 2 (Sanabria Marsh)	3500 BC–1700 BC			AD 856–AD 1850
25	Spain 3 (Lago d Ajo)		1884 BC–552 BC	AD 309–AD 1170	
26	Spain 4 (Puerto de Los Tornos)	4200 BC–AD 395			AD 1200–AD 1750

Table 10.1 (continued)

Area	*Phase 1*	*Phase 2*	*Phase 3*	*Phase 4*
27 Spain 5 (Laguna de la Roya)	4500 BC–2728 BC	968 BC–AD 848		AD 1600
28 Sweden 1 (Agerods Mosse)	3004 BC–256BC	BC	AD 435–AD 1682	
29 Sweden 2 (Kansjon)	3752 BC–AD 978	BC		AD 1647–
30 Switzerland (Lonsigensee)	3920 BC–2170 BC	1253 BC–AD 767		AD 1055–
31 Syria (Ghab)	3592 BC–1505 BC	983 BC–AD 500		
32 Turkey 1 (K'ycegiz G'l)		2306 BC–616 BC	180 BC–AD916	AD 1700–AD 1941
33 Turkey 2 (Beysehir G'l)	3500 BC–2527 BC	243 BC–AD 1100		
34 Ukraine 1 (Karsashinski Swamp)	3673 BC–2170 BC	1338 BC–AD 300		AD 1229–
35 Ukraine 2 (Starniki)		2600 BC–727 BC		AD 93–AD 1400
36 Ukraine 3 (Stoyanov 2)	3900 BC–2020 BC		AD 300–AD 1660	
37 Ukraine 4 (Ivano-Frankovskoye)	3937 BC–500 BC			
38 Ukraine 5 (Dovjok Swamp)		2700 BC–224 BC	AD 40–AD 800	AD 1200–AD 1700

Source: Based on data from Bottema (1974), van Zeist *et al.* (1980), Eronen and Hyvrinen (1982), Amman (1985), Bezusko (1985, 1987), Behre and Kucan (1986), Binka *et al.* (1988), Bradshaw *et al.* (1988), Rankama and Vuorela (1988), Khomutova *et al.* (1994), Penalba (1994), Eisner *et al.* (1995), Lazarova (1995), Stefanova (1995), Watts *et al.* (1996) and Verbruggen *et al.* (1997).

Greece, and becoming acute during the next dark age from 1200 BC to 700 BC, leading to another system crisis (Chew 2001). The trend of deforestation continued, especially during the Classical Greek and Roman periods, ending with another dark age from AD 400 to AD 900. This tendency was followed later by core European powers such as Venice, Spain, Portugal, Holland, France and England deforesting on an increasingly global scale from AD 1200 onwards. Such practices added stress to system reproduction as well (Chew 2002).

Table 10.1 provides time sequences of deforestation covering various areas of the world starting from as early as 4800 BC. Despite the lack of identification of a dark age period in the fourth millennium BC by historians and archaeologists of the ancient world, it seems from some of the pollen profiles that there was a phase of deforestation during the fourth millenium BC. Not only do the pollen profiles exhibit such a period of deforestation, they also reveal the widespread geographical coverage of the degradation of areas in Russia and the Ukraine through to Spain and Syria. In the course of world history, it should not be assumed that this was the first phase of deforestation as the available data are quite limiting. It might perhaps be the first phase of anthropogenically induced deforestation with the advent of the Neolithic Revolution.

The available pollen data profiles (Tables 10.1 and 10.2) suggest three/four subsequent phases of deforestation followed by reforestation towards the later period of the course of a dark age. If dark age phase 1 started around 3800 BC, dark age phase 2 began around 2400 BC. It seems that, nested within this phase 2 dark age, another phase 2A began around 1200 BC. It was followed by dark age phase 3 at around AD 300, and dark age phase 4 at AD 1300. Such an identification of phases does not imply that deforestation follows a cycle. Rather, I am suggesting that there is a length of time when the ecological limit is reached as a consequence of culture–nature relations, thereby requiring a time period for ecological recovery (ecological time) and/or system adaptation (such as reorganization, learning processes, technological adaptation, etc.) to take place. This requires time. Timewise, for ecological recovery, ecological time is the underlying basis. For system adaptation, social time is the case. In this context, the period of social system adaptation is nested within the long duration of ecological time. What this also shows is that there is no systemic cyclical character in these phases other than recurrences over world history when culture–nature relations reached degradative levels whereby ecological regeneration was threatened. What needs to be noted, however, is that the advent of each deforestation phase dovetails with the concentration/urbanization process that Modelski (1999: 390) and Modelski and Thompson (2001: 182) have identified in world history from 3400 BC to 1200 BC. According to them, there were three periods of concentration/urbanization starting around 4000–3400BC, 1200 BC and AD 930. These time points fall within phases 1, 2, 2A and 3 of the deforestation phases outlined in Table 10.2. Phase 4 of deforestation began around AD 1300

Table 10.2 Periodization of dark ages[a]

Phase 1	*Phase 2*	*Phase 2A*	*Phase 3*	*Phase 4*
3854 BC– 2400 BC	2402 BC– 594 BC	1188 BC– AD 689	AD 296– AD 1171	AD 1311– AD 1733

Note
a Mean of 38 pollen profiles of deforestation phases.

and ended around AD 1700. In social time, this time period was also the crisis of the 'long' fourteenth century in Europe and the prelude to the later expansion of the world economy.

The above suggests that deforestation occurs with a long period of economic expansion. These identified periods of economic and political downturns and system collapses that are categorized as dark ages of human history exhibit deforestation and then recovery (reforestation) with the slowdown in socio-economic activity, deurbanization or a drop in human population, enabling the ecology to recover. In the long run, however, with the exception of certain geographical areas and during certain time periods, forest loss has outpaced reforestation. From Neolithic times to the present day, we have lost between seven and eight million kilometres of closed forest and two to three million kilometres of open woodland and shrubland (World Commission on Forests and Sustainable Development 1999). Thus, deforestation has a long history (Chew 2001; Ruddiman 2003).

With deforestation, there are also other consequences such as soil erosion, etc. There is ample evidence even as early as 2200 BC, during the first dark age (2200–1700 BC), in Mesopotamia and Harappa, that soil erosion resulting from deforestation had tremendous consequences for the agricultural economies of these early civilizations. It led to severe economic stress on these social systems and, coupled with climatological changes and natural disturbances, led to crisis in these civilizations (Chew 1997, 2001). Soil erosion was also a condition experienced by Minoan Crete and Mycenaean Greece during the dark age period 1200–700 BC. The occurrence of soil erosion during the period of decline of the Roman Empire prior to the onset of the dark age period AD 300–900 underlines the recurring nature of widespread soil erosion punctuating dark age periods.

Climatological changes, natural disturbances and catastrophes

Considerations of climatological changes, natural disturbances and catastrophes affecting social (world) system reproduction have not warranted much attention in social science analysis in comparison with capital accumulation issues, class and elite dynamics, technological adaptation and ideological/cultural processes. For example, the widespread collapses of cities and civilizations in the Aegean during the dark age period between 1200 BC and 700 BC were believed to result from human agency. Therefore, innovations in sword manufacturing, invasions by foreign armies, internal corruption and economic disintegration as possible explanations for the demise of cities in the Aegean during this dark age period are preferred to other explanations that consider climatological changes, tectonic effects or even comets colliding with earth as possible vectors for the widespread destruction of these communities (see, for example, Yoffee 1988; Drews 1993; Friedman 2003). Such adherence to anthropogenic-induced explanations for political–economic declines, and even the collapse of social systems, is rather unfortunate, for there are some indications linking climatological changes as one of the factors affecting social (world) system reproduction. Through world history, socio-economic and political changes (such as trade collapses and political changes), including large-scale migrations, have occurred during periods of climate change. What is significant is the clustering of climatological changes, natural disturbances and the occurrence of catastrophes during dark age phases.

Climatological changes

The dark age starting around 2200 BC was a systemic crisis of the Bronze Age system. This systemic crisis and the consequent political–economic declines, and even collapses of the core centres of the Bronze Age world system, can be linked, I believe, to factors that are non-anthropogenic in nature. There is evidence of temperature changes (higher temperatures) and increasingly drought-like conditions persisting in the eastern Mediterranean, Egypt, west Asia, Mesopotamia, north-western India, central Asia, Africa and parts of the New World starting from 2200 BC onwards during the onset of the dark age of the third millennium (Ratnagar 1981; Neumann and Parpola 1987; Bentaleb *et al.* 1997; Enzel *et al.* 1999; Chew 2001; Weiss and Bradley 2001).[14]

Time series of temperature changes in terms of warm and cool periods have been offered by Fairbridge *et al.* (1997) categorizing this period as a warm period, meaning increasing aridity of the environment (see Table 10.3). Such conditions have significant impact on social systems that rely on irrigation-based agriculture and on social and political stability (Neumann and Parpola 1987). During this period, besides southern Mesopotamia, we find regional abandonment and selected collapse of social and political systems in Egypt, Assyria, Greece, Indus, Crete, Russia and Palestine from 2200 BC onwards, and another set of upheavals starting around the next dark age at about 1200 BC (Bell 1971; Bottema 1997; Hassan 1997; Krementski 1997; Chew 2001; Weiss and Bradley 2001; Fagan 2004).

Such temperature conditions have significant impact on social systems that rely on irrigation-based agriculture and on social and political stability.[15] Southern Mesopotamia is a case in point. Between 2400 BC and 1700 BC, southern Mesopotamia faced a crisis in agricultural productivity (Jacobsen and Adams 1958; Adams 1981). The stratified society pursued intensive socio-economic activities to produce surplus for domestic consumption as well as for exports (in the form of grains and woollen textiles) to the Gulf and

Table 10.3 Cool and warm periods: Anatolia and adjacent regions

Period	
3385 BC–3250 BC	Cool
3250 BC–2900 BC	Warm
2900 BC–2710 BC	Cool
2710 BC–2345 BC	Warm
2345 BC–2205 BC	Cool
2205 BC–1650 BC	Warm (dark age)
1670 BC–1655 BC	Cool
1650 BC–1410 BC	Warm
1410 BC–1205 BC	Cool
1205 BC–815 BC	Warm (dark age)
815 BC–685 BC	Cold
685 BC–406 BC	Warm

Source: Fairbridge (1997).

beyond. The scale of intensity required extensive deforestation, maximal utilization of agriculture and animal husbandry. Furthermore, with a state structure requiring tax payments, etc., the farmers were required to have an increasing surplus to meet the reproductive needs of the system (Jacobsen and Adams 1958). Besides requiring surplus production, state direction during the Third Dynasty of Ur (2150–2000 BC) also concentrated on certain economic activities such as the production of wool and the development of a large-scale textile industry. This further pushed the need to increase agricultural productivity in the form of feed grains such as barley for sheep (Adams 1981). Population increases and state initiatives to establish new towns peopled by conquered populations for the purpose of pursuing agricultural and textile manufacturing added to the range of economic practices that required heightened resource utilization (Gelb 1973). The end result of these political and economic initiatives was an intensification of agricultural production that pushed the agricultural lands to the limit.

Salinization was a problem in Mesopotamia from the third millennium onwards. Wheat and barley production, grown in the mid-fourth millennium in equal portions, had shifted to more barley cultivation by the end of the third millennium. With the salinity problem, after 1700 BC, the cultivation of wheat was completely given up as barley was a more salt-tolerant grain and more resistant to temperature changes. In addition, barley was also the preeminent feed for sheep, whose end product, wool, was a commodity required for long-distance trade. However, this change in grain cultivation did not solve the issue of soil salinity, which is reflected in the harvest yields. Between 3000 and 2350 BC (Early Dynastic period), crop yields were 2,030 litres per hectare. By 2150–2000 BC (Third Dynasty of Ur), the yield had fallen to 1,134 litres per hectare. By 1700 BC, crop yields had slipped to 718 litres per hectare (Jacobsen and Adams 1958). The agricultural productivity crisis reached its nadir when cultivable land was kept in production with yields of only 370 litres per hectare (Adams 1981). With such yields, the 'burden on the cultivator had become a crushing one' (Adams 1981: 152).

To meet this agricultural crisis, seeding rates were increased. Between 2150 and 2000 BC, 55.5 litres of seed were planted per hectare. This volume doubled in comparison with the previous period between 3000 and 2350 BC Furthermore, with no consideration for the repercussions, alternate-year fallowing was also violated in order to maintain the maximum amount of land available for cultivation (Gibson 1970). Fallowing is the traditional method of handling salinization. In Mesopotamia, by leaving the land to fallow, wild plants such as *shok* and *agul* drew moisture from the water table and dried up the subsoil. This prevented the water from rising and bringing the salts to the surface. When the land was cultivated again, the dryness of the subsoil allowed the irrigation water to leach salt from the surface and drain it below the root level. Fallowing therefore returned the land to its cultivation potential. By reducing or violating fallow times, the productivity of the land was endangered.

For ecological landscapes that are mostly semi-arid, such as in southern Mesopotamia, a drop in rainfall would generate severe stress on agricultural production. Confirmation of these changes via decreased pollen yields, Tigris–Euphrates stream flow, dust spikes and a decrease in lake levels has been made in recent years (Weiss and Bradley 2001). The Dead Sea area reported a 20–30 per cent drop in precipitation from the previous period of 610 mm (Bar-Matthews and Avalon 1997: 155–68; Bar-Matthews *et al.* 1998: 203–14, 1999: 85–95). Pollen records from Lake Zeribar in west Asia suggest extreme drought (Bottema 1997). The Lake Van cores document a dust spike around 2290–2000 BC, a decrease in lake levels and a rapid increase in aridity (Lemcke and Sturm 1997: 653–78). The Lake Van proxies provide a climate record for the Tigris–Euphrates headwaters region.

Given such climatological changes during the first dark age between 2200 BC and 1700 BC, the agricultural sector in southern Mesopotamia was further stressed as increasing temperatures led to a rise in evapotranspiration. For irrigated agriculture, which was the basis of southern Mesopotamian agricultural practices, this would mean a demand for more water. With the drop in rainfall, intensive use of irrigated water had a deleterious effect on agricultural land, which already possessed a salinity problem. In northern Mesopotamia, such climatic conditions also affected towns such as Tell Brak and Tell Leilan under Akkadian imperial rule, which shared the same fate as the urbanized areas in the south (Weiss 2000). Abandonment of towns and settlements in the Habur plains also followed.

During this period, besides Mesopotamia, we find regional abandonment and selected collapse of social and political systems in Egypt, Assyria, Greece,

Indus, Crete, Russia and Palestine from 2200 BC onwards (Bell 1971; Bottema 1997; Hassan 1997; Krementski 1997; Chew 2001).

Temperature increases also affected Egypt. During this period (2200–1700 BC), climate changes led to a reduced flow of the Nile, thus lowering its level and inducing drought conditions that had a systemic impact on the overall economy of Egypt and its surrounding lands (Bell 1971, Hassan 1997). The growth and expansion of Egypt have to be understood within the context of the Nile River. It is this drainage system that is the backbone of the agricultural economy of Egypt. The annual flooding of the Nile valley provides the rejuvenation of the agricultural landscape. On this basis, lower river levels would mean falling Nile flood levels. Such occurrences would have a severe impact on agricultural production, especially in light of the semi-arid conditions of Egypt. Nile flow is a function of the amount of rain that falls in the Ethiopian Highlands and the precipitation stored in Lakes Abhe, Zway-Shala and Turkana. The rainfall in these highlands accounts for 83 per cent of Nile water at Aswan. The seasonality of the rain is dependent on the Indian monsoon that falls between June and August (Barry and Chorley 1992). Therefore, any changes in the monsoon would have an impact on rainfall, which would ultimately lower the flow of the Nile. Around 2200 BC, a severe lake level reduction was reported at Lakes Abhe, Zway-Shala and Turkana (Johnson and Odada 1996; Ricketts and Johnson 1996; Gasse 2000). This led to a lower Nile flow and level, which resulted in aridity and drought conditions in Egypt (Hassan 1986, 1997; Bryson and Bryson 1998).

There were also reports of the invasion of dune sand in the valley near Memphis, suggesting the increasing aridity of the landscape (Hassan 1997). In Middle Egypt, sand dunes also invaded the flood plain. Lack of high floods from the Nile along with the dry climate led to severe pressure on the agricultural system as naturally irrigated areas for crop cultivation were reduced. Famine followed and has been confirmed by the ancient texts of Egypt (Bell 1971; Hassan 1997).

The above climate-induced conditions led to reduced agroproduction which, in turn, had an impact on the Egyptian economy of the First Intermediate period (Weiss 2000). Flood failures occurred between 2180 BC and 2135 BC and again between 2005 BC and 1992 BC (Bell 1975). Signs of famine emerged again around 1750 BC, although they were not as severe as those that occurred in 2200 BC (Bell 1975).

In central Eurasia, preliminary data have also confirmed marked changes in vegetation, beginning around 2200 BC and lasting until around 1700 BC, following increases in temperature (Krementski 1997; Hiebert 2000). Pollen cores indicate a sharp decrease in tree pollen and an increase in steppe pollen. From 2200 BC to 2000 BC, there was a severe drop in forest cover and an increase in steppification, leading to an expansion in the steppe landscape from 1800 BC to 1700 BC. Arid conditions also affected arable land, which caused severe pressure on the animal husbandry of the steppe population. The lush feathergrass steppe that depicted the landscape near Kalmykia from 2500 BC to 2200 BC gave way to dry scrubby vegetation – wormwood steppe – and even desertification by 220–1700 BC. This changed ecological landscape led to outmigration of the sedentary population from river valleys with time, and exploitation of the steppes for animal feed.

Natural disturbances

During this period, in north-western India, tectonic shifts occurred that diverted water courses. In turn, these diversions transformed some rivers into dry riverbeds, further exacerbating the aridity, and thereby impacting on socio-economic life. The drying up of the Sarasvati River had major implications for Harappan urban complexes located on its banks (Possehl 2001). Agrawal and Sood (1982) have noted tectonic shifts that diverted the course of the Satluz and the easterly rivers away from the Ghaggar, which over time became a lake-like depression during this period. Thus, in northern and western Rajasthan, unstable river systems affected socio-economic life. Furthermore, tectonic disturbances also cut off Lothal from its feeder river and eventually the port's access to the sea.

Such climatological changes, tectonic shifts and earthquakes recurred around the next dark age from 1200 BC to 700 BC, affecting the Aegean, with Crete experiencing such shifts as early as 1500 BC. It has been argued that, between 2800 BC and AD 400, a particularly active tectonic regime was in force in the southern Aegean (Manning 1994). Such a pattern of geological conditions meant that volcanic eruptions and earthquakes around 1500 BC provided some of the circumstances for the demise of Crete (Marinatos 1939; Chadwick 1976; Warren 1985). According to Chadwick, earthquakes followed by volcanic eruption on Thera precipitated the delimiting conditions for the Minoans even further (Chadwick 1976; Burgess 1989; Baillie 1995). The volcanic ash not only killed vegetation but also destroyed the Minoan naval fleet. The loss of the latter undermined Cretan naval supremacy that for a long period had provided Minoan Crete with the power to exercise its dominant position in this region of the world system.

For Mycenaean Greece, by 1200 BC, the natural environment was severely stretched. Placed within such a context, the thesis of climatological change proposed by Rhys Carpenter for the demise of Mycenaean Greece needs to be considered (Carpenter 1968). Basically, Carpenter's position is that, with the shift in the tracks of the cyclonic storms that normally bring rain to Mycenaean Greece, a disruption in the rainfall pattern followed for the interior of the Greek mainland. This resulted in drought-like conditions during the thirteenth to the twelfth centuries BC. The persistent drought was also accompanied by an increase in land temperature. As a consequence, the socio-economic structure was affected.[16]

According to Bryson *et al.* (1974: 49), during this period (*c.* thirteenth century), drought conditions and increases in land temperature were also reported in other parts of the world system. The Anatolian plateau had a precipitation rate 20–40 per cent below normal, and the temperature was 2.5–4 degrees Centigrade above normal. The precipitation in Libya was 50 per cent below normal, and the temperature was 1.5 degrees Centigrade above normal. Finally, Bryson *et al.* (1974) also noted that settlements in northern Persia were abandoned because of drought. The precipitation was 50 per cent below normal, and the temperature was 1.7–2.5 degrees Centigrade above normal.

Besides climatological changes, earthquakes have also been suggested as causal factors for the decline of Mycenaean Greece. Earthquakes at Tiryns, Mycenae and the Argolid during the late Helladic period have been suggested for the decline of these two urbanized communities (Zanggar 1993; Mylonas 1996).

Similar climatological changes also occurred during the dark age between AD 300 and AD 900. Temperature increases occurred in Europe, west Asia, China and parts of the Americas (Bryson and Padoch 1980; Broecker 2001; DeMenocal 2001; Weiss and Bradley 2001). In fact, Broecker (2001) has suggested that this warming trend was a global phenomenon and lasted until AD 1200. Analysis of tree rings in Sweden also suggests such climatological shifts.[17] Tree ring evidence from western Europe, Britain and North America also reveals drought-like conditions and slowed growth (Keys 1999). This warming trend resulted in drought-like conditions being felt in the above-mentioned geographical areas, leading to widespread famine, for example in northern China and Korea during AD 530s. Besides the socio-economic tragedies experienced, such as trade route disruption, diseases, etc., there was also political collapse, such as the decline of the Roman Empire, the classic Mayan culture and the Moché civilization of northern Peru. Some scholars have suggested that climate changes might also be a contributing factor besides those of overpopulation, deforestation, soil erosion, social warfare, etc. (Davis and Shaw 2001; Weiss and Bradley 2001).

In summary, what the above shows is that, during periods of what we have termed the dark ages of world history, besides the major ecological damage that occurred as a result of the prior period of intensive and extensive socio-economic expansion and concentration, it seems that climatological changes were also the order of the day. The latter, depending on the ecological landscape, affected the reproduction of social life. Mapping such interactions between climate changes, regime transition and centre–hinterland conflict provides insights into global transformations. Preliminary analyses such as those of Thompson (2000) and Chew (2002) have suggested a correlation between climate change and political–economic transitions for the period commencing 2200 BC onwards for Egypt, Mesopotamia and the Near East. These preliminary studies show that there is much promise in pursuing the interactions between climate changes, environmental deterioration and socio-economic and political transformations.

Socio-economic and political transformations during dark ages

As discussed above, socio-economic and political trends and patterns during dark ages are reversals of what occur during periods of expansionary growth. We note some general trends, such as a fall in population levels for some areas, especially for highly urbanized communities, decline or losses in certain material skills, decay in the cultural aspects of life, decline in living standards and thus wealth, political instability, loss of trading contacts and collapse of trade networks and deurbanization. It is also clear that, if we consider dark ages as periods of ecological crises, the lack of available resources would also mean innovations: in using different materials in the production of commodities, in the establishment of different social and political organizations and in cultural aspects of material life. These innovative ventures seem to occur as the dark ages are receding, and the innovative and learning processes developed as a result of scarcity and societal upheavals are adopted within the social, economic and political fabric of life.

If we examine the first identified dark age period (2200–1700 BC) and its outcomes, political instability is one feature that highlights political–economic events. In Egypt, the climatological changes identified above for this period led to famines, and also brought about the dissipation of central authority. Drought conditions and lowered Nile flooding affected the farmers' ability to pay taxes because of lower harvest yields. This resulted in local administrators and governors, who collected taxes, having to delay their transfer to the royal house. In turn, the king's revenues plummeted, and thus impaired his ability to pay for an army or to deal effectively with the drought and famine. As a result, the stability of the political regime was affected. The sum effects of this in terms of political stability, as Bell (1971) has concluded, were short reigns. For example, between 2190 BC and 2130 BC, there was a succession of about 31–40 kings. Hassan (1997), covering a slightly different period, 2180–2134 BC, reported that 18 pharaohs reigned during this short span. The collapse of the central monarchy of the Old Kingdom around 2180 BC occurred within such dynamics.[18] Later in the period, around 1700 BC, short reigns predominated (Bell 1975). For example, between 1768 BC and 1740 BC, there were 18 kings.

Political instability was also evident in the next dark age period between 1200 BC and 700 BC. Bell (1971) and Braudel (2001), for example, have noted that a second dark age began, starting around 1200 BC, and it was marked by the disappearance of the Hittite empire of Anatolia, the end of Minoan Crete and Mycenaean Greece, the decline of Egypt (Third Intermediary period) and its empire, with Babylonia and Assyria in decline around 1100–1000 BC. Collapse was widespread throughout the region.

Besides political instability in Egypt during the third-millennium dark age of 2200 BC, other reversals also occurred such as artistic degeneration and the scale of monumental buildings being reduced as a result of diminishing resources. The size and elaborateness of the pharaonic tombs were reduced;

by this time, the tombs of kings were one-chambered affairs with less ambitious layouts (Bovarski 1998: 316–19).

In the later dark age period between1200 BC and 700 BC, Greece also encountered a decline or loss of certain material skills, decay in the cultural aspects of life, a fall in living standards and thus wealth, and loss of trading contacts within and outwith Greece (Snodgrass 1971; Desborough 1972). For Greece, the archaeological evidence unearthed suggests socio-economic patterns that are distinctively different from the style and level of socio-cultural life prevailing prior to the onset of the dark age. Pottery and other objects recovered from excavated graves in Greece along with the architecture and design of dwellings from excavated sites reflect ecological stress and scarcity of natural resources.

The above conditions directly affected socio-cultural life in Greece during this dark age phase (1200–700 BC). Pottery styles of the period in Greece became austere, unlike the decadent style of the previous era. The bulk of the pot was usually left plain in the natural colour of the clay and the decorations covered a third of the surface area at most. The lack of intense firing also suggests dwindling energy supplies. As recovery proceeds and the balance of nature is restored, we find the plain, rectilinear or curvilinear patterns in pottery designs giving way to images depicting animals and humans. Such shifts suggest the return of biodiversity to the environment and the loss of biodiversity at the onset of the dark ages.

Beyond pottery styles, other objects recovered indicate a scarcity of natural resources, especially metals, or that the supply sources had dried up. The use of obsidian and bones for blades and weapons underlines such scarcity, and also suggests that trading routes and centres for sourcing the metals might have disappeared or been disrupted.

Ecological scarcity required a downscaling of material and cultural lifestyles. Such changes are reflected in burial practices which exhibited a reorganization of life along modest lines. The design of clothing and shoes was of the plainest kind. The downscaling process is exhibited further in the formation of decentralized communities and associated population losses. Whether this lifestyle trend is one that was actively sought as a consequence of ecological scarcity or occurred as an outcome of the depressive conditions of the dark age is difficult to gauge. What we are sure of is that, as recovery proceeded – we begin to witness this by the middle of the tenth century BC – trading networks were re-established and communities were revived. Such an upswing was characterized by exuberance, materialistic consumption and accumulation. During the dark age, materialistic consumption declined, and most of the trading networks disappeared or were restricted only to the area of the Aegean Sea.

What the dark age of this period represented for the Mediterranean region is one where extreme degradation of the ecological landscape precipitated socio-economic and organizational changes to meet the scarcity of resources in order to reproduce some semblance of cultural and economic life of prior times. As a consequence, systemic reorganization occurred at various levels, from the way commodities were produced to clothing fashions and designs. Hierarchical social structures disappeared during the dark age, as evident by burial practices, and were restored when recovery proceeded (Whitley 1991). In central and eastern Europe, we also witness similar collapses of social hierarchy with communal burials replacing chiefly burials from 1250 BC to 750 BC (Kristiansen 1998).

Another feature of the dark ages – the process of deurbanization – can be witnessed during the first dark age period (2200–1700 BC). Cholistan, in north-western India, experienced a decline in size in terms of settled areas from an average of 6.5 hectares in 3800–3200 BC to 5.1 hectares by 1900–1700 BC, and finally to almost 50 per cent less (2.6 hectares) by 1000 BC. Elsewhere, for the time period of 2200 BC, similar signs of deteriorating conditions were also encountered in Anatolia, with the abandonment of urban centres such as Troy II to Troy III–IV (Mellink 1986: 139–52; Wilkinson 1990). Consequently, depopulation also resulted. Sedentary population settlements on the Anatolian plateau were also abandoned. To the west of Anatolia, Palestine also suffered such crisis conditions. Walled towns were replaced by unwalled villages. There were signs of cave occupation and migratory movements. In some areas, settlements completely disappeared, and remaining settlement sites were reduced to less than half what existed before 2200 BC (Harrison 1997: 1–38).

Across the Mediterranean from Palestine, the Aegean experienced distress, although to a lesser extent. Between 2300 BC and 1900 BC, there was a loss of sedentary population. This was also the case for central Eurasia. The changed ecological landscape led to outmigration of the sedentary population from river valleys over time and exploitation of the steppes for animal feed. Denucleation occurred with the establishment of smaller communities near oases. This spread occurred in central Asia at Korezm (south of the Aral Sea) and Margiana (Murghab delta) in Turkmenistan, Bactria and western China. This process, prompted by ecological degradation and environmental changes, also occurred in Syria, Palestine and Jordan. Migration out of urban centres located on the coast to the interior and the establishment of smaller village-type settlements resulted (McGovern 1987: 267–73).

On mainland Greece and Crete, this deurbanization process was repeated during the next dark age from 1200 BC, giving rise to small communities with lower population levels (Jameson 1994; Watrous 1994). Seen from an ecological point of view, this downscaling provided the necessary timing for nature to restore its balance, and for socio-economic life to start afresh when recovery returned. From these small communities, in the case of Greece, the preconditions for the rise of the Greek *polis* were put into play, and what followed was a flourishing of political and economic life as soon as the social system recovered (Snodgrass 1971). To this extent, the stressed ecological conditions that engendered deurbanization and the formation of small communities precipitated the rise of the *polis* and the Greek city-states. We need to realize, therefore, that perhaps scarcity of resources can also have productive outcomes, which might not otherwise have occurred under bountiful conditions. Stanislawski (1973: 18) has suggested that, instead of seeing the Greek dark ages as periods of darkness, they should be seen as ones of enlightenment with contributions such as the first use of stone-walled agricultural terraces, the use of chicken eggs in the domestic diet, the beginning of the spread of alphabetic writing, the spread of iron, the general use of olives as food and the first use of waterproof plaster.

Systemic reorganization occurred, and the lengthy duration of the dark age is one that we need to note. The fact that it is of such a long duration underlines the length of time required for ecological recovery to take place, and the immensity of the degradation that occurred. What followed in the recovery phase, however, was a dark age-conditioned social–cultural and political lifestyle that formed the basis of western civilization as we know it today.

Beyond the core areas of the eastern Mediterranean littoral, the periphery of the system, such as central, eastern and northern Europe, had a different rhythm *vis-à-vis* economic expansion. Unlike the Near East, the dark age from 1200 BC to 700 BC was a period of population increases, expansion of settlements, agrarian intensification and reorientation of trade and exchange for these regions (Kristiansen 1998; Chew 2001). With the collapse of the Near Eastern Mediterranean trade networks, metal production boomed in central and eastern Europe, and the east–west exchange connection was strengthened, thus establishing a regional system (Urnfield) of trade exchanges and production. Crisis in the regional system emerged much later, around 750 BC, following centuries of intensive resource extraction, land exhaustion and climatological changes in which the climate became cooler and moister. Such differences in economic trajectories between regions suggest that, at this point in time (in terms of world systems development), the synchronicity of relations and processes was not as linked to the extent that crisis in the core was felt throughout the periphery. Despite the lack of synchronicity, systemic change continued to occur. As we have seen above, for central and eastern Europe, regional system changes occurred at a later time after 1200 BC, around 750 BC, following centuries of landscape degradation.

Beyond this region, at the level of the world system, George Modelski and Bill Thompson (2003) have shown some trends in urbanization and population levels since 4000 BC that complement the tendencies we have identified for the dark ages. Colin and Sarah McEvedy (1972) have also reported slow population growth for the second dark age period starting around AD 300–900 when growth of the global population was only about 15 per cent in comparison with the previous period when it was about 100 per cent. Biraben (1980: 5), however, has noted that world population at AD 1 was 255 million and at AD 200 was 256 million; this total was reduced to 206 million by AD 400 and continued at this level until AD 700. Most of the losses were in Europe, the former Soviet Union and Africa. Figure 17 in Biraben (1980) details the global population losses during the dark ages of 1200–500 BC and AD 400–900.

For the dark age that occurred between AD 300 and AD 900, besides the population decreases indicated above, we find social, economic and political reversals, for example, for the Roman Empire, similar to what Greece experienced in the earlier dark age between 1200 BC and 700 BC. We witness these reversals by the fourth century AD. For centuries prior to the onset of the dark ages, the Roman Empire was expanding and, in the course of this expansion, it increasingly developed a complex system of taxation and administration. By the fourth century AD, it was feeling the strain of this infrastructure of support. Furthermore, by the late fourth century, the tribal groups could no longer be kept out of the Roman Empire. Incursions were the order of the day. Hinterland invasions into the core have been documented to be precipitated by deteriorating environmental conditions and climatological changes (Brown 1995, 2001; Modelski and Thompson 1999). The 'barbarian' invasions were into Roman territory in western Europe and north Africa.

In the area of urban complexes, we find that cities were beginning to be reduced in size. For example, in the western part of the Roman Empire, such as Gaul, the cities shrank in size: Lyon was reduced from 160 hectares to 20 hectares and Vienne shrank from 200 hectares to 20 hectares (Hodgett 1972; Randsborg 1991). As the dark age progressed, towns became sparsely populated in Gaul, and there is a lack of evidence in terms of continuity. Deurbanization seems to be the trend in the western part of the Roman empire. The city of Rome itself was depopulating. At AD 367, it had a million persons but, by AD 452, the population was reduced to about 400,000. The latter number was reduced to about 30,000 by the tenth century, which is the end of the dark ages. Urban decay, disintegration, illiteracy and depopulation were the characteristic features depicting the urban landscape.

Along with the urban deterioration, the Roman social hierarchy and bureaucracy were reduced and flattened with local administrators taking over. In the end, the western part of the Roman Empire could no longer sustain itself and collapse followed. The eastern part of the Empire continued, although dark age conditions predominate. In Byzantium, there was little education and literature was non-existent. Cities across Anatolia went through a deurbanization process and contracted to fort-like enclosures located on hills (Haldon 1990; Treadgold 1988, 1997).

Conclusion

If system crisis emerges in the form of dark ages, clearly these dark age phases are interesting moments in terms of mapping the evolution of the world system for they are devolutionary periods of the system. They also demarcate the limits of system reproduction whereby the structural contradictions of world system processes including the nature–culture relations reached systemic limits, and resolution is therefore required before further system evolution can take place.

Depending on the particular epoch of world system history, different base materials, technologies and perhaps even ideas emerge that provide the basis to overcome the systemic contradictions at that particular point in time. All these will not gain traction for further system expansion if the natural environment has not recovered from the prior period of expansionary thrusts, and the relations between culture and nature have not been recalibrated. Over world history, this recalibration has mostly focused on finding new virgin areas for natural resource extraction, and also on the development of new technologies to replace ones that have not been as efficient. In some instances, new ideas emerge as operating guidance for human life. On this basis, Modelski and Thompson's (2003) theory of world system learning processes provides another angle to explain system transition and evolution not from the system crisis point of view that I have undertaken. Both approaches, when combined, I believe provide us with further insights on system transition and evolution as we continue to identify, map and peel away the structures and processes of the world system.

Notes

1 For an exposition of this long-term time duration, see Braudel (1980: 25–54).
2 For an overview of these varied world system/s positions, see Denemark *et al.* (2000); Chew and Knottnerus (2003).
3 The identification of climate as an element in the crisis phase rests on the work of Thompson (2000, 2001).
4 For example, see Drews (1993) for the Bronze Age crisis.
5 For a fuller explication of Braudel's analytical levels of long-term change, see Chew (1997).
6 This endeavour is to move away from a history understood and interpreted within a geospatial-dependent and time-contingent framework. The aim is to abstract a theoretically generalizable account of the dynamics and structures of the evolution of world systems from historical events.
7 If a growth developmental model is assumed, the reproduction levels should be progressively higher rather than lower; hence, instead of developmental evolution, stagnation or devolution would be the more appropriate concept to describe these changes.
8 See, for example, Kristiansen's *Europe Before History* (1998) for an elaborate articulation of the different levels of interaction and connectedness occurring in European transformation over one millennium.
9 Such a multiplicity of levels have been confirmed in the depictions of dark age conditions in prehistoric Greece by Snodgrass (1971).
10 The anthropocentric evaluations of dark ages in terms of conditions and factors leading to the onset of these periods are found quite commonly among the historical literature, especially for the dark age that occurred in the second millennium BC. They included cultural decadence, invasions and conquests by 'barbarians' and nomadic tribes, internal conflicts, overcentralization of authority, famine and diseases, climate changes and tectonic shifts (Toynbee 1939; Childe 1942; Schaeffer 1948; Carpenter 1968; Desborough 1972; Bryson *et al.* 1974; Renfrew 1979; Bintliff 1982; Harding 1982; Weiss 1982; O'Connor 1983; Neumann and Parpola 1987; Snodgrass 1989).
11 By determinative, I mean constraints that do not allow the system to reproduce itself within its social and ecological parameters (see also Kristiansen 1998).

12 For example, in the case of Mycenaean Greece during the dark age, we find several culture–nature trends and patterns that are subdued: fall in population levels, decline or loss in certain material skills, decay in the cultural aspects of life, fall in living standards and thus wealth, and loss of trading contacts within and outwith Greece (Snodgrass 1971; Desborough 1972).

13 See, for example, Snodgrass (1971) and Desborough (1972) for conditions in Greece during the second millennium BC dark age.

14 By no means are these climate changes anthropogenic in origin (Weiss 2000). The cause of these global climatic changes around 2200 BC, of which west Asia is a subset, have been attributed to alterations in solar radiation, thermohaline alterations or ocean tidal cycles with periodicities ranging from 1,800 years to 500 years.

15 For example, it has been estimated that a mere 1 degree Centigrade rise in temperature may reduce annual rainfall by 30 millimetres in the Near East.

16 Wright (1968), Chadwick (1976) and Drews (1993), however, have challenged this thesis of climatological change affecting the socio-economic structure of Mycenaean Greece in the later second millennium. Notwithstanding this, others, such as Lamb (1967), Bryson *et al.* (1974) , Bryson and Padoch (1980) and Braudel (2001), have indicated that the period of drought proposed by Carpenter appears to have prevailed during the time of Mycenaean decline, according to precipitation patterns examined.

17 Dendroclimate charts were provided by Professor Bjorn Berglund, Department of Quaternary Geology, Lund University, Lund, Sweden.

18 Butzer (1997) has challenged this thesis that lower Nile floods induced the demise of the Old Kingdom. Rather, for Butzer, the collapse of the Old Kingdom was a consequence of decentralization, dynastic weakness, a shift of wealth and power to several provincial centres during Dynasty 6, the loss of royal power due in part to the trade monopoly with Syria being undercut by the Akkadian conquest of Byblos, and civil wars, etc.

Bibliography

Abu-Lughod, J. 1989. *Before European Hegemony*. New York: Oxford University Press.

Adams, Robert McC. 1981. *Heartland of the Cities*. Chicago: University of Chicago Press.

Agrawal, D.P. and R.K. Sood. 1982. 'Ecological factors and the Harappan civilization', in G. Possehl, ed. *Harappan Civilization: Contemporary Perspective*. New Delhi: Oxford University Press.

Amman, B. 1985. 'Lobsingensee – Late Glacial and Holocene environments of a lake on the Central Swiss Plateau'. *Dissertations in Botany* 87: 127–34.

Baillie, M. 1995. *A Slice Through Time*. London: Routledge.

Bar-Mathews, M and A. Avalon. 1997. 'Late Quaternary paleoclimate in the Eastern Mediterranean region from stable isotope analysis of speleothems at Soreq Cave, Israel'. *Quaternary Research* 47: 155–68.

Bar-Mathews, Mira, Avner Ayalon and Aaron Kaufman. 1998. 'Middle to Late Holocene Paleoclimate in the Eastern Mediterranean Region', in A.S. Issar and N. Brown, eds. *Water, Environment and Society in Times of Climate Change*. Amsterdam: Kluwer, pp. 203–14.

Bar-Mathews, Mira, Avner Ayalon, Aaron Kaufman and Gerald Wasserburg. 1999. 'The Eastern Mediterranean paleoclimate as a reflection of regional events; Soreq Cave, Israel'. *Earth and Planetary Science Letters* 166: 85–95.

Barry, R. and Richard Chorley. 1992. *Atmosphere, Weather, and Climate*. New York: Routledge.

Behre, K.E. and D. Kucan. 1986. 'Die Reflektion archaologisch bekannter in Pollendiagrammen verschiedener Entfernung', in K.E. Behre, ed. *Anthropogenic Indicators in Pollen Diagrams*. Rotterdam: Balkema, pp 95–114.

Bell, Barbara. 1971. 'The dark ages in ancient history I: the first dark age in Egypt'. *American Journal of Archaeology* 75: 1–20.

——. 1975. 'Climate and history of Egypt'. *American Journal of Archaeology* 79: 223–79.

Bentaleb, I., C. Caratini, M. Fontugne, M. Morzadec-Kerfourn, J. Pascal and C. Tissor. 1997. 'Monsoon regime variations during the Late Holocene in southwestern India', in H. Dalfes and G. Kukla, eds. *Third Millennium BC Climate Change and Collapse*. Berlin: Springer Verlag, pp. 193–244.

Bezusko, L.G. 1985. 'Paleobotanical and radiological studies of deposit from Bog Starniki'. *Ukr. Bot. Zhurn.* 42: 27–30.

——. 1987. 'The oak forest of Maloye Polessie in the late post glacial period.' *Ukrayins'kyi Botanichnyi Zhurnal* 71: 4–8.

Binka, K., T. Madeyska, B. Marciniak, K. Szeroczynska and K. Wieckwski. 1988. Bledowo Lake: history of vegetation and lake development during the last 12 Kyr'. *Bulletin Academie Polonaise des Sciences* 36 (2): 147–58.

Bintliff, J. 1982. 'Climate change, archaeology and Quaternary science in the Eastern Mediterranean region', in A.F. Harding, ed. *Climate Change in Later Prehistory*. Edinburgh: Edinburgh University Press, pp. 143–61.

Biraben, Jean-Noel. 1980. 'Essai sur l'evolution du nombre des hommes'. *Population* 1: 13–25.

Bosworth, Andrew. 1995. 'World cities and world economic cycles', in Stephen Sanderson, ed. *Civilizations and World Systems*. Walnut Creek, CA: AltaMira Press.

Bottema, S. 1974. *Late Quaternary Vegetation History of Northwestern Greece*. PhD dissertation, Groningen University, the Netherlands.

Bottema, Sytze. 1997. 'A third millennium climate in the Near East based upon pollen evidence', in H. Dalfes, G. Kukla and H. Weiss, eds. *Third Millennium BC Climate Change and Old World Collapse*. Heidelberg: Springer Verlag, pp. 488–515.

Bovarski, Edward. 1998. 'First Intermediate Period private tombs', in K. Bard, ed. *Encyclopedia of Ancient Egypt*. New York: Routledge, pp. 316–19.

Bradshaw, R.H.W., T. Young and K. McNeil. 1988. 'The extent and time course of mountain blanket peat erosion in Ireland'. *New Phytologist* 108: 219–24.

Braudel, Fernand. 1980. *On History*. Chicago: University of Chicago Press.

——. 1972. *The Mediterranean and the Mediterranean World in the Age of Philip II*, Vol. 1. London: Fontana.

——. 1981 *The Structure of Everyday Life*, Vol. 1. New York: Harper and Row.

——. 1982 *The Wheels of Commerce*, Vol. 2. New York: Harper and Row.

——. 1984 *The Perspective of the World*, Vol. 3. New York: Harper and Row.

——. 1989 *The Perspective of France*, Vols 1 and 2. New York: Harper and Row.

——. 2001 *Memory and the Mediterranean*. New York: Alfred Knopf.

Broecker, Wallace S. 2001. 'Was the medieval warm period global?' *Science* 291: 1497–9.

Brown, N. 1995. *The Impact of Climate Change: Some Indications from History AD250–1250*. Oxford Centre for the Environment, Ethics and Society Research Papers.

——. 2001. *History and Climate Change: A Eurocentric Perspective*. London: Routledge.

Bryson, Robert and Reid Bryson. 1998. 'Application of a global volcanicity time series on high resolution paleoclimatic modeling of the eastern Mediterranean', in A. Issar and N. Brown, eds. *Water, Environment and Society in Times of Change*. Dordrecht: Kluwer, pp. 1–19.

Bryson, R.A. and C. Padoch, 1980. 'On the climates of history'. *Journal of Interdisciplinary History* X (4): 583–97.

Bryson , R. and T. Swain. 1981. 'Holocene variations of monsoon rainfall in Rajasthan'. *Quaternary Research* 16: 135–45.

Bryson, R.A., H.H. Lamb and David L. Donley. 1974. 'Drought and the decline of Mycenae'. *Antiquity* XLVIII (189): 46–50.

Burgess, C. 1989. 'Volcanoes, catastrophe, and global crisis of the late 2nd millennium BC'. *Current Anthropology* X (10): 325–9.

Butzer, K.W. 1983. 'Long term Nile flood variation and political discontinuities in Pharaonic Egypt', in J.D. Clark and S. Brandt, eds. *From Hunters to Farmers*. Berkeley: University of California Press, pp. 102–12.

——. 1997. 'A socio political discontinuity in the Near East c 2200 BCE: scenarios from Palestine and Egypt', in H. Dalfes, G. Kukla and H. Weiss, eds. *Third Millennium BC Climate Change and Old World Collapse*. Heidelberg: Springer Verlag, pp. 245–96.

Carpenter, Rhys. 1968. *Discontinuity in Greek Civilization*. Cambridge: Cambridge University Press

Chadwick, J. 1972. 'Life in Mycenaean Greece'. *Scientific American* 227 (4): 36–44.

——. 1976. *The Mycenaean World*. New York: Cambridge University Press.

Chase-Dunn, C. and T. Hall. 1997. *Rise and Demise: Comparing World-Systems*. Boulder, CO: Westview Press.

——. 2002. 'Paradigms bridged: institutional materialism and world-systemic evolution', in Sing C. Chew and David Knottnerus, eds. *Structure, Culture, and History: Recent Issues in Social Theory*. Lanham, MD: Rowman and Littlefield, pp.197–216.

Chew, Sing C. 1997. *Accumulation, Deforestation, and World Ecological Degradation 2500 BC to AD 1990*. Advances in Human Ecology 6. Westport, CT: JAI Press.

——. 1999. 'Ecological relations and the decline of civilizations in the Bronze Age world system: Mesopotamia and Harappa 2500 BC–1700 BC', in W. Goldfrank *et al.*, ed. *Ecology and the World System*. Greenwich, CT: Greenwood Press.

——. 2001. *World Ecological Degradation: Accumulation, Urbanization, and Deforestation*. Lanham, MD: AltaMira Press/Rowman and Littlefield Publishers.

——. 2002. 'Globalization, Dark Ages, and Ecological Degradation'. *Global Society* 16 (4): 333–56.

——. 2006 *The Dark Ages: Ecological Stress and System Transformation*. Walnut Creek, CA: AltaMira Press/Rowman and Littlefield Publishers.

Chew, Sing C. and D. Knottnerus, eds. 2003. *Structure, Culture, and History*. Lanham, MD: Rowman and Littlefield Publishers.

Childe, Gordon. 1942. *What Happened in History*. Harmondsworth: Penguin.

——. 1950. 'The urban revolution'. *Town Planning Review* 21: 3–17.

Dales, G.F. 1977. 'Shifting trade patterns between Iranian Plateau and the Indus Valley', in J. Deshayes, ed. *Le Plateau Iranien et l'Asie Centrale*. Paris: CNRS, pp. 67–78.

——. 1979. 'The Decline of the Harappans', in G. Possehl, ed. *Ancient Cities of the Indus*. New Delhi: Vikas, pp. 307–12.

Davis, M. and R. Shaw. 2001. 'Range shifts and adaptive responses to Quaternary climate change'. *Science* 292: 667–73.

DeMenocal, Peter B. 2001. 'Cultural response to climate change during the Late Holocene'. *Science* 292: 674–9.

Denemark, Robert A., Jonathan Friedman, Barry K. Gills and George Modelski, eds. 2000. *World System History: The Social Science of Long-Term Change.* London: Routledge.

Desborough, V.R. 1972. *The Greek Dark Ages*. London: Ernest Benn.

——. 1975. 'The end of Mycenaean civilization and the dark age', in I.E.S. Edwards, C.J. Gadd and N.G.L. Hammond, eds. *Cambridge Ancient History*. Cambridge: Cambridge University Press, pp. 658–77.

Drews, R. 1993. *The End of the Bronze Age*. Princeton: Princeton University Press.

Eisner, W.R., T.E. Tornquist, E.A. Koster, O. Bennike and J.F.N. van Leeuwen. 1995. 'Paleoecological studies of a Holocene lacustrine record from the Kangerlussnaq'. *Quaternary Research* 43: 55–66.

Enzel, Y., L.L. Ely, S. Mishra, R. Ramesh, R. Amit, B. Lazar, S.N. Rajaguru, V.R. Baker and A. Sandler. 1999. 'High resolution Holocene environmental changes in the Thar Desert, northwestern India'. *Science* 284: 125–8.

Eronen, M. and H. Hyvrinen. 1982. 'Subfossil dates and pollen diagrams from northern Fennoscandia'. *Geologis Frem i Stockholm (Finland)* 103: 437–55.

Fagan, Brian. 1999. *Floods, Famines, and Emperors: El Niño and the Fate of Civilizations*. New York: Basic Books.

——. 2004 . *The Long Summer*. New York: Basic Books.

Fairbridge, R., O. Erol, M. Karaca and Y. Yilmaz. 1997. 'Background to Mid-Holocene climate change in Anatolia and adjacent regions', in H. Dalfes *et al.*, eds. *Third Millennium BC Climate Change and Old World Collapse*. Heidelberg: Springer Verlag.

Fairservis, Walter. 1979a. 'The Harappan civilization: new evidence and more theory', in G. Possehl, ed. *Ancient Cities of the Indus*. New Delhi: Vikas, pp. 50–65.

——. 1979b. 'The origin, character, and decline of an early civilization', in G. Possehl, ed. *Ancient Cities of the Indus*. New Delhi: Vikas, pp. 66–89.

Frank, Andre Gunder and B.K. Gills. 1992.'World system cycles, crises, and hegemonial shifts'. *Review* 15 (4): 621–88.

——. 1993. 'Bronze Age world system cycles'. *Current Anthropology* 34 (4): 383–429.

Friedman, Kajsa. 2003. 'Structure, dynamics, and the final collapse of Bronze Age civilizations in the second millennium'. Unpublished MS.

Gasse, F. 2000. 'Hydrological changes in the African tropics since the last glacial maximum'. *Quaternary Science Review* 19: 189–212.

Gelb, I.J. 1973. 'Prisoners of war in early Mesopotamia'. *Journal of Near Eastern Studies* 32: 70–98.

Gibson, McGuire. 1970. 'Violation of fallow and engineered disaster in Mesopotamian civilization', in T. Downing. and M. Gibson, eds. *Irrigation's Impact on Society*. Tucson: University of Arizona Press.

——. 1973. 'Population shift and the rise of Mesopotamian civilization'. in Colin Renfrew, ed. *The Explanation of Culture Change: Models in Prehistory*. London: Duckworth, pp. 447–63.

Gills, B.K. and Frank, Andre Gunder. 1992. World system cycles, crises, and hegemonial shifts. *Review* 15 (4): 621–88.

——. 2002 'A structural theory of the 5,000 year old system', in Sing C. Chew and David Knottnerus, eds. *Structure, Culture and History*. Lanham, MD: Rowman and Littlefield, pp. 151–76.

Goldstone, J. 1991. *Revolution and Rebellion in the Early Modern World*. Berkeley: University of California Press.

Haldon, J.F. 1990. *Byzantium in the 7th Century*. Cambridge: Cambridge University Press.

Harding, A. ed. 1982. *Climatic Change in Later Prehistory*. Edinburgh: Edinburgh University Press.

Harrison, Timothy. 1997. 'Shifting patterns of settlement in the highlands of central Jordan during the early Bronze Age'. *Bulletin of the American School of Oriental Research* 306: 1–38.

Hassan, Fekri. 1986. 'Holocene lakes and prehistoric settlements of the western Fayum'. *Journal of Archaeological Science* 13: 483–501.

——. 1997. 'Nile floods and political disorder in early Egypt', in H. Dalfes *et al.*, eds. *Third Millennium BC Climate Change and Old World Collapse*. Heidelberg: Springer Verlag, pp. 1–23.

Hiebert, Fredrik. 2000. 'Bronze Age central Eurasian cultures in their steppe and desert environments', in G. Bawden and R. Reycraft, eds. *Environmental Disaster and the Archaeology of Human Response*. Albuquerque: University of New Mexico Press, pp. 51–62.

Hodgett, G. 1972. *A Social and Economic History of Medieval Europe*. London: Methuen.

Hooker, J.T. 1976. *Mycenaean Greece*. London: Routledge.

Hughes, Donald. 1994. *Pan's Travail*. Baltimore: Johns Hopkins University Press.

——. 2001. *Environmental History of the World*. London: Routledge.

Jacobsen, T and R.M. Adams. 1958. 'Salt and silt in Ancient Mesopotamian agriculture'. *Science* 128: 1251–8.

Jameson, Michael. 1994. *A Greek Countryside: The Southern Argolid from Prehistory to the Present Day*. Stanford: Stanford University Press.

Johnson, T.C. and E.O. Odade, eds. 1996. *The Liminology, Climatology, and Paleoclimatology of the East African Lakes*. New York: Gordon and Breach.

Kantor, H. 1992. 'The relative chronology of Egypt and its foreign correlations before the first intermediate period', in Robert W. Ehrlich, ed. *Chronologies in Old World Archaeology*, Vol. 1. Chicago: University of Chicago Press.

Keys, David. 1999. *Catastrophe*. New York: Ballantyne Books.

Khomutova, V., K. Pushenko and L. Harrison. 1994. 'Lake status records from the former Soviet Union and Mongolian database'. *Paleoclimatology Publication Report* (2): 86–8.

Knapp, A. Bernard. 1993. 'Thalassocracies in the Bronze Age Eastern Mediterranean trade: making and breaking a myth'. *World Archaeology* 24 (3): 332–47.

Krementski, Constantin. 1997. 'The Late Holocene environmental and climate shift in Russia and surrounding lands', in H. Dalfes *et al.*, eds. *Third Millennium BC Climate Change and Old World Collapse*. Heidelberg: Springer Verlag, pp. 351–70.

Kristiansen, Kristian 1998. *Europe before History*. Cambridge: Cambridge University Press.

Ladurie, L. 1971. *Times of Feast and Times of Famines*. New York: Doubleday.

Lamb, H. 1967. 'R. Carpenter's discontinuity in Greek civilization'. *Antiquity* 41: 233–4.

Lambrick, H.T. 1967. 'The Indus flood plain and the "Indus" civilization'. *The Geographical Journal* 133 (4): 483–9.

Lazarova, M. 1995. 'Human impact on the natural vegetation in the region of Lake

Srebarna and Mire Girvan', in T. Bozilova, ed. *Advances in Holocene Paleoecology in Bulgaria.* Sofia: Pensoft Publication, pp. 47–67.

Lemcke, G. and M. Sturm. 1997. 'd2O and trace element measurement as proxy for the reconstruction of climatic changes at Lake Van', in H. Dalfes *et al.*, eds. *Third Millennium BC Climate Change and Old World Collapse*. Heidelberg: Springer Verlag, pp. 653–78.

McEvedy, Colin and Sarah McEvedy. 1972. *Dark Ages*. London: McMillan.

McGovern, P. 1987. 'Central TransJordan in Late Bronze Age and Early Iron Ages: an alternative hypothesis of socioeconomic collapse', in A. Hadidi, ed. *Studies in the History and Archaeology of Jordan 3.* London: Routledge and Kegan Paul, pp. 267–73.

McNeill, John R. 2000. *Something New Under the Sun.* New York: W.W. Norton.

Mann, Michael. 1986. *The Sources of Social Power*, Vol. 1. Cambridge: Cambridge University Press.

Manning, Sturt W. 1994. 'The emergence of divergence: development and decline in Bronze Age Crete and the Cyclades', in C. Mathers and S. Stoddat, eds. *Development and Decline in the Mediterranean Bronze Age.* Sheffield: J.R. Collins, pp. 221–70.

Marinatos, S. 1939. 'The volcanic eruption of Minoan Crete'. *Antiquity* 13: 425–39.

Mellink, Machfeld. 1986. 'The Early Bronze Age in Western Anatolia: Aegean and Asiatic correlations', in G. Cadogan, ed. *End of the Early Bronze Age in the Aegean.* Leiden: Brill, pp. 139–52.

Modelski, George. 1997. Early World Cities. International Studies Association Meeting, Toronto.

——. 1999. 'Ancient world cities 4000–1000 BC: center/hinterland in the world system'. *Global Society* 13 (4): 383–92.

——. 2003 *World Cities*. Washington, DC: Faros.

Modelski, George, and Thompson, William R. 1996 *Leading Sectors and World Powers.* Columbia, SC: University of South Carolina Press.

——. 1999. 'The evolutionary pulse of the world system: hinterland incursion and migrations 4000 BC to AD 1500', in Nick Kardulias, ed. *World System Theory in Practice*. Lanham, MD: Rowman and Littlefield, pp. 241–74.

——. 2001. 'Evolutionary pulsations in the world system' in Sing Chew and David Knottnerus, eds. *Structure, Culture, and History*. Lanham, MD: Rowman and Littlefield.

Moorey, P.R.S. 1987. 'On tracking cultural transfers in prehistory: the case of Egypt and Lower Mesopotamia in the 4th millennium BC', in M. Rowlands, K. Kristiansen and M. Larsen, eds. *Centre and Periphery in the Ancient World.* Cambridge: Cambridge University Press, pp. 36–46.

Mylonas, George. 1966. *Mycenae and the Mycenaean Age.* Princeton: Princeton University Press.

Neumann, J. and S. Parpola. 1987. 'Climatic change and 11–10th century eclipse of Assyria and Babylonia'. *Journal of Near Eastern Studies* 46: 161–82.

Neumann, J. and R. Sigrist. 1978. 'Harvest dates in Ancient Mesopotamia as possible indicators of climatic variations'. *Climate Change* 1: 239–52.

O'Connor, D. 1983. ' New kingdom and the third intermediate period, 1552–664 BC', in B.G. Trigger, J.D. Faye and R. Oliver, eds. *Ancient Egypt: A Social History.* Cambridge: Cambridge University Press.

Penalba, M.C. 1994. 'The history of the Holocene vegetation in Northern Spain from pollen analysis'. *Journal of Ecology* 82: 815–32.

Perlin, John. 1989. *A Forest Journey*. Cambridge: Harvard University Press.

Ponting, Clive. 1991. *A Green History of the World*. London: Penguin.
Possehl, Gregory. 2001. 'The drying up of the Saravati', in G. Bawden and R. Reycraft, eds. *Environmental Disaster and the Archaeology of Human Response*. Albuquerque: University of New Mexico Press, pp. 63–74.
Raikes, Robert. 1964. 'The end of the ancient cities of the Indus'. *American Anthropologist* 66 (2): 284–99.
Raikes, Robert 1984. *Water, Weather, and Prehistory*. Atlantic Highlands: Humanities Press.
Raikes, Robert and G.F. Dales. 1977. 'The Mohenjo-Daro floods reconsidered'. *Journal of the Palaeontological Society of India* 20: 251–60.
Raikes, Robert and R. Dyson. 1961. 'The prehistoric climate of Baluchistan and the Indus Valley'. *American Anthropologist* 63 (2): 265–81.
Randsborg, Klav. 1991. *The First Millennium AD in Europe and the Mediterranean*. Cambridge: Cambridge University Press.
Rankama, T. and I. Vuorela. 1988. 'Memo. Soc. Fauna Flora'. *Fennica* 64: 25–34.
Ratnagar, Shereen. 1981. *Encounters: The Westerly Trade of the Harappan Civilization*. New Delhi: Oxford University Press.
Renfrew, Colin. 1972. *The Emergence of Civilization*. London: Collins.
——. 1979. 'Systems collapse as social transformation: catastrophe and anastrophe in early state society', in C. Renfrew and K.L. Cooke, eds. *Transformations: Mathematical Approaches to Cultural Change*. New York: Academic Press, pp. 481–506.
Ricketts, R.C. and T.G. Johnson 1996. 'Climate change in Turkana Basin as deduced from a 4000 year-long d^{18}O record'. *Earth and Planetary Science Letters* 142: 7–17.
Ruddiman, William. 2003. 'The anthropogenic greenhouse era began thousands of years ago'. *Climate Change* 61 (3): 261–93.
Schaeffer, C.F.A. 1948. 'Stratigraphie comparée et chronologie de l'Asie Occidentale (III et II millennaire)'. *Economics and Social History of the Orient* 5: 279–308.
Stanislawski, D. 1973. 'Dark age contributions to the Mediterranean way of life'. *Annals of the Association of American Geographers* 63 (4):397–410.
Stefanova, I. 1995. 'Studies on the Holocene history of vegetation in the Northern Pirin Mountains', in T. Bozilova, ed. *Advances in Holocene Paleoecology in Bulgaria*. Sofia: Tonkov, pp. 9–37.
Snodgrass, A.M. 1971. *The Dark Age of Greece*. Edinburgh: Edinburgh University Press.
Snodgrass, A.M. 1989. 'The coming of the Iron Age in Greece: Europe's earliest Bronze/Iron transition', in M.L.S. Sorensen and R. Thomas, eds. *The Bronze–Iron Age Transition in Europe*. Oxford: BAR International Series 483.
Thompson, William R. 2000. 'C-waves, center–hinterland contact and regime change in the Ancient Near East: early impacts of globalization'. International Studies Association Annual Meetings, Los Angeles.
——. 2001. 'Trade pulsations, collapse, and reorientation in the ancient world'. International Studies Association Annual Meetings, Chicago.
Toynbee, A.J. 1939. *A Study of History IV and V.* Oxford: Oxford University Press.
Treadgold, W. 1988. *The Byzantine Revival 780–842*. Stanford: Stanford University Press.
——. 1997. *A History of the Byzantine State and Society*. Stanford: Stanford University Press.
Tucker, Richard. 2000. *Insatiable Appetite: The United States and the Ecological Degradation of the Tropical World*. Berkeley: University of California Press

Van Zeist, W. and M.R. vander Spoel-Walvius. 1980. 'A palynological study of the late glacial and the post glacial in the Paris Basin'. *Paleohistoria* 22: 67–109.
Verbruggen, C., G. Huizer and P. Mol. 1997. 'Paleoecological events in Belgium during the last 13,000 years', in C. Verbruggen, ed. *Paleoecological Events in Europe During the last 15,000 Years. Patterns, Process, and Problems*. Chichester: J. Wiley.
Wallerstein, I. 1974, 1980. *The Modern World-System*, Vols 1–3. New York: Academic Press.
——. 1979. 'Kondratieff up or down'. *Review* II (4): 663–73.
Warren, Peter M. 1985. 'Minoan palaces'. *Scientific American* 253 (1): 94–103.
Watrous, L. Vance. 1994. 'Review of Aegean prehistory. III: Crete from earliest prehistory through the protopalatial period'. *American Journal of Archaeology* 98: 695–753.
Watts, W.A., J.R.M. Allen and B. Huntley. 1996. 'The vegetation and climate of Northwest Iberia over the last 14,000 years'. *Journal of Quaternary Science* 11: 125–47.
Weiss, H. 1982. 'The decline of Late Bronze Age civilization as a possible response to climate change'. *Climate Change* 4: 173–98.
——. 2000. 'Beyond the Younger Dryas', in G. Bawden and R. Reycraft, eds. *Environmental Disaster and the Archaeology of Human Response*. Albuquerque: University of New Mexico Press, pp. 75–98.
Weiss, H. and R. Bradley. 2001. 'Archaeology: what drives societal collapse'. *Science* 291 (5504): 609–10.
Weiss, H. and M.A. Courty. 1993. 'The genesis and collapse of third millennium northern Mesopotamian civilization'. *Science* 261: 995–1004.
Whitley, James. 1991. *Style and Society in Dark Age Greece: The Changing Face of a Pre-Literate Society 1100–700 BC*. Cambridge: Cambridge University Press.
Wilkinson, T.J. 1990. *Town and Country in Southeastern Anatolia*. Chicago: Oriental Institute.
Wilkinson, David. 1995. 'Civilizations are world systems!' in Stephen Sanderson, ed. *Civilizations and World Systems*. Walnut Creek, CA: AltaMira Press.
Williams, Michael. 'Dark ages and dark areas: global deforestation in the deep past'. *Journal of Historical Geography* 26 (1): 28–46.
Wolf, Eric. 1982. *Europe and the People without History*. Berkeley: University of California Press.
World Commission on Forests and Sustainable Development. 1999. *Our Forests Our Future*. Cambridge: Cambridge University Press.
Wright, H.E. 1968. 'Climate change in Mycenaen Greece'. *Antiquity* 42: 123–7.
Yoffee, Norman. 1988. 'The collapse of Ancient Mesopotamian states and civilization', in N. Yoffee and G. Cowgill, eds. *The Collapse of Ancient States and Civilizations*. Tucson: University of Arizona Press, pp. 44–68.
Zanggar, E. 1993. 'Neolithic to present soil erosion in Greece', in M. Bell. and J. Boardman, eds. *Past and Present Soil Erosion*. Oxford: Oxford University Press.

11 Three steps in globalization

Global networks from 1000 BCE to 2050 CE

Joachim Karl Rennstich

The context of globalization

The study of globalization as a conceptual tool for the understanding of our modern global system has been increasingly greeted with criticism from a multitude of directions – and rightly so. Originating in French and American writings in the early 1960s, the term globalization has been used to capture everything from the rise of global financial markets to the fall of the Twin Towers on 11 September 2001. The development of globalization – defined as the process of increasing width and depth of interaction and interdependence among social units in the global world system – as a *theoretical construct*, however, with accompanying testable models, has been rather slow and laden with difficulties. Out of a small number of global system development frameworks that have been put forward recently, this chapter employs a new, world historically based and interdisciplinary framework for the study of global system development, the extended evolutionary world politics (EWP) framework.[1] This chapter uses the EWP framework to study current transitions and the development of a 'post-Fordist' or new global socio-economic system as an evolutionary process with a special focus on the world city system development. It argues that the rise of the Phoenician maritime commercial system provided an important nucleus for the evolution of a global maritime-based external network system, which is currently transforming into an external network system based on digital communication networks. Combining frameworks of political geography (world city and network analysis) with a long-term oriented International Relations and international political economy framework, further evidence is provided for the emergence of an informational network economy, global in extent, cyclical in occurrence and evolutionary in nature. The focus on networks and the re-emergence of global cities as central nodes in the world economy highlight the need to add data beyond the state as the level of analysis for studies of the international system. At the same time, however, it makes evident the need to view these nodes as an embedded part of a state-based international system.

Evolutionary approaches to the study of globalization

Among the multitude of evolutionary approaches, we can identify a number of core assumptions that build their common basis. The special emphasis on change is probably the most commonly associated factor of evolutionary approaches, so it is not surprising that assumptions regarding variation and selection are crucial concepts for the evolutionary paradigm. Change in this view is a constant phenomenon rather than a disruption from the norm. Evolutionary frameworks, therefore, aim to identify and understand the (non-linear or -random) dynamics of any given system and its subsystems. Whereas some changes can have large, immediate effects, other changes develop their impact gradually and more incrementally. Also, the interaction and feedback effects in the system have an important impact on the timing of change. Often, a number of previously insignificant and incremental changes can suddenly grow in importance and scope and quickly diffuse throughout the system when paired with new innovations. Depending on their type, as well as the time point at which they occur, these changes are therefore likely to lead to different outcomes. What becomes crucial from an evolutionary perspective is to uncover the pattern of change within the system of interest, in our case the development of the global world system.[2]

If, as we argue here, globalization is an evolutionary process in the making for an extended period of human history rather than a unique occurrence that started in the latter part of the twentieth century (or 1945, or as a result of industrialization, or any other starting point in recent history), then we must show that the processes usually identified with 'globalization' are part of a *longue durée*. We must demonstrate that these changes resemble past patterns of change and are but a part of a new cycle in the long wave of world politics. A powerful evolutionary theoretical framework that allows us to do so is the EWP framework, based on the work by Modelski (1990, 2000) and extended by Rennstich (2003a).

The extended evolutionary world politics (EWP) framework

The aim of the EWP framework is to provide a way to look at the 'big picture' of the development of the human species, yielding a periodization of world history as a phased evolution of the world system. Here, we argue that globalization is essentially evolutionary in its form and, as a result, has its roots in earlier periods of time. Following Modelski's (1990, 2000; see also Modelski and Thompson 1996) conceptualization, globalization in this view comprises a set of co-evolving processes: global *economic* evolution (of trading systems and world markets); global *political* evolution (of nation state systems, world power competitions and international organizations); *democratization* (i.e. the formation of a potential democratic community); and the creation of a world public opinion[3] (through media and learning processes). The ultimate agents of these processes are individuals and organizations sponsoring and advancing innovation that results in the strengthening of the global layers of interactions.

The EWP framework proposes the following 'evolutionary logic' that explains the creation of 'possibility space' (see Clark *et al.* 1995) or, in other words, the potential options for change open to the systems and its parts.[4] Socio-political and economic change seen in this light is always a historical, dynamic process involving the use, as well as the creation, of resources (as diverse as simple objects, techniques and knowledge, or even entire social organizations). This evolutionary logic is driven, as noted above, by human agency. Second, this agency takes place and is embedded in a social and technological context. In other words, whereas the driving logic (human agency) of this process remains the same, its context changes, constituting a 'social learning algorithm' of evolutionary change that is at work at all levels of the global system process (from the individual to the change of the global system as a whole). Within the EWP framework, the four mechanisms driving the evolutionary globalization process and constituting a 'social learning algorithm' are:

1. variety creation (very broadly: cultural process);
2. cooperation or segregation (social process);
3. selection (political process); and
4. preservation and transmission (economic process).

As such a synthesis has to be an ordered one, all world system processes have a time structure that allows for successive optimizations of these mechanisms in a formal logical 'learning sequence' (following the numbered sequence above). Global system processes in this view, then, are seen as nested[5] and synchronized (i.e. co-evolving), four-phased temporal learning experiments driven by common evolutionary logic inherent in all these processes.

Global system processes, globalization and the world city system

Viewed with help of the EWP model, the phase of the global world system process that comes closest to the most common perception of globalization (i.e. the idea of an interdependent 'one world') has begun to develop around 900 CE,[6] developing the preconditions (global system process) through variation generation and experiments during the build-up of a global community (global community process; see Table 11.1). This process is driven by the dynamics of nested political and economic processes, extending the possibility space during each phase and moving the globalization process forward through the trial and error process of the evolutionary drive logic and the punctuations of a selection of the fittest organizational and institutional setting.

Figure 11.1 graphically summarizes this model of the modern era globalization process as laid out in the EWP model. In this view, the global

Table 11.1 Extended evolutionary world politics model of process of globalization, 930–2080 CE

Starting (≈year)	*Global system process*	*Global community process*	*Global political evolution (long cycles)*	*Global economic evolution*	*Network structure*
930	Preconditions	**Experiments**	**Eurasian Transition**	**Sung Breakthrough**	Build-up
		Reforming	North Sung		Transition
			South Sung		External
1190		Republican	Genoa	**Commercial/Nautical**	External
			Venice	**Revolution**	
1430	Global nucleus	Calvinist	**Atlantic Europe**	**Oceanic Trade**	External
			Portugal		
			Dutch Republic		
1640		Liberal	Britain I	**Industrial Take-Off**	Transition
			Britain II		Internal
1850	Global organization	**Democracy**	**Atlantic Pacific**	**Information**	
		Democratic groundwork	USA	K17 Electric, steel	Internal
				K18 Electronics	Transition
				Digital	
				K19 Informational	External
				industries	External
				K20 Digital network (?)	
2080					

Source: Based on Modelski (2000) and own additions. All years CE.

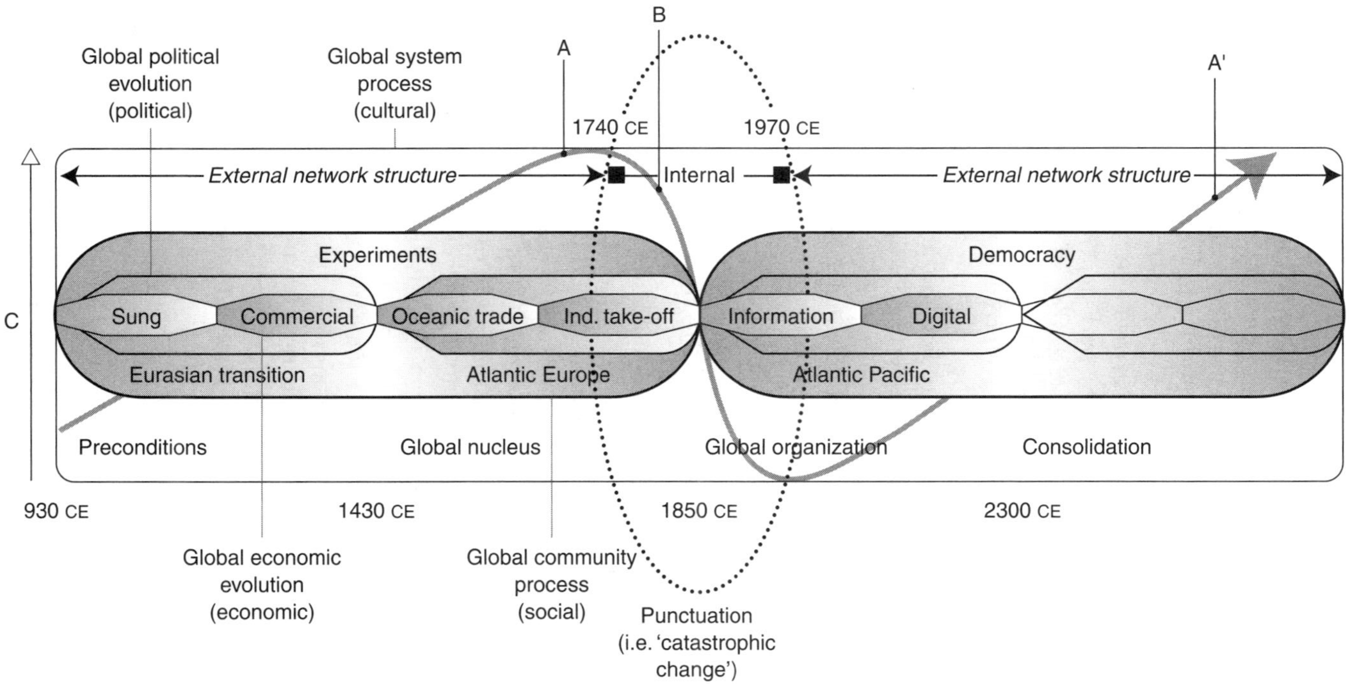

Figure 11.1 Evolutionary model of globalization, based on the extended EWP framework, 930–2300 CE.

system process driven by the nested processes of economic (innermost octagon, labelled 'Sung', 'Commercial', 'Oceanic trade', 'Industrial take-off', 'Information' and 'Digital'), political (bullet-formed boxes, labelled 'Eurasian transition', 'Atlantic Europe' and 'Atlantic Pacific') and social (rounded boxes, labelled 'Experiments' and 'Democracy') development. Together, they constitute the global system development (represented by the thin grey box framing all other processes). This global system increases in reach and overall complexity (with the *y*-axis label 'C' being short for 'system complexity' and represented by the bold grey, wave-like arrow) until – during the nineteenth century – it reaches a state in which the path-dependent system eventually runs out of future possible choices, a state also referred to as 'hypercoherence'[7] that regularly occurs in any complex system.[8] In other words, the global system experiences a 'punctuation' (also referred to as 'catastrophic change') around 1850, resulting in the end of the experimental phase in the global community process and starting with the democratic phase as its selected fittest global social system. During this punctuation, the global system process changes from an external structure to an internal one (starting around the middle of the eighteenth century), manifesting the selected organizational and institutional structures, until a new phase of evolutionary dynamic sets in during the late twentieth century.[9]

Evolution of the world city system: the first two steps

In the following section, we shall discuss in greater detail the emergence of the evolution of the global system as presented in Figure 11.1, with a special focus on the main nodes of connection, namely world cities (see, for example, Bosworth 2000; see also Chase-Dunn and Hall 1997). We will do so highlighting the three main points of its development: (1) the rise of a (crude) external, maritime network system as the result of the rise of the Phoenician city system; (2) the renewal of the system after its levelling-off period with the emergence of the (complex) external, maritime Italian city systems; and (3) the transition of the (complex) external maritime network system towards a new system based on digital communication networks.

World cities constitute the major nodes of external socio-economic and -political networks, lately also referred to as 'human webs' (McNeill and McNeill 2003), that create the ecology in which global system formation takes place. As pointed out earlier, adaptation to changing environments is a crucial factor for the development of the global system process. Following Bosworth (2000: 279), we argue here that adaptive behaviour in the case of the development of the world city system emerges in the face of 'blockages' brought about by military and political 'choke-holds on world trade'. Within our framework, these blockages correspond with punctuations of the global system process, forcing active innovative agents to adapt in the form of circumvention and the development of new connections. Connections of this sort can either involve a recombination of existing nodes in the current system or even the development of new nodes and consequently a new system.

Table 11.2 lists five blockages crucial in the development of the world city system. The first two blockages mark the transition from a land-based Silk Road to a maritime-based Spice Route system. The third and fourth blockages represent important turning points of the system from a preindustrial Spice Route to an industrial Atlantic system. The fifth blockage marks the transition to an informational system based on digital communication networks. The cycles of Silk Road and Spice Route alternation reflect the tension between continental (i.e. land-based) and maritime systems, where each represents a strategy for building an increasingly complex systemic structure, expanded connectivity and thus higher differentiation of the system as a whole. This pulsating shift towards an external node (maritime) network system is captured in Figure 11.2. The figure highlights the increasing shift – following the traditional 'learning curve' of evolutionary processes – from land-based to maritime (i.e. port-centred) world cities as major nodes of the emerging global system.

Our expectation of the global system process as a learning structure is also reflected in the shape of the complexity curve in Figure 11.1, representing the level of complexity of the global system as a whole. After an initial progress towards a crude external, maritime system, the development levels off (after the second blockage) into a crude land-based external system, until it slowly resumes its development with the rise of the increasingly maritime Sung China system (after the third blockage). It is important to note that

Table 11.2 World city blockages and circumventions

Blockage	*Circumvention*	*Network structure*	*City rise*
I. Parthia blocks Silk Roads (*c.* 25 BCE)	Romans develop Red Sea route	Crude external network structure (maritime)	Rome, Alexandria, Anuradhapura
II. Persia blocks Byzantium (*c.* 550 CE)	Byzantium develops northern steppe route	Crude external network structure (land)	Constantinople, Changan
III. Northern tribes in China (*c.* 800–1100 CE)	Sung dynasty expands maritime trade	Crude external network structure (transitory maritime)	Hangchow, Canton, Cairo, Genoa, Venice
IV. Muslim powers block Europe (*c.* 1400–1500 CE)	Europeans find Cape route, Atlantic crossing	Complex external network structure (maritime)	Lisbon, Seville, Amsterdam, London
V. Colonial western powers block Britain (*c.* 1850 CE)	UK/US create independent communication networks	Complex external network structure (informational)	New York, San Francisco, London, Tokyo, Seoul

Source: Based on Bosworth (2000: 280), with own additions and changes.

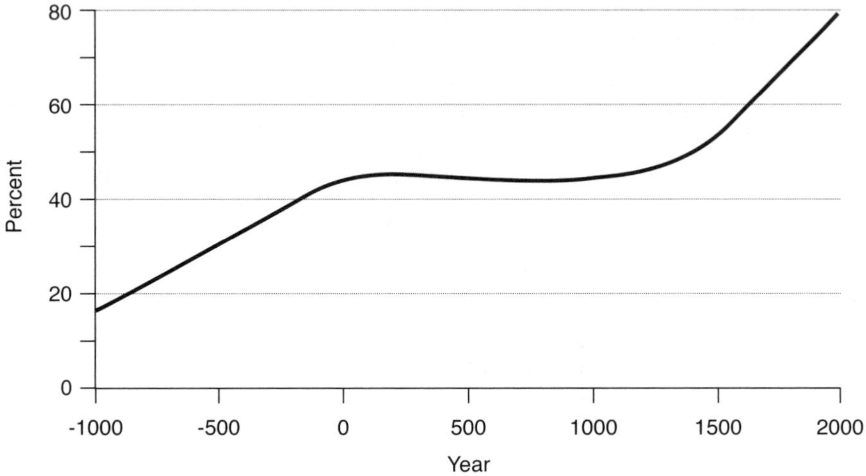

Figure 11.2 The 25 largest world cities, percentage external nodes, 1000 BCE–2000 CE.

each of these blockages represents punctuations of the system in the form of internal network systems blocking the emergence of a global system process based on increasingly complex external networks (see discussion below).[10]

Network trajectories

So far, we are able to identify the unfolding of a pulsating global process system, with periods characterized by internal network structures, followed by periods of external network structure dominance. Elsewhere (Rennstich 2003a), we have demonstrated in greater detail the development of three distinct network systems arising in the modern global system: (1) the commercial maritime system; (2) the industrial production system; and (3) the emerging new digital commercial system. Both the commercial maritime and the digital commercial systems are characterized by their emphasis on external network relations, whereas the industrial production phase (as an outgrowth of the 'punctuation' of the global world system process in our model) is primarily reinforcing existing organizational and institutional patterns through internal networks.

As laid out in our model (see Tables 11.1 and 11.3), the formation of the modern global system – and thus globalization as we experience it today – has emerged roughly around 900 CE with the rise of complex and diversified organizations (including nation states, as well as more complex business enterprises[11]) and the formation of networks of organization at the global level. As Modelski and Thompson (1996: 45) have argued, these organizations could not have taken place without significant innovation in the fields of information processing (e.g. printing, oceanic communication), military

Table 11.3 Co-evolutionary world system processes, EWP matrix, 3400 BCE–2080 CE

Start (≈year)	*World system process (eras)* *System structure → world*	*World socialization* *System structure → community*	*Active zone process* *System structure → collective organization*	*World economy process* *System structure → production/commerce*
3400 BCE	Ancient	**Crude structured world** (centre-building)	**Mid-Eastern** (Uruk) (Sumer)	**Command economy** Bronze
2300 BCE		(Dispersal)	(Mesopotamia) (Egyptian)	Fertile crescent
1200 BCE	Classical	(Concentration)	**Eurasian** (East Asian) (Indian)	Iron
100 BCE		(Dispersal)	(Mediterranean) (Mid-Eastern)	Silk Roads
930 CE	Modern	**Fine structured world** (reconcentration)	**Oceanic** (Eurasian transition) (Atlantic Europe)	**Market economy** National Market
1850 CE		(Democratic base)	(Atlantic Pacific)	World Market

Source: Based on Modelski (2000: 40).

technology (e.g. gunpowder weapons) and economic innovations (e.g. media of exchange). Sung China is widely regarded as the geographic space where this inception (or emergence of 'preconditions' in our model) has occurred (e.g. Reischauer *et al.* 1960; Elvin 1973; McNeill 1982; Jones 1988; Gernet 1996).

Sung China's four consecutive waves of innovative socio-economic leadership and their accompanying leading sectors – printing and paper; formation of a national market; the development of an effective fiscal and administrative framework; and the expansion of maritime trade – provided the basis for the emergence of the commercial maritime system, the first instance of an expanding, global commercial system characterized by its reliance on external network structures. Asia, however, was not to be the centre of the development of the emerging commercial maritime system. Although Asia remained a crucial and integral part of the emerging commercial maritime system, it was due to the dynamics of leading sectors developing in Europe that the system evolved fully.

It is important to note, however, that the modern global system process has evolved out of a previous set of economic, political, social and cultural world system processes. The EWP framework thus includes an analysis of the development of the premodern system structure ('crude structured world') as the 'community-building' step in the evolution of the global world system. Table 11.3 lists the steps from a less complex set of world systems processes that provide the path (and evolutionary selection) for the systems providing the basis for the modern global system process. Here, we shall focus on the innovations emerging during the Phoenician external and maritime-based network system as the basis for the following evolution of further external, maritime network city systems, and highlight the development of its next step in the form of an external, information-based system.[12]

Phoenician trade network system

Arising in a relatively narrow strip of coastal land (and what is now Lebanon and Syria), the Phoenicians emerged around 1100 BCE as the leading trading and seafaring power of the ancient Near East, lasting until roughly 850 BCE, although the main system nodes in the form of world cities such as Tyre would continue to hold a central position for much longer.[13] With networks across the Mediterranean and into the Indian and Atlantic Oceans, the sturdy longboats and galleons of Ugarit, Sidon, Byblos and Tyre foreshadowed the ocean-going ships to be employed in the next major extension of a then global maritime-based external network system with the emergence of the modern global system 2,000 years later. Further improving initial models of Mesopotamian-managed enterprises, the system emerging from the networks of the merchants of Tyre can be best understood as an evolution of the Mesopotamian system, but remains unique in that it was the first truly transcontinental system with a set of central (maritime) nodes in three different continents.

Moore and Lewis (1999: 72–3) point out an important similarity between the first and second steps of the evolution of the world city system, arguing that 'the similarities between the Near East in the late second millennium and Europe in the century and a half before the Industrial Revolution were quite remarkable' marked by a balance-of-power system, a common set of clear rules and common norms as expressed in the equal treatment of courts and a common diplomatic language.

Indeed, this environment mirrors in many respects that of the world city network system and mix of competing state systems during the next phase of commercial/nautical revolutions and the co-evolving political, social and cultural world system processes after 1200 (see Table 11.1). From an evolutionary perspective, this description reflects the stage of 'cooperation and segregation', followed by the 'selection' process of the system best adapted to the environment in which it operates (reflected in the flattening of the learning curve pictured in Figure 11.2). It is characterized by the emergence of a common system with a common set of standards of interaction (in social, linguistic, political and economic terms) and thus higher system complexity. This not only limits what Allen *et al.* (1992) have termed the 'possibility space' within the increasingly complex system, but also as a result increases the 'evolutionary heat' in the form of competition, ultimately driving a selection process.

In respect to the importance for world city system development, it is important to note that it was during this phase that the coastal cities, such as Byblos, Tyre and Arward, took on a special role as central nodes of the new maritime external network system, but remained firmly embedded in the Assyrian Empire (Buzan and Little 2000: 213). Their role as central network nodes was reaffirmed by the fact that their relationship with the empire was itself contractually based, allowing these nodes to maintain the needed degree of independence to operate within their maritime commercial system network while remaining locked in to the greater socio-political environment of the world system as a whole.

Featuring a dense and increasingly urbanized population, well-kept harbours, an ample supply of wood and a ready supply of a highly skilled and educated workforce, the cities of the Levant were ideally suited to develop a commercial maritime-based external network economy not dissimilar to the Genoan/Venetian, Dutch or even the first British system emerging in the second major 'cooperation and segregation' stage of the evolution of world city system (and ultimately the global system process as a whole). It is to this second stage that we turn briefly now, before discussing in greater detail the transition towards a new world city system based not on maritime but on digital informational networks.

Genoese and Venetian trade network system

Emerging from the Venetian and Genoese trade network systems, through the Dutch commercial network to the British trading system, each long wave (of co-evolving two economic K waves and one political leadership cycle) in the Modelski and Thompson (1996) sense, has witnessed an increase in complexity and geographical widening of the system as a whole.[14] By the tenth to eleventh century, after medieval Europe emerged from its 'dark ages', European development and population growth was expanding again, and with it demand for luxury goods (such as spices and silk) and the ability to pay for them (Lopez 1987). Trade, or as Bernard (1976: 274) put it, 'links with the outside world more over, the very essence of commerce', was to provide the dynamics behind Europe's progress. Similar to the earlier bursts of innovation in Sung China (see Table 11.1), this pattern repeated itself, although now centred on the Genoese and later Venetian trading operations. Thus, the ultimate focus of leading sector trade for the European subsystem was the reordering of the flow of high-value goods from Asia to Europe. Whereas Genoa led in the development and expansion of the commercial space, namely the development of the Champagne Fairs as a major trading platform for the trade network nodes, shifting later to an emphasis on the Black Sea trade, Venetian maritime advancements manifested and institutionalized this system, developing into a dominating commercial network node in the expanding world trade system (see Modelski and Thompson 1996: ch. 10).

Portuguese trading network system

In a further widening of the maritime-based network (over the less efficient land-based networks), the Portuguese were able to eliminate a layer in the distribution of goods, establishing a presence on the coast of west Africa, gaining direct access to the sources of gold in the interior. This turned out to be a crucial innovation in a century when all Europe was suffering from a shortage of precious metal, creating in its turn a new leading sector (see Table 11.1). Even more important was the further expansion of the maritime network (opened by the voyage of Vasco da Gama, 1497–99) into a truly oceanic trading network. Not only did it link the rich and complex maritime trade of Asia with the Atlantic, enabling a (relatively short-lived) monopoly over the extremely lucrative spice trade (pepper in particular) and thus in its wake the creation of a new leading sector, but it also initiated the movement of the hub of European intercontinental trade away from the Mediterranean to the Atlantic.

Dutch and British network systems

As Curtin (1984: 179) has pointed out, maritime trade, in particular, has constituted the leading sector of commercial growth in the world economy, perhaps as early as the ninth century, but certainly between the fifteenth and nineteenth centuries. The emergence of the Netherlands' trading supremacy was founded on its strong role in intra- and intercontinental trade. Its success was rooted in the transportation of bulky, low-priced commodities (e.g. grain, herring, salt and timber) to and from the Baltic region. This enabled early Dutch specialization in inexpensive but numerous freight-carrying ships and the development of an efficient shipbuilding industry. As a consequence, the Dutch were able to move into, and in the end control, the richer trades of Europe and the world, namely with the capturing of the Eastern trade routes after 1580 (Israel 1989). Together with its function as a distribution centre of Spanish-American silver to the northern European area (including Germany and the British Isles; see Braudel 1972), the Netherlands developed into the central node of the world trading network, in terms of both trading activity and finance (for an extensive review, see Modelski and Thompson 1996: 79–83; Arrighi *et al.* 1999: 97–109).

Again, we witness the now familiar pattern of the establishment of a superior network infrastructure, followed by an extension of this advantage in the advancement of superior organizational capital accumulation[15] and enterprise structures. The development of cheap yet reliable freight-carrying ships such as the *fluyt* and the build-up of an efficient shipbuilding industry clearly fit our description of technological innovations that enable the creation of extraordinary growth and the evolution of a new leading sector. Only through the clustering of various innovations in the sixteenth-century Netherlands were the Dutch able to create their expertise and advantage in transportation necessary for the generation of their trade routes and shipping dominance. It is thus in the seventeenth-century Netherlands where we can find the first and most successful example of a worldwide corporate business organization, the Dutch joint-stock chartered companies. A prime example of the manifestation of this organizational form was the Dutch East Indies Company or, in its original name, the *Verenigde Oost-Indische Compagnie* (VOC), established in 1602.[16] Together with the *West-Indische Compagnie* (WIC), founded in 1621, the Dutch not only dominated important parts of the eastern trades, but also pioneered the Atlantic triangular trade, linking European manufacturing communities with slave-procuring communities in Africa and the plantation communities of the Americas (Emmer 1981; Unger 1982; Postma 1990).

This predominant position as a central node of the worldwide trade network was successfully contested by England after its trade underwent a substantial transformation (Richardson 1987: ch. 4 and 5). As Scammell (1989: 232) notes, the major commercial focus for England after 1650 was largely on oceanic expansion, 'with the impetus coming from a surge in Asian and American imports and the simultaneous growth of a lively market in the Americas (North, South, and Caribbean) for domestic exports and reexports'. Another crucial factor became the advancement of production techniques, transforming former luxury goods into mass-consumed goods by substantially lowering their price of production and thus increasing availability to a larger market (Mintz 1985; see also Davis 1954). Thus, Britain was able to extend the Dutch trading network, not only in size but, maybe even more importantly, in 'depth' (i.e. vertical integration/control of production), accompanied by the increasing importance of London as the major financial node of world capital.

As argued earlier, it is helpful for our understanding of the evolution of the global system as a whole to focus specifically on the blockages of the central nodes in the world city system. These blockages manifested themselves in the form of internal network systems with the explicit attempt to block existing external network systems (either land or maritime based). From an evolutionary perspective, they acted as punctuations of the global system process (based on an external network structure), forcing a circumvention of these blockages and ultimately driving the global system process towards greater complexity. Here, we shall argue that the fifth blockage (see Table 11.2) arrived in the form of the build-up of internal network structures, forcing the creation of independent communication lines connecting the dispersed patches of mainly British but also other players in the imperial game. We have discussed this punctuation in greater detail elsewhere (Rennstich 2003a). Our focus here is on the outcome of this punctuation in the form of the transition from a maritime-based external network structure to one based on a wholly new network: an informational external network based on digital communication networks.

The new global digital commercial system: the third step

The development surrounding the emergence of the fifth blockage (see Table 11.2) is the main focus here. It is especially significant for the further evolution of the global system in marking the development of a new external world city system. Rather than relying on oceanic port cities as the central nodes of the global system, the global economic shift towards an information-based system (see Table 11.1) marks the rise of digital communication clusters as the central nodes of the world city system.[17] With the increasingly apparent demise and unravelling of the Fordist model of the dominance of internal networks beginning in the 1970s, the punctuation of the global system seemed to have given birth to a new phase of extending external network dominance. This holds true not only on the macro or world systemic level but also on less aggregated levels as well. As Best (2001: 54) has demonstrated in his study of production systems, this process has entailed 'moving from a closed network to a business model organized around the leadership and design dynamic internally and open systems externally'. A business policy of 'focus and network' facilitated the implementation and diffusion of the principle of systems integration not only in the organization of technology but, maybe even more importantly, in the business organization as well (Miles *et al.* 1997). This created the decentralized environment for the emergence of new innovative clusters that allowed for the crucial diffusion characteristic of all previous new leading sector developments.

Initially, these external networks remained mainly within the boundaries of national economies. With networking emerging as a means of coordination enhancing the resource creation activities of enterprises (Richardson 1972), these networks now increasingly tend to extend across national borders and regions (Miles *et al.* 1997). Fostered by the rise of digital communication interfaces – most visibly so in the various forms of the Internet[18] – lowering significantly the cost of access and the creation of open systems and the availability of standardized and truly global logistical solutions, a multitude of cost-efficient organizational open systems have replaced previously closed systems or open national systems. As Dicken (1999, 2003) argues, in effect, the global economy is made up of a variety of complex intraorganizational and interorganizational networks intersecting with geographical networks structured particularly around linked agglomerations or clusters of activities.

Previous authors have focused on the close relationship between the expansion of transportation infrastructures and the expansion of industrial economies (e.g. Hall and Preston 1988; Berry 1991). Even a superficial study of this linkage makes it obvious that the close relationship between communication and transportation networks thus makes it necessary to study the development of communication systems and their impact as well. We agree with Hall and Preston's (1988: 187) argument that the information infrastructure may be just as important as the infrastructure of physical transport, or even more so. In the following section, we shall identify in greater detail the institutional and organizational characteristics of this newly emerging external network-based global system. What differentiates it from the previous external network system is its digital nature with implications for its scale – both horizontally (i.e. geographic diffusion) as well as vertically (i.e. connected units) – and its impact on the creation of new leading sectors. A closer look at the network trajectories of this new system will help to make this development more transparent.

Network trajectories

Information and knowledge are two separate although intertwined concepts, and the centrality of both in the new digital external network system requires a closer look at the historical development of their organization and development. A classic definition of information (from a mathematic and scientific viewpoint) refers to the reduction of uncertainty in a communication system (Shannon 1948). It thus includes any pattern of energy or matter we can find in nature as a container of information. Knowledge, however, does not simply equal information, but rather refers to 'ideas and facts that human mind has internalized and understood' (Headrick 2000: 4), often acquired and assembled in a complex fashion, a complexity that makes its nearly impossible to simulate in a mechanical fashion (i.e. 'artificial intelligence'). As societies grow more complex and the amount of accumulated knowledge rises, the need for information handling becomes an important determinant of successful organization and mastery of this complexity. Rather than aiming to identify a starting point for a 'knowledge society' that will necessarily be somewhat arbitrary, it seems more useful in respect to the framework employed in this work to view the entire development of humankind as the development of a knowledge society. This, as our framework suggests, has not been a linear progress, however, but rather a process marked by periods of sharp accelerations in the amount of information that people had access to and in the creation of information systems to deal with it (Headrick 2000: 8).

To understand the evolution of the new digital network, it is thus necessary to have an understanding of the forms of information systems that mark its development. Headrick (2000: 4–5) defines information systems as the 'methods and techniques by which people organize and manage information, rather than the content of the information itself'. Information systems in this understanding are supplements of the mental functions of thought, memory and speech and thus the technologies of knowledge. Headrick uses five dimensions on which to categorize information systems, namely information (1) gathering; (2) classification; (3) transformation; (4) storage; and (5) communication. Employing these dimensions, he identifies the rise of a new information system, driven as the previous information systems by the combination of information demand, supply and organization, emerging in the period 1700–1850. This new information system ultimately provided the basis for the digital informational system that is now emerging as the main central nervous system of the global system. Rather than the result of new (mechanical) technological tools, Headrick (2000: 9, 217) argues that it was a cultural change driven by social, economic and political upheavals and transformations.

Similarly, Hobart and Schiffman (1998) argue for a dynamic interplay between technology and culture, shaping and being shaped by it, resulting in three distinctive information ages: classical, modern and contemporary. Hobart and Schiffman also argue for the roots of the contemporary information system in the cultural (combined with the technological) developments in the eighteenth and nineteenth centuries. Whereas Headrick, as a historian, focuses more on the past evolution of the new information system, Hobart and Schiffman extend their analysis and identify in addition the rise of a distinct new information system based on its digital character.[19] In this system, they argue, information no longer acts as a universal, abstract model of the world, either classifying or analytical, but rather has become a world unto itself, in which abstract symbols can be assigned arbitrarily to any objects and procedures whatsoever. As an important precursor, the rise of relational mathematics in the modern age realized the information potential of number and organized it in a broad-reaching, reductionist hierarchy;

digital information has elicited the information potential of purely abstract symbols, fabricating a realm of pure technique apart from any foundation in knowledge (Hobart and Schiffman 1998: ch. 8).[20]

What unites these authors is their perspective that control over space differs with the types of politico-economic organization employed (roughly a division between 'trading' and 'territorial' states), an argument of course further explored here in terms of the relationship between control over space and the network structure of the global system. In particular, Rosecrance's (1999) latest extension of his argument as well as Hugill's (1999) study of the relationship between communication systems and geopolitics bear great importance on the study undertaken here.

Taking Innis's (1950) analysis a step further, Hugill (1999), in his study of the relationship between communication systems, geopolitics and the global system, also emphasizes the 'two-way flows of information that predominate as mechanisms of military [i.e. political] and economic control' (Hugill 1999: 4). He argues that the geopolitical interests from trading states (in the framework of this work, states that exert their power mainly in external networks) and territorial states (i.e. internal network-based states) differ in terms of the military and communications systems they employ. Whereas trading states have an interest in exerting weak control over long distances, territorial states wish to exert strong control over short distances (Hugill 1999: 7). The former thus tend to invest in long-range military and communications systems, in other words, they aim to establish external networks of control. Hugill's extensive study of the evolution of four crucial communications technologies (i.e. telegraphy, telephony, radio and radar) starting at 1844 – our noted point of punctuation of the global system and ultimately the birth point of the newly emerging external network system – demonstrates how especially long-range radio and the digital (i.e. programmable) computer both evolved into enablers of external network establishment and control. The pattern of existing technology being transformed in innovative spurts and clusters again proves the breeding ground for the emergence of a new long cycle of global system development (see Table 11.1). As noted earlier, however, a crucial difference from the former cycle is that it marks the return to a global system based on external network structures.

From a more technological perspective, Hall and Preston (1988) make the similar argument that the origins of the newly emerging system must be traced back to the transformations in communication system technologies beginning roughly around the middle of the nineteenth century, with the invention of the electrical telegraph (1830s) as well as the telephone and typewriter and gramophone (1875–90). These new inventions mark the emergence of what the authors call 'new information technology' industries, embracing the technologies – mechanical, electrical, electromechanical, electronic – that record, transmit, process and distribute information (Hall and Preston 1988: 5). This, of course, is congruent with the framework presented here and consistent with the argument of a punctuation of the global system development around this period, resulting in a connected, yet new and distinct, external network system based on the digital central nervous system.

The third step: the digital external network structure

What characterizes the current technological revolution that enables the basis of innovative clustering of K19 is not the *centrality* of knowledge and information, but the *application* of such knowledge and information to knowledge generation and information processing/communication devices, in a cumulative feedback loop between innovation and the use of innovation (Hall and Preston 1988; Saxby 1990; Castels 1996). Whereas the leading sectors of the former external network-based global system (i.e. the Baltic and Atlantic trade routes and later the eastern trades) were dominantly maritime based, the leading sectors of this external network system are increasingly digital in nature. As in previous cycles, the development of a new infrastructure sets the 'tone' of the following leading sectors. It is thus not surprising to see the emergence of a 'digital trade route' in the form of information and communication technology (ICT)-based digital networks as the precursor of a more complex digital-based external network system.

The Internet (i.e. the backbone of the digital external network system) serves as a trade route in the sense that the new commodity of the global economic system – digitalized information – is transported along its lines. However, digitalized information itself is not the only commodity. E-commerce, or the electronically enabled retailing of software, digital books, digital services (e.g. online brokering and e-banking), and digital outsourcing (e.g. data processing) are now common phenomena. It is reasonable to add the growing number of web-enabled transactions ('e-business') of non-digital items and services, both business-to-business and consumer-to-business, to this count.

Its impact goes beyond a mere distributive advancement of external networks. Similar to organizational changes apparent in earlier external network systems, it enables dramatic organizational change as well. As Castells (2001: 102) points out, 'e-Business is not the business that is exclusively conducted online but a new form of conducting business, by, with, and on the Internet'. Digital networks thus develop into a truly commercial and organizational central nerve system connecting both digital (e.g. the Internet, mobile communication networks, etc.) and non-digital (e.g. distributional networks, production facilities, etc.) systems. The digital nature of the system allows for relative ubiquity and low cost of provision and access to the system, and thus for a qualitative and quantitative deeper integration than in previous external systems. This is a crucial difference from the previous maritime-based external system: despite its use and availability as a 'trade route', the wider impact of the digital nervous system spanning the globe must be seen as a facilitator of organizational and thus institutional change at all level of human interaction, ranging from individual peer-to-peer exchanges[21] to exchanges between states and the structure of the global system as a whole (for an excellent discussion, see Singh 2002).

Harvey (1989) goes so far as to argue that *all other* aspects of late modern societies, including cultural transformations, are in fact residue effects of this restructuring of the socio-spatial logic of modern economies into a new socio-spatial axis: as capitalist systems of production mutate to take advantage of globalizing technologies and flexible modes of accumulation (i.e. in our framework, the transition to an increasing reliance on external network relationships) in an attempt to find a new 'spatial fix'. The main enablers of this change are ICTs and the development of 'cyberspace', together constituting a digital external network structure (see, for example, Poster 1995; Dodge and Kitchin 2001).

Shapiro and Varian (1999) argue that the main pillar of what is identified elsewhere (Rennstich 2002) as the informational network economy is not a fundamental shift in the 'nature' or even 'magnitude' of the information itself but, rather, advances in information technology and infrastructure. The crucial difference from previous paradigms is the dramatic increase in the ability to manipulate information (Shapiro and Varian 1999: 8–9). The changes that led to the increased networking described above are rooted in the information technology infrastructure but also reinforce its development. As noted earlier, Borrus and Bar (1993) mark three major technological trends that have had the widest impact on ICT as the infrastructure for the above-described property of networking: (1) the digitization of networks; (2) the emergence of broadband transmission; and (3) the increase in the functionality, performance and variety of the non-computer technology connected to networks. Increasing the system's intelligence permits increasing differentiation of network performance, of service (or application) choices and ever more intimate management and control. Increases in capacity, speed and digitalization now permit transport integration and unprecedented flexibility and performance in network use as infrastructure to economic activities. The trend towards large numbers of highly sophisticated devices increasingly relying upon a network also constitutes a discontinuous transformation in the demands being placed upon the network infrastructure in terms of both the transmission volumes and the new pattern of use it will have to support (Borrus and Bar 1993).[22]

Digital world cities

The United States takes a central position within this new digital network (not only in geographical terms). As a result of the emergence of the Internet as a global common standard of the digital network, the US still maintains its central role in this global network. By the early 1990s, the US possessed the most developed computer networks in the world. As the result of the telecommunications and later 'dot.com boom' in this period, it was also left with the most widely dispersed digital infrastructure, making it a priority for other countries to focus on links to the US rather than on links between themselves and thus reinforcing the centrality of the US in the digital hierarchy. Cukier (1999), for example, notes that it is often cheaper for national service providers to lease high-capacity Internet connections (from US companies) from any European capital to the US than from one capital to another within the continent (and thus through European providers).

As Townsend (2001b) demonstrates, whereas every region and nearly every country is now tied into the digital network in the form of a direct Internet connection to the US, direct connections between other countries are less common. This is especially visible in the connection structure between different major regions, such as Europe and Asia, where direct connections are almost non-existent. As a result, the US still serves as a central switching facility for inter-regional data traffic and thus as a central node in the digital external network system.

In his study of the development of the modern international telecommunication network, Barnett (2001) also finds evidence for a network that he describes as one large interconnected group of nations arrayed along a centre-to-periphery dimension. His findings indicate that:

> as the world moves into the information age, the international telecommunications network has become more denser, more centralized, and more highly integrated. The fact that the network is becoming more centralized during this period [from 1978–1996] indicates that an increasing amount of information is flowing through the core countries rather than being exchanged directly among the more peripheral nations.
>
> Barnett (2001: 1649)

Also recognizable is the re-emergence of major cities as important nodes of the external network development. During the transition from an internal network-based system to an external-based one, so-called 'global cities' acted mainly as sites (or network nodes) where transnational flows of goods, capital and people were tied into national and regional economies (Sassen 1991, 1997). In other words, they tied the internal network-structured economies to the global system. As new studies (Zook 2000, 2001; Townsend 2001a, 2001b) focusing on digital communication networks – and thus primarily Internet based – have shown, many large, dense metropolitan clusters of Internet activity exist outside the archetypical global cities of New York, London and Tokyo.[23] Evidence thus exists to demonstrate that new telecommunications networks reflect a more complex system of interurban information flows than implied by earlier works centring on the global city hypothesis, connecting a wider range of cities in a more complex way (Townsend 2001a, 2001b).[24]

This renewed focus on a 'centres and hinterlands' structure of the global system as well as the geographical centrality of the US for the functioning (and control) makes it clear that, despite its increasingly digital nature, the global system is still very much a geopolitical one in the traditional sense of the meaning. Far from creating a sphere of 'space- and placelessness' (e.g. Benedikt 1991; Cairncross 2001), the new external network-based system, despite its transformative dynamics, does not render the spatial logic of existing modernist societies obsolete. As Kitchin (1998) argues, geography continues to matter as an organizing principle and as a constituent of social relations (see also Mattelart 2000; Dodge and Kitchin 2001: ch. 2). It cannot be entirely eliminated because of the interaction of the virtual space with the world beyond ICT networks and cyberspace, which only in combination constitute the external networks on which the global world system is based. Thus, it is more useful to distinguish spatial logic, as both Castells (1996) and Rosecrance (1999) point out, between the 'space of flows' and the 'space of places'. As Morley and Robins (1995) put it:

> If we have emphasized processes of delocalization, associated especially with the development of new information and communications networks, this should not be seen as an absolute tendency. The particularity of place and culture can never be done away with, can never be transcended. Globalization is, in fact, also associated with new dynamics of *re*-localization. It is about the achievement of a new global–local nexus, about new and intricate relations between global space and local space. Globalization is like a jigsaw puzzle: it is a matter of inserting a multiplicity of localities into the overall picture of a new global system.
>
> Morley and Robins (1995: 116)

Rethinking globalization

For students of world history and the *longue durée* in the Braudelian tradition, the emergence of world cities as central nodes of the new digital global system network is all too familiar. Braudel (1992b) identified so-called 'world cities' (i.e. single cities dominating the world economy in which they operate), notably Venice, Antwerp, Genoa and Amsterdam, as crucial drivers of modern social change in Europe. Later replaced by the sequence of what Lee and Pelizzon (1991) have termed 'hegemonic cities', or rather economic centres of hegemonic states, these centres have experienced a three-phased development from adaptation to later integration (or nationalization), followed by the demise of this new focus on territoriality and the return of a network of central nodes of a global commercial, social and cultural (and thus political) network (Taylor 1995). Here, however, we extend the *longue durée* far beyond Braudel's view and connect the rise of his world cities with the world city system emerging during the rise of the Phoenician commercial maritime network system around 1000 BCE. The blockages of world city system networks – and thus, ultimately, the increasingly complex external network system as a whole – fits not only our proposed model of a punctuation of the global system before the rise of Sung China around 900 CE, marking the beginning of the modern global system process, it also fits with our identification of the rise of internal network structures during the industrialization phase (with its focus on global internal networks and thus a stronger emphasis on territoriality) as a major blockage of the external global system, setting the stage for the emergence of a new, external network-based system with a renewed emphasis on world or, rather, global cities as its central nodes. In the same manner as the first stage of the codification of information in the form of the alphabet during the Phoenician system, the second stage of this codification, in the form of a binary (i.e. digital) code encapsulating every form of biological, social and economic structure during the rise of the digital commercial system under US leadership, has proved a crucial innovation for the evolution of the global system. Although we cannot foresee the future, we can assuredly get a better understanding of the processes leading to its unfolding. If the far-reaching consequences that occurred as a result of the shift in network structure during the Phoenician system are any guide, the shift towards an informational digital system will prove to be a watershed in the development of the global system process far beyond the realms of organizational structures of firms or the hierarchical power distribution within the world system. The new digital network structure will, and to some degree has already started to, profoundly change all co-evolving world system economic, political, social and cultural processes.

Notes

1 For a discussion of this and alternative frameworks, see Rennstich (2003a).
2 Rather than arguing for a deterministic outcome through structure, evolutionary studies instead examines the 'evolutionary drive' (Allen *et al.* 1992) that creates what Clark *et al.* (1995) have called 'possibility space' or the range of potential options for change open to the system and its parts.
3 The term 'world public opinion' does not mean to imply the existence of a single, uniform, globally accepted public opinion but rather an increasing (if largely elite) acknowledgement of matters outside one's own immediate local environment. See, for example, McNeill (1967; 1991); Curtin (1984); Abu-Lughod (1989); Plattner (1989); Braudel (1992a); Bentley (1993).
4 Dark (1998: 116) prefers to call it the creation of 'system of systems' and their interaction dynamics. For a discussion of some of the underlying epistemological assumptions of evolutionary economics, which also build the basis of this work, see Andersen (1994: 15).
5 Nesting here refers to 'large-scale processes enfold, and are in turn animated by, smaller scale processes of determinate proportion in conditions of synchronization' (Modelski 2000: 30).
6 This work follows the increasing use of CE (Common Era) and BCE (before the Common Era), which replaces the traditional dating system employing AD and BC, respectively, for the same periods.
7 The terms 'hypercoherence' or 'catastrophic change' refer not to the overall breakdown of the global system process, but rather to the terminology used in chaos and catastrophe theory. They represent an 'option narrowing' as a result of the selection of a new organizational and institutional setting in the global

community process. After a relatively short period of internal network structure dominance, the system reverts to an external system structure, setting in motion a new rise in complexity, bringing with it a new phase of externally open systems and, consequently, leading to a new stage of hypercoherence.

8 For a discussion of complex systems theories, see Auyang (1998).

9 For a more detailed account, see Rennstich (2003a).

10 For a discussion of the impact of internal network system versus external network systems, see Rennstich (2003a, 2003b).

11 For an argument of earlier complex 'multinational' enterprise organization, see Moore and Lewis (1999).

12 It is may not be a coincidence that one of the major innovations with a far reaching impact on all co-evolving world system processes occurring during this period was the complex 'coding' of language in the form of an alphabet (see Bentley 1993: 23). This innovation has its roots, like all such major innovations, in previous advancement in coding of language, but stands out as an important evolutionary step nonetheless (Hobart and Schiffman 1998: ch. 2). It advanced the creation of a more complex world system in a similar manner to the next step of coding not only communication but indeed all elements of life in a single, binary (i.e. digital) code.

13 The following discussion is largely based on Moore and Lewis (1999: ch. 5). See also Curtin (1984: 75–80).

14 Our intention here is not to suggest that only the Venetian or British trading networks existed. Far from it: what characterized the maritime commercial system was rather a vast multitude of local and regional networks, stretching, as in the case of Asia, across vast amounts of geographical space (see, for example, Subrahmanyam 1996; Frank 1998). What remains crucial for the 'rise of the West' (as McNeill put it) as a leading 'trendsetter' or driver of evolutionary logic (in terms of the global economic and political processes) was the attempt of the network system described here to act as central nodes, connecting the divergent existing networks rather than replacing them.

15 During the high time of Genoese and Venetian trade, it was in Italy where the first systems of 'high finance' emerged (Arrighi 1994: ch. 2). It was in Amsterdam, however, that the first stock exchange in permanent session developed, with a volume and density of transactions that outshone all past and contemporary stock markets (Israel 1989; Braudel 1992b, 1992c). This feature of a combination of leading sector development and centre financing node has characterized all subsequent systems, in external as well as internal network environments alike.

16 Boxer (1979: 51) describes the VOC as a 'colossal organization, comparable to one of the modern great multinational firms, when due allowance is made for differences in time, space, and demography'. For a discussion of the VOC as an institutional innovation, see Steensgaard (1982); see also Meilink-Roelofsz (1986). For an argument of earlier developments of 'multinational' (i.e. cross-border active) corporations, see Moore and Lewis (1999).

17 See, for example, Mitchell (1995, 1999); Wheeler *et al.* (2000); Dodge and Kitchin (2001); Townsend (2001a, 2001b).

18 For in-depth treatments of the development of the Internet, see Abbate (1999) and Naughton (2000).

19 For a similar argument, see Robertson (1998). Robertson, however, focuses more on the importance of the digital computer as the enabler of this information system transformation.

20 Similar to the argument developed in a broader context of networks (not limited to communication systems) in this work, Innis (1950: 216) argues that a crucial element of the interaction between cultures is their adoption and use of different communication systems to control space. In other words, Innis' focus on com-

munication systems as a determinant for political and economic organization analyses the same phenomenon that authors such as Mackinder (1904, 1981), Rosecrance (1986, 1999), Tilly (1989), Fox (1991) and Hugill (1999) have studied from a more socio-political organizational perspective.

21 For a summary of peer-to-peer standards in progress, see http://peer-to-peerwg.org. See also Oram (2001) and Lessig (2001: 134–8).

22 For a review of the structure of commercial Internet markets, see Greenstein (2000).

23 See also Kotkin (2000) who focuses on the effect of digital networks on urban development; see also Fujita *et al.* (1999) for a formal economic analysis of this development.

24 Sassen (2001), in the second edition of *Global City*, recognizes these changes and discusses the emergence of a new global urban system (ch. 7).

References

Abbate, Janet. 1999. *Inventing the Internet*. Cambridge, MA: MIT Press.

Abu-Lughod, Janet L. 1989. *Before European Hegemony: The World System AD 1250–1350*. New York: Oxford University Press.

Allen, Peter M., Norman Clark and Francisco Perez-Trejo. 1992. 'Strategic planning of complex economic systems'. *Review of Political Economy* 4 (3): 275–90.

Andersen, Esben Sloth. 1994. *Evolutionary Economics: Post-Schumpeterian Contributions*. London: Pinter Publishers and St Martin's Press.

Arrighi, Giovanni. 1994. *The Long Twentieth Century: Money, Power, and the Origins of our Times*. London: Verso.

Arrighi, Giovanni, Beverly J. Silver and Iftikhar Ahmad. 1999. *Chaos and Governance in the Modern World System*. Minneapolis: University of Minnesota Press.

Auyang, Sunny Y. 1998. *Foundations of Complex-System Theories: In Economics, Evolutionary Biology, and Statistical Physics*. Cambridge: Cambridge University Press.

Barnett, George A. 2001. 'A longitudinal analysis of the international telecommunication network, 1978–1996'. *American Behavioral Scientist* 44 (10): 1638–55.

Benedikt, Michael. 1991. 'Introduction', in M. Benedikt, ed. *Cyberspace: First Steps*. Cambridge, MA: MIT Press, pp. 1–26.

Bentley, Jerry H. 1993. *Old World Encounters: Cross-Cultural Contacts and Exchanges in Pre-Modern Times*. New York: Oxford University Press.

Bernard, Jacques. 1976. 'Trade and finance in the Middle Ages, 900–1500', in C.M. Cipolla, ed. *The Fontana Economic History of Europe: The Middle Ages*. Hassocks: Harvester Press.

Berry, Brian Joe Lobley. 1991. *Long-Wave Rhythms in Economic Development and Political Behavior*. Baltimore: Johns Hopkins University Press.

Best, Michael H. 2001. *The New Competitive Advantage: The Renewal of American Industry*. Oxford: Oxford University Press.

Borrus, Michael and François Bar. 1993. *The Future of Networking* (research paper) [online]. Berkeley Roundtable on the International Economy, University of California Berkeley (BRIE), 16 March [cited 9 April 2000]. Available from http://Brie.Berkeley.Edu/~Briewww/Pubs/Rp/Network.Html.

Bosworth, Andrew. 2000. 'The evolution of the world-city system, 3000 BCE to AD 2000', in R.A. Denemark, J. Friedman, B.K. Gills and G. Modelski, eds. *World System History: The Social Science of Long-Term Change*. New York: Routledge, pp. 273–84.

Boxer, Charles R. 1979. *Jan Compagnie in War and Peace, 1602–1799: A Short History of the Dutch East-India Company*. Hong Kong: Heinemann Asia.

Braudel, Fernand. 1972. *The Mediterranean and the Mediterranean World in the Age of Philip II*, trans. by S. Reynolds. London: Collins.

——. 1992a. *Civilization and Capitalism, 15th–18th Century*. 3 Vols. Berkeley: University of California Press. Original edn, 1982–1984.

——. 1992b. *Civilization and Capitalism, 15th–18th Century: The Perspective of the World*. Vol. 3. Berkeley: University of California Press. Original edn, 1984.

——. 1992c. *Civilization and Capitalism, 15th–18th Century: The Wheels of Commerce*. Vol. 2. Berkeley: University of California Press. Original edn, 1983.

Buzan, Barry and Richard Little. 2000. *International Systems in World History: Remaking the Study of International Relations*. Oxford: Oxford University Press.

Cairncross, Frances. 2001. *The Death of Distance: How the Communications Revolution is Changing our Lives*. 2nd rev. edn. Boston, MA: Harvard Business School Press.

Castells, Manuel. 1996. *The Rise of the Network Society*. Malden, MA: Blackwell Publishers.

——. 2001. *The Internet Galaxy: Reflections on the Internet, Business, and Society*. Oxford: Oxford University Press.

Chandler, Tertius. 1987. *Four Thousand Years of Urban Growth: An Historical Census*. Lewiston, NY: St David's University Press.

Chase-Dunn, Christopher K. and Thomas D. Hall. 1997. *Rise and Demise: Comparing World-Systems*. Boulder, CO: Westview Press.

Clark, Norman, Francisco Perez-Trejo and Peter M. Allen. 1995. *Evolutionary Dynamics and Sustainable Development: A Systems Approach*. Aldershot: Edward Elgar.

Cukier, Kenneth Neil. 1999. 'Bandwidth colonialism? The implications of internet infrastructure on international e-commerce'. Paper read at INET '99, 22–25 June, at San Jose, CA. Available from http://www.Isoc.Org/Inet99/Proceedings/1e/1e_2.Htm.

Curtin, Philip D. 1984. *Cross-Cultural Trade in World History*. Cambridge: Cambridge University Press.

Dark, K.R. 1998. *The Waves of Time: Long-Term Change and International Relations*. London: Pinter.

Davis, Ralph. 1954. 'English foreign trade, 1660–1700'. *Economic History Review* 7 (2): 150–66.

Dicken, Peter. 1999. 'Globalization: an economic-geographical perspective', in W.E. Halal and K.B. Taylor, eds. *Twenty-First Century Economics: Perspectives of Socioeconomics for a Changing World*. New York: St Martin's Press, pp. 31–51.

——. 2003. *Global Shift: Transforming the World Economy*, 4th edn. Thousand Oaks, CA: Sage Publications.

Dodge, Martin and Rob Kitchin. 2001. *Mapping Cyberspace*. London: Routledge.

Elvin, Mark. 1973. *The Pattern of the Chinese Past*. London: Eyre Methuen.

Emmer, P.C. 1981. 'The West India Company, 1621–1791: Dutch or Atlantic?', in L. Blussé and F.S. Gaastra, eds. *Companies and Trade: Essays on Overseas Trading Companies During the Ancien Régime*. Leiden: Leiden University Press, pp. 71–95.

Fox, Edward Whiting. 1991. *The Emergence of the Modern European World: From the Seventeenth to the Twentieth Century*. Cambridge, MA: Blackwell.

Frank, Andre Gunder. 1998. *Reorient: Global Economy in the Asian Age*. Berkeley: University of California Press.

Fujita, Masahisa, Paul R. Krugman and Anthony Venables. 1999. *The Spatial Economy: Cities, Regions and International Trade*. Cambridge, MA: MIT Press.

Gernet, Jacques. 1996. *A History Of Chinese Civilization*, trans. by J.R. Foster and C. Hartman, 2nd edn. Cambridge: Cambridge University Press. Original edn, 1972 (French).

Greenstein, Shane. 2000. 'The evolving structure of commercial internet markets', in E. Brynjolfsson and B. Kahin, eds. *Understanding the Digital Economy: Data, Tools, and Research*. Cambridge, MA: MIT Press, pp. 151–84.

Hall, Peter Geoffrey and Paschal Preston. 1988. *The Carrier Wave: New Information Technology and the Geography of Innovation, 1846–2003*. London: Unwin Hyman.

Harvey, David. 1989. *The Condition of Postmodernity: An Enquiry into the Origins of Cultural Change*. Oxford: Blackwell.

Headrick, Daniel R. 2000. *When Information Came of Age: Technologies of Knowledge in the Age of Reason and Revolution, 1700–1850*. Oxford: Oxford University Press.

Hobart, Michael E. and Zachary Sayre Schiffman. 1998. *Information Ages: Literacy, Numeracy, and the Computer Revolution*. Baltimore, MD: Johns Hopkins University Press.

Hugill, Peter J. 1999. *Global Communications since 1844: Geopolitics and Technology*. Baltimore, MD: Johns Hopkins University Press.

Innis, Harold Adams. 1950. *Empire and Communications*. Oxford: Clarendon Press.

Israel, Jonathan Irvine. 1989. *Dutch Primacy in World Trade, 1585–1740*. Oxford: Clarendon Press, Oxford University Press.

Jones, E.L. 1988. *Growth Recurring: Economic Change in World History*. Oxford: Oxford University Press.

Kitchin, Rob. 1998. *Cyberspace: The World in the Wires*. Chichester: J. Wiley.

Kotkin, Joel. 2000. *The New Geography: How the Digital Revolution is Reshaping the American Landscape*, 1st edn. New York: Random House.

Lee, Richard and Sheila Pelizzon. 1991. 'Hegemonic Cities in the Modern World-System', in R. Kasaba, ed. *Cities in the World-System*. New York: Greenwood Press, pp. 43–54.

Lessig, Lawrence. 2001. *The Future of Ideas: The Fate of the Commons in a Connected World*. New York: Random House.

Lopez, Robert. 1987. 'The trade of Medieval Europe: the south', in M.M. Postan and H.J. Habakkuk, eds. *The Cambridge Economic History of Europe: Trade and Industry in the Middle Ages*, 2nd edn, Ch. 4. Cambridge: Cambridge University Press. Original edn, 1952.

Mackinder, Halford J. 1904. 'The geographical pivot of history'. *Geographical Journal* 13: 421–37.

Mackinder, Halford John. 1981. *Democratic Ideals and Reality*. Westport, CT: Greenwood Press. Original edn, 1919.

McNeill, John Robert and William Hardy McNeill. 2003. *The Human Web: A Bird's-Eye View of World History*. New York: W.W. Norton.

McNeill, William Hardy. 1967. *A World History*. New York: Oxford University Press.

——. 1982. *The Pursuit of Power: Technology, Armed Force, and Society since AD 1000*. Chicago: University of Chicago Press.

——. 1991. *The Rise of the West: A History of the Human Community; with a Retrospective Essay*. Chicago: University of Chicago Press. Original edn, 1963.

Mattelart, Armand. 2000. *Networking the World, 1794–2000*, trans. by L. Carey-Libbrecht and J.A. Cohen. Minneapolis, MN: University of Minnesota Press. Original edn, 1996.

Meilink-Roelofsz, M.A.P., ed. 1986. *All of One Company: The VOC on Biographical Perspective: Essays in Honour of Prof. M.A.P. Meilink-Roelofsz, under the Auspices of the Centre for the History of European Expansion, Rijksuniversiteit Leiden*. Utrecht: Hes Uitg.

Miles, Raymond E., Charles C. Snow, John A. Mathews, Grant Miles and Henry J. Coleman, Jr. 1997. 'Organizing in the knowledge age: anticipating the cellular form'. *The Academy of Management Executive* 11 (4): 7–20.

Mintz, Sidney Wilfred. 1985. *Sweetness and Power: The Place of Sugar in Modern History*. New York: Viking.

Mitchell, William J. 1995. *City of Bits: Space, Place, and the Infobahn*. Cambridge, MA: MIT Press.

——. 1999. *E-Topia : 'Urban Life, Jim – But Not as we Know It'*. Cambridge, MA: MIT Press.

Modelski, George. 1990. 'Is world politics evolutionary learning?'. *International Organization* 44 (1): 1–24.

——. 2000. 'World system evolution', in R.A. Denemark, J. Friedman, B.K. Gills and G. Modelski, eds. *World System History: The Social Science of Long-Term Change*. London: Routledge, pp. 24–53.

——. 2003. *World Cities: –3000 to 2000*. Washington, DC: Faros2000.

Modelski, George and William R. Thompson. 1996. *Leading Sectors and World Powers: The Coevolution of Global Politics and Economics*. Columbia, SC: University of South Carolina Press.

Moore, Karl and David Lewis. 1999. *Birth of the Multinational: 2000 Years of Ancient Business History – From Ashur to Augustus*. Copenhagen: Copenhagen Business School Press.

Morley, David and Kevin Robins. 1995. *Spaces of Identity: Global Media, Electronic Landscapes, and Cultural Boundaries*. London: Routledge.

Naughton, John. 2000. *A Brief History of the Future: Radio Days to Internet Years in a Lifetime*. Woodstock, NY: Overlook Press.

Oram, Andrew, ed. 2001. *Peer-To-Peer: Harnessing the Benefits of a Disruptive Technology*. Beijing: O'Reilly.

Plattner, Stuart, ed. 1989. *Economic Anthropology*. Stanford, CA: Stanford University Press.

Poster, Mark. 1995. *The Second Media Age*. Cambridge, MA: Polity Press.

Postma, Johannes M. 1990. *The Dutch in the Atlantic Slave Trade, 1600–1815*. Cambridge: Cambridge University Press.

Reischauer, Edwin O., John King Fairbank and Albert M. Craig. 1960. *A History of East Asian Civilization*. 2 vols. Boston, MA: Houghton Mifflin.

Rennstich, Joachim K. 2002. 'The new economy, the leadership long cycle, and the nineteenth K-wave'. *Review of International Political Economy* 9 (1): 150–82.

——. 2003a. *Globalization and the Evolution of the Informational Network Economy: Past, Present, and Future Technological Change*. Dissertation, Department of Political Science, Indiana University, Bloomington, IN.

——. 2003b. 'The future of great power rivalries', in W.A. Dunaway, ed. *Emerging Issues in the 21st Century World-System: New Theoretical Directions for the 21st Century World-System*. Westport, CT: Praeger, pp. 143–61.

Richardson, David. 1987. 'The slave trade, sugar, and British economic growth, 1748–

1776', in B.L. Solow and S.L. Engerman, eds. *British Capitalism and Caribbean Slavery: The Legacy of Eric Williams*. Cambridge: Cambridge University Press.

Richardson, G.B. 1972. 'The organisation of industry'. *The Economic Journal* 82 (327): 883–96.

Robertson, Douglas S. 1998. *The New Renaissance: Computers and the Next Level of Civilization*. New York: Oxford University Press.

Rosecrance, Richard N. 1986. *The Rise of the Trading State: Commerce and Conquest in the Modern World*. New York: Basic Books.

——. 1999. *The Rise of the Virtual State: Wealth and Power in the Coming Century*. New York: Basic Books.

Sassen, Saskia. 1991. *The Global City: New York, London, Tokyo*. Princeton, NJ: Princeton University Press.

——. 1997. 'The new centrality: the impact of telematics and globalization', in P. Droege, ed. *Intelligent Environments: Spatial Aspects of the Information Revolution*. Amsterdam: Elsevier.

——. 2001. *The Global City: New York, London, Tokyo*. Princeton, NJ: Princeton University Press.

Saxby, Stephen. 1990. *The Age of Information: The Past Development and Future Significance of Computing and Communications*. New York: New York University Press.

Scammell, Geoffrey Vaughn. 1989. *The First Imperial Age: European Overseas Expansion, c. 1400–1715*. London: Unwin Hyman.

Shannon, Claude E. 1948. 'A mathematical theory of communication'. *Bell System Technical Journal* 27: 379–423, 625–56.

Shapiro, Carl and Hal R. Varian. 1999. *Information Rules: A Strategic Guide to the Network Economy*. Boston, MA: Harvard Business School Press.

Singh, J.P. 2002. 'Introduction: information technologies and the changing scope of global power and governance', in J.N. Rosenau and J.P. Singh, eds. *Information Technologies and Global Politics: The Changing Scope of Power and Governance*. Albany, NY: State University of New York Press, pp. 1–38.

Steensgaard, Niels. 1982. 'The Dutch East India Company as an institutional innovation', in M. Aymard, ed. *Dutch Capitalism and World Capitalism*. Cambridge: Cambridge University Press, pp. 235–57.

Subrahmanyam, Sanjay, ed. 1996. *Merchant Networks in the Early Modern World*, 15 vols. Vol. 8. Aldershot: Variorum.

Taylor, Peter J. 1995. 'World cities and territorial states: the rise and fall of their mutuality', in P.L. Knox and P.J. Taylor, eds. *World Cities in a World-System*. Cambridge: Cambridge University Press, pp. 48–62.

Tilly, Charles. 1989. 'The geography of European statemaking and capitalism since 1500', in E.D. Genovese and L. Hochberg, eds. *Geographic Perspectives in History*. Oxford: B. Blackwell, pp. 158–81.

Townsend, Anthony M. 2001a. 'The Internet and the rise of the new network cities, 1969–1999'. *Environment and Planning B: Planning and Design* 28 (1): 39–58.

——. 2001b."Network Cities And The Global Structure Of The Internet." *American Behavioral Scientist* 44 (10):1697–1716.

Unger, W.S. 1982. 'Essay on the history of the Dutch slave trade', in M.A.P. Meilink-Roelofsz and M.J.L.v. Yperen, eds. *Dutch Authors on West Indian History: A Historiographical Selection*. The Hague: M. Nijhoff, pp. 46–98.

Wheeler, James O., Yuko Aoyama and Barney Warf, eds. 2000. *Cities in the Telecommunications Age: The Fracturing of Geographies*. New York: Routledge.

Zook, Matthew A. 2000. 'The web of production: the economic geography of commercial Internet content production in the United States'. *Environment and Planning A* 32 (3): 411–26.

——. 2001. 'Old hierarchies or new networks of centrality?' *American Behavioral Scientist* 44 (10): 1679–96.

12 Globalization began in 1571[1]

Dennis O. Flynn and Arturo Giráldez

Introduction: problems in defining globalization

Globalization is said to be the most ubiquitous term found today in both popular and academic publications worldwide. We have been disappointed, however, to discover that few authors offer operational definitions of the term 'globalization', and fewer still attempt to place the origins of globalization in the context of world history. The purpose of this essay is twofold: first, to discuss the birth of globalization in world history terms and, second, to do so with the aid of an explicit definition that permits identification of a precise year of globalization's birth. Our central argument – that globalization was born in the specific year 1571 – comprises the body of this essay. The general outlines of our contention are summarized later in this introductory section.

We have been unable to discover a satisfactory definition of the term 'globalization' in the most widely cited reference works. The *New Palgrave Dictionary of Economics* (Eatwell *et al.* 1998) offers no definition at all. *The New Encyclopaedia Britannica* (Encyclopaedia Britannica 2002) attempts a definition in cultural terms:

> Globalization is the process by which the experience of everyday life, marked by the diffusion of commodities and ideas, is becoming standardized around the world. An extreme interpretation of this process, often referred to as globalism, sees advanced capitalism, boosted by wireless and Internet communications and electronic business transactions, destroying local traditions and regional distinctions, creating in their place a homogenized world culture.

The following paraphrase (Teulon 1996) captures the essence of the entry for 'globalisation' in *Vocabulaire Économique*, published by the University Presses of France:

> Globalization involves intensified internationalization of production and exchange. Due to convergence of living standards and uniformity

> of consumption patterns in developed countries, corporations increasingly reason in global terms and adopt global strategies in order to take advantage of economies of scale.

Social scientists, journalists, politicians and others use the term constantly, but without attribution of any explicit meaning to the term. It seems that each speaker is permitted to use the term in any way that serves a particular purpose. No wonder the ubiquitous term 'globalization' arouses such deep emotions among people around the world today. Business interests favour an increasingly open global marketplace because it produces profitable opportunities, while other businesses simultaneously oppose globalization because overseas products threaten existing markets. Pro-labour forces harbour reservations about promised benefits, because international competition threatens domestic jobs in specific industries. Economists invariably cite David Ricardo's law of comparative advantage (first enunciated in 1819), which states that unfettered trade elevates overall living standards in both rich and poor participating countries. Economists recognize that certain parties suffer in consequence of free trade forces, of course, but they argue that overall gains are sufficiently large so that winners could compensate losers, while still leaving residual gains that permit rising living standards for all citizens. Environmentalists remain unconvinced by such free trade arguments, to say the least, tending to view consumerism as a threat to fragile global ecologies. Religious leaders argue about whether or not market forces are destructive of moral values. In sum, the globalization debate contains a cacophony of contradictory positions, except that nearly everyone agrees on one point: globalization appears to be a recent phenomenon that is hurling humanity worldwide into uncharted waters.

The reader will find no opinion or advice in these pages about current political debates. Our decision has nothing to do with timidity about expressing our views, but rather because we use the term 'globalization' to refer to a set of *historical* processes. We neither approve nor disapprove of the evolutionary forces that led to the birth of globalization, just as we neither approve nor disapprove of the law of gravity. Following the advice of Joseph Schumpeter (1954: 12–13), it is essential that we understand the genesis of economic processes:

> First, the subject matter of economics is essentially a unique process in historic time. Nobody can hope to understand the economic phenomena of any, including the present, epoch who has not an adequate command of historical *facts* and an adequate amount of historical *sense* or of what may be described as *historical experience*.

For those who do adopt historical perspectives, globalization is normally portrayed as a twentieth-century phenomenon, indeed mostly rooted in the post-Second World War era:

> For some, the global connectedness of our age is its distinguishing characteristic, a new reality and a change in consciousness of which interest in global history is but one manifestation. This global era and its origins, including perhaps the last 50 or 100 years, should therefore be the subject matter of global history.
>
> (Grew 1999: 5)

This perception of recent globalization is buttressed by widespread recognition that the world has 'become smaller' as a result of recent technological innovations, such as commercial aviation and the computer revolution. For a nineteenth-century example, consider the sparsely populated regions of western North America. Completion of the transcontinental railways about 140 years ago in the US effectively reduced the formidable barriers presented by the Rocky Mountains (the 'Great Continental Divide') and the Sierra Nevadas. The point is, world regions have become more and more integrated over time, and globalization is a term applied to a final stage that eventually emerged during the second half of the twentieth century.

We agree that, in general, regions have become increasingly connected through time. Yet a central question remains: at what point does integration of world regions become 'globalization'? The non-historical literature offers neither objective criteria for determining a date for the inception of globalization nor identifiable causes. But globalization trends today must be seen in evolutionary terms. The present is an inheritance from the past, and explanations of globalization must include its origins. We speak today of the 'age of aviation' in terms of the Wright brothers' first flight a century ago, and the 'nuclear age' as having begun with an initial atomic blast towards the end of the Second World War. The point is that all historical 'ages' must be defined in terms of identifiable origins. Any operational definition of the 'age of globalization' must allow for the identification of a start date. Historically oriented scholars are currently engaged in debate about globalization's origins.

A powerful 'world history' movement has been sweeping the United States in recent times (a nationwide advanced placement examination in world history for US high school seniors began in Spring 2002). Spearheaded by the World History Association, this intellectual movement is expanding worldwide.[2] 'World historians' reject conventional, nation state units of analysis and focus attention instead on long-distance connections, including climatic, geographic, economic, epidemiological, ecological, demographic and cultural aspects. These scholars are, of course, correct in emphasizing the existence of deep interconnections throughout the Afro-Eurasian world for thousands of years, via both overland routes and connecting waterways. Where we take exception, however, is when some world historians describe such long-distance connections as 'globalization'. The 'Old World' long-distance connections they emphasize do indeed play a crucial role in our interpretation of the birth of globalization, but true globalization did not evolve until the Old World was directly connected with the Americas in 1571. The Pacific Ocean alone comprises one-third of the surface area of the earth. The Americas and the Atlantic Ocean account for around another one-third. Thus, the Afro-Eurasian complex – the 'Old World' – comprises approximately the remaining one-third of the surface area of the globe. We believe that it is inappropriate to label Old World historical connections as 'global'. Any definition of 'globalization' that excludes two-thirds of the globe – most of the Atlantic, the Americas and most of the Pacific – is an oxymoron.

We contend that globalization occurred when all heavily populated land masses began sustained interaction in a manner that deeply linked them all through global trade.

> The discovery of America, and that of a passage to the East Indies by the Cape of Good Hope, are the two greatest and most important events recorded in the history of mankind. Their consequences have already been very great: but, in the short period of between two and three centuries which has elapsed since these discoveries were made, it is impossible that the whole extent of their consequences can have been seen. What benefits, or what misfortunes to mankind may hereafter result from those great events, no human wisdom can foresee.
>
> (Smith 1965/1776: 590)[3]

Global trade emerged when (1) all heavily populated land masses began to exchange products continuously – both directly with each other and indirectly via other land masses – and (2) they did so in values sufficient to generate lasting impacts on all trading partners. It is true that important intercontinental trade existed prior to the sixteenth century, but there was no direct trade link between America and Asia before the founding of Manila as a Spanish entrepôt in 1571. Prior to that year, the world market was not yet fully coherent or complete; after that year it was.

After more than 10,000 years of isolation, contacts between the Old World and the New World altered the trajectory of human evolution in profound (and sometimes disturbing) ways. For example, Old World diseases decimated the indigenous population of the Americas because New World inhabitants lacked immunity to Afro-Eurasian diseases, partly explaining why the importation of African slaves was deemed a commercial necessity for exploitation of the vast resources of the New World. Europeans also introduced large domestic animals (e.g. horses and cattle) and numerous plants (e.g. wheat, sugar and oranges) into the Americas, permanently altering New World landscapes in the process. It is difficult to imagine places such as Argentina, Mexico and the United States in the absence of horses, cattle and wheat today, for instance, yet these building blocks of society were entirely absent prior to contact with Europeans. Indeed, environments throughout the Americas were redirected along completely different trajectories as a result of new linkages with the Old World. Many such powerful forces of globalization were set in motion soon after Europeans arrived in the Americas, momentous forces that remain visible into the twenty-first century. However, it would be a mistake to think that the New World was merely an importer of agents of change. On the contrary, unique American plants and seeds were also exported, thus altering Old World landscapes fundamentally and permanently. At least one-third of today's human foodstuffs were introduced exclusively from the Americas, including corn, potatoes, sweet potatoes, the peanut, beans and scores of other plants (including tobacco).

Scholars (Crosby 1972, 1986) have admirably documented the history of these global linkages, and they make it clear that ecological and demographic consequences reverberated in multiple directions throughout planet earth once the Americas were brought into the mix. Our research (Flynn and Giraldez 1995) attempts to explain the role played by the global silver market as an economic engine that helped to initiate and sustain structural transformations throughout the world. We explain how and why silver markets provoked the birth of global trade and the central role played by the world's dominant economic power, China. In addition, we also emphasize that oceanic trade routes provided necessary vectors through which economic, ecological and demographic forces spread globally. Today's modern global system dates from the sixteenth century and China's marketplace led the way.

A number of scholars of the Enlightenment period believe that thinkers first began to conceptualize reality in global terms in the eighteenth century. Our problem with this contention is factual: innumerable merchants, government bureaucrats, religious leaders and intellectuals were in fact fully aware of global connections during the sixteenth and seventeenth centuries. Besides, if global consciousness were the determining factor, then exactly how many global thinkers would there have to be in order to initiate a globalization? We contend that eighteenth-century globalization conceptualizations were (1) not unprecedented and (2) sprang forth from a globalization reality that began in the sixteenth century.

Influential economic historians Kevin O'Rourke and Jeffrey Williamson (2002a, 2002b) contend that globalization began in the 1820s, based upon econometric evidence showing that international commodity prices only began to converge in the 1820s. We disagree with the conclusions of O'Rourke and Williamson, although they are to be commended for offering both an explicit definition of the term globalization as well as empirical evidence in support of their thesis. According to our definition of globalization provided above, the birth of globalization did not require international price convergence.[4] The history of price convergence is important, but the nineteenth-century phenomenon identified by O'Rourke and Williamson occurred during the Industrial Revolution, well after globalization's sixteenth-century birth.[5]

European dynamism?

After having explored the west coast of Africa earlier, Europeans traversed the Atlantic to the Americas (1492), sailed around the Cape of Good Hope (1497) and crossed the Pacific (1521), all within 30 years. Broadly speaking, this Age of European Exploration is overwhelmingly depicted by historians as having resulted from dynamism emanating from within Europe. European dynamism has been attributed to a variety of unique forces, including European science, advantageous geographic conditions, competition among numerous nation states, favourable institutions and even pro-capitalistic religious doctrines (in conjunction with other cultural factors). In other words, scholars have generally disagreed about the sources of European dynamism. The existence of western Europe as a prime driving force on the world stage, on the other hand, has generally gone unquestioned.[6]

Perceptions of European pre-eminence characterize the literature on precious metals history as well. Specifically, sixteenth- and seventeenth-century monetary relations between Europe and Asia have been couched in terms that attribute dynamism to Europe and lassitude to non-Europe. The conventional interpretation can be summarized as follows. There was tremendous European demand for certain Asian products, including spices, ceramics and silks, that Europeans were incapable of producing. As a result, Europeans imported prodigious quantities of Asian products. Asian imports of European wares were paltry by comparison, on the other hand, partly because inward-looking Asian consumers were less adventuresome about purchase of foreign wares than their European counterparts. From a European point of view, European imports from Asia were huge, while European exports to Asia were meagre. Europeans responded to massive net imports from Asia – a European balance-of-payments deficit – by sending cash monies to Asia decade after decade. Thus, the centuries-long flow of precious metals from Europe to Asia is ultimately attributable to lively purchasing habits by Europeans (compared with Asian consumers). Precious metals had to flow eastward to pay for net purchases from Asia. Again, this conventional explanation for global flows of precious metals is consistent with traditional 'European dynamism' hypotheses. European consumers were far more receptive to Asian products than Asian consumers were regarding European products. A flow of monies from Europe to Asia was but a reaction to European demand for non-monetary items produced in Asia.

Our research casts a dramatically different light on monetary events and actors throughout the world, permitting a more balanced and less Eurocentric interpretation of the birth of globalization during this time period. We unequivocally reject the conventional interpretation outlined immediately above. In other words, we dismiss the assertion that monetary metals flowed from Europe to Asia as passive balancing items that merely responded to an imbalance between the import and export of non-monetary items. For, if the conventional trade deficit argument were true, then a variety of types of monies would have been expected to flow from Europe to Asia. As several monetary substances were internationally recognized (e.g. silver, gold, copper and cowrie shells), recipient merchants in Asia should have been indifferent about the particular mix of monies sent in payment by European purchasers. For example, reputable gold monies should have been just as welcome as reputable silver monies. Various monies would therefore be expected to flow from west to east. But nothing of the sort actually happened. What did happen is that American silver flowed through (not 'from') Europe on its way to China (not to abstract 'Asia'). Indeed, substantial volumes of another major monetary substance, gold, flowed in precisely the opposite direction simultaneously – from China to Europe – between the 1540s and 1640. Nor was this silver-for-gold exchange a uniquely Europe–China phenomenon. Japan produced perhaps half as much silver as did all of Spanish America during the sixteenth and seventeenth centuries. Virtually all Japanese silver was exported to the Chinese marketplace, and Japan simultaneously imported gold from China (as had Europe). Moreover, the Acapulco–Manila galleons carried 50 tons of American silver to China annually via the Pacific Ocean throughout the 1600s, while gold flowed out of China and back to the Americas simultaneously. Thus, historical facts simply contradict the dominant trade deficit hypothesis found in the historical literature today. The conventional thesis is powerless to explain why one particular monetary substance alone – silver – persistently flowed west-to-east along the Eurasian landmass and maritime routes, while another crucial monetary substance – gold – flowed east-to-west along these same trade routes. And it is obviously erroneous to portray these monetary events in Europe-versus-Asia terms in any case; what would it mean to claim that Japan was 'western' in the sixteenth and seventeenth centuries? And a negligible fraction of the silver shipped through Europe was produced within Europe during our period. It was produced in America and was largely destined for China. Europeans also acted as intermediaries in the trans-shipment of Japanese silver to China. Not only are trade imbalance arguments ineffective in elucidating why monetary substances flowed globally as they did, this conceptual apparatus precludes clear thinking on the topic.[7]

Historical evidence also contradicts trade imbalance reasoning when we look at the other two main monetary substances in the world during this time period, copper and cowrie shells. Sweden was the most important source of copper within Europe, but Japan produced perhaps twice as much copper as Sweden by the late seventeenth century. China again presented the largest end-market for Japanese copper, but substantial shipments of Japanese copper also found their way to Europe. That is, Japanese copper flowed from Asian mines during a time when American silver continued to flow through Europe to Chinese markets. These monies never flowed systematically together. The world's leading producer of cowrie monies was the Maldive Islands in the Indian Ocean. Maldivian cowries were exported to markets throughout Asia, but European merchants also imported immense quantities of cowries (as ballast items) for the purpose of re-exporting them to end-markets in west Africa at huge profit. Our central conclusion with respect to the world's four leading monies, in other words, is that they *never* flowed in tandem anywhere in the world during these centuries. As the conventional explanation claims that 'money' in general flowed from Europe to Asia as a passive balancing item, contrary historical facts allow us to reject quite dogmatically the European trade deficit hypothesis.

Modern economic theory, which teaches us all to aggregate together various monetary substances (including silver coins, gold coins, copper coins and cowries), has inadvertently precluded understanding of global monetary events during our time period. Thus, we are forced conceptually to disaggregate individual monies and treat each separately, including silver. Doing so at a global level reveals immediately that it is a mistake to couch things in 'east–west' terms. There was no imbalance of trade – east–west, north–south, Europe–Asia or otherwise – for which monetary substances had to compensate. There was just trade. The singular market most responsible for the birth of globalization was the silver trade. The most dynamic end-markets for silver in the world resided in China. Europeans were important middlemen, as were innumerable non-Europeans who also devoted considerable energies to the pursuit of profit emanating from the global trade in silver and related products.

Cycles of silver

There were two silver cycles prior to the Industrial Revolution. We label one the Potosí/Japan silver cycle, spanning a 'silver century' from the 1540s to 1640s, because a preponderance of the world's silver production was concentrated at mines in Potosí (modern-day Bolivia) and Japan. Thousands of tons of silver were trans-shipped throughout the world towards China; and the high price of silver in China descended to silver's world price by 1640. The world price of silver simultaneously fell to its cost of production by 1640, signalling the end of a century of superprofits emanating from the global silver trade. Later on came the Mexican silver cycle of 1700–1750, marked by an unprecedented eruption of Mexican silver production also destined for Chinese markets.

From the 1540s onwards, it became common knowledge among merchants, government officials, clerics, scholars and others that China was the end-market for American and Japanese silver. Indeed, there was no question about this later during an early stage of the Industrial Revolution. Adam Smith doubted neither the importance of silver in stimulating world trade, nor the central role of China. This is unsurprising because the relentless flow of American silver to China continued throughout Smith's lifetime:

> The silver of the new continent seems in this manner to be one of the principal commodities by which the commerce between the two extremities of the old one [Europe and China] is carried on, and it is by means of it, in great measure, that those distant parts of the world are connected with one another.
>
> (Smith 1965/1776: 207)

If it is permissible to designate any region of the earth as a dynamic centre, then China is the prime candidate for centrality at the time globalization was born. China contained a larger proportion of world population in the sixteenth century than it does today (roughly 20 per cent today versus 25 per cent plus then). China also contained cities of a million and more by the year 1600, when the largest cities in western Europe (London and Paris) contained perhaps 200,000 inhabitants each. With huge urban centres, vast rice lands and per capita living standards among the highest in the world, no economy on earth dominated to the extent that the Chinese economy did at that time. European economies paled in comparison.

No one would consider writing a twentieth-century world history of the oil business without heavily emphasizing the centrality of the world's most prominent oil consumers. Yet trade histories routinely ignore the fact that China was the world's dominant end-market for silver for centuries. Failure to look at trade relations from truly global points of view has caused twentieth-century historians and social scientists to lose sight of the fact that access to Asian markets guided merchant behaviour worldwide. Among those merchants, however, the consolidation of Muslim trading networks since the fifteenth century and the arrival of Europeans in Asian waters in the sixteenth century had a lasting impact on world history:[8]

> East Asia had been in contact with the West for more than a millennium, largely through overland migrations and trade routes, but occasionally, indirectly by sea. Nothing in the previous experience of the peoples of the region prepared them, however, for the infinitely more intensive interaction of the sixteenth and seventeenth centuries.
>
> (Cohen 2000: 215)

It is important to understand that the European presence in Asia prior to the Industrial Revolution was confined to the archipelagos and fringes of mainland Asia. Confrontations with mainland powers were out of the question. Manila was the headquarters of Spain's Asian operation, while the Portuguese were located in Goa (India) and Macao. The Dutch and English arrived early in the seventeenth century; the former were based in Batavia (Jakarta), while the latter gained a foothold with trading posts in Bombay, Madras and Calcutta in coastal India. Europeans could not begin to threaten Japan or the powers on Asia's mainland. After expelling the Portuguese in the 1630s, for example, the Japanese used Dutch merchants as replacements. The Dutch were confined to a tiny artificial island called Deshima in Nagasaki Bay, and the Shogun strictly controlled the terms of trade. But why were Europeans anxious to reach the fringes of Asia? The answer is that they desired to plug into the world's most lucrative markets. Nobody could compete with Asian producers of spices, silks and ceramics – and, in the eighteenth century, tea – all highly prized commodities the world over. But what could Europeans offer to exchange for such valuables? The answer is one dominant product: silver.

As mentioned already, silver gravitated overwhelmingly to end-market China. The reason is simply that the price of silver in China was double its price in the rest of the world. A paper money system had existed in China since at least the eleventh century, but fiscal problems led to overissue and collapse of the Ming monetary system in the middle of the fifteenth century. Merchants, especially in maritime regions of China, converted to the use of silver as a monetary base.[9] As this trend towards conversion to silver money expanded, local and regional government entities increasingly converted tax payments to silver as well. Although the Ming Dynasty long opposed the silverization movement, which had moved 'from the bottom up', Ming acquiescence to this irresistible trend was eventually institutionalized in the form of the 'Single-Whip Tax Reform' of the 1570s; a multitude of taxes were consolidated into a single empire-wide tax, payable exclusively in silver (even by peasants). As China contained at least a quarter of the world's population and huge cities (e.g. 1 million in Nanjing and 660,000 in Beijing), the conversion of China's monetary and fiscal systems to a silver base was of momentous impact. Moreover, because of China's extensive tributary system, domestic silverization created a ripple effect reaching far beyond Chinese borders:

> The entire tribute and interregional trade zone had its own structural rules that exercised a systematic control through silver circulation and with the Chinese tribute trade at the center. This system, encompassing East and South-East Asia was articulated with neighboring trade zones such as India, the Islamic region and Europe.
>
> (Hamashita 1994: 97)

The Chinese economy was so enormous that its conversion to silver caused the market value of the white metal to soar far higher in China than in America, Japan, Europe and elsewhere in the world. Regionally divergent bimetallic ratios provide a clear indicator of the elevated value of silver in China *vis-à-vis* the rest of the world. In the early sixteenth century, the gold/silver ratio in China stood at 1:6, while in 'contrast the gold/silver ratio hovered around 1:12 in Europe, 1:10 in Persia, and 1:8 in India' (von Glahn 1996: 127). No wonder that the specific metal, silver, flooded into China for centuries; the Chinese simply offered the best price for this product. Rather than depicting the flow of silver to China as a passive *effect* of disequilibrium in non-monetary trade, therefore, it is better to recognize that disequilibrium within the silver market itself was an active *cause* of global trade. Thousands of tons of silver entered China via trade networks throughout the world, glutting even the immense Chinese marketplace. The price of silver in China sank to the world price by 1640, ending the 'Potosí-Japan silver cycle' and its extraordinary worldwide profit structure.

After a half-century interlude, a 'Mexican silver cycle' (1700–50) followed the formula established by its 1540s–1640s predecessor, but it also involved shocking environmental dynamics (see Flynn and Giraldez 2002b). China's population increased dramatically during the eighteenth century at a time when its cultivated acreage expanded by perhaps half. According to a prominent Sinologist (Spence 1990: 95), much of China's 'population growth in the 18th century was speeded up by a massive ecological change: the introduction of new crops into China from the New World' (especially sweet potatoes, peanuts and maize of Latin American origin).[10] These population dynamics were related to increased commercialization and further ecological changes within China (see Marks 1999). In simple terms, China's eighteenth-century population explosion and market growth implied yet another immense increase in China's demand for silver. It was this resultant demand-side pressure that caused the value of silver within China to spike some 50 per cent above silver's price in the rest of the world (as divergent bimetallic ratios again make clear). Along with supply-side dynamics within Mexico's mining industry, China's demographic revolution was responsible for the world's second silver boom during the first half of the eighteenth century. More Spanish American silver was produced in the eighteenth century (mostly from Mexican mines) than in the sixteenth and seventeenth centuries combined. High-quality pieces of eight coined in Mexico became by far the most dominant monetary substance in history. Trade circuits worldwide were inundated with silver headed for Chinese markets and, by 1750, the Chinese price of silver had once again (as in 1640) descended to its price in the rest of the world. Superprofits disappeared and a global trade crisis emerged once again.

The trends outlined above help to clarify a sea change in foreign commerce in the middle of the eighteenth century in Asia. The Battle of Plassey in 1757 led to British control of Bengal. British profits from the China trade solidified Britain's position 'in the East during the three decades of the 1750s, 1760s and 1770s . . . decades of rising British power and of French and Dutch decline' (Furber 1976: 176) The British managed to gain control of a new, rapidly growing market involving the importation of Bengali opium into China in exchange, in part, for Chinese exports of tea. The point is not that silver discontinued its journey into China during the second half of the eighteenth century – it did not – but rather that opium and tea became the high-profit markets, with silver playing a complementary role in terms of profitability. London tea imports reached 2.5 million pounds by 1760, 9 million pounds by 1769–70, 14 million pounds in 1785–86 and 23 million pounds by the end of the century (Furber 1976: 175), and this opium 'traffic grew more than twentyfold between 1729 and 1800, which helped to staunch the flow of bullion from Britain to China' (Pomeranz and Topik 1999: 103). But the Chinese history of opium consumption was itself linked to American tobacco introduced via the Philippines in the sixteenth century: 'The habit of opium smoking in China was an offshoot and development of tobacco smoking' (Spence 1992: 231). Once again, an important biological exchange involved an American crop. This time, tobacco was tied to the consumption of opium, a more lucrative (for the British) Chinese import than was the (complementary) American silver during the second half of the eighteenth century. So lucrative was the British opium monopoly that the East India Company earned clear profit of at least 100 per cent even on sales in Calcutta to the Dutch (Troki 1999: 54). The British tea-and-opium connection itself was part and parcel of complex trade connections at the global level. English people consumed sugar with tea during this period, for example, which required importation of prodigious quantities of slave-produced sugar from the Americas.

No one questions European and US superiority in military and economic terms after the Industrial Revolution, including their ability to dominate land-based Asian powers as the nineteenth century progressed. It is important to recognize, however, that economic dominance by Europe, the United States (and later by Japan) is a post-Industrial Revolution phenomenon:

> Just 200 years ago, two other countries – India and China – accounted for two thirds of the world's economic output . . . How did industry and European-style countries called nation-states – rather than highly developed agrarian empires like China and India – come to define our world?
> (Marks 2002: 2)

Lest the reader be tempted to dismiss statements concerning Asian economic prowess as current fashionable opinions, consider the words of prominent eighteenth-century analysts writing about their own times. David Hume (1970: 198) stated that a 'Chinese works for three-halfpence a day, and is very industrious. Were he as near us as France and Spain, every thing we use would be Chinese . . .'. Adam Smith (1965/1776: 189) asserted matter of factly: 'China is a much richer country than any part of Europe, and the difference between the price of subsistence in China and in Europe is very great. Rice in China is much cheaper than wheat any-where in Europe'.

Kenneth Pomeranz's (2000) award-winning *The Great Divergence* contains a systematic comparison of standards of living in Europe *vis-à-vis* China. He concludes that Europe's most advanced regions had achieved a per capita standard of living roughly equal to those of advanced regions in China by the time of the Industrial Revolution:

> In sum, core regions in China and Japan circa 1750 seem to resemble the most advanced parts of western Europe, combining sophisticated agriculture, commerce, and nonmechanized industry in similar, arguably even more fully realized, ways. (p. 17) . . . [And] eighteenth-century China (and perhaps Japan as well) actually came closer to resembling the neoclassical ideal of a market economy than did western Europe (p. 70).

Pomeranz contends that all advanced regions within the Eurasian landmass were facing serious problems in terms of exhaustion of natural and manmade resources prior to the Industrial Revolution. It appeared unlikely that any such region could have sustained existing standards of living, never mind vaulting into a new industrial era. One of the crucial advantages enjoyed by certain European powers (especially England), according to Pomeranz, was access to the vast natural resources of the Americas. His book is filled with quantitative estimates of the significance of this European advantage.

No Asian power enjoyed access to a parallel environmental bonus. It remains to be seen whether Pomeranz's hypothesis will withstand waves of current and future scepticism. His impressive scholarship and bold stance, however, ensure that future debates on the Industrial Revolution must necessarily be cast in global terms. Henceforth, all competing hypotheses must respond at a global level of analysis.

Conclusion

Absence of consensus concerning a workable definition of the term 'globalization' has produced debates that lack intellectual rigour. Our contention is that globalization is a historical process with characteristics that can be identified and studied systematically. As stated in the introduction, global trade emerged when (1) all heavily populated land masses began to exchange products continuously – both directly with each other and indirectly via other continents – and (2) they did so in values sufficient to generate lasting impacts on all trading partners. The birth of globalization occurred in 1571, the year that Manila was founded as a Spanish entrepôt connecting Asia and the Americas. After more than 10,000 years of isolation, the 'Columbian Exchange' (Atlantic) and the 'Magellan Exchange' (Pacific) (see McNeill 2001) permanently linked all populated continents in terms of trade, diseases, ecologies and cultures. For the sixteenth to the eighteenth centuries, silver was an essential commodity that linked the world, and China was its dominant end-market. A new historiography has emerged that also places the Industrial Revolution and a subsequent of western pre-eminence in a global context.

Today's 'age of globalization' did not begin in the post-Second World War era, as is routinely portrayed by non-historians in popular and academic presses. Neither was globalization initiated by price convergence in the 1820s, nor by eighteenth-century European global consciousness, as some historically oriented scholars claim. And long-distance connections across the Afro-Eurasian landmass over thousands of years cannot be properly labelled global, as some world historians claim, because the Afro-Eurasian 'Old World' comprises only one-third of the surface area of the globe. How can a system be considered global when two-thirds of the globe is disconnected from it? The voyages of Columbus resulted in connection of the Americas – one-third of the surface area of the earth, including the Atlantic Ocean – to the Old World beginning in the late fifteenth century. But it was not until permanent connection between the New World and Asia beginning in 1571 – via the silver-laden Acapulco–Manila galleons – that the final one-third of the globe (the Pacific world) was brought into the mix.[11] Connection of the New World with the Old World profoundly influenced the shape of today's world. Connection of the Americas to the rest of the world yielded ecological and social transformation of sufficient profundity that Alfred Crosby (1986: 271) has depicted the post-fifteenth century global exchange of flora, fauna and diseases as 'a revolution more extreme than any seen on this planet since the extinction at the end of the Pleistocene'. We recognize that specific eras involve unique circumstances and transformations that alter the rhythms of the global system. For example, new Asian exports in the eighteenth century (e.g. tea and opium) were added to traditional exports of preceding centuries (e.g. silks, porcelain and spices). Technological innovations continue to increase the speed of production and exchange, but our global system today is a consequence of historical forces that continue to evolve since sixteenth-century beginnings.

Some may criticize us for overemphasizing economic aspects of globalization's birth, because our story provides such a prominent role for the silver trade. But decades of study of the worldwide silver trade have forced us to acknowledge a crucial insight: recognition of interdisciplinary connections is unavoidable when trying to decipher multicentury cycles at a global level. Long-term global history forces the observer to abandon the confines of traditional academic disciplines.

> To understand what is distinctive about human history, we must have some idea of how a biologist or a geologist might approach the subject. We cannot *become* biologists or geologists, and our understanding of these fields will have its limits; but we do have to use as skilfully as we can the expertise of specialists in other fields. And we have much to learn from their different perspectives on the past. Excessive respect for disciplinary boundaries has hidden many possibilities for intellectual synergy between disciplines.
>
> (Christian 2004: 9)[12]

In terms of the birth of globalization, the relentless search for profit led inadvertently to the spread of deadly diseases, and subsequently to dissemination of unknown forms of flora/fauna throughout the globe. Manifold ecological, demographic and cultural reactions literally reshaped the world. Reshaped physical and cultural landscapes then reverberated back into the economic sphere, in a series of feedback loops with no end in sight. In this context, globalization forces today are best visualized against the backdrop of sixteenth-century origins.

Notes

1 A shorter version of this essay appeared in Flynn and Giráldez (2002a).
2 For further information, see www.thewha.org.
3 We agree with Smith, but add that connections between the Americas and the East Indies via the Pacific Ocean were also of critical importance.
4 See O'Rourke and Williamson (2002a, 2002b). For our more complete criticism of O'Rourke and Williamson, see Flynn and Giráldez (2004).
5 For criticism of O'Rourke and Williamson, see Flynn and Giráldez (2004); O'Rourke and Williamson (2004) responded in the same issue of the journal. The *European Review of Economic History* has rejected publication of our rejoinder to O'Rourke and Williamson (2004).
6 For recent exceptions to the European pre-eminence hypothesis, see Blaut

(1993), Lewis and Wigen (1997), Frank (1998) and Marks (2002). For a recent restatement of traditional views, see Landes (1998).

7 K.N. Chaudhuri has long recognized the need to separate conceptually intercontinental movements of gold from intercontinental movements of silver. Chaudhuri (1978: 156) urged a return to the reasoning of classical economists such as David Ricardo.

8 Zheng He, famous commander of Ming China's fleets of the early fifteenth century, was himself a Muslim.

9 For a long-term monetary history of China, see the landmark treatise by von Glahn (1966).

10 According to Crosby (1972: 199): 'No large group of the human race in the Old World was quicker to adopt American food plants than the Chinese. While men who stormed Tenochtitlan with Cortes still lived, peanuts were swelling in the sandy loams near Shanghai, maize was turning fields green in south China and the sweet potato was on its way to becoming the poor man's staple in Fukien'. Our emphasis on the global silver market leads us to focus on the central role of China, but the impact of American plants throughout the world cannot be ignored. For example, Crosby (1972: 185) also states that: 'The importance of American foods in Africa is more obvious than in any other continent of the Old World, for in no other continent, except the Americas themselves, is so great a proportion of the population so dependent on American foods'.

11 Perhaps global 'reconnection' is more accurate than initial 'connection', as humans did indeed populate much of the globe prior to the end of the last Ice Age (when rising oceans isolated the New World from the Old World). Even so, today's globalization was uniquely shaped by the intensity and nature of post-1571 connections worldwide.

12 David Christian's (2004) timeframes extend 13 billion years to the origins of the universe, compared with our timespan of a few centuries, but the point is that long-term analysis requires bridging among academic disciplines.

References

Blaut, J.M. 1993. *The Colonizer's Model of the World: Geographic Diffusionism and Eurocentric History*. New York: Guilford Press.

Chaudhuri, K.N. 1978. *The Trading World of Asia and the East India Company, 1660–1760*. Cambridge: Cambridge University Press.

Christian, David. 2004. *Maps of Time: An Introduction to Big History*. Berkeley: University of California Press.

Cohen, Warren I. 2000. *East Asia at the Center: Four Thousand Years of Engagement with the World*. New York: Columbia University Press.

Crosby, A.W. 1972. *The Columbian Exchange: Biological and Cultural Consequences of 1492*. Westport, CT: Greenwood.

Crosby, A.W. 1986. *Ecological Imperialism: The Biological Expansion of Europe, 900–1900*. Cambridge: Cambridge University Press.

Eatwell, J., M. Milgate and P. Newman, eds. 1998. *The New Palgrave: A Dictionary of Economics*. London: Macmillan.

Encyclopaedia Britannica (2002) 'Globalization and culture', in *The New Encyclopaedia Britannica*, Vol. 20. Chicago, IL: Encyclopaedia Britannica.

Flynn, Dennis O. and Arturo Giráldez. 1995. 'Born with a "silver spoon": the origins of world trade in 1571'. *Journal of World History* 6: 201–21.

Flynn, Dennis O. and Arturo Giráldez. 2002a. 'Cycles of silver: globalization as historical process'. *World Economics* 3: 1–16.

Flynn, Dennis O. and Arturo Giráldez. 2002b. 'Cycles of silver: global economic unity through the mid-18th century'. *Journal of World History* 13 (2): 391–427.

Flynn, Dennis O. and Arturo Giráldez. 2004. 'Path dependence, time lags and the birth of globalisation: a critique of O'Rourke and Williamson'. *European Review of Economic History* 8: 81–108.

Frank, Andre Gunder. 1998. *Re Orient: Global Economy in the Asian Age*. Berkeley: University of California Press.

Furber, Holden. 1976. *Rival Empires of Trade in the Orient, 1600–1800*. Minneapolis: University of Minnesota Press.

Grew, Raymond. 1999. 'Food and global history', in Raymond Grew, ed. *Food in Global History*. Boulder, CO: Westview Press.

Hamashita, Takeshi. 1994. 'The tribute system of modern Asia', in A.J.H. Latham and H. Kawakatsu, eds. *Japanese Industrialization and the Asian Economy*. London: Routledge.

Hume, David. 1970. 'Hume to Oswald, 1 November 1750', in Eugene Rotwein, ed. *David Hume Writings on Economics*. Madison, WI: University of Wisconsin Press.

Landes, David. 1998. *The Wealth and Poverty of Nations: Why Some Are So Rich and Some So Poor*. New York: Norton.

Lewis, M. and K. Wigen 1997. *The Myth of Continents: A Critique of Meta-geography*. Berkeley: University of California Press.

Marks, Robert B. 1999. *Tigers, Rice, Silk and Silt: Environment and Economy in Late Imperial South China*. New York: Cambridge University Press.

Marks, Robert B. 2002. *The Origins of the Modern World: A Global and Ecological Narrative*. Lanham, MD: Rowman and Littlefield.

McNeill, John R., ed. 2001. *Environmental History in the Pacific World*. Aldershot: Ashgate.

O'Rourke, Kevin and Jeffrey G. Williamson. 2002a. 'When did globalization begin?' *European Review of Economic History* 6: 23–50.

O'Rourke, Kevin and Jeffrey G. Williamson. 2002b. 'After Columbus: explaining Europe's overseas trade boom, 1550–1800'. *The Journal of Economic History* 62: 417–55.

O'Rourke, Kevin and Jeffrey G. Williamson. 2004. 'Once more: when did globalization begin?'. *European Review of Economic History* 8: 109–17.

Pomeranz, Kenneth. 2000. *The Great Divergence: China, Europe, and the Making of the Modern World Economy*. Princeton, NJ: Princeton University Press.

Pomeranz, K. and S. Topik. 1999. *The World that Trade Created: Society, Culture, and the World Economy, 1400 to the Present*. Armonk, NY: M.E. Sharpe.

Schumpeter, Joseph. 1954. *History of Economic Analysis*. New York: Oxford University Press.

Smith, Adam. 1965/1776. *An Inquiry into the Nature and Causes of the Wealth of Nations*. New York: Random House.

Spence, Jonathan D. 1990. *The Search for Modern China*. New York: W.W. Norton.

Spence, Jonathan D. 1992. *Chinese Roundabout: Essays in History and Culture*. New York: W.W. Norton.

Teulon, Frederic. 1996. *Vocabulaire Economique*, 3rd edn. Paris: Presses Universitaires de France.

Troki, Carl A. 1999. *Opium, Empire and the Global Political Economy: A Study of the Asian Opium Trade, 1750–1950*. London: Routledge.

von Glahn, Richard. 1966. *Fountain of Fortune: Money and Monetary Policy in China, 1000–1700*. Berkeley: University of California Press.

13 Colonies in a globalizing economy, 1815–1948

Patrick Karl O'Brien

International trade for colonial and autonomous regional economies of the Third World, 1815–1948

Under the international economic order that prevailed between the end of mercantilism and decolonization (referred to in this essay as liberal imperialism), the costs of transacting, transporting and trading commodities, both within and across national and imperial frontiers, declined sharply.[1] To some discussable but unmeasureable degree, the opportunities to realize enhanced gains from trade also depended upon the political status of regional economies operating and interacting (through trade in commodities, capital flows, labour migration and the diffusion of useful knowledge) within a global economy – expanding along cycles of faster, slower and even negative rates of growth – but expanding, nevertheless, more rapidly than ever before.

Contextualized within a key metanarrative in global history concerned with imperialism, the question addressed by this essay can be posed as follows: were the macroeconomic benefits potentially available from the expansion and extension of international trade over the nineteenth and twentieth centuries less accessible to or more or less politically constrained for regional economies and populations of polities that continued or passed under colonial rule after 1815 than for societies that remained formally under indigenous and/or autonomous forms of governance?[2]

In theory, multiple regression analysis – based upon a fully specified growth model and applied to an acceptable base of data for a satisfactory sample of regional economies for benchmark years between 1815 and 1948 – could conceivably isolate and even quantify the significance of forms of rule for the realization of gains from international trade during an age of liberal imperialism.[3]

Alas, and even if this contentious method produced plausible conjectures, the possibilities for completing cross-country, let alone cross-regional, exercises in multiple regression analysis are entirely remote for any of the years between the end of mercantilist warfare (1815) and the onset of decolonization marked by Indian independence in 1948. Data are not there! Meanwhile, Tables 13.13 and 13.14 reveal that commodity exports per capita by region for

1900, 1937 and 1948 (the best index available to compare 'scales of involvement' in international trade for a large sample of colonized and autonomous economies) display no clear correlations between types of governance and 'potential' gains from participation in foreign trade.[4]

Perhaps the only viable entrée into any reconfigured discussion of this important question will be to elaborate upon the macroeconomic context for achieving gains from trade, namely the growth and structural charges that occurred for the world economy as a whole, as the context for achieving gains from trade increased through time and conditioned prospects for economic growth across the geographical spaces and political boundaries of an evolving international economic order of colonized and autonomous regions of an integrating world economy. My essay will present data that reveal how ostensibly equal, or random, prospects for realizing potential gains from trade tended to be skewed in favour of particular zones of that evolving and integrating global economy.

My suggestion, flowing from an analysis of bodies of data available for world trade, international capital flows and the migration of labour, is that, for long stretches of the past two centuries, prospects for trade (with potential for growth) for almost all regional economies of the present-day Third World (colonized or formally autonomous) seems *prima facie* to have operated as a far weaker engine for growth than for regions of western Europe and particularly for European settlements overseas. If this hypothesis can be clarified and supported with some acceptable statistics, then the representation of colonial rule (1815–1948) as any kind of widespread and significant constraint upon convergence derivable from participation in world trade ceases to be credible.

Of course, this thesis could become congenial for apologists for Europe's imperial record over this period. They now maintain that European governance and institutions may well have helped numerous colonial economies and indigenous workforces to realize enhanced gains from trade before decolonization. Nevertheless, the view developed here is rigorously agnostic on this contentious and ideologically charged issue because *prima facie* the data currently available suggest that the size of economies, their geographical endowments, natural advantages, distance from European markets, networks of internal transportation linking interior regions to seaports and baseline ratios of exports and imports to gross domestic products all mattered more than alien or indigenous rule for the achievement of gains from foreign trade during an era of liberal imperialism.[5]

Furthermore, and insofar as participation in foreign trade was either a (or even the) major source for growth and structural change available to the agrarian economies of the Third World, the persistence of imperialism and extension of colonial rule over the nineteenth and twentieth centuries on balance probably neither restrained nor promoted any marked degree of convergence in productivity levels and standards of living between today's developed and underdeveloped countries. In opposition to a dominant view that argues for stronger 'correlations' between indigenous forms of governance and national economic progress, this essay will maintain that colonial rule, at least over its final phase from 1815 to 1948, hardly altered prospects for long-run growth across the spectrum of sovereign and non-sovereign regions of the world economy one way or the other. I have, moreover, argued elsewhere that this seems to be less true for Europe's imperial states who ran their economies and societies into the awesome destruction of two world wars. For this era, colonizers made limited, if any, economic gains, and their populations suffered massively from their prolonged geopolitical and atavistic commitments to the maintenance, extension and defence of empires (O'Brien 1997).

Liberal imperialism

But, as a preface, we must define liberal imperialism, which refers to an international economic order of rules and conventions governing all forms of commerce across frontiers that came onstream over the nineteenth century and marked a departure from the previous violent and unstable system for the conduct of international economic relations. Under that *ancien régime*, 'mercantilism', the operation of international, interimperial and intra-imperial commerce, had been regulated by states claiming sovereignty over trade, transportation, investment, migration and the diffusion of knowledge across national frontiers, as well as the borders of provinces, dominions and colonies under their jurisdiction.

There will be no need to review the underlying ideological assumptions behind a long tradition of mercantilist regulation. Only historians of economic theory in retrospect (taking cues from Adam Smith) represent mercantilism as approximations to a coherent doctrine or theory (Coleman 1969). As an 'episteme' of widely shared assumptions behind the conduct of international and intraimperial economic relations of early modern commerce, mercantilism appears in legal texts representing complex sets of national laws promulgated by governments throughout the world primarily to favour the economic interests of their subjects over the economies and citizens of other rival states and empires; and secondly, to ensure that the economies and workforces of their colonies and dominions operated in ways that complemented and minimized competition with the economies and workforces of the metropolis (Magnusson 1994).

In practice, the mercantilist 'mission' (often published as preambles to statutes and decrees that claimed to accord priorities in commercial and imperial policy to augmenting the power and profit of states, their fiscal systems, external commerce and domestic economies) was not that easy to formulate as rules commanding a metropolitan, let alone any imperial, consensus of economic interests. Furthermore, and in the absence of either widespread compliance with laws or the organizational capacity required for efficient implementation and coercion, the attempts by medieval and early modern states (almost everywhere in Eurasia) to regulate the commerce of their realms, empires and subjects with the rest of the world economy continued to be aspirational and liable to degenerate into widespread, persistent and uncontrollable evasion (Tracy 1991).

Enduring pretensions at the heart of mercantilism rather than conversions to the precepts of classical political economy eventually led governments to 'loosen up' and, in several classic cases, to abandon 'futile' efforts to regulate connections of domestic with colonial and foreign economies.[6] Intellectual arguments for freer trade had, moreover, appeared long before 1776 or 1815. Nevertheless, the Congress of Vienna (or rather the Battle of Trafalgar in 1805) marked a conjuncture in geopolitical relations when the Royal Navy had clearly established undisputed primacy at sea (Gomes 1987; Glete 1993). Wisely and because its victory in a long mercantilist quest for competitive superiority in global trade, shipping and the provision of commercial services (1651–1805) allowed for magnanimity, the Victorian state refrained from any direct interference with the seaborne trade of any of its economic rivals (even in wartime). Over the nineteenth century, Britain used its overwhelming naval power only to 'open up' the Ottoman, Qing and Siamese empires and several South American republics to possibilities for maritime trade, to restrain commerce in slaves, to countervail piracy and, above all, to effectively contain colonial rivalry and deter further ventures by Portugal, Spain, Holland, France and other European powers to take over territory, assets and populations in the western hemisphere (Semmel 1986).

Prompted by an emerging ideology of free trade, ruling monarchical and aristocratic elites of that period became more realistic in their ambitions to control economies and more easily persuaded that a stance of *laissez-faire* towards movements of commodities, capital, labour and knowledge across both national and imperial frontiers might serve the interests of their states and societies more effectively than regulation.

Although European colonization and territorial expansion continued unabated (see Table 13.2), it was no accident that liberal forms of imperialism came onstream after 23 years of intensified and costly conflict – the Revolutionary and Napoleonic Wars, 1793–1815 (Clesse and O'Brien 2002). That new international economic order matured at the same time as the industrialization of western Europe, which, together with technological and institutional possibilities for rapid, more secure and, above all, cheaper transactions and lower transportation costs for the distribution of commodities, people, investible funds and knowledge, by land and sea, created possibilities for a vastly augmented level of commodity exchange and commercial intercourse across an expanding world economy (Arrighi 1994).

The growth of international trade and the integration of a world economy, 1815–1914

Alas, data required to plot the expansion of world trade, capital flows and migrations of labour over the long nineteenth century are neither secure nor comprehensive enough. Nevertheless, research by scholars into disparate bodies of official sources, together with Mulhall's (1892 and subsequent editions) poorly referenced *Dictionaries of Statistics*, have allowed the publication of useable figures for the volumes, geographies and commodity compositions of world trade, as well as accepted estimates for migrations of capital and labour across frontiers for more than a century between 1815 and 1948.[7]

For example (see Table 13.1), once recovery from the Revolutionary and Napoleonic Wars was under way, annual average rates of growth for world trade advanced at within a modal range of three to five per cent per annum (Kenwood and Lougheed 1999). Trends and cycles cannot be properly established, but a climacteric (1872–99) followed by an upswing appears in tables calibrated by Arthur Lewis (1981) from the US government's *Statistical Abstract of Foreign Countries* (1909). Rates for the long nineteenth century are nearly three or four times the rates estimated by Walt Rostow (1978) for the previous century and reported by Angus Maddison (1982) for the interwar years 1919–39. Paul Bairoch (1976: tables 1 and 2) reckoned that per capita trade may have multiplied 16 times, and the ratios of imports plus exports to aggregated global production probably rose (according to Simon Kuznets 1959: 100–8) from insignificant proportions (around three per cent) into the 20–30 per cent range over the century preceding the First World War.

Behind the accelerated growth and augmented macroeconomic significance of world trade is that familiar sequence of industrialization, whereby Britain, Belgium, northern France, Switzerland, Germany, Holland, Scandinavia and, by the end of the century, regions of Iberia and Italy matured at different rates, along their own path-dependent trajectories into industrial market economies. Higher proportions of the 'core's' growing populations came to reside in towns and found employment in industry and urban services. Productivity per worker and, eventually, standards of living rose as the outcome of a process driven by investment in technically superior varieties of capital goods, new commodities and more efficient forms of organization for production in agriculture, mining, communications, commerce and, above all, in manufacturing industry.[8]

Industrialization at the core led to ever-increasing surpluses of machine-made commodities available for sale on world markets and to an enormous uplift in demand for imported foodstuffs, minerals and organic raw mate-

Table 13.1 Growth rates for world and Third World commodity trade, 1820–1913

Period	*World trade (%)*	*Tropical exporters (%)*	*Less developed economies (%)*
1820–40	3–4	–	–
1840–60	5–6	–	4.9
1860–80	4–5	3.2	4.4
1880–1900	3–4	3.0	3.0
1900–13	4–5	4.6	4.3

Sources: Rostow (1978: 66) (includes an estimate of 1.1 per cent for growth in world trade 1730–80), Kuznets (1966) and Lewis (1970).

rials required to sustain accelerated population growth, urbanization and structural change across several economies of western Europe. Markets integrated initially at regional and then national levels. Eventually intra- and intercontinental economies (that had been linked for centuries) became more closely and regularly connected because technological and organizational innovations radically reduced the risks and costs of supplying the information, establishing business networks and constructing the transportation required to transfer goods, services and personnel across time and distance.

Geographical boundaries for decisions affecting industrial and primary production and commerce widened. For both new and expanding areas of economic activity, what to produce, how to design and manufacture commodities, where to buy raw materials and sell final outputs, to raise capital and to hire skilled and even unskilled labour ceased to be spatially confined, politically controlled and culturally constrained. As an age-old process of connection, maturing into integration, gathered momentum and foreign competition intruded into more domains of regional and national production, and as ratios of exports and imports to domestic output and consumption increased, prices of tradable commodities of comparable quality 'moved towards' convergence and 'pulled' prices of the inputs and factors of production engaged in cultivating mining or manufacturing for international markets in the same direction. That tendency could, however, only push or pull the prices of traded goods and services (and, by derivation, the returns and payments to the land capital and labour utilized as inputs in their production) at speeds and in directions that were both theoretically plausible and potentially possible. Among the world's plurality of regional economies, the timing and degree of convergence towards higher levels of productivity remained highly 'conditional' on the extent and intensity of integration for particular commodity and factor markets, as well as the specific capacities of local, regional, national and colonial economies to respond to opportunities to participate in world trade.[9]

Zones and economic geographies for world trade, 1815–1914

Responses and eventual long-term outcomes varied enormously. Case-by-case historical surveys swamp prospects for generalization with detail that could not be subsumed in 'averages' or 'regressions'.[10] Following the approach pioneered by Arthur Lewis, this essay seeks to arrive at middle-range hypotheses by distinguishing the long-term effects that growth of the core and the integration of world markets exercised upon three 'separable zones' of the world economy.

First and foremost, international trade exercised its most benign effects upon a zone of European settlements overseas, located for the most part in temperate climatic latitudes and in places that had been recognized long before the nineteenth century as favourably endowed with underutilized and accessible supplies of fertile land, arboreal forests, fishing grounds and mineral deposits. During the age of liberal imperialism, the populations inhabiting or migrating into this fortunate zone became citizens of the United States, Canada, Argentina, Chile, Uruguay, Australia, New Zealand and South Africa – territories that had been colonized by white European settlers as part of their incorporation of an Atlantic into a global economy. The political and military actions, but particularly the pathogens carried by the initial waves of European settlers, reduced indigenous populations to fractions of pre-Conquest levels (Crosby 1986). By the end of an imperial meridian (1783–1825), most European settlements overseas enjoyed virtual autonomy over their internal economic affairs, including more or less unfettered control over the expropriation and reallocation of local property rights (Bayly 2004). In Latin America and the south of the United States, before the emancipations of 1862–84, the rights of settlers also included the ownership of large and growing populations of black slaves.[11] In addition, settler societies carried negligible burdens of taxation for external security, which was implicitly guaranteed by the Royal Navy funded by British taxpayers. If a 'World Bank' had been around and had reported to the Congress of Vienna on the world's natural resources potentially available for exploitation by European capital and labour, the territories and assets of this relatively empty zone (partially surveyed and/or under exploration) could only have been presented as highly promising.

Less promising, but certainly better known and more easily accessed to support growing demands from the core for food, raw materials and minerals, we distinguish a second zone of the world economy consisting of established countries or provinces located along the northern, eastern and southern peripheries of western Europe. Russia, Poland, Scandinavia, southern Italy, Iberia and the Balkans had long been connected to the industrializing economies by waterborne transportation moving along the coasts and rivers that flowed into the Mediterranean, Baltic and North Seas. Within this established zone, intra-European trade, based on natural variations in endowments, geographies, soils and climates, had persisted for millennia. At the onset of industrialization, several regions along this 'semi-periphery' still possessed considerable potential to respond to opportunities to trade their primary produce and minerals for manufactured goods, to attract capital from their European neighbours, to import and adapt new technology, to send surplus emigrants to the Americas and to embark on their own national paths towards industrial market economies (Pamuk and Williamson 2000).

Our third zone of the rapidly growing and increasingly integrated global economy provides a heuristic geographical and political context for investigations into the impact of European imperialism (formal and informal) on the development of the economies and standards of living for a majority of the world's inhabitants. That context or frame is difficult to demarcate and will be referred to anachronistically (as the label is modern) as the 'Third World'. In political and economic terms, the Third World considered here as a zone of the liberal world economy looks enormous and amorphous because it: (1) includes territories, resources and populations that either remained within or were incorporated, after the Congress of Vienna, into the empires of Britain, France, Spain, Portugal, Holland, Germany, Russia, the United States and Japan; (2) excludes settlements of largely British populations overseas formally under British sovereignty (such as Australia), which enjoyed considerable local autonomy in the formulation of laws and the construction of institutions for the conduct of their internal and external (but not strategic) affairs; (3) envelopes nominally sovereign empires, polities and economies that had been either coerced into or had prudently abrogated varying degrees of sovereignty over external economic relations with the rest of the world (e.g. the Ottoman, Qing, Japanese and Siamese empires).[12]

In summary, this third zone of a globalizing economy will be demarcated as a residual category, located in large part between the Tropics of Cancer and Capricorn on the continents of Asia, Africa and South America. It includes a majority of the world's population and numerous regions possessing considerable endowments of land, mineral wealth, forests, fishing grounds and, above all, cheap labour, employable ('exploitable') for purposes of meeting rising demands for primary produce from societies in the European core.

Shares of that zone's resources and population falling under effectively exercised colonial rule by metropolitan powers fluctuated over time. Between 1783 and 1825, the incorporation of the states of Mughal India more than compensated (in strictly demographic terms) for the cessation of land and people to independent governments of the United States, Brazil and other states of Central and South America. Thereafter (and with increased intensity during the scramble for Africa – 1882–1902), transfers from indigenous to alien (largely European) rule proceeded the other way so that, by 1914, the shares of world's surface, populations and total product under the direct control of metropolitan governments approximated to ratios set out in Table 13.2.

For purposes of the macroeconomic analysis pursued in this essay, there is no reason to become involved in debates about types and intensities of imperial rule compared with intrusions of external power (explicit or implicit) into the formulation and enforcement of regulations by ostensibly autonomous governments that affected the commerce undertaken by their subjects with Europeans or other outsiders. Even the 'degrees' of freedom to trade enjoyed by businessmen operating under several styles of colonial rule remain to be established.[13]

Furthermore, liberal imperialism implies that, after 1815, the international economic order had changed so that, after centuries of violent predation, colonization and mercantilist forms of exploitation, the proportions of the world's population and resources restrained from participating in opportunities for foreign trade by direct forms of alien (usually European) rule diminished sharply. Some historians might still claim that nominally independent national (and regional) economies continued, however, to be

Table 13.2 Europe and its colonial empires 1760–1963 (rounded to millions)

	Populations (millions)						
	1760	*1830*	*1880*	*1913*	*1938*	*1950*	*1963*
Europe	125	180	244	320	396	392	437
European colonies	27	205	312	554	724	160	30
African colonies	0	1	9	113	144	0	0
American colonies	21	3	9	12	17	0	0
Asian colonies	6	201	292	421	552	0	0
Oceania colonies	0	0	3	8	1	0	0
	Areas (in million sq km)						
	1760	*1830*	*1880*	*1913*	*1938*	*1950*	*1963*
Europe	5	5	5	5	5	5	5
African colonies	0	0	2	26	29	0	0
American colonies	24	1	10	10	10	0	0
Asian colonies	0	4	5	8	9	0	0
Oceania colonies	0	3	8	9	9	0	0
	Gross domestic production in $ of 1990 in billions						
	1820	*1900*	*1950*				
Western Europe	140	555	1,223				
European settlements	13	346	1,629				
European periphery	185	323	878				
Africa	35	52	184				
Latin America	14	69	405				
Asia	461	629	1,035				

Sources: Maddison (2001: 365) provides data for 'merchandise' exports as a percentage of GDP in 1990 prices for 11 countries, and his GDP data are cited in this table; Bairoch (1997) and Etemad (2001).

constrained by their 'heritage' of mercantilist domination, and that regions under European rule were never 'really free' to trade beyond limits and boundaries established by imperial regulations (Condcliffe 1951). Even where legal and/or cultural constrictions prevailed, that merely shifts enquiries towards comparisons of indigenous and post-Conquest regulations for the operation of economic activities or to speculations concerning trajectories that colonized economies may have been on before takeover, or moved on to after independence. Such counterfactual investigations could be instructive to pursue, but less inconclusive histories might emerge from this exercise that will attempt to measure and contrast the considerable variations in outcomes that emerged among four interacting zones of the world economy as they responded to opportunities for trade with development presented by the industrialization of the core. By proceeding at this macroglobal level of generalization, the problems of incoherence involved in the proliferation of one case study after another are circumvented. Data can be marshalled and some hypotheses elaborated to suggest why the Third World (including the colonized and non-colonized Third World; amalgamated here into a single zone) responded 'less elastically' to opportunities to trade than either the zones of European settlement or the European periphery?[14]

Any attempt to quantify the global context within which zones and their regional economies operated between 1815 and 1914 will be difficult because data on the changing volume, economic geography and commodity composition of world trade are neither comprehensive nor calibrated into a form that displays the performance of the three zones demarcated for the purposes of reaching middle-range generalizations. For most of this period, no international institutions existed to prompt scholars to think globally or to amalgamate and calibrate data into forms that would help them. Fortunately, Paul Lamatine-Yates, Paul Bairoch, Bouda Etemad, John Hanson, Walt Rostow, the Woytinskys, Simon Kuznets and others have aggregated and reclassified an imperfect range of national data under headings that allow for conjectures and distinctions supportable with reference to statistics for exports, imports and international factor flows that at least are of superior accuracy to anything available for outputs, incomes and other indicators of macroeconomic performance on a global scale (Woytinski and Woytinski 1955; Yates 1959; Kuznets 1966; Rostow 1978; Hanson 1980; Bairoch and Etemad 1985).

Let us begin to comprehend the structural basis for world trade by using their published statistics to reference and modify that familiar generalization: namely, that international trade in commodities (no global figures for trade in services are in print) continued, down to and beyond 1913, to be based on an exchange of primary products for manufactured goods (Table 13.3).

Of course, it is merely heuristic to represent global trade (over this period) as an exchange of primary products (produced by three zones of the world economy) for the manufactured goods and commercial services sold by another zone, namely the industrializing core of western European economies. All four zones exported both manufactures and primary products. Nevertheless, we may safely conjecture that, by the last quarter of the nineteenth century, some 70 per cent of the commodities traded on international markets by the core (Britain, Belgium, Holland, France, Germany and Switzerland) consisted of manufactures, while the primary produce imported by that same zone from neighbouring countries within western Europe and from the three other zones of the world economy accounted for approximately the same percentage of its imports (Foreman-Peck 1995).

Data are not available to trace these ratios back to the period when manufactures assumed a high degree of prominence in exports emanating from core economies. For the United Kingdom, that pattern of specialization became established during the seventeenth century. Apart from the Netherlands, other core economies continued to depend upon a more resource-intensive range of exports until later in the eighteenth and nineteenth centuries. They then moved more rapidly into the production of manufactures

Table 13.3 Primary products and manufactured exports by region in 1830, 1876–80 and 1913

	*Circa 1830**		*1876–80*		*1913*	
Region	*Primary produce (%)*	*Manufactures (%)*	*Primary produce (%)*	*Manufactures (%)*	*Primary produce (%)*	*Manufactures (%)*
United Kingdom[a]	9	91	12	88	30	70
North-west Europe[b]	–	–	44	56	48	52
East and south Europe	–	–	78	22	76	24
North America	–	–	86	14	74	26
Third World	92	8	98	2	89	11

Sources: Kenwood and Lougheed (1999: 87); Bairoch (1996: 92) estimated the share of manufactures in exports for the whole of Europe as 65 per cent for *c.* 1830; 65 per cent for *c.* 1840, 64 per cent for *c.* 1850, 61 per cent for *c.* 1860 and 58 per cent for *c.* 1870. For the Third World, Bairoch and Etemad (1985: 34) have estimated the following ratios for manufactured exports: *c.* 1839 8 per cent; 1860 4 per cent; 1900 12 per cent; 1912 9 per cent; 1928 10 per cent; 1937 9 per cent.

Notes

a The figures for 1831 for UK are from Crafts (1985: 143).

b North-west Europe includes Scandinavia and, as late as 1913, primary products constituted 60 per cent of Swedish exports.

for export than either the peripheries (of southern, northern and eastern Europe) or European settlements overseas (Minchinton 1969; Milward and Saul 1977).

Right up to the conjuncture of 1914, exports from all three zones outside the European core continued to be dominated (overwhelmingly so and until 1948 in the case of the Third World) by primary products (Tables 13.4 and 13.5). Historically, it is almost certainly the case that shares of manufactures in the exports emanating from Mediterranean Europe, India, China and other parts of the world had been higher *c.* 1675–1700 than the reduced percentages that appeared in records for the last quarter of the nineteenth century would indicate. By then, metropolitan prohibitions upon investment in colonial industries had all but disappeared (even in the most mercantilist of European empires), and exports from North America and Australasia and Japan included rapidly rising proportions of manufactured goods.

Throughout this period, only a small share of exports from the Third World sold on world markets consisted of manufactures. Kenwood and Lougheed cite an implausibly tiny ratio of 2.4 per cent for 1876–80, which suggests a half-century of severe de-industrialization followed by some semblance of restoration over the next six decades. De-industrialization only occurred in particular regions and sectors of industry and, because the processing of exports (classified in official statistics) as primary products shades into

Table 13.4 Destinations for Third World exports, 1840–1938

Year	*Europe (%)*	*North America (%)*	*Third World (%)*
1840	67	7	26
1860	68	8	24
1880	62	12	26
1900	66	16	28
1913	60	17	22
1928	55	23	22
1938	55	18	27

Sources: Hanson (1980) and Bairoch and Etemad (1985).

manufacturing, there is no need, *pace* Marx, to exaggerate its significance.[15] Meanwhile, several now famous attempts by states to force the pace of industrialization failed (Batou 1990). Apart from Japan, virtually no recovery of competitive capacity to manufacture commodities for sale on world markets occurred in Asia, or developed in southern America (let alone the Middle East and Africa), until the industrialization of the 'rest' began to advance later in the twentieth century (Amsden 2001).

Most governments and their economic advisers who considered the prospects for raising standards of living for majorities of the world's populations still attached to agricultures concluded that a (if not the) way forward would be to increase sales of cash crops (and minerals, wherever accessible) on world markets, particular European markets, to which they sent the highest proportions of exports (Arndt 1987: ch. 1).

Yet over decades (1830–1953) of population growth, urbanization, industrialization and rising incomes per capita (which proceeded at discernibly more rapid rates in Europe and zones of European settlement), the 'proportions' of imports purchased from the Third World display no tendency to rise (Table 13.6). This fact prompts the obvious question of why that zone could not exploit opportunities to export at rates that might at least have maintained (or, better still, significantly augmented) its share of primary products sold upon world markets?

Perhaps the first observation to make (Table 13.4) is that no fundamental shift occurred over time in the destinations of exports from Third World

Table 13.5 Shares of primary products sold on international markets, 1830–1937 (by zone)

Emanating from	*1830 (%)*	*1860 (%)*	*1900 (%)*	*1913 (%)*	*1928 (%)*	*1937 (%)*
Europe	40	44	42	40	35	34
European settlements	13	19	29	25	26	23
Third World	47	37	29	35	39	43

Source: Bairoch and Etemad (1985), Bairoch (1973) and Yates (1959) for the ratios of 1928 and 1937.

Table 13.6 Geographical origins of European imports, 1830–1953

Year c.	*Europe (%)*	*North America (%)*	*South America (%)*	*Asia (%)*	*Africa (%)*	*Oceania (%)*	*Third World (%)*[a]	*Third World (%)*[b]
1830	63	10	12	13	2	–	27	25
1856	62	13	8	12	3	2	25	25
1860	61	14	8	12	3	2	25	23
1870	68	11	8	9	3	2	21	19
1880	65	16	6	8	3	2	19	16
1890	65	15	6	9	3	2	20	17
1900	60	18	7	9	3	3	22	17
1910	60	14	8	10	5	3	26	21
1928	56	16	10	9	5	3	27	23
1938	53	15	10	10	7	5	27	25
1953	57	11	7	11	10	4	32	26

Sources: Bairoch (1974, 1976).

Notes
a Includes South America, Asia and Africa.
b Excludes Argentine, Chile and Uruguay, South Africa and Japan.

economies. Before 1913, something like 65 per cent of their foodstuffs, raw materials and minerals were purchased by Europe and European settlements, and the rise in the share going to Europeans overseas (in North America and elsewhere) moves in line with the relative shift in the distribution of the populations among these two zones of rapid development.

Europe never became 'dependent' on the Third World for primary products, and the continued significance of its own primary production and intra-European trade in providing by far the largest source for the food, raw materials and minerals required for the industrialization of the core is clear. Furthermore, Table 13.6 also displays clear rises in the 'relative' importance of North America and Australasia and a trend of decline to *c*. 1900 of Third World sources of supply for the development of Europe. In summary, while industrialization proceeded over the long nineteenth century within the context of a growing world economy (linked by commerce, migrations of capital and labour and imperial ties), that process occurred without any profound structural shifts in the geography of global trade. Western Europe's own farms, forests and mines continued to produce most (around 60 per cent) of the food, organic inputs and minerals required to sustain the development of the core. Supplies from European colonies and settlements overseas played a complementary role that increased in scale and scope, but even their significance has been exaggerated by the excessive attention accorded by the historiography of modern industrialization to that precocious case of the first industrial revolution. Located upon a smallish offshore island, the domestic economy of the United Kingdom had long been (and continued to be) more closely connected to the Americas and Australasia as well as the Third World than the mainland ever became.

Indeed, the realm's pattern of long-run development based on favourable natural endowments, position and sustained investment in naval power never represented a paradigm or set of comparative advantages for other European economies to pursue. After all they (Portugal, Spain, Holland and France) had effectively become 'also-rans' in the mercantilist quest for power, profits and economic growth based upon expansion overseas. As follower countries, they pursued trajectories for development that became far less path dependent upon trade, investment and colonization in Africa, Asia and the Americas. Their levels and growth of demand for imports from other continents remained altogether more circumscribed. Although the volume of primary products delivered from the Third World for sale on mainland markets increased at faster rates over the long nineteenth century, Europe (as a whole) continued to meet virtually stable shares of its needs from the continent's own agricultures, forests and mines and, at the margin, depended far more on settlements in the Americas and Australasia than upon imports from other zones and regions of the world. Indeed over time, the share of European (but not British) demand met by imports from Asia, Africa and Southern America declined, not only from a 25 per cent level, measured for 1830, but from ratios that may well have been higher when precious metals, slaves and tropical groceries dominated European trades with other continents during the sixteenth, seventeenth and eighteenth centuries (Table 13.6). Comparable impressions emerge from tabulations which expose the destinations of Europe's exports. Although the ratios are not accurate (see Tables 13.7 and 13.8) or calibrated into the categories required for analysis by zones, they point to long-term stability in the significance of intra-European trade and to an altogether slight rise in the importance of Third World markets for European commodity exports. Again, the figures also display the United Kingdom as the 'outlier' in its extra-European trading relationships.

The performance of the Third World in a globalizing economy, 1815–1914

For only a century after 1815, the response of the Third World to opportunities presented by trade and the integration of global markets depended upon natural rather than the comparative advantages of diverse regional economies, on indigenous entrepreneurship and investment and the capacities of particular zones to attract European capital and skilled labour as well as the help or hindrance offered by different forms of colonial and traditional governance.

Although geography is not destiny, the commodity composition of exports from the Third World exposes strong dependence on latitudes, locations, climates, soils and other ecological factors (Table 13.9). Diversification among a narrow range of foodstuffs, organic raw materials and a sample of mineral

Table 13.7 Geographical origins of UK imports and destinations for UK exports, 1830–1910

'M' means imports emanating from and 'E' exports sold to	*1830 M*	*1830 E*	*1860 M*	*1860 E*	*1880 M*	*1880 E*	*1910 M*	*1910 E*
Europe	–	48	31	34	41	36	45	35
North America	–	26	26	17	31	17	24	12
South America	–	12	10	12	6	10	9	13
Asia	–	13	23	26	12	25	10	24
Africa	–	3	5	3	4	4	5	7
Oceania	–	1	5	8	6	8	7	9

Source: Bairoch (1974).

ores exported from Asia, Africa and tropical America does not appear to have proceeded far between 1830 and 1937, and the composition of exports had changed only marginally by the beginnings of decolonization in 1948. Before crude oil came onstream, exports from the Third World continued to be dominated by a limited range of tropical groceries, agrarian raw materials and a small selection of drugs. Manufactures, minerals and precious metals made up residual categories and the concentration (up to 80–90 per cent measured in dollars f.o.b. at current prices) upon foodstuffs, organic materials and botanical drugs persisted until very late in the twentieth century.

Of course, the diversity, quality and sources of Third World supplies of these 'natural' products had altered over the centuries, and long-run changes cannot be mapped statistically before the 1830s, when the proportions represented by precious metals and manufactures were almost certainly lower than they had been during the sixteenth, seventeenth and eighteenth centuries.

Table 13.8 Destinations for European exports 1750–1953

Year c.	*Europe (%)*	*North America (%)*	*South America (%)*	*Asia (%)*	*Africa (%)*	*Oceania (%)*	*Third World (%)*
1750	72	1	11	7	–	–	–
1790	76	10	8	5	1	–	14
1800	74	12	8	4	2	–	14
1830	72	12	8	6	2	–	16
1860	68	9	8	10	3	2	20
1890	70	9	7	9	3	2	18
1910	68	8	8	10	4	2	21
1928	66	8	7	10	7	2	21
1938	64	7	7	10	9	3	23
1953	61	7	5	13	11	3	27

Sources: Bairoch (1974) and Rostow (1978).

Table 13.9 Commodity composition of Third World exports, 1830–1937 (ratios in dollars at current prices and rounded)

Categories	*1830*	*1860*	*1900*	*1912*	*1928*	*1937*
Agrarian raw materials						
Textile fibres	14.6	14.8	17.2	15.5	13.3	11.9
Indigo	3.7	2.4	0.5	0	0	0
Metals and mineral ores	1.9	3.9	3.1	1.8	2.3	3.8
Fuels	0	0	0.4	2	6.1	12.6
Hides and skins	3.5	4.0	3.3	4.2	2.9	2.1
Rubber	0	0.2	3.5	3.9	6.0	6.6
Wood	1.6	0.9	0.4	0.9	0.7	0.6
Gum	1.2	0.6	0.1	0	0	0
Other	3.4	5.0	3.6	6.4	3.4	2.3
Totals	29.9	3.8	32.1	34.7	34.7	39.9
Foodstuffs						
Sugar	25.1	18.1	8.6	8.2	8.7	7.8
Cereals	1.9	5.0	10.7	13.6	13.0	10.6
Coffee, tea, cocoa, spices	15.9	18.7	14.2	12.9	13.1	10.2
Vegetable oils, seeds, fats	2.3	1.7	5.2	7.7	7.7	7.0
Meat and fish	1.0	1.2	3.2	3.2	3.6	3.4
Fruit, vegetables, etc.	1.0	3.5	4.2	4.6	6.2	7.3
Totals	47.2	48.2	46.1	50.2	52.3	46.3
Drugs						
Tobacco	1.4	4.0	3.9	2.8	2.1	1.7
Opium	6.5	7.9	2.0	1.0	0	0
Totals	7.9	11.9	5.9	3.9	2.1	1.7
Precious metals	7.0	4.4	3.8	2.8	1.0	3.2
Manufactures	8.0	3.7	12.1	8.5	10.0	8.9

Sources: Reconstructed from tables 2.4, 2.6 and 3.3 in Bairoch and Etemad (1985).

Alas, the sources did not allow us to separate out the small percentage (rising to 18 per cent by 1912) of 'Third World' exports from regions of white settlement in temperate latitudes in Africa and South America, namely Argentina, Chile, Uruguay and South Africa. Nevertheless, Table 13.10 reveals that primary products emanating from this populous zone of the world economy can be characterized as embodying natural advantages of soil, climate and location as well as the accumulated experience acquired over centuries from the cultivation and marketing of a range of foodstuffs, tree crops and agricultural raw materials adapted to grow well in specific environmental niches located in the tropical latitudes of Asia, Africa and Southern America.

Furthermore, the share of such exports based on natural endowments and emanating from economies under European colonial rule fluctuated over time. The proportion may well have been higher before 1830 when imports from Iberian, Dutch, British and French possessions in the Caribbean and Southern America dominated their trades with the Third World. After the imperial meridian (1783–1830) when Britain, Spain, Portugal and France reluctantly ceded independence to most of their colonies in the Americas, roughly half of all exports originating from the Third World came from regional economies (that remained or passed under direct European rule). That 'colonial' or 'imperial' proportion of the South hardly changed right down to the Scond World War (Table 13.6).

For more than a century after 1830, the maintenance and extension of imperial rule (European, Japanese and American) to include ever increasing proportions of the world's territory, natural resources and populations hardly altered the overall share of primary products that 'colonized' agrarian regions sold on world markets (compare Tables 13.2 and 13.9).

Their exports, indeed exports from the entire Third World (colonized and independent alike), rose in line with world trade (Table 13.1), but not at rates required either to jack up the shares of primary products sold on international markets (Table 13.5) or to make much difference to the potential for development as measured in Table 13.13. Neither indigenous nor foreign skills, enterprise and investment provided the abundant and elastic supplies of labour available in Asia, Africa and Southern America with the cultivable land, irrigation, water, technology knowledge, institutions and transportation required to generate the export surpluses required to raise levels of labour productivity in agriculture (or mining) to western levels that could conceivably have led to structural change and rising levels of per capita income.

Constrained by ecologies that promoted trade based to a large extent upon natural advantages and under intensified competition from the agrarian and mineral sectors of the core and periphery of Europe, and above all from European settlements overseas, for decade after decade, the primary producers of the Third World never managed to attract more than a modest fraction of Europe's rising exports of surplus capital, skilled labour and entrepreneurs – migrating (not as Lenin postulated) to colonies and regions with cheap exploitable labour, but in overwhelming proportion to the United States and other white settlements overseas.[16]

Liberal imperialism had relaxed constraints, increased the incentives and reduced risks (omnipresent under mercantilism) for the migration of capital and labour to many more regions of a growing world economy. Unfortunately, comprehensive data for annual flows of gross and net investment moving across the frontiers of countries, empires and zones of that global economy over the very long run will never allow us to plot trends and cycles in 'foreign' investment. We may, however, assume that, for centuries before 1815, investment moving across frontiers funded the accumulation of stocks of fixed and circulating capital, owned by metropolitan capitalists and utilized within the

Table 13.10 Shares of total exports emanating from independent polities and colonial regions of the Third World, 1830–1937

	1830	*1860*	*1900*	*1912*	*1928*	*1937*
South America						
Tropical regions[a]	91	85	63	59	57	65
Temperate regions[b]	9	15	37	41	43	35
Colonies[c]	49	34	17	15	13	18
Independent polities	51	66	83	85	87	82
South American share of Third World exports	48	45	38	38	37	37
Asia						
India	43	45	43	40	29	26
China	21	19	15	15	17	7
Far East[d]	74	86	85	92	93	89
Middle East[e]	26	14	14	8	7	11
Colonies[f]	53	57	71	77	76	82
Asian share of Third World exports	44	47	48	48	50	45
Africa						
North Africa[g]	57	61	69	69	56	46
Sub-Saharan Africa[h]	14	8	25	27	42	52
Sugar Islands[i]	29	31	9	4	2	2
Colonies	32	34	97	98	96	95
African share of Third World exports	8	8	13	13	13	11

Source: Reconstructed from data in Bairoch and Etemad (1985), tables 5.1, 6.1 and 7.1.

Notes
a All other countries on the mainland plus the islands offshore.
b Includes Argentine, Chile and Uruguay.
c Colonies exclude colonies on the mainland.
d Far East includes India, China, Ceylon, Indo-China, Indonesia, Malaya, Philippines, Borneo, Korea, Taiwan, Hong Kong, Nepal, Sarawak, Thailand, French and Portuguese India.
e Middle East includes Iran, Turkish Empire, Aden, Cyprus, Crete, Oman.
f Colonial excludes China, Iran, Turkish Empire, Cyprus, Crete, Afghanistan, Oman.
g North Africa includes Mahgreb, Egypt and Libya. Most of north Africa had been colonized by European governments by 1900.
h Includes countries south of the Sahara and the sugar islands of Mauritius and Réunion.
i Colonial is all Africa less Morocco.

colonial economies of empires, ruled and defended (more or less effectively) by the states (navies) of Portugal, Spain, the Netherlands, Denmark, France and Britain.[17] That politically determined scale and pattern of investment overseas changed over the era of liberal imperialism. During a more peaceable order that followed the Congress of Vienna, net annual flows of European capital increased and fluctuated in a rather predictable cyclical fashion (between home and foreign investment). The trend accelerated, and both the levels and the shares of domestic savings invested outside national economies went up and up. According to one estimate, the stock of long-term foreign investment emanating from Britain, France, Germany, Belgium, Switzerland and Sweden may have risen 35 times (measured in current prices) between 1825 and1913 and from three per cent to nearly five per cent of the core's gross national product (Edelstein 1994; Bairoch 1997: 316–17).

O'Rourke and Williamson's (1999) data for the United Kingdom, France and Germany for 1850–54 to 1910–13 refer to foreign investment as percentages of domestic savings, and display considerable fluctuations and no clear tends, but testify again to the exceptional propensities of British capitalists (compared with their French and German counterparts) to invest overseas. Efficiently serviced by the City of London, British investors placed between a third and a half of their savings in foreign assets so that the share of the kingdom's wealth invested beyond its borders rose from around six per cent in 1850 to 26 per cent by 1910. Their participation in the stock of European capital invested outside Europe rose from one-third *c.* 1815 to just over half *c.* 1913 (O'Rourke and Williamson 1999: 226–34). Meanwhile, French and German investors placed far higher proportions of their savings in assets on the mainland – 52 per cent and 44 per cent (as at 1913) compared with five per cent for the United Kingdom (Edelstein 1994; Bairoch 1976: 316–17). By then, capitalists from the United States had emerged as foreign investors (overwhelmingly in Canada and South America) and owned around seven per cent of the stock of foreign capital – quoted on the world's major stock exchanges (O'Rourke and Williamson 1999: 229). At that conjuncture in the growth of the world economy, the aggregated value of the stock of recorded paper assets which (as a lower bound estimate) excludes unrecorded but rather considerable sums for direct foreign investment in both fixed and circulating capital could have amounted to some 18 per cent of world output (Bairoch 1997: 317–18).

By 1913, the populous Third World enjoyed benefits of less than 20 per cent from this stock of foreign capital, and there is no reason to anticipate that the geographical distribution just before the First World War misrepresents patterns of investment from 1815 to 1913 (Table 13.11). On the contrary, Africa, Asia and tropical regions of South America probably obtained a rising share of capital invested abroad during the long boom from 1899 to 1914. Before that, a favoured zone of white 'settlement' with close and significant commercial connections with Europe, located in temperate latitudes, with independent or dominion forms of government may well have attracted an overwhelming share of total private capital invested across frontiers, as well as subsidized defence from Britain during the era of liberal imperialism.[18]

Outside sugar, tea, coffee and rubber plantations, European investors contributed tiny proportions of the funding for machinery, equipment, tools, buildings and working capital used by firms for agricultural or industrial production anywhere in the Third World. Although venture capital and buccaneer entrepreneurs are infamous in the histories of empires, most European money migrated to Asia, Africa and South America in search of secure opportunities to earn marginally higher rates of return payable on bonds issued either by governments or on the debentures and equities of companies engaged in mining, forestry, land clearance, irrigation, the building of roads, docks, harbours, houses, urban infrastructures and, above all, to fund the construction and operation of railways which linked cultivable land, forests and mineral deposits of the Third World to towns, ports and international markets.[19]

Railways happened to be the one (albeit significant) component of the capital stock funded (in large part) by European investors that can be compared and presented in statistical form as kilometres of track laid down to cross and to penetrate into the interiors of continents. Yet it would be more heuristic to compare evidence on the formation of social overhead capital (including railways) across countries and regions so that polities under colonial rule could be contrasted with countries and empires under autonomous governments. Meanwhile, the 'big picture' – as represented by data in Table 13.12 – exposes the lower scales of kilometres of railway per capita and per hectare of cropland compared with the advantages derived from modern and superior forms of steam-powered inland transportation enjoyed by Europe and European settlements in the Americas (including settlements in South America) over the economies of Asia and Africa between 1850 and 1930.[20]

As a byproduct of their political status, India and other regions of the colonized Third World may (counterfactually) have enjoyed favoured treatment from British and other European investors placing their savings in 'protected' (sometimes subsidized) forms of social overhead capital than, say, China,

Table 13.11 Geographical distribution of recorded foreign investment (measured in dollars at current prices *c.* 1913)

	Estimate (a) (%)	*Estimate (b) (%)*
Europe	26	36
North America	24	–
South America	20	8
European settlements[a]	–	45
Africa	9	5
Asia	16	6
Oceania	5	–
Total	100	100

Sources: Bairoch (1976); Bulmer-Thomas (1994).

Note
a North America, Argentine, Chile, Uruguay, South Africa and Australasia.

Brazil or other autonomous polities of the Third World. Nevertheless, and despite repeated claims made by apologists for liberal imperialism, it is clear that colonies never became preferred destinations for the bulk of European investment overseas.[21] The post-1815 departure from mercantilistic patterns of private investment virtually confined to empires became all too clear for the British and other cases. Only 36 per cent of the money raised on the London capital market between 1865 and 1914 funded the formation of capital within the British Empire, and only 35 per cent of that share (or a mere 13 per cent of total overseas investment raised on the London capital market) became available to India and other colonies containing abundant supplies of politically manipulable property rights and economically exploitable labour. Europe's surplus capital migrated in overwhelming proportion to support, sustain and subsidize European settlements overseas (Davis and Huttenback 1986). Ironically (from any Leninist perspective), unsettled debates about the costs and benefits of imperialism are now concerned to measure 'potential losses' to Britain and other European societies that flowed from their sustained commitment to rule and defend colonies for more than a century after the malign geopolitical legacy of mercantilism for economic growth had become merely 'ornamental' for the social welfare of western populations (O'Brien and Prados De La Escosura 1998).

White settlements not only attracted the bulk of European funds required to construct social overhead capital that supported the direct exploitation of cultivable land and minerals available in the Americas, Australasia and other settlements, but they also remained favoured destinations for millions of adolescent and healthy workers (including a significant minority of skilled and entrepreneurial Europeans) who migrated across frontiers and oceans over the long nineteenth century. In all, some 44 million people emigrated from Europe between 1821 and 1915; a majority came from countries of the core and 44 per cent from the peripheries of Mediterranean and eastern Europe. They 'travelled' in a large proportion (81 per cent) to the United States, Canada, Argentine and Australasia and as 'human capital' made variable but significant contributions to the development of both the economies in which they spent their working lives as well as the European countries they left behind (Castles and Miller 1993).

Although material benefits from migration for the overall growth of an Atlantic and global economy are not disputed, at the time and as pessimistic assessments about the effects of emigration (particularly the emigration of skilled labour) upon the long-term development of particular 'national' economies has generated conclusions that the settlements may have been gained at the expense of the metropole (Bairoch 1997: 177–85). That argument is nationalistic and is more often elaborated for outflows of capital than labour (Pollard 1985; Lazonick and Elbaum 1986).[22]

Recently, that view has been satisfactorily reconsidered (if not refuted) in a series of monographs in cliometric history synthesized by O'Rourke and Williamson's seminal book *Globalization and History* (Harley 2000). Their cen-

Table 13.12 Railways, areas, croplands, populations by continent, 1820–1930

		Europe	*North America*	*Oceania*	*South America*	*Asia*	*Africa*
Year *c.*	Total area in hectares (millions)	473	1,839	843	2,053	2,679	2,966
1850	Population (millions)	164	26	–	38	801	111
	Croplands (hectares, millions)	132	50	6	18	153	84
	Railways (thousand km)	23	15	–	–	–	–
1870	Population (millions)	187	44	2	40	864	90
	Croplands (hectares, millions)	140	80	7	21	166	91
	Railways (thousand km)	89	90	–	4	8	2
1900	Population (millions)	203	83	6	74	925	133
	Croplands (hectares, millions)	145	133	14	33	190	110
	Railways (thousand km)	234	341	–	62	51	11
1913	Population (millions)	261	105	6	80	976	124
	Croplands (hectares, millions)	146	156	17	39	202	120
	Railways (thousand km)	286	456	–	112	92	27
1930	Population (millions)	301	129	7	112	1,141	164
	Croplands (hectares, millions)	149	196	22	57	231	150
	Railways (thousand km)	211	472	–	136	112	48

Sources: Bairoch (1976, 1997), Rostow (1978), Maddison (2001), Turner *et al.* (1990) amd World Resources Institute (1986–9).

tral conclusion that mass outmigration from Europe prior to the First World War probably accounted for about 70 per cent of wage rate convergence for the Atlantic economy as a whole rests, however, upon a database for a sample of European economies, the United States, Argentine and Brazil and refers to a span of years 1870–1913. The book did not set out to explore implications flowing from the integration of an Atlantic economy for the rest of the world economy, particularly for densely populated regions of the Third World? Yet the problems involved in extending their sophisticated methods to include the rest of the world seem insuperable and raise the counterfactual question of what the growth rate of the American economy, its demands for labour, wages convergence and levels of development across the Atlantic economy might have been if Asians had replaced European immigrants over the entire century 1815–1914? Presumably, the slave trade would have persisted for longer and on a far greater scale. Given that transport costs declined, the 'pull' on labour supplies from other continents would, over centuries, have intensified and raised wage rates in potential sending regions of several economies, including India, China, Japan, Java and other eastern societies with 'surplus' labour (Hatton and Williamson 1995).

Although the redistribution of populations across the Atlantic attracted complementary flows of capital, which pushed up wages and generated higher rates of productivity growth for Europeans along with their settlements overseas, that process might not, however, have operated to anything like the same degree for the densely populated regions of the Third World. Firstly, the scenario seems improbable because established political elites and vested interests of workforces of European origin in place in the Americas and Australasia would almost certainly have resisted the influx of anything more than tightly controlled quotas of immigrants from Asia (Foreman-Peck 1992; Wong 1997). Secondly, and despite the radical decline in fares and travelling times by ships and trains, transportation and start-up costs for migrants remained high for young men from low-wage economies to finance. That is why millions of Chinese and Indian workers (who also became more mobile during the nineteenth century) emigrated across shorter distances and took advantage of indentures and other forms of temporary servitude in order to obtain employment overseas (Cohen 1995). Thirdly, the potential scale and extent of underemployment among the agrarian workforces of many regions of Asia implies that supply curves for labour may have been more elastic than was the case, even for regions of the European periphery (Iberia, southern Italy and Ireland) with the highest ratios of labour to cultivable land and incidence of poverty (Table 13.12). Labour inputs from workers with low marginal productivities are easily replaced, and their 'voluntary', 'enforced' or 'distressed' migration exerts limited upward pressures on local wage rates and prospects for development. Thus, and even if the option became politically possible and economically feasible for Asia, with given baseline densities of populations to cultivable land and other natural resources, the sheer scale of outmigration required to generate the kind of increases in real wages that followed even from the emigration of poor Irish, Italian and

Iberian workers could only have flowed from non-feasible resettlement of populations from the densely populated regions of Asia by migration – far in excess of the 60 million or so workers who left Europe for the Americas over the long nineteenth century.[23]

During an era of liberal imperialism, 1815–1948, differentials in labour productivities, real wages and standards of living between the European core and its settlements overseas on the one side and the colonized and autonomous societies of the Third World on the other widened monotonically. By 1913, model gaps in real wages stood at around six to one (Williamson 2000). This 'great divergence' emanated from sources that have been discussed by historians and demarcated by economic theories, macroproduction functions and multiple regression analysis concerned to explain our modern north–south divide (Pomeranz 2000). Global historians invariably emphasize favourable access enjoyed by 'surplus' European labour to virtually empty new worlds with ghost acres and abundant natural resources in the Americas (Jones 2003).

Since Marx, problems of 'exploitation' have dominated debates about connections between imperialism and European investment overseas. With hindsight, that perspective now seems irrelevant, and historians have become concerned with imperfections in international markets for capital and the myopias displayed by foreign (and domestic) investors towards opportunities to integrate abundant supplies of cheap labour, inaccessible land and underexploited mineral wealth available in many parts of the Third World long before the age when transnational corporations appeared in large numbers (Latham 1978; Harley 1996).

Crowded out or excluded from access to the Americas and starved of foreign and metropolitan capital for local development, the agrarian workforces of the Third World concentrated on securing subsistence. For growth, they worked hard at margins where cash crops could be exported and where a rather restricted range of natural advantages allowed by their ecologies provided opportunities for more intensive participation in international trade. In their pursuit of that obvious and viable option for profit, any suggestion that colonial governance positively discouraged regional economies under European sovereignty in Asia, Africa and Southern America from actively competing to sell primary products on world markets seems *prima facie* implausible, contradicts most histories of colonial policy and derives no support from the data tabulated below.[24]

Table 13.13 compares calculations, based on official statistics, of exports per capita for three benchmark years during the closing half-century of liberal imperialism. As an index, the figures offer some indication of the potential capacities of a large sample of both nominally sovereign and colonized (but soon to be independent) agrarian economies of the Third World to purchase imports on international markets for purposes of consumption, defence and development. This data set also provides proxies for their relative capacities to service foreign loans that could be used for investment and/or consumption.

Table 13.13 Exports per capita for national (N) and colonial (C) economies in US dollars at current prices for 1900, 1937 and 1948

		Exports per capita in US dollars		
National economy		*1900*	*1937*	*1948*
Group 1 (population 0–5 million)				
Bolivia	N	0	11	28
Costa Rica	N	28	15	58
Cuba	C	33	35	139
Dominica	N	0	11	37
Ecuador	N	9	3	14
El Salvador	N	4	9	23
Guatemala	N	5	6	14
Haiti	N	0	3	8
Honduras	N	12	24	46
Nicaragua	N	6	1	17
Panama	N	0	6	16
Venezuela	N	9	53	236
Chile	N	21	40	60
Paraguay	N	0	8	23
Uruguay	N	36	37	78
French West Indies	C	0	35	128
British Guyana	C	34	43	78
British West Indies	C	13	34	69
Surinam	C	0	15	70
French Cameroon	C	0	5	13
French Equatorial Africa	C	0	3	12
Madagascar	C	0	6	11
French Togoland	C	0	4	11
Tunisia	C	0	16	19
Réunion	C	0	40	100
Angola	C	0	6	13
Cape Verde	C	0	0	50
Libya	C	0	8	11
Gold Coast	C	0	18	55
Mauritius	C	0	35	110
Sudan	C	0	12	126
Sierra Leone	C	0	7	11
Spanish Morocco	C	0	4	16
Liberia	C	0	1	10
Malaysia	C	0	118	170
Taiwan	C	0	42	5
Sarawak	C	0	45	162
Iraq	C	0	6	7
Jordan	C	0	10	30
Palestine	C	0	18	3
Cyprus	C	0	28	46
Syria	C	0	5	8

		Exports per capita in US dollars		
National economy		*1900*	*1937*	*1948*
Group 2 (population 5–10 million)				
Colombia	N	4	10	28
Algeria	C	0	23	48
French Morocco	C	0	7	22
Mozambique	C	0	3	7
Rhodesia	C	0	20	37
Kenya/Uganda	C	0	7	13
Ceylon	C	10	22	44
Peru	N	6	14	20
Group 3 (population 10–20 million)				
Mexico	N	5	12	20
Argentine	N	0	54	87
French West Africa	C	0	4	10
Belgian Congo	C	0	7	23
South Africa	N	0	22	50
Egypt	C	8	13	31
Burma	N	0	12	14
Philippines	C	3	10	17
Thailand	C	2	5	5
Afghanistan	N	0	2	4
Turkey	N	0	7	10
Group 4 (population 20–50 million)				
Brazil	N	9	9	25
Nigeria	C	0	5	6
Indo-China	C	0	5	3
Korea	C	0	9	7
Group 5 (population 50+ million)				
British India	C	1	2	4
Indonesia	C	3	8	5
Japan	N	0	17	3
China	N	0	2	1

Notes and sources: All figures have been rounded to the nearest dollar. The figures for 1900 are from Hanson (1980). The figures for 1937 and 1948 refer to the devalued dollar of 1934 and are not comparable with Hanson's estimates for 1900. Exports valued in dollars are from United Nations (1955). Population totals were taken from United Nations (1949a) and the groups are based on total populations for 1937 and 1948.

For all regions of the Third World (including colonies), exports per capita (or relative capacities to import and service foreign debts) had accumulated gradually over varying spans of engagement with the world economy. Evidence for that engagement goes back no further than 1830 and is only available for continents and subcontinents, which means that the figures for South America include 'high exports per capita' from three temperate locations of white settlement (Argentine, Chile, Uruguay) (see Table 13.13). Although imports flowing into Third World economies certainly rose over time, the zone's overall potential to buy commodities, services and capital goods and to borrow money on European financial markets remained clearly and consistently below the capacities to import commodities and services available to the UK, to the western European core and to European settlements overseas. For more than 133 years (1815–1948), these fortunate zones and populations of the world economy enjoyed levels of consumption and funds for domestic investment derived from engagement with international trade that exceeded the modest gains achieved by the Third World by considerable (but not by growing!) margins. The competitive superiority of the 'west' over the rest of the world in securing gains from trade had developed over centuries of time and was based upon three separable, but ultimately connected, sources of comparative advantage. First, from higher levels of economic efficiency in transforming inputs into final outputs (which included surpluses of commodities sold on world markets – factoral terms of trade); secondly, from fluctuating but consistently favourable prices obtained for the mix of manufactures and primary produce exported compared with products imported (mainly primary products) – net barter terms of trade; and, thirdly, from an extraordinary and growing share of profits, wages and interest obtained by the 'west' from the organization, transportation, financing and servicing of international trade in commodities.[25]

Factoral and barter terms of trade are familiar to economists analysing the 'proximate' determinants and observed divisions or gains from trade (Kindleberger 1962). Until recently, they have however been less interested in the historical origins of comparative advantages enjoyed by particular zones, countries or regions of the world economy. With conspicuous exceptions, theorists of international trade have also accorded limited attention to 'large facts' that preoccupied their mercantilist precursors, such as the balance of merchandise trade (Woytinski and Woytinski 1955; Frank 1978). Their concentration on the balance of payments emanated from a core theoretical concern to refute the 'bullionist errors' that dominated economic thought before Adam Smith (Hutchison 1988). Nevertheless, and long after mercantilist theories of international trade had been consigned to history, it continued to be the case that the total values of 'commodity' imports consumed and/or invested by the economies of a core of western European economies exceeded the total values of the commodities they exported and by a growing margin.

According to Bairoch's (1974) estimates, Europe's surplus of commodity imports (c.i.f.) over exports (f.o.b.), which amounted to approximately eight per cent of total imports in 1830 had risen to 23 per cent a century later. Unfortunately, international payments data exposing just how each zone of the world economy funded deficits on its balance of trade with all other zones are virtually impossible to reconstruct for periods before national governments began to publish detailed balance of payments accounts.[26] Bairoch's data refer only to Europe's commodity trade and for the period after 1830. His estimates show rising trade deficits with all other continents, particularly and significantly with European settlements in North America and Australasia, but also with the Third World of Asia, Africa and South America, which supplied something like a modal 30 per cent of Europe's 'excess' merchandise imports over exports between 1850 and 1938. To fund these rising deficits on balance of trade accounts with other zones, European economies sold and/or provided the rest of the world with commercial services – particularly shipping, but also international transportation, banking, insurance, mercantile and governmental services and other 'invisibles'. Europeans also transferred long-term loans required to expand both production and trade within and beyond the borders of colonies and national economies in Asia, Africa and the Americas.

The build-up of the expertise, organization, social overhead capital, political protection and stable systems of property rights to secure and sustain comparative advantages in almost all forms of transportation and intermediation between producers and consumers for regular commerce between regions of the world economy emerged after centuries of mercantilism and imperialism. Along the way, the inputs and subsidies from European states committed to mercantile enterprise, political conquest and colonization overseas were vital for success (Tracy 1990). Eventually, 'pay-offs' in the form of flows of interest, dividends, 'home charges', payments for governance and protection and for the services of all kinds supplied by European middlemen and intermediaries emerged as 'invisibles' on Europe's balance of payments accounts, particularly for the UK and the Netherlands, but for several other mainland powers as well. Promoted and protected by states, the export of 'services' matured into one of the most profitable and enduring of Europe's comparative advantages and, through a complex system of multilateral payments, allowed the 'core' to circumvent the problem of balancing commodity trade on a bilateral basis and to run growing deficits between the import and export of commodities. Import surpluses consumed and invested by western Europe expanded by a factor of 70 between 1830 and 1953 (Frank, unpublished manuscript, 2004).[27]

For the Third World, the history of enforced (and/or unavoidable) dependence on 'European middlemen' did not necessarily signify exploitation, if services from European firms (including governance) became available at 'competitive prices'. Apologists for imperialism maintain that government and all other services supplied by Europeans could well have been cheaper and more efficient. Nevertheless, the 'diffusion/intrusion' of European middlemen across the service sectors of many regional economies of the Third World and the core's position of politically acquired dominance in international shipping and other services implied a massive reallocation over time from earnings derived from external trade (and domestic) to alien (European) minorities, which effectively reduced revenues from commodity exports 'retained' for expenditure and investment within the countries of origin. Thus, decolonization of both governmental and private services at least shifted 'some' share of the gains from trade back towards and into the hands of middlemen from the economies of the Third World.[28]

Yet, even within the circumscribed prospects for making and retaining gains from trade available to all agrarian economies of the Third World, no correlation can be detected between the long-term success of particular regions in realizing relatively high levels of exports per capita and their political status. For example, in 1900, that index exposes several colonies (Cuba, British Guyana, British West Indies, Ceylon and Egypt) performing very much better than other colonies (Philippines, India and Indonesia), while the records of subtropical national economies (El Salvador, Guatemala, Colombia, Mexico, Thailand and China) indicate a very low potential for export-led growth in real per capita incomes. By the eve of decolonization (1948), a long list of Europe's colonies, old and new, had achieved exports per capita of more than $50 per capita. But a longer list of both colonized and autonomous economies earned revenues from gross commodity exports that fell way below even that low level. Export revenues were, moreover, shared between local producers and Europeans for the services that they profitably provided as intermediaries in facilitating their participation in international trade.

No doubt a fully specified model replete with a data set constructed to test the hypothesis by deploying 'regional' (countries are not the relevant units for this purpose) regression analysis could conceivably come up with some kind of 'averaged coefficients' to suggest that connections between colonial governance and the growth of exports per capita had at some general level been positive, although it is not clear whether historians are entitled to call upon the findings of cross-country regression analysis in order to offer valid measures of the statistical significance of institutional and policy variables inspired by underspecified models of long-term growth.[29]

Meanwhile, even a cursory survey of the economic histories of the colonial regions and countries and simple correlations serve to expose the unavoidable and profound significance of geography and demography in explaining levels of exports per capita achieved by colonized and autonomous economies during the era of liberal imperialism.[30] For example, no surprise could be occasioned by the high degree of correlation exposed in Table 13.13 in the data available for 1900, 1937 and 1948 between the size of a country's population and exports per capita.[31] World demand for imports of primary products cultivated and grown in the Third World growing at rates of three to four per cent per annum could hardly have a significant impact upon average standards of living for British India or Qing China by jacking up their revenues from exports per capita to levels that could conceivably have created real prospects for the allocation of revenues from international trade that would lead to rising standards of living for such large countries.

Geographies can be decomposed into clusters of natural inputs (including tropical environments hospitable to obliterating human diseases such as malaria, yellow fever, bilharzias) that *ceteris paribus* could be more or less favourable to the expansion of exports (and to population growth). Histories of regions that experienced successful, less successful and unsuccessful export-led intensive growth from 1815 to 1948 seem to have been much more closely connected to such factors than to the promotional or restraining influences from colonial, compared with home, rule.[32]

In retrospect, and by the beginning of an era of decolonization and American hegemony, persistent and widely shared 'Ricardian expectation' that increased exports of primary products could (given time) act as an engine of growth for many economies of the poorest parts of the world seemed to have had little going for it as a strategy for long-term development outside zones and regions of European settlement (Tables 13.13 and 13.14). With the conspicuous exceptions of an explicable sample of smaller, well-endowed and/or fortunately located economies (including Costa Rica, Cuba, Venezuela, Ceylon, the French and British West Indies, Guyana, Surinam, Réunion, Cape Verde, Gold Coast, Mauritius, Malaysia, Sarawak, Cyprus and Taiwan), potential capacities to import the commodities and investible funds required to kick start a process of structural change look too small as a macroeconomic policy for transformation that either colonial or autonomous governments might have pursued with much greater success. Thinly populated independent countries (e.g. Venezuela) or colonies (Malaysia), well endowed with fuel or minerals and new products such as rubber did build up 'prospects' for development based upon high levels of per capita exports, but that potential had hardly emerged for British India, Qing China, independent Siam and the equally populous Philippines (colonized first by Spain and after 1898 by the United States).

As elaborated in this chapter, the explanation of why the predictions of an extremely influential economic theorist from a small but well-endowed island economy embodied such limited provenance for the poorest agrarian regions of Asia, Africa and Southern America has been located within the structural parameters of an evolving and integrating global economy. Within that context, the development of economies and the policies of governments emerge as responses conditioned by connections and interactions of four zones of an integrated international economy. As Paul Krugman insisted, 'world trade must be regarded as the outcome of a process in which trade flows, world prices and employment are all simultaneously determined'.[33]

For several reasons (which had something, but not much, to do with the persistence and extension of colonial governance), one zone (the Third World) made significantly lower gains from trade than the core, European settlements and Europe's periphery (Table 13.14). First, bullion and Oriental manufactures had clearly declined from the positions they enjoyed in intercontinental trade during the centuries of mercantilism, while the zone's potentially rich endowments of crude oil and natural advantages for the cultivation of rubber emerged after 1900. Discoveries of mineral ores boosted exports here and there, but total tons mined hardly made a difference to

Table 13.14 Exports per capita (relative capacity to import and to raise loans, measured in US dollars at current and constant prices), 1830–1948

		1	*2*	*3*	*4*	*5*	*6*	*7*
	Continent/zone	*1830*	*1860*	*1900*	*1913*	*1928*	*1937*	*1948*
1	South America	5.1	8.4	10.5	19.6	28.6	11.0	43.8
	(Deflated)	*(5.1)*	*(12.0)*	*(18.1)*	*(23.6)*	*(25.1)*	*(12.0)*	*(19.6)*
2	Africa	0.2	0.5	1.6	3.2	6.0	3.3	22.5
	(Deflated)	*(0.2)*	*(0.7)*	*(2.7)*	*(5.2)*	*(6.1)*	*(3.4)*	*(10.1)*
3	Asia	0.2	0.4	0.9	1.98	3.9	1.5	4.5
	(Deflated)	*(0.2)*	*(0.6)*	*(1.6)*	*(3.0)*	*(3.9)*	*(1.6)*	*(2.0)*
4	Third World	0.3	0.8	1.6	3.4	6.2	2.6	10.4
	(Deflated)	*(0.3)*	*(1.1)*	*(2.8)*	*(5.5)*	*(6.2)*	*(2.7)*	*(4.7)*
5	European core	5.2	13.1	21.76	36.3			
	(Deflated)	*(5.1)*	*(11.4)*	*(28.6)*	*(31.8)*			
6	United Kingdom	6.0	28.6	36.3	54.3			
	(Deflated)	*(6.0)*	*(24.4)*	*(47.7)*	*(65.4)*			
7	European periphery	1.1	3.3	5.7	9.0			
	(Deflated)	*(1.1)*	*(4.7)*	*(0.98)*	*(10.8)*			
8	European settlements	4.6	10.2	18.3	35.6			
	(Deflated)	*(4.6)*	*(14.6)*	*(31.6)*	*(58.4)*			

Notes and sources: The data for 1830–1937 in current price dollars are from Bairoch and Etemad (1985). Their figures for 1937 are in the devalued dollar of 1934. Column 7 data for 1948 are from United Nations (1949b), and the population data for continents are from United Nations (1949a) for 1948.The figures for column 1, rows 5, 6, 7 and 8, are calculated from data in Hanson (1980). The European Core, UK, European periphery and European settlements for 1860 to 1913 are taken from Lewis (1981) divided by population figures in Maddison (2001). Constant price dollars are placed in brackets, and the deflators are price indices for UK exports and imports as reported in Mitchell (1962: 331). Only the UK figures in current price dollars have been deflated by a UK index for prices of UK imports. All other figures are deflated by a price index for UK exports and refer to 1830 as the reference year and provide a perception of trends from 1830 to 1948.

world output and never constituted more than five per cent of aggregate exports from Africa, Asia and Southern America.

Apart from 'tropical groceries' (coffee, tea, cocoa and spices, palm oil and rice), most of the foodstuffs, drugs and raw materials exported from the Third World could also be procured from agricultures located in more temperate zones. Furthermore, along with falling costs for transportation, and transactions that intensified competition for most forms of primary produce (however bulky, heavy or distant from points of consumption), substitutions for traditional, ecologically based advantages (such as beet for cane sugar and synthetics for natural fibres, chemicals for indigo and other natural dyes, metals for timber, etc.) also came onstream and exerted downward pressure on the prices obtainable for almost all the commodities exported from the Third World listed in Table 13.9.

Third, over the era of liberal imperialism (1815–1948), the potential for greater gains derived from vents for surpluses obtainable by cultivating previously inaccessible fertile land, mining mineral deposits and exploiting abundant supplies of cheap labour depended on inflows of foreign investment, local entrepreneurship and governmental assistance for the construction of social overhead capital designed to integrate the resources and workforces of the Third World into global markets.

Interestingly, all three preconditions came together in that remarkable but short-lived boom of the '*belle époque*' (1900–13) that preceded the First World War and then tragically ran into the buffers of the great depression and the Second World War (Latham 1981).

The growth rates in Table 13.15 for 1830–1900 are from Bairoch and Etemad's (1985) data deflated by an index for British export prices taken from Imlah (1958) and current price estimates for 1900–13, 1913–37, 1937–48 and 1913–48 by the official price index for manufactured goods exported by the United States as reported in the US Bureau of the Census, *Historical Statistics of the United States*. The weights used to calculate growth of Third World exports are for 1913 except for 1913–48, where paasche weights for 1948 generate a growth rate of 1.7 per cent. These rates are estimates of averaged changes in income terms of trade for exports of primary produce from Third World economies (Table 13.15).

Trade data from several sources testify that capacities to import manufactured and capital goods derived from exports from the Third World accelerated to reach rates of six to seven per cent per annum (1900–13), compared with an average rate of around three per cent over the previous seven decades. Although the impact of the First World War upon Third World economies has not been investigated, that expansion continued at more modest rates up to 1928, but collapsed during the years of the great depression. Over an interregnum of warfare, neomercantilism and depression (1913–48), exports from economies in South America and Africa fell back and grew at rates below trend rates for 1830–1900. But warfare, revolutions and struggles for colonial freedom and transitions to independence had seriously depressing effects on the trade of most Asian economies throughout that period.

Given the potential significance for growth of enhancing capacities to import – by augmenting exports and attracting foreign investment – the interregnum of warfare, neomercantilism, cyclical instability and depression that afflicted the world economy between 1913 and 1948 stands out as singularly unfortunate for standards of living throughout the Third World. For something close to four decades which succeeded the 'first long boom' (1900–13) and preceded decolonization and the reconstruction of a reformed international economic order, growth of total real earnings from exports for most economies (particularly Asian economies) fell well below the record

Table 13.15 Rates of growth and purchasing power of commodity exports from the Third World, 1830–1948

	Rate of growth (%)				
Continent	*1830–1900*	*1900–1913*	*1913–1937*	*1937–1948*	*1913–1948*
South America	2.6	6.5	2.0	3.7	2.5
Africa	3.6	6.3	1.3	3.6	2.0
Asia	3.0	6.5	3.3	–5.1	0.6
Third World	2.9	6.4	2.5	–0.5	1.5 1.7

Notes and sources: Estimates of the total exports from South America, Africa and Asia valued in dollars for 1830, 1860, 1880, 1900, 1912, 1913, 1928, 1937 and 1948 at current prices are available from the following sources: United Nations (1955), Lamartine-Yates (1959), Hanson (1980), Lewis (1981) and Bairoch and Etemad (1985).

rates achieved during the cycle and remained significantly lower than long-run average annual rates estimated for 1830–1913.

The implications of some two decades of disruption to the growth of the international economy can be represented by comparing estimates of per capita income terms of trade for the Third World societies with counterfactual values based on an assumption that the growth of exports of primary products from 1913 to 1948 remained on a trend (defined as the annual average rate for 1830–1913).

This counterfactual speculation reveals how seriously geopolitical conflicts (1914–18 and 1939–45) and macroeconomic policy failures by governments in Washington and London constricted opportunities for export-led growth based upon sales of foodstuffs, organic raw materials, minerals and fuels on world markets (Table 13.16). Unfortunately, political shocks to the world economy appeared at a time that coincided with the beginnings of widespread declines in crude death rates which led, in short compass, to a near doubling in natural rates of increase of the populations in many regions of Asia, Africa and Southern America (Bairoch 1975; Kitson and Michie 1995).

Table 13.16 Exports per capita in 1948 deflated by the price index for manufactures sold on world markets

	Actual levels in $	*Counterfactual levels in $*
South America	19.6	71.1
Africa	10.1	20.5
Asia	2.0	10.5
Third World	4.7	17.7

Sources: see Tables 13.13 and 13.15.

Conclusions: governance and the performance of colonized and autonomous Third World economies

Over the years from 1815 to 1948, the constricted prospects of the economies of the Third World to afford rising standards of living for their populations depended to some 'considerable' degree upon their capacities to respond to opportunities to realize gains from international trade by exploiting underutilized natural resources, minerals, cultivable land and particularly their elastic supplies of cheap labour.[34] Although western techniques for the exploration, mining and refining of mineral ores and crude oil raised productivities in extractive industries, flows of innovatory knowledge for the more efficient cultivation, processing and marketing of food and cash crops produced by agricultures of the Third World remained virtually confined to traditional methods of transplanting seeds, plants and tools from region to region and from continent to continent. New knowledge of how to raise the productivities of land and labour in tropical environments hardly appeared until well into the twentieth century; and certainly much later than the emergence of agronomic science that augmented the efficiency of agricultures located in more temperate latitudes (Federico 2000). Throughout large areas of Asia, Africa and Southern America, increased outputs depended far more upon extending land under cultivation and upon multiple cropping. At those margins, Europe and European settlements doubled the area of cropland available to farmers between 1850 and 1930, while hectares under crops in the Third World rose by an impressive but lower percentage – 72 per cent (Table 13.12). Further extensions to areas cultivated and cropped continued to be constrained by shortages of water and access to markets for cash crops. These obstacles on the supply side waited to be alleviated by higher rates of investment in irrigation systems and transportation networks. No macrodata exist to measure increases to flows of water into agricultural production, but the already inadequate mileage of railways, which had grown from just 14,000 kilometres of track in 1870 to 231,000 by 1913, hardly changed over the next 40 years (Table 13.12).

Geopolitical conflicts initiated by Europeans and the macromismanagement of the world's largest economies certainly depressed prospects for growth among regional economies all over Asia, Africa and Southern America during that malign interregnum, 1913–48. Nevertheless, even without two decades of slower and disrupted growth, unfavourable secular trends in demand for primary products from the industrialized and industrializing market economies of the European core, North American, Australasia and Japan restrained the rise in consumption for the foodstuffs, raw materials, minerals and other primary products traditionally supplied by the agricultures and mines of the Third World.

These trends arose, persisted and intensified for two main reasons. First, several economies (including the United States, Canada, Australia, Scandinavia, Russia, Austria–Hungary, but not Japan), industrializing and urbanizing rapidly after 1873, obtained higher shares of the foodstuffs, raw materials and minerals that they required either from the agricultural and mineral sectors located within their own frontiers or from the increasingly efficient primary producers of Europe and European settlements overseas.

Second, and this major secular influence from demand could not be bucked, scientific research sponsored by European firms and governments to discover and develop synthetic substitutes, technologies for conservation and alternative products for the foodstuffs, organic raw materials, minerals and fuels supplied by the agricultures, forests and mineral sectors of Asia, Africa and Southern Africa emerged during the last quarter of the nineteenth century and became relentlessly competitive over the twentieth century. Propelled by geopolitical and sustained by economic incentives, flows of new knowledge (emanating from discoveries in organic and inorganic chemistry, physics, botany, biotechnology and engineering) continued to generate an ever-widening range of cheaper manufactured substitutes, which steadily reduced the values and advantages of natural endowments enjoyed for millennia by primary producers from Africa, Asia and Southern America.

For more than a century, national and world markets for almost all 'basic' foodstuffs, raw materials and minerals exported by Third World economies (including cereals, cotton, coffee, sugar, hides and skins, gums, tea, tobacco, gold, wool, seeds, fruit and vegetables, cocoa, jute, crude oil, silk, wood, palm and vegetable oils, indigo, botanical drugs, spices and copra) came under competitive pressures of varying intensity from synthetic fibres, artificial rubber, plastics, light metals, chemical dyestuffs, pharmaceuticals, enzyme sugars, instant coffee, tea bags and 'concocted' foods of many varieties, designed, developed and manufactured basically in the 'north' to reduce millennia of dependence of consumers and industries everywhere upon the 'primary produce' of the world's agricultures, mines and forests. In the course of competition between science and technology and industry, on the one side, and agriculture, forestry and mining on the other (which intensified from the mid-nineteenth century onwards), the significance of primary production, measured in terms of shares of national and global expenditures of world trade, diminished (Hayami and Ruttan 1985).

Secular trends, which had been gathering momentum for more than two centuries, accelerated and held down commodity prices and returns to the factors of production (land, labour and capital) engaged in primary production throughout the world economy. During this era of liberal imperialism, all traditional organic-based economies and sectors of production confronted three challenges – how (1) to improve the efficiencies of their agricultural and extractive sectors; (2) to diversify agrarian outputs into cultivation of foodstuffs benefiting from higher income elasticities of demand and into raw materials with low elasticities of substitution; and (3) to reallocate capital and other resources into manufacturing services and other activities up the commodity chain.[35]

Smithian and Ricardian theory correctly identified gains from trade that could and did accrue to economies of the Third World through the exploitation of vents for surpluses and, less commonly, through specialization along the lines of comparative advantage (Theberge 1968; Little 1982). Despite Ricardo's tendency to focus on long-run equilibrium, the theory never prompted those impressed by its logic to predict that intensified applications of science-based technologies and complementaries across industries of the core would, over time, operate to depress the growth of global demand for the foodstuffs and raw materials and other primary products produced by agricultures everywhere and particularly by traditional agrarian economies of Asia, Africa and Southern America. With hindsight, economists and historians now appreciate that policies and investments that encouraged regional economies from the Third World to respond to opportunities to trade in primary produce and build up capacities to import did not take into account secular trends in demand or recognize that the diversifications and linkages required to cope with changes in the composition of international trade, coupled with rapid population growth and technological change, would turn out to be more difficult than the (albeit painful) adjustments became for the agricultures of the European core and North America.[36]

Over the long run, the yields per hectare for Third World agricultures rose but slightly and, although total factor productivities for certain crops improved (particularly for crops produced on plantations), there is no evidence of any widespread increase in the productivity of labour between 1815 and 1948. On the contrary, the onset of Malthusian problems promoted by improvements in public health, cheaper food and easier access to markets for cash crops led to an intensification of labour inputs and declines in marginal productivities and real wages in many regions of Asia, Africa and Southern America. Thus, despite unfavourable trends in world demand for primary produce (which the wars and downturns in world trade during the interregnum 1914–18 intensified), encouraged by improved access to world markets provided by the collapse of shipping charges for freight overseas after the First World War and the investments in infrastructures for international trade, put into place during the boom from 1900 to 1913, the increasingly elastic supplies of cheap labour available to the agrarian economies of the Third World continued to exploit traditional natural advantages of soil, location and climate (Bairoch 1975).

To conclude: over a brief 'age' of liberal imperialism, which succeeded the 'era' of warfare, predation and plunder, labelled as mercantilism, the persistence of colonialism meant the extension of alien rule and control over agrarian economies, trading within a globalizing world economy. World commerce 1815–1948 has been 'represented' in this chapter in terms of integrations and interactions through commodity and factor flows across four separable zones: a European core, the European periphery, European overseas settlements and a Third World of both colonized and autonomous economic regions. My narrative, based upon tabulations culled from secondary sources, has suggested that the potential for development among and across these zones and regional economies depended on their capacities to respond to opportunities to participate in overseas trade. Observed variations in response (measured as exports per capita) depended far more on baseline populations, geographies, natural endowments, distance and access to and from markets than forms of rule. At the macro level, elaborated in this chapter, contrasts across the regional economies of the Third World are not clear or salient enough to provide a basis for validated general conclusions about 'benign or malign economic effects' of colonial compared with indigenous governance. Consensus could emerge from critical surveys of cases region by region, economy by economy. Such histories are more likely, however, to undermine any prospects for generalization (Albertini and Wirtz 1982; Waites 1998).

Meanwhile, the debate for and against the proposition that the maintenance and extension of colonial rule in a 'liberal' world order could only have retarded the development of colonial economies may have reached the impasse of irreconcilable, ideologically based and untestable positions.[37] Given the pervasiveness of a Ricardian 'episteme', in which rulers (colonial and non-colonial alike) together with indigenous businessmen formulated strategies for the growth of local economies throughout the Third World, *post hoc*, it is not clear whether imperial governments could be arraigned at the bar of historical opinion either for failing to anticipate the instabilities and disruptions of 1914–18 or for their myopias in not perceiving that secular trends in scientific discoveries, technological innovation and income elasticities of demand would operate over time to diminish the role and rewards for primary production in world trade.

In formulating shorter term policies designed to encourage production for world markets, colonial rulers might, however, be indicted for neglecting to pursue strategies for export-led growth to their optimal extent by providing sufficient social overhead and other capital required to integrate agrarian economies into world trade. Few of these alien regimes did enough to attract foreign investment, skilled labour and transnational corporations to invest in territories under their control. Of course, European governors, viceroys and proconsuls did almost nothing to tax away the rents and excessive profits garnered and repatriated by European civil servants, soldiers, merchants, bankers and other privileged 'mediators' and 'middlemen' for the 'services' that they supplied to 'connect' the farmers, workforces and natural resources of colonies to world markets. Perhaps, however, we will never know to what degree the transactions costs of operating within a colonial economy exceeded the costs of investing, working and innovating under alternative forms of indigenous rule. Given the structural constraints imposed by location, climate and geography or the way that the world economy evolved, as well as the entrenched positions of privilege that Europeans had already acquired from centuries of successful mercantilism, comparisons between the colonized and autonomous economies of the Third World do not, however, leave an impression that any potential or counterfactual gap in transactions costs could have been wide enough to proclaim that the continued divergence in standards of living between the west and the rest could be strongly linked to the persistence of imperialism between 1815 and 1948.

Notes

1 See Foreman-Peck (1995). The relative weights and time trends for falls in transportation, transactions and information costs are discussed in Kuakiaren (2001).
2 The bibliography on imperialism in world history is now a library of books: an excellent recent text replete with references is Abernethy (2000) and see Johns (1988).
3 An exemplar of the genre dominated by a family of models based on cross-sectional regression analysis is Acemoglu *et al.* (2001). For a sceptical review of the data used in these exercises, even for recent years, see Rozanski and Yeats (1994) and Srinivasan (1994). For a critique of the methods and assumptions of such exercises, see Kenny and Williams (2001).
4 Maddison (2001: 365) provides data for merchandise exports as percentages of GDP in 1990 prices. His ratios are cited as a footnote to Table 13.2.
5 By using cross-country multiple regression analysis, Gallup (1994) and Gallup *et al.* (1998) maintain that geography matters more than institutions in explanations for current differentials in real per capita incomes.
6 For the other view, see Irwin (1996).
7 I have referenced the data sources under each table presented in this chapter.
8 Major survey articles with full bibliography on European industrialization are included in O'Brien (1994) and Church and Wrigley (1994), vols 4 and 5.
9 The Heckscher–Ohlin model of integration among economies of the Atlantic economy has been well analysed and quantified by O'Rourke and Williamson (1999). A global model of interconnections between the industrialization of the core, the expansion of trade and divergence in incomes has been published by Baldwin *et al.* (1998).
10 For example, I do not anticipate that the methods and models surveyed in Hall and Jones (1999) could be applied to the question of why some countries achieved higher levels of exports per capita over the period 1815–1948. At present, there is more illumination from an historical approach; see, for instance, Crafts (2000).
11 The role of Africans in the making and maintenance of an Atlantic and a world economy has been analysed by Inikori (2002).
12 See the following references for the external economic relations of: (1) the Qing Empire: Deng (1999); (2) the Ottoman Empire: Pamuk (1997); Quartaert (2000); (3) Japan: Howe (1999); (4) Siam: Ingram (1971).
13 The debate on formal versus informal imperialism, which addresses this question, continues and has been surveyed by Platt (1973) and Louis (1976), and is reviewed by Winks (1998).
14 My approach has been inspired by the attempts of Arthur Lewis (1970, 1978) to formulate generalizations that apply to the operations of a world economy as a whole.
15 See Roy (1999) and, for Marxist views of de-industrialization, see also Brewer (1980) and Warren (1980).
16 The Marxist–Leninist theory of European investment overseas is outlined by Mandel (1975) and critically reviewed by Fieldhouse (1973).
17 Tracy (1990) contains relevant articles and bibliographies to overseas investment before 1815.
18 See Bairoch (1996) and Crafts (2000: 27). Hirst and Thompson (2003) have an estimate for foreign direct investment for 1914 of around $16 million, which comes to around 16 per cent of Bairoch's estimate of Europe's gross domestic product (GDP) – see Bairoch (1976: 99). On subsidised defence of Britain's dominions and colonies, see Davis and Huttenbach (1986, ch. 5).

19 The risk-averse preferences of foreign investors have been discussed extensively (see Edelstein 1982, 1994). See also the references in O'Brien (1988).

20 Hugill (1993) is a good text on the history of global transportation, and see Davis and Wilburn (1973).

21 See Ferguson (2003); Hall and Jones (1999: 107) used cross-country regressions to report that 'Countries most influenced by Europeans in past centuries have social infrastructures conducive to high levels of output per worker'. Alas, at the time of colonial rule, investors did not see them that way.

22 Most European histories of capital exports include the view that the national economies involved might have used the capital more productively within domestic economies

23 See O'Rourke and Williamson (1999) for emigration from Ireland, Italy and Spain to the Americas.

24 The thrust of imperial histories is to suggest that pressures and policies from colonial governments were to engage in trade. See Gifford and Louis (1971); Havinden and Meredith (1993); Seavoy (2003).

25 Theoretical discussions of comparative advantage and the divisions of gains from trade have been largely concerned with factoral and net barter terms of trade. See Meier (1968) and Myint (1976); the balance of trade is discussed by Condcliffe (1951).

26 But see Hilgert (1942); Frank (1976) and the references cited by Frank.

27 I am indebted to Andre Gunder Frank for drawing my attention to the significance of unbalanced trade in the development of the world economy. Alas, his manuscript, *ReOrient: the Nineteenth Century*, was unpublished at the time of his death.

28 Bagchi (2002) has summarized his estimates of the scale of these transfers and payments for services rendered for India and Indonesia. For comparisons between India and Java, see Bayly and Kolff (1986).

29 But see Acemoglu *et al.* (2001), and their critics noted in footnote 3 for a favourable 'perception' and contestible 'view' of colonial institutions. As for their methods, I simply note the conclusions of Levine and Renelt (1992: 959). They find that 'very few economic variables are robustly correlated with cross-country growth rates or the ratio of investment expenditures to GDP' and that 'a large assortment of political indicators are not robustly correlated with growth or the investment share'.

30 The bibliography of Third World economic histories available for survey is extremely long, and recent attempts were made by Reynolds (1985) and Waites (1998).

31 The correlation coefficient comes to 0.78.

32 The significance of geographical variables in explaining levels and rates of growth in real incomes per capita has support from economic theory and from an array of presumably contestible statistical correlations generated by economists using cross-country regression analysis. The classic text in trade theory is Krugman (1997) and recent tests cited in footnotes 5 and 29.

33 On the need to consider the world economy as the unit for analysis, see Krugman (1995).

34 The continued significance of connections between trade based upon natural resources and growth has theoretical support from gravity models now fashionable in economics. See Frankel and Romer (1999).

35 The commodity chain approach to comprehending evolving divisions of gains from trade is the paradigm for programmes of research conducted by the world systems school of historical sociology. See Chase-Dunn and Hall (1993) and Wallerstein (2000).

36 The models behind my prosaic conclusions have been formulated in Matsuyama (1995); for recent data, see Radetzski (1990).

37 May I refer to a long-standing and stimulating debate I have conducted with my friends Giovanni Arrighi, Andre Gunder Frank and Immanuel Wallerstein over this issue. See Arrighi (1994), Frank (1998) and Wallerstein (1974, 1984 and 1989).

References

Abernethy, B. 2000. *The Dynamics of Global Dominance: European Empires, 1415–1980*. New Haven, CT: Yale University Press.

Acemoglu, D., J. Robinson and S. Johnson. 2001. 'The colonial origins of comparative development: an empirical investigation'. *American Economic Review* 91: 1369–401.

Albertini, R. and A. Wirtz. 1982. *European Colonial Rule: The Impact of the West on India, South East Asia and Africa*. Oxford: Clio.

Amsden, A. 2001. *The Rise of the Rest*. New York: Oxford University Press.

Arndt, H.W. 1987. *Economic Development: The History of an Idea*. Chicago, IL: University of Chicago Press.

Arrighi, Giovanni.1994. *The Long Twentieth Century: Money, Power and the Origin of our Times*. London: Verso.

Bagchi, A.K. 2002. 'The other side of foreign investment by imperial powers'. *Economic and Political Weekly* 37: 2229–38.

Bairoch, P. 1973. 'European foreign trade in the XIX century'. *Journal of European Economic History* 2: 5–37.

Bairoch, P. 1974. 'Geographical structure and trade balance of European foreign trade'. *Journal of European Economic History* 3: 582–8.

Bairoch, P. 1975. *Economic Development of the Third World since 1900*. Berkeley: University of California Press.

Bairoch, P. 1976. *Commerce Exterieur et Developpement Economique de l'Europe au XIX Siecle*. Paris: Mouton.

Bairoch, P. 1996. 'Globalization, myths and realities: one century of foreign trade and investment', in R. Boyer and D. Drache, eds. *States Against Markets: The Limits of Globalization*. London: Routledge.

Bairoch, P. 1997. *Victoires et Deboires 11: Histoire Economique et Sociale du Monde du XVIe Siecle a Nos Jours*. Paris: Gallimard.

Bairoch, P. and B. Etemad. 1985. *Structure par Produits des Exportations du Tiers Monde, 1830–1937*. Geneva: Droz.

Baldwin, R., P. Martin and G.I.P. Ottaviano. 1998. 'Global income divergence, trade and industrialization: the geography of growth take-offs'. *Journal of Economic Growth* 6 (1): 5–37.

Batou, J. 1990. *Cent Ans de Resistance au Sous-Developpement: Etude Compare des Tentatives d'industrialization du Moyen-Orient et de l'Amerique Latine, 1770–1870*. Geneva: Droz.

Bayly, C.A. 2004. *The Birth of the Modern World, 1780–1914*. Oxford.

Bayly, C.A. and D.H.A. Kolff, eds. 1986. *Two Colonial Empires*. Boston: Dordrecht.

Brewer, A. 1980. *Marxist Theories of Imperialism: A Critical Survey*. London.

Bulmer-Thomas, V. 1994. *The Economic History of Latin America since Independence*. Cambridge: Cambridge University Press.

Castles, S. and M. Miller. 1998. *The Age of Migration: International Population Movements in the Modern World*. New York: Guilford.

Chase-Dunn, C. and T. Hall. 1993. 'Comparing world systems: concepts and working hypotheses'. *Social Forces* 71: 851–86.
Church, R.A. and E.A. Wrigley, eds. 1994. *The Industrial Revolutions*. Oxford: Blackwell.
Clesse, A. and P.K. O'Brien, eds. 2002. *Two Hegemonies: Britain, 1846–1914 and the United States, 1941–2001*. Aldershot: Ashgate.
Cohen, R., ed. 1995. *The Cambridge Survey of World Migration*. Cambridge: Cambridge University Press.
Coleman, D.C., ed. 1969. *Revisions in Mercantilism*. London: Methuen.
Condcliffe, J.B. 1951. *The Commerce of Nations*. London: Longmans.
Crafts. N.F.C. 1985. *British Economic Growth during the Industrial Revolution*. Oxford: Clarendon.
Crafts, N.F.C. 2000. *Globalization and Economic Growth: An Historical Perspective*. Working Paper Wp/00/44. Washington, DC: IMF.
Crosby, A.W. 1986. *Ecological Imperialism: The Biological Expansion of Europe, 900–1900*. Cambridge: Cambridge University Press.
Davis, C.B. and K.E. Wilburn, eds. 1991. *Railway Imperialism, 1830–1914*. New York: Greenwood.
Davis, C. and R.A. Huttenback. 1986. *Mammon and the Pursuit of Empire: The Political Economy of British Imperialism, 1860–1912*. Cambridge: Cambridge University Press.
Deng, G. 1999. *Maritime Sector, Institutions and Sea Power of Pre-modern China*. Westport, CT: Praeger.
Edelstein, M. 1982. *Overseas Investment in the Age of High Imperialism*. New York: Columbia University Press.
Edelstein, M. 1994. 'Foreign investment and accumulation', in R. Floud and D. McCloskey, eds. *The Economic History of Britain since 1700*, Vol. 2. Cambridge: Cambridge University Press.
Etemad, B. 2001. *La Possession du Monde*. Brussels: Complexe.
Federico, G. 2005. *Feeding the World: An Economic History of Agriculture, 1800–2000*. Princeton, NJ: Princeton University Press.
Ferguson, N. 2003. *Empire: How Britain Made the Modern World*. London: Allen Lane.
Fieldhouse, D. 1973. *Economics and Empire*. London: Macmillan.
Foreman-Peck, J. 1992. 'A political economy of international migration, 1815–1914'. *Manchester School* 60: 359–76.
Foreman-Peck, J. 1995. *A History of the World Economy*. Hemel Hempstead: Harvester-Wheatsheaf.
Frank, A.G. 1976. 'Multilateral merchandise trade imbalances and uneven economic development'. *Journal of European Economic History* 2: 407–38.
Frank, A.G. 1978. *World Accumulation, 1492–1789*. New York: Monthly Review Press.
Frank, A.G. 1998. *ReOrient: Global Economy in the Asian Age*. Berkeley: University of California Press.
Frank, A.G. unpublished. *ReOrient: The Nineteenth Century*.
Frankel, O.A. and D. Romer. 1999. 'Does trade cause growth'. *American Economic Review* 89: 379–99.
Gallup, J., J.D. Sachs and A.D. Mellinger. 1999. 'Geography and economic development'. Center for International Development, Harvard University Working Paper 1: 1–41.
Gifford, P. and W.R. Louis, eds., 1971. *France and Britain in Africa*. New Haven, CT: Yale University Press.

Glete, J. 1993. *Navies and Nations: Warships, Navies and State Building in Europe and America*, 2 vols. Stockholm: Almqvist and Wiksell.

Gomes, L. 1987. *Foreign Trade and the National Economy*. Basingstoke: Macmillan.

Hall, R.E. and C.I. Jones. 1999. 'Why do some countries produce so much more output per worker than others?' *Quarterly Journal of Economics* February: 891–116.

Hanson, J.R. 1980. *Trade in Transition: Exports from the Third World, 1840–1900*. New York: Academic Press.

Harley, C.K., ed. 1996. *The Integration of the World Economy, 1850–1914*, Vol. II. Cheltenham: Edward Elgar.

Harley, C.K. 2000. 'A review of O'Rourke and Williamson's "Globalization and History"'. *Journal of Economic Literature* 38: 926–35.

Hatton, T. and J.G. Williamson, eds. 1995. *Migration and the International Labour Market*. London: Routledge.

Havinden, M. and D. Meredith. 1993. *Colonialism and Development: Britain and its Tropical Colonies*. London: Routledge.

Hayami, Y. and V. Rutton. 1985. *Agricultural Development*. Baltimore, MD: Johns Hopkins University Press.

Hilgert, F. 1942. *Network of World Trade*. Geneva: League of Nations.

Hirst, P. and G. Thompson. 2003. *Globalization in Question: The International Economy and the Possibilities of Governance*. Cambridge: Cambridge University Press.

Howe, C. 1999. *The Origins of Japanese Trade Supremacy*. London: Hurst.

Hugill, P. 1993. *World Trade since 1431*. Baltimore, MD: Johns Hopkins University Press.

Hutchinson, T.W. 1988. *Before Adam Smith: The Emergence of Political Economy*. Oxford: Basil Blackwell.

Imlah, A. 1958. *Economic Elements in the Pax Britannica*. Cambridge, MA: Harvard University Press.

Ingram, J.C. 1971. *Economic Change in Thailand*. Stanford, CA: Stanford University Press.

Inikori, J. 2002. *Africans and the Industrial Revolution in England*. Cambridge: Cambridge University Press.

Irwin, D. 1996. *Against the Tide: An Intellectual History of Free Trade*. Princeton, NJ: Princeton University Press.

Johns, R. 1988. *A Colonial Trade and International Exchange*. London: Pinter.

Jones, E.L. 2003. *The European Miracle*, 3rd edn. Cambridge: Cambridge University Press.

Kenny, C. and D. Williams. 2001. 'What do we know about economic growth?' *World Development* 29: 1–22.

Kenwood, A.G. and A.L. Lougheed. 1999. *The Growth of the International Economy, 1820–2000*. London: Routledge.

Kindleberger, C. 1962. *Trade and the National Economy*. New Haven, CT: Yale University Press.

Kitson, M. and J. Michie. 1995. 'Trade and growth: a historical perspective', in M. Kitson and J. Michie, eds. *Managing the Global Economy*. Oxford: Oxford University Press.

Krugman, P. 1995. 'Growing world trade: causes and consequences'. *Brooking's Economic Activity* 1: 327–62.

Krugman, P. 1997. *Development, Geography and Economic Theory*. Cambridge, MA: Harvard University Press.

Kuakiaren, Y. 2001. 'Shrinking the world: improvements in the speed of information transmission'. *European Review of Economic History* 5: 1–29.

Kuznets, S. 1966a. *Six Lectures on Economic Growth*. London: Frank Cass.

Kuznets, S. 1966b. *Modern Economic Growth*. New Haven, CT: Yale University Press.

Lamartine-Yates, P. 1959. *Forty Years of Foreign Trade*. London: Allen & Unwin.

Latham, A.J.H. 1978. *The International Economy and the Underdeveloped World*. London: Croom Helm.

Latham, A.J.H.1981. *The Depression and the Developing World*. London: Croom Helm.

Lazonick, W. and B. Elbaum, eds., 1986. *The Decline of the British Economy*. Oxford: Oxford University Press.

Levine, R.E. and D. Renelt. 1992. 'A sensitivity analysis of cross-country growth regressions'. *American Economic Review* 82: 942–63.

Lewis, W.A. 1970. *Tropical Development, 1880–1913*. London: Allen & Unwin.

Lewis, W.A. 1978. *Growth and Fluctuations, 1870–1913*. London: Allen & Unwin.

Lewis, W. A. 1981. 'The rate of growth of world trade, 1830–1972', in S. Grassman and E. Lundberg, eds. *The World Economic Order: Past and Prospects*. London: Macmillan, pp. 1–81.

Little, I.M.D. 1982. *Economic Development: Theory, Policy and International Relations*. New York: Basic Books.

Louis, R., ed. 1976. *Imperialism: The Robinson Gallagher Controversy*. New York: New View Point.

Maddison, Angus. 1982. *Phases of Capitalist Development*. Oxford.

Maddison, Angus. 2001. *The World Economy: A Millennium Perspective*. Paris: OECD.

Magnusson, L. 1994. *Mercantilism: The Shaping of an Economic Language*. London: Routledge.

Mandel, E. 1975. *Late Capitalism*. London: Verso.

Matsuyama, K. 1995. 'Complementarities and cumulative processes in models of monopolistic competition'. *Journal of Economic Literature* 33: 701–29.

Meier, G.M. 1968. *The International Economics of Development*. New York: Harper and Row.

Milward, A. and B. Saul.1977. *The Development of the Economies of Continental Europe, 1850–1914*. London: Allen & Unwin.

Minchinton, W., ed. 1969. *The Growth of English Overseas Trade in the Seventeenth and Eighteenth Centuries*. London: Methuen.

Mitchell, B.R. 1962. *Abstract of British Historical Statistics*. Cambridge: Cambridge University Press.

Mulhall, M.G. 1892 and subsequent editions. *Dictionaries of Statistics*. London: Routledge.

Myint, H. 1976. *The Economics of Developing Countries*. London: Hutchinson.

O'Brien, P.K. 1988. 'The costs and benefits of British imperialism, 1846–1914'. *Past and Present* 120: 163–200.

O'Brien, P.K., ed. 1994. *The Industrial Revolutions in Europe*. Oxford: Blackwell.

O'Brien, P.K. 1997. 'The security of the realm and the growth of the economy, 1688–1914', in P. Clarke and C. Trebilcock, eds. *Understanding Decline: Perceptions and Realities of British Economic Performance*. Cambridge: Cambridge University Press.

O'Brien, P.K. and L. Prados De La Escosura. 1998. 'The costs and benefits of European imperialism from the Conquest of Ceuta, 1415, to the Treaty of Lusaka, 1974'. *Revista de Historia Economica* 1 (special issue).

O'Rourke, K. and J.G. Williamson. 1999. *Globalization and History: The Evolution of a Nineteenth Century Atlantic Economy*. Cambridge, MA: Harvard University Press.

Pamuk, S. 1997. *The Ottoman Empire and European Capitalism, Trade, Investment, and Production*. Cambridge: Cambridge University Press.

Pamuk, S. and J.G. Williamson. 2000. *The Mediterranean Response to Globalization before 1850*. New York: Routledge.

Platt, D.C.M. 1973. 'Further objections to and for the imperialism of free trade'. *Economic History Review* 26: 77–91.

Pollard, S. 1985. 'Capital exports, 1870–1914'. *Economic History Review* 38: 489–514.

Pomeranz, K.P. 2000. *The Great Divergence: China, Europe and the Making of the Modern World*. Princeton, NJ: Princeton University Press.

Quartaert, D. 2000. *The Ottoman Empire, 1700–1922*. Cambridge: Cambridge University Press.

Radetzksi, M.A. 1990. *A Guide to Primary Commodities*. Oxford: Basil Blackwell.

Reynolds, L.G. 1985. *Economic Growth in the Third World, 1850–1980*. New Haven, CT: Yale University Press.

Rostow, W.W. 1978. *The World Economy*. London: Macmillan.

Roy, T. 1999. *Traditional Industry in the Economy of Colonial India*. Cambridge: Cambridge University Press.

Rozanski, J. and A. Yeats, 1994. 'On the inaccuracy of economic observations'. *Journal of Development Economics* 44: 103–30.

Seavoy, R.E. 2003. *Origins and Growth of the Global Economy*. Westport, CT: Praeger.

Semmel, B. 1986. *Liberalism and Naval Strategy*. London: Allen & Unwin.

Srinivasan, T.N. 1994. 'Database for development analysis: an overview'. *Journal of Development Economics* 44: 3–27.

Theberge, J., ed. 1968. *Economics of Trade and Development*. New York: Wiley.

Tracy, J.D., ed., 1991. *The Political Economy of Merchant Empires: State Power and World Trade, 1350–1750*. Cambridge: Cambridge University Press.

Turner, B.L., *et al.*, eds. 1990. *The Earth as Transformed by Human Action*. Cambridge: Cambridge University Press.

United Nations. 1949a. *Demographic Yearbook for 1948*. New York: United Nations.

United Nations. 1949b. *Yearbook of International Trade Statistics*. New York: United Nations.

United Nations. 1955. *Yearbook of International Trade Statistics*. New York: United Nations.

Wallerstein, I. 1974, 1984, 1989. *The Modern World System*, 3 vols. London: Academic Press.

Wallerstein, I. 2000. 'Commodity chains in the world economy, 1590–1990'. *Review* 23: 1–13.

Waites, B. 1998. *Europe and the Third World from Colonization to Decolonization, 1500–1998*. New York: Macmillan.

Warren, B. 1980. *Imperialism: Pioneer of Capitalism*. London: Verso.

Williamson, J.G. 2000. 'Globalization Factor Prices and Living Standards in Asia Before 1940,' in J. Latham and H. Kawakatsa, eds., *Asia Pacific Dynamism, 1550–2000*. London: Routledge.

Winks, R. 1998. 'Historiography' in W.R. Louis, ed., *The Oxford History of the British Empire*, vol. 5. Oxford: Oxford University Press.

Wong, G., ed. 1997. *Global History and Migration*. Boulder, CO: Westview.

World Resources Institutes. 1986–1989. *Reports*. PDF versions.

Woytinski, W.S. and E.S. Woytinski. 1955. *World Commerce and Governments*. New York: Twentieth Century Fund.

Index